Religion and Conflict in Modern

Religion and Conflict in Modern South Asia is one of the first single-author comparisons of different South Asian states around the theme of religious conflict. Based on new research and syntheses of the literature on 'communalism', it argues that religious conflict in this region in the modern period was never simply based on sectarian or theological differences or the clash of civilisations. Instead, the book proposes that the connection between religious radicalism and everyday violence relates to the actual (and perceived) weaknesses of political and state structures. For some, religious and ethnic mobilisation has provided a means of protest, where representative institutions failed. For others, it became a method of dealing with an uncertain political and economic future. For many, it has no concrete or deliberate function, but has effectively upheld social stability, paternalism and local power, in the face of globalisation and the growing aspirations of the region's most underprivileged citizens.

William Gould is Senior Lecturer in Indian history at the University of Leeds. He is the author of *Hindu Nationalism and the Language of Politics in Late Colonial India* (2004) and *Bureaucracy, Community and Influence in India: Society and the State, 1930s–1960s* (2011).

Religion and Conflict in Modern South Asia

WILLIAM GOULD
University of Leeds

CAMBRIDGE UNIVERSITY PRESS
Cambridge, New York, Melbourne, Madrid, Cape Town,
Singapore, São Paulo, Delhi, Tokyo, Mexico City

Cambridge University Press
32 Avenue of the Americas, New York, NY 10013-2473, USA

www.cambridge.org
Information on this title: www.cambridge.org/9780521705110

First published 2012

Printed in the United States of America

A catalog record for this publication is available from the British Library.

Library of Congress Cataloging in Publication Data
Gould, William, 1973–
Religion and conflict in modern South Asia / William Gould.
p.   cm.
Includes bibliographical references and index.
ISBN 978-0-521-87949-1 – ISBN 978-0-521-70511-0 (pbk.)
1. South Asia – Religion.   2. Social conflict – South Asia – History.
3. Social conflict – Religious aspects – History.   I. Title.
BL1055.G68   2011
306.60954–dc22   2011001009

ISBN 978-0-521-87949-1 Hardback
ISBN 978-0-521-70511-0 Paperback

For Dylan

Contents

Abbreviations

AIADMK	All India Anna Dravida Munnetra Kazagham
AICC	All India Congress Committee
AL	Awami League, Bangladesh
BHU	Banaras Hindu University
BJP	Bharatiya Janata Party
BJS	Bharatiya Jana Sangh
BLD	Bharatiya Lok Dal
BNP	Bangladesh National Party
BSP	Bahujan Samaj Party
CIDL	Central Record Room, CID, Lucknow
CM	Chief Minister
DMK	Dravida Munnetra Kazagham
ENLF	Eelam National Liberation Front
EPDP	Eelam People's Democratic Party
EPRLF	Eelam People's Revolutionary Liberation Front
EROS	Eelam Revolutionary Organisation of Students
FP	Tamil Federal Party
FSF	Federal Security Force, Pakistan
IJI	Islamic Jamhoori Ittihad
IPKF	Indian Peace-Keeping Force
ISI	Inter-Services Intelligence, Pakistan
JI	Jamaat-e-Islami, Bangladesh
JP	Jatiya Party, Bangladesh
JSS	Jatika Sevaka Sangamaya
JVP	Janatha Vimukthi Peramuna

LTTE	Liberation Tigers of Tamil Eelam
MMA	Muttahida Majlis-i-Amal
MQM	Mohajir Quami Movement
NAI	National Archives of India, Delhi
NAP	National Awami Party
NMML	Nehru Memorial Museum and Library, New Delhi
NRI	Non-Resident Indian
NWFP	North-West Frontier Province
OBC	Other Backward Castes
OIOC	Oriental and India Office Collections, British Library, London
PAC	Provincial Armed Constabulary
PLOTE	People's Liberation Organisation of Tamil Eelam
PMK	Paattali Makkal Katchi
PNA	Pakistan National Alliance
PPP	Pakistan People's Party
PRODA	Public and Representative Office Disqualification Act
PSP	Praja Socialist Party
RSS	Rashtriya Swayamsevak Sangh
SC	Scheduled Caste
SLFP	Sri Lanka Freedom Party
SM	Sipah-I Muhammed
SP	Samajwadi Party
SRC	States Reorganisation Commission
SSP	(Sunni) Sipah-I Sahaba Pakistan
TELO	Tamil Eelam Liberation Organisation
TJP	(Shia) Tahriki Jafaria Pakistan
TNFJ	Tahrik-I Nifaz-I Fiqh-I Ja'fariyya
TUF	Tamil United Front
TULF	Tamil United Liberation Front
UNP	United National Party, Sri Lanka
UP	Uttar Pradesh
UPSA	Uttar Pradesh State Archives
VHP	Vishwa Hindu Parishad

Glossary

Adharmi	ancient religion
adi	original
Adivasi/Adibasi	umbrella term for original and indigenous peoples of a region
ahimsa	nonviolence
Ahir	Hindu agricultural caste associated with cattle rearing
Ahmadi	Muslim sect with difference of belief with orthodox Muslims surrounding prophet
Ahrar	liberal; Muslim party
Akali	admirer and follower of the 'supreme power'; Sikh party
akhara	gymnasium
andolan	movement
anna	one-sixteenth of a rupee
arora	mercantile caste community
Arti	ceremony or form of worship
Arya Samaj	Arya Society – Hindu reform organisation
awami	people
badmash	ruffian
Bahujan	people in the majority
Bania	trader/business caste
basti	settlement or suburb
Batgama	low-caste agriculturalists/soldiers in Sri Lanka

bhadralok	gentlefolk; refers mostly to high-caste groups in Bengal
bhakti	devotion/devotional movement or practice
Bharatiya	Indian
Caliphate	Islamic system of government under constitutional head of Caliph
Chamar	low caste often associated with tanning and leather work; today Scheduled Caste
chanda	contribution
chauraha	roundabout/junction
Chehlum	Shia religious observation
Chettiar	trading and agricultural community, South India of Vaishya varna
Chitpavan	Brahman community of Konkan, Maharashtra
crore	ten million
Dadhkando	Hindu festival in UP cities
dal	party/corps
Dalit	'suppressed'; caste groups previously referred to as 'outcaste' or 'untouchable'
Damdami Taksal	Sikh educational organisation
dar al-harb	'abode of war'; territory not under Islamic control
dar al-ulum	'abode of sciences'; Muslim establishment for higher learning
dharma	religious duty
Dharmarakshana Sabha	society for temple reform
Dravidian	people of Dravidian language group in south India
Eelam	Tamil name for Sri Lanka
fatwa	religious opinion on Islamic law
garbhadan	traditional life-cycle rite
gari	song
gaurakshini sabha	cow-protection society
gharana	system of social and ideological formation, linking musicians
goonda	gangster/hooligan/lout
Gounder	community of Tamilnadu and Karnataka
goyigama	dominant caste in Sri Lanka

Gujar	north Indian caste now defined as OBC
Hanafi	school of Islamic jurisprudence named after Abu Hanifa al-Numan
hartal	strike
hindutva	'Hinduness', coined by Vinayak Damodar Savarkar
Holi	Hindu festival around February–March
iddat	waiting period for widow or divorced Muslim woman
Jagran	night worship of mother goddess
jamiat/jamaat	society/organisation
Jamnabhoomi	birthplace
Janata/Janatha	populace/people
Jat	agricultural caste mainly from western UP, Punjab and Rajasthan
Jatav	sub-caste of Chamar, Scheduled Caste
jati	community, family or tribe, fixed by birth
Jatiya	national
jhanda	flag or standard
joy bangla	long live Bangladesh
Julaha	Muslim weaver community
kafir	unbeliever
kajal	song
Kallar	caste of Tamilnad
Kanbi	sub-caste of Maharashtra
kar sevak	volunteer to a religious cause
Karaiyar	sea-faring and warrior caste of Tamilnad
Kayastha	caste of scribes
Kazagham	organisation/federation (Tamil)
khadi	home-spun cloth
Khattri	administrative and commercial caste
kirtan	devotional song
kisan	farmer
kotwal	officer in charge of a police station
Koviar	Sri Lankan Tamil caste of agriculturalists and temple workers
krishak	farmer
Kshattriya	Hindu upper caste of martial or royal status
Kurmi	agricultural caste

lajja	shame
lakh	one hundred thousand
lashkar	army
ma-bap	mother-father
madrasah	educational institution
mahajan	moneylender
Mahar	largest Scheduled Caste group in Maharashtra
Mahasabha	'great' assembly/association
Mahvamsa	historical poem of Sri Lankan kings, Buddhist text
Majlis	assembly
mandal	society, association, committee
mandir	temple or place of worship
masjid	mosque
maulvi/moulvi	Muslim priest or learned man
mela	festival/company of dancers taking part in a festival
Mizo	Ethnic community of the North-East of India
mohalla	neighbourhood
Mohurram	Islamic festival
Momin	Muslim community associated with weaving
mudaliyar	Tamil/Sri Lankan high caste
mufti	Islamic scholar
muhajir	Urdu-speaking migrants to Pakistan
Muhurram	Islamic mourning festival
mulla	Islamic scholar
Munda	Adivasi people of Jharkhand and Bihar
munnetra	progress
muttahida	united
Nadar	caste group of Tamilnad
natukal	hero stone
nawab	regional ruler under Mughal dynasties
octroi	local tax
panchayat	caste council or council of elders
pandit	Hindu scholar teacher/brahman
pargana	revenue or administrative unit
parishad	council

patidar	caste group of Gujarat often using surname Patel
pir	Sufi spiritual leader
praja	people
puja	prayer
Qadiani	derogatory term for follower of Ahmadiyya community
qaum	people/nation/community
Qawwali	Sufi devotional music
Rajput	major group within Kshattriya varna
raksha	protection
Ramdasia	caste of weavers, ethnic group within Sikh community
Ramlila	Hindu festival
rashtriya	national
Rath yatra	festival of chariots
ryotwari	system of revenue administration based on cultivator
sabha	assembly, congregation or association
salagama	caste traditionally associated with cultivation of cinnamon in Sri Lanka
salish	village judgement
samaj	society
samajwadi	socialist
samiti	association
sammelan	conference/convention/meeting
sampradaya	disciplic succession around a Hindu tradition
samyukta	united
Sanatan Dharma	'eternal law/religion'
sangathan	organisation
sangh	association
sankh	conch shell
sati	ritual involving immolation of a widow
satyagraha	'truth force', nonviolent resistance
Satyashodhak Samaj	society of the seekers of truth
sena	army
seva	service
sharif	noble/high-born

sheth	merchant
shuddhi	'purification' and Hindu reconversion movement
Suba	province
sudra	lowest varna
swadeshi	self-sufficiency/ home industry
swaraj	self-rule, independence
swatantra	free/independent
swayamsevak	volunteer
tabligh	Muslim proselytisation movement
tahsil	revenue division
tamasha	spectacle/show
tanzim	religious movement for the unity and organisation of Muslims
tazia	representation of the shrine of Hasan and Husain, carried in procession
Teli	low-caste oil pressers
Thakur	Kshattriya Rajputs
'ulama	Islamic learned man
ummah	community of believers
Vaishnavite	worshipper of Vishnu and his avatars
Vaishya	Upper varna – usually traders of commercial communities
Vanniar	Tamil caste group
Varna	fourfold division of Hindu society
Vellalar	landlord community of Tamilnad
vishwa	world
waqf	religious property trusts
Yadav	agricultural caste associated with cattle rearing
Zakat	alms giving
zamindar	landlord, landowner

Acknowledgements

This book is the result of research and writing carried out intermittently since 1996, during my time at the University of Cambridge and then since 2003 at the University of Leeds. It is the product of three converging interests over that period. First is a long-term fascination with the politics of religious community mobilisation in India, which formed the basis of archival research in Uttar Pradesh in the late 1990s. Second, it has also connected to a more recent focus on the nature of the Indian state, and how ordinary citizens have historically made contact with that state, especially at local levels over the period of independence. Finally, and perhaps most importantly, it has come about as a result of collaborations built up since 2006 with Sarah Ansari, Taylor Sherman and Yasmin Khan in looking at the comparative histories of India and Pakistan. This collaboration was based on uneasiness with the tendency of scholars working on the subcontinent to concentrate on *either* India *or* Pakistan, and the paucity of comparative studies that consider developments on both sides of the new borders. There were, we thought, various limitations implicit in the dominant mode of 'national' studies within the context of South Asia, and we were lucky enough to receive an Arts and Humanities Research Council (AHRC) award to fund a comparative project, 'From Subjects to Citizens: Society and the Everyday State in India and Pakistan, 1947–1964'. This book, therefore, would hardly have been possible in its present form without this assistance from the AHRC, and in this connection, I am first and foremost grateful for the opportunity to collaborate with Sarah, Taylor and Yasmin since 2006, as a result of the AHRC project. In association with 'From Subjects to Citizens', I have also benefited greatly from conversations with Francis Robinson, Ian Talbot, Paul R. Brass,

Markus Daechsel, Craig Jeffrey and Nicolas Jaoul, as well as all of the
attendees at the project's three workshops in Leeds and London.

Much of the material and arguments that appear here were already
forming during research for my PhD from 1996 and for my first book
Hindu Nationalism and the Language of Politics in Late Colonial India
(Cambridge: Cambridge University Press, 2004). There were a number of
broader and comparative issues that *Hindu Nationalism* was unable to
address, and some research material that, unused in the first instance, has
been refined and developed for this book. In this connection, I am deeply
indebted to all of my colleagues during my time at Cambridge, and
particularly those who introduced to me the interconnections between
the everyday concerns of Indian subjects/citizens and the politics of 'communalism'. Principal here was the late Raj Chandavarkar, my PhD super-
visor, who constantly interrogated my ideas on themes associated with this
book and encouraged my wider-ranging interests in South Asia. Also
important at this time were two other highly influential historians of
labour in India – Subho Basu and Nandini Gooptu – and a colleague
working on ethnic conflict in Gujarat – Ornit Shani. Around this time
too, the attendees of the Cambridge Centre of South Asian Studies seminar
were a constant source of interaction and ideas, and in this connection, I
would like to thank Chris Bayly, Gordon Johnson, Justin Jones, Magnus
Marsden, Eleanor Newbigin, Francesca Orsini, Norbert Peabody and
Carey Watt. More widely, my time at Cambridge brought me into contact
with other influential advisers, notably Thomas Blom Hansen, Joya
Chatterji, Roger Jeffery and Sudipta Kaviraj. As all Smuts Research
Fellows at the Centre in Cambridge know, these kinds of interactions are
made all the more significant as a result of conversations (and coffee
breaks) with Kevin Greenbank and Barbara Roe based at the Centre. At
that time and since, I made extensive use of a range of libraries and archives
(including the Centre of South Asian Studies), and I would like to thank the
staff of the University Library, Cambridge; the Oriental and India Office
Collections of the British Library; the National Archives of India, Delhi;
the Uttar Pradesh State Archives, Lucknow; Bharatiy Bhavan, Allahabad;
the Gyan Prasad Library, Kanpur; the Indian Institute of Public
Administration, Delhi; and the Nehru Memorial Museum and Library,
Delhi.

Since 2003, my ideas for *Religion and Conflict in South Asia* were
developed further via interactions with colleagues and students at the
University of Leeds. The experience of exploring and articulating issues
of religious mobilisation and conflict with students at all levels, and their

responses to my research, has certainly helped me to form some of the principal arguments presented here. To this end, I am grateful to all those students who took the plunge to study India with me over the last seven years, particularly Catherine Coombs, Susanne Kranz, Rabia Dada and Oliver Godsmark. The School of History and the Faculty of Arts at Leeds have also been extremely fertile environments for the development of this project. In this connection, I would like to thank my colleagues on 'Race and Resistance', particularly fellow Indianist Andrea Major, and my collaborators in South Asian Studies – Sean McLoughlin, Emma Tomalin, Ananya Kabir and David Hall-Matthews – all of whom listened to research papers, which have informed this work. Perhaps most important of all has been the patience and time granted to me by my family, in particular my partner Olivia Gould and my parents Richard and Elizabeth Gould, as I juggled research time in India with fatherly duties. Finally, I dedicate this book to a young man who has managed to keep me upbeat through the last three years of the project. He too has enjoyed roaming the streets of Delhi during one of my research trips there, but has also, along with Olivia, tolerated my absences.

I

Introduction

Community and Conflict in South Asia

In the aftermath of one of the most dramatic British colonial retreats – that of the summer of 1947 – two entirely separate states were created out of British India – one on the extraordinary basis of religious community and the other on its denial. Each was founded upon apparently contrary ideas about what constituted a 'nation'. On the one side lay the outwardly secular democratic state of India. The leading political movement of late colonial India – the Indian National Congress – representing itself as the only truly 'national' organisation in the region, had to claim to represent all Indians. On the surface at least, it eschewed the politics of religious community from its very beginning in 1885, as a colonial tactic to divide and rule Indian society. From the very beginning too, though, the Congress's commitment to secularism became more vague and inapplicable the closer it came to local politics. This could be seen in the 1880s and 1890s when the interests of urbane Congress publicists from the great cities of Bombay, Calcutta and Madras came into conflict with the radical Hindu mobilisers of western and northern India. It could also be seen in the late 1940s, when the secular modernist Jawaharlal Nehru struggled for control of the Congress with the UP leader, Purushottam Das Tandon. The former shunned the self-proclaimed champions of the 'Hindu community' as reactionaries. The latter, while taking a leading role in the Congress, actively organised the *Hind Raksh* Dal (Protection of India Party) around the principles of Hindu mobilisation, which involved militaristic protection of the 'homeland' from anti-national (Muslim) elements. Independent India was a secular state, but it was clearly a fragile and contested secularism.

On the other side lay the new state of Pakistan, divided by thousands of miles between the western part of Punjab and the eastern half of Bengal,

[handwritten margin note: Secular vs. religious]

and founded on the principle that the Muslim community of India represented a separate nation. For its champion, Mohammad Ali Jinnah, the 'two-nation theory', as it came to be known from the early 1940s, did not necessarily imply a push for an entirely separate sovereign state, cut off completely from the rest of India. Yet the clear principles underlying the Muslim League were that the Muslims of India should be seen as a separate political-interest group, with separate rights that could only be represented by co-religionists. This contradicted a powerful tradition in radical Muslim leadership in India, which had, since the first decade of the twentieth century, often worked within or alongside the Congress (a tradition that included Jinnah himself). It also made no sense to large swathes of the Indian Muslim population, who lived comfortably side by side with their co-religionists, took part in Hindu festivals or who worshipped according to regional devotional practices. And when Pakistan was finally formed, not only did a greater number of Muslims remain in India than migrated to the new state, but many who had migrated returned to India in the years following the violence of partition.[1]

These events affected millions of people in India, but for many, the transition from a colonial to a democratic state did not suddenly or radically transform their lives. It is this dichotomy – the apparent gulf between the high politics of antagonism between different religious communities and its highly differentiated and problematic effect on the ground – that will form a central focus of this book. Tracing the high politics of India's partition and similar events is now a relatively easy matter. What is not so easy is explaining why so many ordinary citizens of South Asia's states came then and later to be involved in religious controversy and conflict, when such events had little bearing on their local communities. This book will look at the ways in which the practice of religion was associated with the development of India's religious traditions as 'world religions', whose adherents formed particular 'communities', but for whom identification with such communities did not necessarily relate to everyday religious practices. The question then arises as to how and why such communities were defined as such. Terminology itself is produced by the politics and hierarchies of representation and power relationships that underpinned them. Therefore, throughout, this book will also explore how the very terms 'religion' and 'community', and

[handwritten left margin: Found at the bottom]

---

[1] For a detailed study of this process in the north-west of India, see Vazira Zamindar, *The Long Partition and the Making of Modern South Asia: Refugees, Boundaries, Histories* (New York: Columbia University Press, 2007).

its associated term 'communalism' (used to describe conflict and violence between religious communities in South Asia), transformed in significance. It will argue that the association of ordinary Indians with a sense of religious community was locally contingent, and complicated by local experiences. On the other hand, it will suggest that the phenomenon of religious conflict or 'communal' conflict needs to be looked at by viewing the interconnection of local politics with broader systems of political representation as they changed between the colonial and post-colonial periods. In particular, it will look at religious community mobilisation in response to actual (and perceived) actions, failures, weaknesses and powers of the state in India, and will argue that these factors were central to the escalation of conflict around religious identity. Central to this process was the specific transition from an authoritarian colonial state, to post-colonial systems in which democratic practices overlay older structures of authoritarian power. And, as will be unravelled more below, it is via a comparison of different nation states in the region that the full implications of these state interactions can be explored.

(1) SITUATING RELIGIOUS COMMUNITY AND CONFLICT

Writing about South Asia for the late colonial period has, for obvious reasons, been dominated by narratives of India's 'freedom struggle' or by the building of political institutions that went hand in hand with anti-colonial politics. In these narratives, partition in 1947 often becomes the final tragic outcome of a politics infused with competing national and communal visions – a kind of pristine march to freedom, which loses its way in the tide of growing communal sentiment among Hindus, Muslims and Sikhs. Most histories of Indian nationalism, where they have been concerned with ideology, have tended to depict a scenario of polarised, competing ideological visions. This would include not only some of the old contemporary accounts such as that of Chadhuri Khaliquzzaman,[2] but also some of the 1970s and 1980s writing that traced histories of the main national institutions and state transformations, albeit in different ways.[3] The first set of ideological visions identified religious community or a notion

---

[2] Chaudhuri Khaliquzzaman, *Pathway to Pakistan* (Lahore: Longmans, 1961).

[3] For example, David Page, *Prelude to Partition: The Indian Muslims and the Imperial System of Control 1920–1932* (Delhi: Oxford University Press, 1982); Peter Hardy, *The Muslims of British India* (Cambridge: Cambridge University Press, 1972); and Gyanendra Pandey, *The Ascendancy of the Congress in Uttar Pradesh: A Study in Imperfect Mobilisation* (Oxford: Oxford University Press, 1978).

of Hinduness as the core of national identity. A second ideological position apparently promoted secular identities as the basis of nationhood.[4] In more recent work of this type, India's past, specifically the colonial past, has been researched with one eye to the events of 1947 or more recently through consideration of the rising political authority of the Hindu right in contemporary Indian politics since the early 1990s. It is perhaps these two events more than anything else that have led historians to consider Indian history in terms of secular/non-secular polarisations. The outcome has been to create an impression that the most significant political cleavages in Indian society and politics related to broad differences between its two most important religious communities – the Hindu and the Muslim – without necessarily asking the central question of why parties and groups at certain moments chose to privilege such artificial group identities, and how they can be disaggregated.[5] To some extent, this is a continuation of colonial representations of community. But it has more modern manifestations, as we will see throughout this book.

This book argues that the dichotomy between the 'religious' and 'secular' in South Asia is itself problematic, when we examine in detail organisations of religious or secular mobilisation. It will also attempt to challenge the division of South Asian politics along the line of religious community. Popular and academic representations of Indian society and politics continue to delineate the interests and politics of broadly defined religious communities, most classically for India and Pakistan – Hindu, Muslim, Sikh and Christian – or in the case of Sri Lanka, Buddhist, Muslim and Christian. A prominent sociologist working on India has marked this in terms of a Western fascination or obsession with delineating the religious essence of pre-independent India.[6] Religious 'community' should not be taken as a given from the start.[7] The terms 'Hindu' and 'Muslim', particularly the former, are broad generalisations of religious tradition, which only vaguely capture the complex realities of identity. Yet, such communal labelling has clearly stuck at the level of representation, as

---

[4] This idea of polarised and competing ideological visions is set out clearly by Paul R. Brass, *Theft of an Idol: Text and Context in the Representation of Collective Violence* (Princeton: Princeton University Press, 1997), pp. 279–80.

[5] This has given rise to a specific stress on such broad religious cleavages, for example, Peter van der Veer, *Religious Nationalism: Hindus and Muslims in India* (Berkeley: University of California Press, 1994).

[6] Ronald Inden, *Imagining India* (London: Hurst, 2000).

[7] Gyanendra Pandey, 'Liberalism and the Study of Indian History: A Review of Writings on Communalism', *Economic and Political Weekly*, 18, 42, 1983, 1789–1791, 1794.

discussed above. Even more startlingly, these generalised representations of community appear to have had a profound effect on the political lives of citizens in nearly all of South Asia's states. This is despite the fact that such representations rarely capture the everyday urban or rural affairs of most Indians, even where they are related to religious practice.

This dichotomy between the politics of representation of religious identity, and the everyday experiences of ordinary citizens, has colonial roots that will be explored more below. It has also been driven by the popular media: newspapers in India intermittently discuss the ongoing issue or 'problem' of what is described as 'communalism' – the apparent opposition of broad religious communities, often resulting in violence (although since 1947, communities are rarely directly identified), which is quantified in terms of casualties on each side. Also significant is the nature of the political process. Since the establishment of formal representative institutions in India, elections at all levels have often been fought around such anticipated 'communal' differences. Political parties in post-independent India, Pakistan, Bangladesh and Sri Lanka have mobilised around political factions, many of which have been defined, at strategic moments, by religion, caste or ethnic community. Histories of South Asia continue to make reference to the clumsy cleavage between 'Hindus' and 'Muslims' or between broadly defined ethnic groups. And yet academic observations on these states usually agree that there is something unsatisfactory in placing too much stress on religious or communal identity in the lives of South Asian peoples. All of this leads us to the questions of what exactly 'religion' and 'community' mean in the Indian subcontinent, both in public spheres of political action and in everyday life, and what role religious and communal identity play in the political lives of its citizens at different moments over the last century.

Throughout, this book will attempt to move away from thinking about religious community solely or largely in terms of identity, since such approaches largely fail to provide satisfactory answers to these questions. For most historians and political scientists looking at 'communalism', analyses have frequently revolved around questions of group identity and the ways in which political processes and ideologies have allowed public men and women to emphasise religious or communal identities over others. However, it is necessary to pinpoint the specific political, economic and social pressures that, over time, have created the context for such political decisions. This book does not argue that ordinary people in South Asia have no agency when it comes to political identity. But it will argue that 'identity' as a framework of analysis is problematic in understanding the broader processes of religious conflict, since its multifaceted and complex nature does not connect satisfactorily to the broader dynamics of community violence over extended periods of time. Neither does it account for the contradictions of political behaviour, in which unexpected participants apparently encourage or engage in all kinds of conflict. The notion of 'identity' does not explain very sufficiently either why a sense of religious community appeared to matter at certain moments or in certain periods and places and not others. Most importantly, it is not a very useful tool in helping the historian to understand why religious communities appear to act in unison, even when their specific religious affiliations or beliefs were quite different from those of their co-religionists.

However, there is clearly a level at which individuals and groups decide or are persuaded to act on the basis of a loyalty to religious community. And here, identity does play a part, albeit one that can only be analysed in relation to wider contextual factors, and in particular, the explicitly *political* aspects of those identities. One of the questions that is implicitly, but rarely directly, tackled by research on communalism is why, despite holding a range of identities relating to home, family, caste, religion, nation, region or language, did colonial subjects and post-colonial citizens apparently privilege a sense of religious identity over other loyalties? This book argues that 'Hindu' or 'Muslim' identities were never held as exceptional. They were never entirely independent of a range of other political and social identities that cut across and complicated moments of religious unity. It is impossible therefore to isolate or extract elements of identity entirely, and perhaps the best a historian can do is to examine how particular forms of political identification reinforced each other. For this reason, this book will examine other kinds of identity in relation to religious community – and specifically will look in detail at caste and ethnicity. Both of these terms incorporate, in most of our case studies, notions of 'religion', although conflict over sectional interests based on region or language (as in Pakistan) or caste (as in parts of India) complicate manifestations of religious conflict. Throughout, this book will argue that it is practically impossible to separate out religious community conflict from ethnic community conflict in many instances, especially as the bases for sectarian antagonism are rarely related to primordial differences of belief.

In popular debate and media responses to communalism, religious identities and loyalties are considered as phenomena that can be separated from other social formations. This book will argue that this was rarely if ever the case, by looking, for example, at caste, social status, health and sexuality on the one hand, and their interrelationship with broader religious mobilisations on the other. It will argue that a range of contingent social and occupational circumstances for individuals, families and larger social institutions led to differential and fluctuating expressions of religious mobilisation. It has, however, been far too easy for historians and social scientists to employ the notion that 'popular consciousness' is defined by religious sentiment, even where the complex and varied nature of religious belief and the changing nature of class identifications are clearly apparent. To some extent, this tendency is the result of a modern fascination with statistical and demographic mapping of religious communities: in the 2001 census of India, those defined as 'Hindus' made up roughly 80.5% of the population, 'Muslims' 13.4%, 'Christians' 2.3% and 'Sikhs' 1.9%. According to the pre-partition Indian census of 1931, 'Hindus' made up 68.2%, 'Muslims' 22.2%, 'Buddhists' 3.7%, 'Christians' 1.8% and 'Sikhs' 1.8% of the total population. In 1931, there were Muslim majorities in the important (and later divided) provinces of Bengal and Punjab of 55.8% and 53.2% respectively, and a significant Muslim minority in the United Provinces (UP) of just under fifteen per cent. Such official statistics, as this book will argue throughout, recreate and reinforce political projects for religious community assertion and, despite the detailed census disaggregation, tend to present simplified and consolidated views of community (especially in the case of 'Hindus'), thereby misrepresenting more complex realities.[8] This book also aims to survey the history and politics of religious community in South Asia, against the context of other colonial policies. In particular, it looks at how the particular phase of intermittent British expansion and retreat between the wars served to generate moments of broad religious identification as new spheres of colonial authority expanded and older traditional power brokers within the colonial system became defensive.

There are, of course, many scholars who have consistently questioned the unity of religious community categories, casting doubt on the extent to which identification with broad religious groupings is based in political

---

[8] As the final section of Chapter 4 will explore, the approaches of community pressure groups to the Indian Census operations of 1931 were very different to those of 1941, with an aggressive increase in pressure groups in the second operation. Efforts to 'represent' communities in different ways therefore materially affected the results of such official surveys. This is also recognised in K. Hill, W. Seltzer, J. Leaning, S. J. Malik, S. S. Russell, 'The Demographic Impact of Partition: Bengal in 1947' (Weatherhead Center for International Affairs, Harvard University, 2004), http://iussp2005.princeton.edu/download.aspx?submissionId=52236 accessed on 25 November 2010.

realities, rather than strategic compulsions[9] or much more disaggregated and localised cultural identities.[10] This latter approach dates back to the early 1980s, when a group of Delhi-based historians initiated a broad and diverse field of historical analysis, which critiqued the grand, hegemonic and over-arching empirical models of social science research, just as it rejected histories concerned only with the powerful. Important for these historians in looking at religious conflict were the hitherto 'marginal', subordinated and contingent identities of ordinary poor Indians, whose voices were given as much explanatory power as studies of political economy. In this work, Indians' cultural identities were approached as relatively autonomous – an idea that will be critiqued more below.[11] And in the aftermath of the cultural historical turn, in which writers began to embrace identities and representations more than political narratives, some very valuable work has looked at deeper issues of gender, sexuality, demography and health against the background of 'communalism'.[12]

Since the late 1980s, historians have most commonly explored 'communalism' as a form of political representation,[13] and this book will also look at how social hierarchies underpinned these political representations. In the late colonial period, a common official and Congress observation was that ordinary, low-status populations might be best mobilised by reference to their apparently primordial religious attachments. And for those with the resources to influence political institutions and the state machinery, recourse to religious community mobilisation indicated the essential corruptibility of India's poor. It apparently delineated their primitive and pre-capitalist sensibilities. This was the presumed violence of the uneducated, low-status and (usually) low-caste, faceless figure, who, standing outside the demographic boundaries of bourgeois civil society,

---

[9] See David Ludden, ed., *Contesting the Nation: Religion, Community and the Politics of Democracy in India* (Philadelphia: University of Pennsylvania Press, 1996).

[10] Gyanendra Pandey, *The Construction of Communalism in Colonial North India* (Delhi: Oxford University Press, 1990).

[11] The clearest examples of this approach can be seen in the first three volumes of *Subaltern Studies*, Ranajit Guha, ed., 1982–1985.

[12] Some of the most sustained work on sexuality and communalism can be found in Charu Gupta, *Sexuality, Obscenity, Community: Women, Muslims, and the Hindu Public in Colonial India* (Delhi: Permanent Black, 2001). See also Patricia and Roger Jeffery, *Confronting Saffron Democracy: Religion, Fertility and Women's Status in India* (New Delhi: Three Essay Collective, 2006).

[13] The most famous example of this is Gyanendra Pandey, *The Construction of Communalism in Colonial North India*. This text will be explored in more detail later in the chapter.

expressed his/her rights through direct action.[14] These populations, to make their claims, had to be invested with the moral context of 'community' by high-level observers, government and the media.[15] Political messages to the uneducated in all South Asian States are therefore (according to this theory) most effectively delivered with reference to their 'own' ethnic or religious traditions. Late colonial political leaderships based their strategies on the same assumptions, and the official historical archives in India are littered with commentaries on the religious sentiments aroused by the soapbox. 'Communalism' became, as a message, a political weapon, and historians and commentators alike too easily took up such messages as the expression of a political reality.

India's leading politicians over our period both before and after independence in 1947 therefore associated the politics of religion with the 'underdeveloped' sentiments of the urban and rural poor. The idea that religious sentiment underpinned the 'autonomous' politics of India's poor has, ironically, also been one theme in the 'Subaltern Studies' literature.[16] Shortly after independence in India, governments and bureaucracies were organised around the assumption that as state and society 'modernised', such primordial attachments would naturally disappear. But these discourses conveniently served the interests of existing elites in South Asia. At other moments, for example shortly after independence in India, Sri Lanka and Pakistan, governments promoted the idea of national interest and 'loyalty' to the state on the basis of relationships between religious 'majorities' and 'minorities'.[17] Once again, this was a means of propping up dominant, usually majority, communities, who associated their power with secularism and modernisation and those of minorities with superstition, tradition and obscurantism.

Yet those disempowered communities who were the subject of this reasoning had always made reference to their varied and often conflicting religious traditions on their own terms too. The political demands of urban and rural labour became increasingly strident in the interwar

---

[14] Partha Chatterjee, *The Politics of the Governed: Reflections on Popular Politics in most of the World* (New York: Three Essays Collective, 2004), pp. 53–68. Chatterjee argues that the disempowered groups living outside of 'civil society' are unable to assert their rights according to established law or administrative procedure.

[15] Ibid., p. 75.

[16] Gyanendra Pandey, 'Liberalism and the Study of Indian History: A Review of Writings on Communalism'.

[17] Sarah Ansari, William Gould and Taylor Sherman, 'The flux of the matter: loyalty, corruption and the everyday state in the post-partition government services of India and Pakistan, c. 1946–1956', unpublished manuscript, 2010.

period, particularly as forms of mass mobilisation allowed workers and peasants to critique both the colonial state and nationalist leaders. This book will briefly look in Chapter 4 at the ways that class identifications were interlaced with religious sensibility, and how the organisation of rural and urban workers could revolve around the specific indices of caste and religious cohesion as a means of challenging the everyday impositions of the local state.[18] Religious or ethnic community mobilisation could be a means of collective defence or pressure against quotidian forms of suppression, not in a way that was entirely autonomous to other ideologies, such as those of the left, but which nevertheless challenged religious nationalists. While the role of religion in political mobilisation was, for many of India's leading politicians in the interwar period, indicative of India's lack of 'modernity', for many without the means to influence the authoritarian colonial state directly, it could be a means of liberation or rebellion. The assertion of ethnic or religious community became a means for many of opposing regimes and the arms of the state, in different periods and circumstances over our study.

Leaders could not force followers to follow, and religious controversy, or 'communalism', by no means had a purely functional significance. However, attempting to identify pure agency – either of political leaders or of India's poor – is a largely fruitless exercise. Instead, this book looks at how belief and action surrounding religious community were always produced by a complex interplay of influences, decisions, forms of political pressure, or rebellion and reaction. To this end, as well as explicitly political manifestations of community politics, Chapters 2–4 will also explore how the changing formulations of 'Hindu' and 'Muslim' communities, for example, were informed by changing ideas about the relationships between men and women, public health and the structure of the family. These changes, and transformations in communication and the use of language, patterns of consumption or ways of surviving, and experience of the arts and culture, reinforced the desire in many parts of South Asia to

---

[18] In this connection, the book will look at the work, for example, of Rajnarayan Chandavarkar, *Origins of Industrial Capitalism* (Cambridge: Cambridge University Press, 1994); Nandini Gooptu, *The Politics of the Urban Poor in Early Twentieth Century India* (Cambridge: Cambridge University Press, 2001); Subho Basu, 'Strikes and "Communal" Riots in Calcutta in the 1890s: Industrial Workers, Bhadralok Nationalist Leadership and the Colonial State', *Modern Asian Studies*, 32, 4, 1998, 949–83; Dipesh Chakrabarty, 'Trade Unions in a Hierarchical Culture: The Jute Workers of Calcutta 1920–1950', in Ranajit Guha, ed., *Subaltern Studies III: Writings on South Asian History and Society* (Delhi: Oxford University Press, 1984), pp. 151–2.

reconsider their relationship to religious practice and community. Increasingly over our period, it became apparent to many that the content of their religious beliefs provided answers or mediated the insecurities, dangers and conflicts of the rapidly changing political world. More often than not, where organisations were formed largely around the interests of a specific religious community, their agendas were based on political insecurity: either the insecurity of minority status or the need to defend and 'organise' against another community. This could involve a politics of hate or a response to a rapidly changing world in which expectations about tradition, the family and the familiar rites of passage were breaking apart. In many cases, as we will see in later chapters, this meant that the exponents of 'Hindu' or 'Muslim' mobilisation co-opted the strong arm of the state as a means of 'controlling' threatening minorities.

This book will relate manifestations of broad religious loyalty closely to significant moments of political, social and cultural change. It will do so by looking in detail at the nature of the ideologies underpinning the politics of religious community, and how they were informed by other kinds of political identification. For example, throughout, the book will examine the relationship between religious community and caste, as well as ethnicity. In particular, Chapter 4 will examine the interaction between caste and religious community in the late colonial period, and Chapters 6, 7 and 8 will explore how the politics of 'ethnicity' in Pakistan and Sri Lanka, and the politics of caste reservations in India, related to moments of conflict and violence. There has been some important research exploring interconnections between religious community and caste for colonial India. For example, the work of Nicholas Dirks, building on the argument of scholars such as Ronald Inden, looks at caste as a product of a colonial desire to order, discipline and represent Indian society in terms of a fundamental sense of religiosity and tradition. Dirks looks at colonial ethnographies and sets out how caste identities were reinscribed by the way in which the colonial state sought to 'imagine' caste differences.[19] An important implication of this work is that *all* state-defined identities are to a great extent transformed by structures of rule and order. Religious identities become part of a larger array of colonially defined ethnic identities, set out as part of a framework for ruling and controlling the subcontinent. Dirks is not arguing that caste was 'invented' entirely, but that its meaning was transformed into a category that had a very new kind of political purchase. Susan Bayly

---

[19] Nicholas B. Dirks, *Castes of Mind: Colonialism and the Making of Modern India* (Princeton: Princeton University Press, 2001).

puts more stress on the longer-term significance of 'caste' as an ethnographic category,[20] but also deepens the intellectual links between caste and religious identity formation, through her work on caste ethnographers and Hindu reformers. Perhaps most significantly, she has shown how the colonial fascination with caste and race was as much about European academic debate as it was about the realities of Indian social organisation.[21] More recent work has looked at the connections between 'caste' prejudice and communal conflict in post-independent India. Ornit Shani, using case studies from Gujarat, has argued that a number of supposedly religious riots since the mid-1980s have only really made sense in the context of wider political debates about caste reservations.[22]

Another group of writers has examined the specific social and cultural movements that ran alongside or produced the constituencies that supported Hindu nationalist ideologues. This theme will be explored principally for the late colonial period in Chapter 4. John Zavos, for example, looks at the emergence of Hindu nationalism in relation to the changing state and movements for social and religious reform.[23] In a different vein, Vasudha Dalmia and Francesca Orsini have both written about how the changing literary sphere in the late colonial period was interlaced with ideologies defining the Hindu community.[24] Janaki Bakhle has recently shown how the cultural sphere of music, changing through the period of anti-colonial nationalism, also refracted religious identity ideologies in complex ways.[25] Some of these authors have used the idea of the 'public sphere' to explore the social bases of support for projects of religious community organisation. The arts provided a means of mediating relationships between domestic and public spheres, and reading, listening and performance were increasingly set out as functional projects in nation building and community consolidation. But just as battle lines were drawn in the area of representative politics, so too did other organisations

[20] Susan Bayly, *Caste, Society and Politics in India from the Eighteenth Century to the Modern Age* (Cambridge: Cambridge University Press, 1999).
[21] Susan Bayly, 'Caste and Race in the Colonial Ethnography of India', in Peter Robb, *The Concept of Race in South Asia* (Delhi: Oxford University Press, 1997).
[22] Ornit Shani, *Communalism, Caste and Hindu Nationalism: The Violence in Gujarat* (Cambridge: Cambridge University Press, 2007).
[23] John Zavos, *The Emergence of Hindu Nationalism in India* (Delhi: Oxford University Press, 1999).
[24] Francesca Orsini, *The Hindi Public Sphere 1920–1940: Language and Literature in the Age of Nationalism* (Oxford: Oxford University Press, 2002).
[25] Janaki Bakhle, *Two Men and Music: Nationalism in the Making of an Indian Classical Tradition* (Oxford: Oxford University Press, 2005).

challenge the standardisation of the arts and culture into spheres relating to religious community.

(II) RELIGION, COMMUNITY AND THE STATE IN SOUTH ASIA

The nature of the changing state in late colonial and early independent South Asia and the attempts of pressure groups to influence its agents are crucial to the arguments presented here. This book will consider the state over our entire period, not as a background entity, but as something frequently contested and subverted as a result of government officers' interaction with powerful men on the one hand and the general public on the other. In these interactions, the representation of religious and ethnic community was often vital. As the modern nation state took shape over the late nineteenth and early twentieth centuries, the Raj often permitted community-based interest groups to bid for influence and leverage within the bureaucracy, assemblies and other institutions of the state. However, because the Raj continually sought new ways to bolster its rule on the cheap and to forestall opposition by co-opting powerful regional elites, it needed to reform representative institutions and to 'Indianise' the services. In periods when uncertainty surrounded the degree of influence and authority Indians would exercise within the colonial system, it was important for leaders to give the impression that they could mobilise large numbers of people. Such postures gave them legitimacy in the face of the Raj's proclaimed interest from the 1910s in 'responsible self-government'. Association with large-scale religious community movements provided, for many, a means of mobilising large numbers of people who were otherwise disenfranchised, especially when the colonial state distributed the power on the basis of communal categories. Despite the constitutional reforms of 1892, 1909, 1919 and 1935, which gradually allowed some Indians to gain power in representative institutions that affected the lives of increasingly large numbers of constituents, the franchise was minuscule throughout, and the British had no intention of leaving India until the effects of war made it essential.

The histories of these states also involved a process of transformation from a colonial system based on thinly spread bureaucratic and police control to democratic governance. And in this sense, older pockets of quasi-autonomy from the gaze of the state survived across the region, with powerful interest groups either usurping or controlling bureaucratic offices.[26] Since state power varied from locality to locality, and was disaggregated and weak in many places, particularly in phases like the mid to late 1940s, local power brokers could under certain circumstances therefore take control of some of its functions. In the 1940s, and in other phases in parts of South Asia after independence, for example the mid-1980s in Sri Lanka, local militias and 'volunteer' movements took on quasi-policing roles, intimidated political opponents, or became a means of defending specific communities. In these cases, state sovereignty could be challenged. And the exercise of local power in these instances was both legitimised via reference to religious community and organised on the basis of community loyalty. This book will also explore where, how and why association with religious community movements appeared to lead ordinary people to extreme acts of violence, in a context where, for the most part, practitioners of different religious beliefs had peacefully coexisted for generations.

Using specific case studies, historians and political scientists have examined how state agents seem to perpetuate or control violence,[27] whether certain institutions of civic engagement in specific urban regions are more prone to riotous and conflict-ridden populations,[28] or whether such apparent violence grows out of political mobilisations against the state.[29] Yet few have, in this process, continued to ask the perhaps more important question of how state power was constituted and what that meant for India's population over this period. One important exception is work that has considered the long-term failure of the 'consociational' periods of state power in India (i.e. phases when the state empowered minorities by providing them with proportionality in government). This includes the half-century before 1947 and the years since the late 1980s. This book agrees that such apparent failures are probably related to the 'multidimensional and oppositional' nature of ethnic identities in India, making it difficult for political leaders to peacefully broker deals between broad communal groups.[30] However, this book also looks below this level of the state,

[26] See Rajnarayan Chandavarkar, 'Customs of Governance: Colonialism and Democracy in Twentieth Century India', *Modern Asian Studies*, 41, 3, 2007, 441–70.
[27] Paul R. Brass, *The Production of Hindu–Muslim Violence in Contemporary India* (London: University of Washington Press, 2003).
[28] Ashutosh Varshney, *Ethnic Conflict and Civic Life* (New Haven: Yale University Press, 2002).
[29] Sandria Freitag, *Collective Action and Community: Public Action and the Emergence of Communalism in North India* (Berkeley: University of California Press, 1989).
[30] Steven Ian Wilkinson, 'India, Consociational Theory and Ethnic Violence', *Asian Survey*, 40, 5, 2000, 767–91.

and suggests that incidents of violence should not necessarily guide analysis. Equally significant are anthropolgal approaches to the 'everyday state' in contemporary India, which suggest that what observers think of as the 'state' in India is not a concrete, uniform or homogenous entity that can be reified into a corporate decision-making body.[31] This framework probably strikes a chord for those studying the nature of the state in any part of the world. But it is especially the case for India, where the colonial system effectively permitted the ongoing exercise of pockets of traditional local power and influence.[32] And if the state is not uniform but itself is composed in part of powerful social interest groups, then its implication within moments of conflict between Indian communities is highly contingent.

Clearly, participants within 'communal' conflicts, and publicists and report writers about such events, evoke or mobilise the idea of the state and/or its structures and nominated personnel. In almost every case, the role of state agents is thought to be crucial by witnesses, often critically so in terms of explaining the events themselves. Often, such violence is represented in terms of the failure of the state or the 'authorities'. At other moments, there is suggestion of acquiescence by police and bureaucrats in the moments of conflict, or even the idea of a state-driven political conspiracy, either involving men of 'local influence' or, commonly, outsider 'goonda' or 'badmash' elements with links to the powerful factions of the urban space. Nearly all consideration of the phenomenon of 'communalism', including the meaning and resonance of the term itself as a discourse then, involves some reflection on the nature of the state. And in some cases, it provides us with quite a new way of thinking about what the state is and what it meant to ordinary Indians affected by such moments of violence and their aftermath.

The significance of this kind of local reflection of the state was not entirely lost on two of the leading historians of India in the mid to late 1980s and early 1990s. In 1985, C. A. Bayly published an essay looking at the phenomenon of communalism as something that preceded formal colonial state power in India by discussing, for example, the Sikh land-wars of the early eighteenth century. The implications of Bayly's argument, although in many respects just a light foray into a subject that had not

---

[31] For an interesting discussion on the ambiguous 'boundaries' of the state in South Asia, which crosses disciplinary boundaries, see C. J. Fuller and John Harriss, 'For an anthropology of the modern Indian state', in C. J. Fuller and Veronique Benei, eds., *The Everyday State and Society in Modern India* (London: Hurst and Co., 2001), pp. 1–30.
[32] For the most explicit statement of this idea, see Rajnarayan Chandavarkar, 'Customs of Governance: Colonialism and Democracy in Twentieth Century India'.

figured centrally in most of his principal work on India up to that point, was that 'communalism' should not be seen necessarily just as a product of the late colonial context. But the essay went on to argue that it was possible to trace general patterns of state transformation in explaining the apparent appearance of conflict along the lines of religious community. For Bayly, wherever and whenever there had been circumstances of dramatic or rapid state transformation, where the stakes were high in the redistribution or consolidation of political power, conflicts between religious communities often featured.[33] Bayly was very likely (although indirectly) writing in the context of a tendency in the nationalist historiography in India to relate 'communalism' to the presence of the colonial state system. Although much of Bayly's most detailed work has been on early colonial India, his essay is important for thinking more generally about how state transformations between colonial and post-colonial systems affect the nature of communalism.

Responding to Bayly's argument, Gyanendra Pandey suggested more firmly that since 'communalism' should be seen as much as a discourse and representation of conflict and 'religious' antagonism, it was important to establish the moments in time when the idea of communalism had political purchase. For Pandey, communalism was 'constructed' in the late colonial period as a phenomenon that related to the development of Indian nationalism as an ideology. As a notion of 'secular' national mobilisation developed, so its other side – 'communalism' – was represented as something 'taboo' and, in that representation and changed meaning, became something very different to what might have appeared as religious or sectarian conflict in the pre-colonial period. Effectively, for Pandey, 'communalism' was a form of colonial knowledge. For a whole range of local conflicts to become 'communal' was a matter of representation. 'Communalism' therefore became a political and ideological framework that provided a context for the discussion of a whole range of more complex conflicts, and thereby determined their political purchase.

One of the differences between the arguments of Bayly and Pandey surrounds the chronology of communalism and religious conflict. But the debate also throws up questions about how we might think about the relationship between such conflict and how it is represented (for Pandey) or managed (for Bayly) by the state. For Bayly, it appears to be possible to make comparisons between different forms of state involvement in such

[33] C. A. Bayly, 'The Pre-History of "Communalism"? Religious Conflict in India, 1700–1860', *Modern Asian Studies*, 19, 2, 1985, 177–203.

conflict by examining the concrete and pragmatic responses of their bureaucracies. In contrast, for Pandey, such comparisons are at best unfruitful and at worst teleological, since 'communalism' is a distinctively modern product of a particular kind of colonial state interaction. For Pandey, when it comes to the comparative nature of the state, the modern state is more centralised, more interventionist and importantly makes claims to be more 'neutral'.[34] In a similar way, the work of Stanley Tambiah on Sri Lanka has suggested that there was nothing primordial about the Sinhalese–Tamil tension or confrontation, in the sense that the 'communal' nature of this conflict, relating essentially to ethnic identity, did not occur before the British conquest of Kandy in 1815. The bureaucratic ordering of the modern state was critical in the shaping of ethnic identities, and therefore manifestations of anything approaching 'communalism' could not have taken place, in a comparable way, before the appearance of modern state structures.[35]

But neither Pandey nor Bayly seem to knit into their accounts fully the point that these views of the state are, themselves, the product of ideologies that have artificially separated state and society. Both accounts of the phenomenon of communalism effectively assume a uniform pattern of state power, which exists as a background entity or as a structured and fluctuating canvass of authority. Once the historian begins to disaggregate the state fully, and to look at how it is itself composed of powerful social forces, we can view state authority in terms of reshaping processes. For example, so-called Muslim separatism and Congress majoritarianism can be viewed as continual attempts to give the idea of the state a particular shape, to contest the allocation of resources through it and to look towards anticipated future structures. We can see that beneath and beyond even these dynamic processes of the constantly morphing image of the state is the disaggregated and contested nature of power networks within it. While politicians in the assemblies and institutions at the centre or province/state (or those knocking on its doors) discussed the direction of state authority, the experience of the state for the vast majority of Indian subject/citizens was very different. For example, for many, the state was a machinery through which things could be done or fixed, and its formal rules and mechanisms could be diverted or even manipulated with the right contacts or through the exercise of influence, sometimes through institutions of

---

[34] Pandey, *Construction of Communalism*, pp. 15–17.
[35] Stanley Jeyaraja Tambiah, *Buddhism Betrayed? Religion, Politics and Violence in Sri Lanka* (Chicago: University of Chicago Press, 1992).

'civil society' (explored more in Chapters 2 to 4). In this way, the state in India (particularly in its working at local levels) did not stand above the political negotiations between representatives of different religious communities. It was not an autonomous entity. Indeed, the very way in which a 'community' leader set up his/her leadership and his representative status was with one eye on how he or she might influence local state structures.

(III) COMMUNALISM AND VIOLENCE

Another common assumption about the state is that it largely stands above or adjudicates the moments of direct conflict and confrontation between different communities in South Asia. This section will explore how the state, via its agents, was directly implicated in moments of violence, and that the association of 'communalism' with violence was itself problematic. The subject of 'communalism' and religious identity politics in India has generated a lot of interest in rioting, violence and conflict. Most of this work has been on contemporary violence,[36] but some older works, most notably Gyanendra Pandey and Sandria Freitag, looked at the anatomy of communal riots in the colonial period.[37] Again, in most work on the subject since the 1980s, one of the central questions has surrounded why so many people appeared to acquiesce or actively participate in conflicts having very little to do with their immediate circumstances. Some of the *Subaltern Studies* writers, for example, suggested that, in many cases, direct public action, including riots and violence, represented the natural (and largely autonomous) expression of workers and peasants.[38] The danger with ascribing this kind of autonomy to peasant and worker activity is that it can recreate contemporary official (and Indian nationalist) observations on the 'natural' tendencies of India's poor, as described above. Suggesting that cultural identities are 'autonomous' is not far from arguing that they are relatively resistant to change from the outside,

---

[36] See, for example, Achin Vanaik, *The Furies of Indian Communalism* (London: Verso, 1998); Paul R. Brass, *Theft of an Idol* (Princeton: Princeton University Press, 1997), Ashutosh Varshney, *Ethnic Conflict and Civic Life: Hindus and Muslims in India*; Steven I. Wilkinson, *Votes and Violence: Electoral Competition and Ethnic Violence in India* (Cambridge: Cambridge University Press, 2004); and Ornit Shani, *Communalism, Caste and Hindu Nationalism: The Violence in Gujarat*.

[37] Gyanendra Pandey, *The Construction of Communalism in Late Colonial India*; Sandria Freitag, *Collective Action and Community*. See also Suranjan Das, *Communal Riots in Bengal, 1905–1947* (Delhi: Oxford University Press, 1991).

[38] Partha Chatterjee, 'Agrarian Relations and Communalism in Bengal', in Ranajit Guha, *Subaltern Studies I* (Delhi: Oxford University Press, 1982).

political contexts and broader social conflicts.[39] And this argument was used by colonial officialdom as a way of resisting state-driven social reform.

The work of the *Subaltern Studies* authors has been extremely important in demonstrating how the everyday politics of the disempowered could be very different to those of India's elites, and to this end, it is used throughout this book. These differences are extremely important. The best of this work, too, has not been so clearly integrated into mainstream accounts of Indian nationalism: as a result, the story of India's supposed march to freedom remains just that – a historical movement towards a tragic conclusion, perhaps constructed to appease popular desires for an alternative outcome to events. However, it also tends to oversimplify the ways in which no action involving violence, particularly at the level of mass politics, was ever entirely autonomous or based on 'free' choices. This book will also critique the idea that the riot provides the archetypal manifestation of religious identity politics then, and in particular, the assumption that violence epitomises the politics of the 'subaltern'. Such suggestions ultimately lead to the conclusion that the essential political motivations of the poor are located in pre-capitalist consciousness and ideologies.

Researchers on communalism have also tended to adopt the idea that religious riots or religious violence provide a key or route into understanding communalism or the mobilisation of religious identities in politics. However, as Paul R. Brass has pointed out in his most recent work on the subject, the task of finding a set of causes or roots to the communal riots is largely fruitless and misleading, when the key agencies in the production of such violence are implicated in state actions and political processes.[40] Throughout, this book argues that events resulting in large numbers of casualties, ostensibly fought on the grounds of religious community difference, have a significance that moves well beyond the immediate or direct causes of conflict. In fact, it is more valuable to examine the larger political effects of religious and sectarian violence, the way 'communal' conflict has become a political theme in struggles between parties and regimes and the local circumstances in which political capital is gained from conflicts. Here, reporting on violence, the quantifying of casualties and the

[Handwritten marginal note: Paul Brass argument]

---

[39] David Washbrook, 'Orients and Occidents: Colonial Discourse Theory and the Historiography of the British Empire', in Robin Winks, ed., *The Oxford History of the British Empire Volume V: Historiography* (Oxford: Oxford University Press, 1999).

[40] Paul R. Brass, *The Production of Hindu–Muslim Violence in Contemporary India*.

soul-searching around 'remedies' form part of the whole project of how violence becomes a part of the political process in South Asia. But even more importantly, this book attempts to trace the means in which the real, everyday concerns of ordinary people are connected to moments of violence that have a significance that reaches beyond their localities. And it also looks at the ways in which communities (as those working on institutions of civil society have suggested) sometimes avoid violence on the basis of religion.[41] As we will explore, violence is often an extreme manifestation of a much more complex array of confrontations and negotiations between individuals and communities.

Two specific examples serve to show how analyses of 'violence' need to be treated with caution. The mid to late 1940s is universally acknowledged as a time of repeated and sustained violence between India's main 'religious communities' – described in the literature as Hindus and Muslims and Sikhs and Muslims. It is also generally accepted that most of this violence came about as a result of the political expectations, promises and upheavals of the final years and months of British power in India. Many historians have suggested that this phase of conflict in India is unique. However, even if we suggest that, in these moments of large-scale violence, there are contingent and specific rivalries that are better explained with reference to local and disaggregated factors, specific issues of 'identity' are not necessarily helpful.[42] For example, a huge amount of the violence took place specifically around the process of migration and displacement between 1947 and the early 1950s (and into the 1960s in Bengal). There were multilayered reasons for these later sets of conflict, which may have related to the partition but which also connected to specific localities and points of migration. In any account, the coexistence of Hindus, Muslims and Sikhs does not adequately explain this violence in the name of 'religious community'. Instead, we need to investigate how the notion of 'community' among these groups linked to structures of state (and non-state, civil institutions or quasi-state) power at all levels. Although influenced by the very geopolitical conflicts of the subcontinent itself after 1947, the effect of religious identity and conflict on politics was highly ambiguous and differential across the region. For example, the 'secularism' of India, as this book will discuss, was challenged (both before

[41] See Ashutosh Varshney, 'Ethnic Conflict and Civil Society: India and Beyond', *World Politics*, 53, 3, 2001, 362–98.
[42] Brass writes about 'repertoires' of violence, in which local feuds and conflicts are decided or resolved. See Paul R. Brass, *Forms of Collective Violence: Riots, Pogroms and Genocide in Modern India* (New Delhi: Three Essays Collective, 2006).

and after independence) by powerful interest groups inside and outside the mainstream, who sought to establish the 'religious' basis of Indian identity.

The second example concerns the dramatic changes of the early 1990s in India. Riots between Hindus and Muslims spread across north India, in response to the demolition of a sixteenth-century mosque built on the alleged site of the birthplace of the Hindu god, Ram – the Babri Masjid in Ayodhya, Uttar Pradesh. But this violence was not the outcome of simmering animosity between the two communities across the region, although the mosque-temple dispute did have a deep history. Rather, it was directly stimulated by the political mobilisation of the BJP, alongside associated institutions, the Vishwa Hindu Parishad (World Hindu Council), the Rashtriya Swayamsevak Sangh (RSS) and the Bajrang Dal. And this mobilisation was made possible for reasons that in some cases had very little to do with any specific sense of antagonism between religious communities and much more to do with longer-term decisions of local governments and political reactions to the developing politics of caste reservations.[43] The specific turn of politics in the late 1980s and early 1990s in UP had allowed the mosque dispute to take on a symbolic significance. But most importantly, over the 1980s, the institutions of the Hindu right had grown in political strength in northern and western India and had benefited directly in areas of community controversy.

Drawing the analysis of 'communalism' and the violence associated with it away from considerations of identity has implications for how far we seek to explore 'causes' of violence. Questions about causes often assume that a linear explanation exists for a moment of violence, when in fact the very questions surrounding causation are problematic. Whereas the documented 'spark' for a riot in an Indian city might have been a bazaar quarrel between members of two different communities, the conditions that allow violence to spread are very rarely explained by reference to the original and specific differences at the local level. There are often, however, clear points of comparison between conflicts in different parts of any particular region or across regions. What sorts of histories emerge when we compare these contexts and moments, not only over broad phases of India's political past, but also with other colonial and post-colonial contexts in South Asia? The chapters that follow will tackle some of these questions and provide some synthesis for what is a complex

---

[43] See Chapter 8 for more detail on this dispute.

and divided historiography on religious conflict or 'communalism' in South Asia.

There are other reasons for treating the study of pure moments of violence with care. The terms 'communalism', 'religion' and 'violence' themselves have a form of descriptive power in South Asian society and politics, and it is through the employment of such categories that scholars produce knowledge about South Asia. Recent work on Sri Lanka is instructive here, in thinking about the relationship between the categories of violence and religion. The work of Ananda Abeysekara has suggested that much of the writing on 'ethnic' conflict in Sri Lanka has posited Buddhism and violence as essential opposing cultural categories – that the resurgence of violence on the island somehow represents the 'betrayal' of the true spirit of the tradition. Here, Abeysekara suggests that the categories of Buddhism and violence are taken as self-evident by the likes of other authors on Sri Lanka's violence – principally Stanley Tambiah and Bruce Kapferer. Was, as Tambiah suggests, Buddhism 'betrayed' in the widespread emergence of violence in the mid-1980s? As we will see in Chapters 6 and 7, Tambiah posited the idea of a political Buddhism that was opposed to a doctrinal one.[44] But opposing the two creates problems, because so much of this scholarship takes each category as a given and does not explain why something that is described as Buddhism today becomes violence tomorrow and vice versa.

Abeysekara's point about the dangers of making assumptions about the terms we use is convincing, as is the invitation to scholars to unpack and question the idea that humanism implies automatic or unquestioned commitments to safe 'non-violent' political practices. What counts as 'religious action' or 'violence' is contingent and should be related to the detailed contexts in which each term is constituted – contexts that may allow the meanings of such terms to shift. Approaching the terminology in this way hopefully allows us to disentangle violence from official and state-driven concerns about stability and instability and to relate it rather to the exercise of power. This is important to some of the main arguments of this book, which are concerned with the ambiguous points at which state actors, sometimes informally empowered, assumed the mantle of physical force and indeed legitimised themselves using violence.

However, in focussing on difference, contingency and context, this book will not lose sight of the real interconnections that existed between events in different parts of the subcontinent. In attempting to anatomise

---

[44] Stanley Jeyaraja Tambiah, *Buddhism Betrayed.*

violence without atomising it, we should bear in mind that the human subjects of historical enquiry lived and experienced politics across a range of regional, national and global spaces. Deconstruction of analytical categories has been fashionable for a long time, and much of this work is useful. There have been many attempts to break apart completely, older ideas about 'communal' conflict on the basis of broadly defined religious communities. Most recently, detailed research has allowed scholars to employ critiques that directly break down and complicate identities such as 'Hindu' and 'Muslim' via close studies of particular regions – sometimes provinces or states, sometimes districts, sometimes cities or even villages.[45] India, its regions, cities and villages are also considered to be quite exceptional, not easily related to other contexts. However, there has been very little attempt to compare even the states of South Asia, apart from at the level of high politics, despite the fact that people moved across these spaces, learned about them and were in many cases materially affected by events thousands of miles away.[46]

This book will also suggest further that there is not, and never has been, any clear line of demarcation between the institutions ostensibly espousing secularism and those of religio-political mobilisation.[47] Second, it will argue that since 'Hindu–Muslim' conflict is never an uncomplicated matter of a clash of civilisations or religious outlook, we need to examine how contexts and circumstances are negotiated by the ideological and political choices of those involved in conflict. Finally, in looking at violence, we need to move away from looking at it as an aberration, a moment of madness, and more in terms of an everyday struggle of people attempting to make sense of their predicament. All too often, 'communalism' has been represented as largely a momentary aberration in an otherwise peaceful context.[48] Important, here, is the sense in which so much writing on violence in states such as those of South Asia has tended to quantify and collectivise such violence and, in the process, has dehumanised its victims. In this sense, not only is it important to attempt to narrate experiences of

---

[45] See Magnus Marsden, *Living Islam: Muslim Religious Experience in Pakistan's North West Frontier* (Cambridge: Cambridge University Press, 2005).

[46] Sarah Ansari, William Gould and Taylor Sherman, 'The flux of the matter'. Another notable exception here would be Ayesha Jalal, *Democracy and Authoritarianism in South Asia: A Comparative and Historical Perspective* (Cambridge: Cambridge University Press, 1995).

[47] For examples of this approach, see Janaki Bakhle, *Two Men and Music*, and William Gould, *Hindu Nationalism and the Language of Politics in Late Colonial India* (Cambridge: Cambridge University Press, 2004).

[48] Gyanendra Pandey, *Routine Violence: Nations, Fragments, Histories* (Palo Alto: Stanford, 2005), pp. 13–15.

individuals in violence – to prevent their experiences from being swamped by figures – but also to move beyond the analysis of violence in terms of casualty statistics and to consider its longer-term implications.[49] The traumas and displacements of violence affected not only the nations and the living spaces of communities, it also affected relationships within families and between individuals.

(IV) HISTORIES OF SOUTH ASIA: A COMPARATIVE APPROACH

The region of South Asia[50] or the Indian subcontinent is often depicted not just as a convenient geographical description, but also as a collection of states with distinctive and cross-comparative social and political elements. It has formed a consolidated region of study and research throughout the academic world outside the subcontinent itself. Yet to some extent, this is a fictional unity, created by the historical demands of nation-state building. Over the period of our study, it has been divided and mapped around borders both imaginary and real – divisions created around competing identities and the limited political attempts to contain or represent them. One of the themes of this book will be to investigate how far this tension – between the artificial grouping of regions on the one hand and the apparent building of concrete geopolitical, national and regional identities on the other – created the conditions for particular kinds of social, religious and ethnic conflict.

The nation-states of this region today and the administrative subdivisions within them have encompassed almost every possible political system – from the communist state governments of North East and Southern India (West Bengal and Kerala), through to periods of right-wing party rule under 'Hindu nationalist' regimes and military dictatorships. The region includes the largest, most socially complex democracy in the world (India), a nation built upon religious separatism (Pakistan), another on regional and linguistic separatism (Bangladesh) and states based on totalitarian and monarchical regimes (Nepal).[51] The most populous and

---

49 Gyanendra Pandey, 'India and Pakistan, 1947–2002', *Economic and Political Weekly*, 37, 11, 2002, 1027–33.

50 The term 'South Asia' was a geopolitical, as well as a geographical, term used in the United States and UK during the Cold War, and formed the basis for regional studies in the Universities of Michigan, Virginia and Cambridge.

51 The focus of this book is on India, Pakistan, Bangladesh and Sri Lanka, and for reasons of space, Nepal and Burma have not been included.

internationally powerful of these states (India, Pakistan, Bangladesh, Burma and Sri Lanka) were part of British India and Ceylon – an enormous imperial territory, whose fragile unity was central to the immediate political instabilities of the region shortly after independence from colonial rule in 1947. And in historical writing about the subcontinent, it is this colonial past that has to a great extent forged the sense of the 'subcontinental' region. Most significantly, as this book will explore in subsequent chapters, the very project of 'nation building' in this region involved processes of colonial partition and was therefore, as Partha Chatterjee has pointed out, intimately tied to the colonial experience.[52] The approach of this book inevitably causes some distortions. It focuses more on north India than on the South, principally because some of the main primary research material has been drawn from the region of Uttar Pradesh or from archives dealing with the central government. Some states and regions have been covered in more detail than others, some have been excluded and not every theme in this vast subject has been treated.[53]

The danger of writing about religion and conflict over such a vast geographical area is that the nuances of case studies in particular regions can be missed. However, it is not the intention of this book to repeat what has been done in the many pieces of detailed research on specific localities or to recreate something on a similar scale. It will attempt to suggest, using both those case studies and some original primary research, that there are both empirical and theoretical advantages to a comparative approach. First of all, at key moments in the period this book is concerned with, the political identities of significant north Indian communities were directly affected by international developments. Francis Robinson, Mushirul Hasan, Ayesha Jalal and Farzana Shaikh have shown how the political ideologies of north Indian Muslims in the 1910s and 1920s were in some cases moulded in response to international developments in the Islamic world.[54] Indirectly too, it is important to look at developments in other

---

[52] Partha Chatterjee, *Nationalist Thought and the Colonial World: A Derivative Discourse* (Minneapolis: University of Minnesota Press, 1993).

[53] Burma (Myanmar) and the monarchies of Nepal, Bhutan and Sikkim have traditionally been included in definitions of 'South Asia', and for others Afghanistan and Tibet. However, for reasons of coherence and clarity, this book does not explore these states.

[54] Francis Robinson, *Separatism Among Indian Muslims: The Politics of the United Provinces Muslims 1860–1923* (Cambridge: Cambridge University Press, 1973); Mushirul Hasan, *Nationalism and Communal Politics, 1885–1930* (New Delhi: Manohar Publications, 1991); Farzana Shaikh, *Community and Consensus in Islam: Muslim Representation in Colonial India, 1860–1947* (Cambridge: Cambridge University Press, 1989).

colonial contexts. Susan Bayly has shown how colonial ethnography in turn-of-the-century India was immersed in wider international academic debates about ethnographic mapping.[55] How the state recorded, studied and ruled different Indian communities had international implications, especially within other imperial contexts. Moving into contemporary India, it is clear that modern Hindu nationalism has been nourished by transnational connections.[56]

Second, the principal states of South Asia today have deep-rooted historical connections. The history of their divergence into separate nation states, for example in 1947 and 1971, is very much at the heart of this book's concerns. Since 1947, the politics of religious community in both India and Pakistan cannot be examined without some reference to the 'other' state. Very few studies of the politics of either state attempt to compare the experiences of both places. Third, the politics of each of these states, particularly when it comes to themes surrounding religious communities, has involved the direct involvement of one or more of the others. The politics surrounding the Sinhalese–Tamil conflicts in Sri Lanka relates to regions of India and the actions of its central government; Bangladesh came into existence in 1971 partly as a result of the involvement of India against West Pakistan; and significant reactions to the rise of the Hindu right have taken place since the early 1990s in both Pakistan and Bangladesh. Finally, there are theoretical advantages in taking on board the work of those looking at different regions of South Asia, particularly around ideas of 'communalism' or violence. For example, some of the most insightful work on everyday violence and the question of how ordinary people come to be involved in religious community conflicts has been done in the context of Sri Lanka. And much of this research can be related to India, Pakistan and Bangladesh.

It is also useful to compare the colonial and post-colonial politics of religious and ethnic community, and to move over the divide of 1947. For example, a consideration of early manifestations of the idea of the 'Hindu' community allows us to have a more nuanced sense of Hindu nationalism after 1947. Equally, some of the more sophisticated approaches to 'communalism' in colonial India can be related to the material in more recent times. Work on colonial India can be used then to reflect on post-colonial

---

[55] See, for example, Susan Bayly, 'Caste and "race" in the colonial ethnography of India'.
[56] For some discussion of this, see Chetan Bhatt, *Liberation and Purity: Race, New Religious Movements and the Ethics of Postmodernity* (London: UCL Press, 1996) and Arvind Rajagopal, *Politics after Television: Hindu Nationalism and the Reshaping of the Indian Public* (Cambridge: Cambridge University Press, 2001).

South Asia and vice versa.[57] In this connection, the book will explore colonial imaginings of religious communities in the subcontinent. There is a danger that scholars sometimes simplify colonial notions of community, as though it is possible to talk of a consolidated 'British approach' or the policy of 'the Raj'. The colonial state and its forms of knowledge have often been homogenised once historians start to look at communal politics. Some important work has questioned this oversimplification of colonial knowledge in relation to religious community.[58] I will argue further that it was the specific practical imperatives facing institutions of the state (the police and bureaucracy, for example, but also the municipalities and district boards) rather than simply loosely defined colonial ideologies that generated differentiated views on religious mobilisation in India. And the actions of these institutions, being quite different in different localities, naturally varied the real meaning of colonial approaches to community. The book will look at how state agents were so easily implicated in religious violence or conflict and why state institutions have had such an important part to play in hardening religious or communal identities. In looking at the colonial state in this way, the historian gains a clearer sense of how democratic polities continued to mobilise in ways that co-opted state agents, and did so with reference to local ideas about religious or ethnic community interests.

In looking at religion and conflict between 1860 and the 2000s in South Asia, one of the key questions of the book, then, is why particular forms of political community emerged to privilege religious identity over others at certain moments. This book will argue that there were specific political and social changes, particularly between the 1870s and 1930s, which not only shaped the *representation* of religious identities themselves, but which also determined the interrelationship between religion and other social identities, such as family, kinship, caste, region or linguistic group. In this connection, Chapters 2, 3 and 4, as well as covering the period from the 1860s to the 1930s, will survey how notions of religious community cut across other forms of identity politics or political structures. First, they will consider the relationship between the functions of the state itself and religious/ethnic community mobilisations. Second, they will briefly look at how recent work has investigated the crucial interrelationships between

---

[57] This approach is followed in a different way by Steven Wilkinson, in 'India, Consociational Theory, and Ethnic Violence'.

[58] John Zavos, *The Emergence of Hindu Nationalism in India*, and Norbert Peabody, 'Tod's Rajast'han and the Boundaries of Imperial Rule in Nineteenth Century India', *Modern Asian Studies*, 30, 1, 1996.

caste, class/occupation and religious mobilisation. The book will outline, for example, how social and ritual disabilities and advantages associated with caste identities cut across or encouraged particular forms of religious mobilisation and how these mobilisations related to political power. Third, these chapters will explore the relationship between the politics of religious community and class and, in this connection, will look at the development of new forms of consumerism, the status concerns of professionals, changes in the family and public health and the ways in which working-class politics interacted with religious community mobilisation. Finally, these chapters will explore how ideas about the 'Hindu' or 'Muslim' politics were also created by changes in cultural production and output, particularly in relation to language and music.

Chapter 5, which focuses on the 1940s, contains some of the main primary research material. It also elaborates some of the principal arguments of the book, which connect colonial with post-colonial histories of communalism and violence. First, it will explore the ways in which the colonial state began to fracture in the 1940s, and how quasi-state organisations, often militaristic in their orientation, became a means for powerful local leaders to further their political agendas. In the context of a polarised political situation, especially in places like Uttar Pradesh, this meant that a range of volunteer organisations, some of them armed, were based around ideas about religious community difference. They faced off around some of the key political moments of the period and, importantly, often took up policing functions. Second, this section looks at violence and displacement shortly following independence, not in terms of the well-documented mass violence of the partition itself, but the immediate aftermath in terms of its effects on the local state, the position of Muslims as a minority in India and the connection between local events and broader political agendas. Often quite localised and specific forms of communal mobilisation fed into wider agendas of conflict and reprisal. In particular, it argues that partition created multilayered conflicts of great longevity, which extended well beyond the disputes around statehood, borders or political identity.

Chapters 6, 7 and 8 explore the histories of religious community, ethnic and caste mobilisation and conflict between 1947 and the 2000s in the states of India, Pakistan, Bangladesh and Sri Lanka. Chapter 6 explores the central issue of 'national integration' and how the regimes of each state developed overarching ideologies of national belonging. These cast a different light on the politics of religious community and brought into play in new ways the tension between the centralising drives of national governments and regional movements. The latter evoked, in some cases, similar strategies to the mobilisers of religious communities. Second, it considers the meaning of state 'secularism', particularly in the Indian context, but also the significance of religion and religious ideologies in the states of Pakistan and Sri Lanka. Finally, it explores the interconnections between caste mobilisation (in India) and ethnic/regional mobilisation (in Pakistan and Sri Lanka) and how they related to ideologies of 'communal' politics. Chapters 7 and 8 continue these narratives into the period of the 1970s to the 2000s, exploring the creation of Bangladesh in 1971, the apparent 'Islamicisation' drives of regimes in Pakistan and Bangladesh and the background to the violence between Sinhalese and Tamils (as well as other communities) in Sri Lanka from the early to mid 1980s. Finally, these chapters explore the rise of the Hindu right in the 1980s and 1990s in India, and the nature of 'communal' violence in the 1980s, 1990s and 2000s. Most crucially, the final two chapters explore the appropriation of local state power by parties and organisations that sought to challenge and destabilise incumbent regimes, often on the basis of language, region, ethnicity or religion.

2

Building Spheres of Community

1860s–1910s

In 1890, an eleven-year-old Bengali girl by the name of Phulmonee became the subject of intense public debate across India. She had died as the result of rape by her twenty-nine-year-old husband, Hari Maiti, who had acted on the basis of a traditional life-cyle rite – *garbhadan* – which permitted a husband to have sexual intercourse with his wife within sixteen days of her first period. A year later in 1891, an Age of Consent Bill was passed that raised the minimum age of consent for married girls to twelve years. The Bill was passed despite the reluctance of representatives of the colonial state itself, and under pressure from Indian reformers. The debate surrounding the Age of Consent Bill created new and urgent discussions about the nature of domestic 'Hindu' life. The existence of authoritative religious codes on the rights of husbands to control the lives of girl brides had hindered any suggestion of colonial reform. Indeed, some of the key communities, on which the colonial system depended, backed a vociferous campaign in opposition to the Bill and, most importantly, in opposition to the colonial state. This intrusion into the religious customs of the Hindu family was depicted by journals in Bengal, such as the *Bangabasi*, as an attack on the sovereignty of the 'Hindu people' to control the bodies of women. Some lower-caste communities in north India too in this period aspired to higher ritual status by practicing infant marriage of girls.[1]

The very definition of the Hindu family and 'community', the legal rights (or non-rights) of women within it, was therefore, in this debate, played out in relation to a colonial state that sought to recognise and

---

[1] See Tanika Sarkar, 'A Pre-History of Rights: The Age of Consent Debate in Colonial Bengal', *Feminist Studies*, 26, 3, 2000, 601–22.

protect vital sources of 'community' identity. But, as this chapter will explore, it did so on the basis of fundamental tensions in the relationship between the state and Indian society, which constantly threatened to delegitimise state agencies. In this debate too, new discussions emerged about the relationship between the individual, family and community; about the importance of religion to Indian society; and about the legal and civic rights of women in relation to men. It exposed the means whereby the colonial state sought to 'discover' religious custom and the means of communication and publicity that promoted certain selected ideas about religious custom. Throughout the debates on the Age of Consent Bill, as this chapter will explore around broader themes, traditional notions of community rights were being challenged not only in a broad ideological defence against Western modernity, but also from other, non-Brahmanical visions of what constituted a religious community in India.

(1) RELIGION AND POLITICAL MOBILISATION IN THE LATE NINETEENTH CENTURY

In order to understand the complex actions of the colonial system, reformers and 'conservatives' around issues like the age of consent in the 1890s, it is necessary to move back at least to the aftermath of the 1857 mutiny-rebellion. In 1858, the Act for the Better Government of India finally transferred the entire administration of India from the Company to the Crown. A Secretary of State for India received the powers of the Company's Court of Directors, and the former was to control the reorganised Indian Civil Service. However, the events of 1857–8 did not represent a sudden transformation in British power in India. The basis of the colonial system had been changing from the late 1780s, and had accelerated through the Charter Acts of 1813 and 1833, which progressively transformed the power of the Company. But the Queen's Proclamation of 1 November 1858 did represent an important shift in the state's intentions in relation to Indian religion. The Proclamation suggested that the Raj would

disclaim alike the right and desire to impose our convictions on any of our subjects. We declare it to be our royal will and pleasure that none be in anywise favoured, none molested or disquieted, by reason of their religious faith or observances, but that all alike shall enjoy the equal and impartial protection of the law.[2]

---

[2] See Papers of Charles Canning, Brotherton Library, Leeds.

In theory, the state was restricted in its interference in what administrators considered to be the 'religious' interests of Indians. In making such a statement, the Government of India (and other representatives of the colonial state) presumed that tangible and clearly defined religious communities could be 'discovered' or codified.[3] These definitions were essentially based on Western notions of 'religion', through which India's religious cultures were read, as a means of collecting information on the Raj's subjects.

Colonial interpretations of religious community in India could be varied and contradictory, however,[4] and the whole process of collecting information about Indians changed the nature of the contacts made between Indian subjects and state authority in uneven ways. Indians could gain leverage in relation to state agencies by promoting 'community' identities. And the dynamics of this interaction transformed over the last third of the nineteenth century, as more Indians gradually became involved in local administration and municipal/district politics. This varied greatly from region to region, and had a differential impact over the last quarter of the nineteenth century. To some extent, as we will see in this chapter, Indian discussions about religious community related to increased involvement by the state in the everyday lives of the Raj's subjects; for example, via a more formalised civil service from the 1860s: new areas such as public health and hygiene fell under the remit of the bureaucracy in most Indian localities.[5] More generally, the steady formalisation of colonial bureaucratic power aimed to establish greater official control over the resources of the land and the revenues to be derived from it. And as this process developed, trading and moneylending intermediaries brought the gaze of the state more directly to rural and urban communities across the country. In India over the late nineteenth century, official definitions of religious communities then were tied up with the whole exercise of colonial power itself. For some historians, this was a direct process, with the very definition and discovery of 'religion' being a facet of orientalist 'knowledge' about the colonised world.[6] For others, it was a colonial project of

[3] Bernard Cohn, *Colonialism and Its Forms of Knowledge: The British in India* (Princeton: Princeton University Press, 1996). See also Vasudha Dalmia, *The Nationalisation of Hindu Traditions: Bharatendu Hariscandra and Nineteenth Century Banaras* (Oxford: Oxford University Press, 1997).
[4] Norbert Peabody, 'Tod's Rajast'han and the Boundaries of Imperial Rule in Nineteenth Century India', *Modern Asian Studies*, 30, 1, 1996, 185–220.
[5] Claude Markovits, ed., *A History of Modern India, 1480–1950* (London: Anthem, 2002), p. 348.
[6] Ronald Inden, *Imagining India.*

'organisation' as a cultural language of modernity, which was picked up by Indian intellectuals and used to authorise social and political institutions.[7] In other ways, we could view this process as a gradual 'nationalisation' of selected 'traditions' by Indian intellectuals, involving institutions that sought to reform, revive or set out the traditions of religious community that drove the process.[8] All of these ideas will be explored more in this chapter. Most historians are agreed that the practice of defining 'religious' community had far-reaching consequences in India from the middle part of the nineteenth century, which overlapped with the building of 'national' organisations, and the eventual occurrence of 'religious' or 'communal' conflict.

All religious traditions in India were subject to this renewed intellectual scrutiny in the late nineteenth century, but it was Hinduism and the 'Hindu' community that was the subject of the most intense and prolonged debate. First, investigations of Hinduism as a set of religious traditions and system of social organisation were at the root of British colonial ideas about Indian (or 'oriental') society in general and the forms of government that were 'best suited' to the region. Hinduism and the idea of the Hindu community were therefore subject to changing traditions of European political thought in the early to mid-Victorian period. To take one important example, Benthamite utilitarian thinkers in the 1830s presupposed the sense that the 'corruption' of 'oriental' systems of government and social organisation might be remedied via a rational system of governance. European secular 'rationalism' was juxtaposed with the idea of an essentially non-rational Indian population, whose social structures were embedded in religious hierarchies, recognised by outsiders as 'Hindu'. But these ideas transformed in the decade leading up to the mutiny-rebellion. For J. S. Mill and the Romantic thinkers of the mid to late nineteenth century, Indian social and political organisation was better understood with reference to 'sentiment' rather than simply reason. Indian social institutions therefore should not necessarily be subject to reform, since the essential character of their 'cultures' defined how Indian peoples represented themselves and built institutions of social and political organisation.[9] These Romantic traditions in political philosophy suggested that primordial identities were at the root of Indian political behaviour – a premise that

---

[7] See John Zavos, *The Emergence of Hindu Nationalism in India*, p. 2.

[8] Vasudha Dalmia, *The Nationalization of Hindu Traditions*.

[9] See Lynn Zastoupil, 'J. S. Mill and India', *Victorian Studies*, 32, 1, 1988, 31–54. See also Eric Stokes, *The English Utilitarians and India* (Oxford: Oxford University Press, 1959), ch. IV.

also later led, although through different debates and circumstances, to the biological essentialism of late Victorian racial science.[10] It also led to the project of 'discovering' the essential religious cultures of the Indian people, in a way that directly compared them to European religious organisation. In particular, what was seen as the essential 'corruption' of Brahmanical Hinduism was compared unfavourably to the reformist spirit supposedly evident in Christian civilisation and which lay at the root of Victorian notions of 'progress'.[11]

However, Indians played the major role in setting the actual terms of these debates about social change and religious reform. In response to European discourses of racial and cultural superiority that underpinned colonial power, a range of cultural movements and institutions were developed to take up the project of delineating 'Hindu' culture, practice and community in particular – the very area in which Europeans had posited their notions of racial superiority. We will examine some of these in more detail in this chapter. But by way of introduction, the debates of Indian intellectuals from different regions, and the institutions that drove and publicised their views, transformed the conception of Hinduism and the Hindu community from all angles. What in the premodern period was largely a 'juxtaposition of flexible religious sects',[12] rather than a monolithic religion, was increasingly compared by these intellectuals with other 'World Religions'. Religious practice in India continued to be heterogeneous throughout our period – in fact, there never was and never has been coherency and unity in religious belief within Hindu traditions. However, 'Hinduism' and 'Hindu' as meaningful signifiers of religion in India certainly did develop in the late nineteenth century.[13] It was this development that will form the focus of this chapter.

The idea of the 'Hindu' community, 'Hinduism' or the 'Muslim' community in India therefore became more palpable for both literate and illiterate communities over the last four decades of the nineteenth century, despite the real divergencies of tradition and religious practice across India. But extremely important in this process was who, specifically, was instrumental in such redefinitions and for what purposes. Since the groups and individuals here were varied and diverse, this chapter will

[10] See Kenan Malik, *The Meaning of Race: Race, History and Culture in Western Society* (Basingstoke: Macmillan, 1996).

[11] Thomas Metcalf, *Ideologies of the Raj* (Cambridge: Cambridge University Press, 1994).

[12] Romila Thapar, 'Syndicated Moksha?', *Seminar*, 313, 1985, 14–22.

[13] See the essays in G. Sontheimer and H. Kulke, eds., *Hinduism Reconsidered* (Delhi: Manohar, 1997).

sketch out some of the principal patterns of interaction and debate. Those involved in the process of defining religious communities were often also in a position to 'represent' or lead them. This meant that literary, intellectual and political elites were, at first glance, best qualified to mobilise resources to define Hindu history and tradition, usually on the basis of their reading of 'greater' high-caste traditions than those representing any one of the vast array of 'smaller' localised traditions across India.[14] Yet, as we will see, this project of representation did not accurately represent the realities of religious community interaction in most cases, and a range of localised religious mobilisations challenged the attempts of elites to standardise a sense of the 'Hindu' community.

The definition of 'Hindu' and (in different ways) 'Muslim' was therefore an exercise in the power of representation at multiple levels: between European administrator and Indian intellectual, and between dominant Indian publicist and relatively disempowered Indian subject. For the Muslim elites of northern India, it was related to increasing European impact on other parts of the Muslim world, and the decisions by the Government of India to placate potentially dangerous opposition to their rule as *dar al-harb*.[15] Important above all from the Indian perspective was the ability to mobilise social and cultural resources – the skill to mediate ancient texts, or the capital and expertise to set up a publishing house, or the building of an educational institution. These activities nearly always took place in a context of negotiation with or resistance to colonial authorities. However, the many different types of people engaged in the intellectual project of defining 'Hinduism' meant that it was very difficult to categorise institutions in terms of either 'revivalism' or 'reformism'.

These varied approaches might have involved the work of individual publicists and intellectuals like Harischandra Bharatendu – a leading Hindi journalist who, through the promotion of Hindi, began to develop the notion of a unified Hindu community in the region of the United Provinces.[16] Alternatively, we might explore the process with reference to specific institutions, such as the Sanatan Dharma Sabhas – orthodox organisations supported by Bharatendu, which set out, in cities like Banaras, to establish and define authoritatively correct/standard procedures in religious practice. Or we might look at reform and revival in

---

[14] For a detailed discussion of the interrelationship between 'greater' and 'lesser' traditions in Indian religions, see Chris Fuller, *The Camphor Flame: Popular Hinduism and Society in India* (Princeton: Princeton University Press, 1992).
[15] Peter Hardy, *The Muslims of British India*, pp. 56, 118–24.
[16] Dalmia, pp. 5–11.

Hinduism in relation to a much more active organisation – the Arya Samaj. This movement was founded in 1875 by Swami Dayanand in Punjab, and focussed on the ancient Vedas as the core texts of 'Hinduism', which posited an idealised, four-*varna* basis for Indian society in rejection of caste as *jati*. Certainly, most representations of 'Hinduism' were formed in response to changing political contexts in which Indian governments and administrations adjudicated 'community' representation on local boards and bureaucracies. Outside these formal institutions, debates about religious communities and traditions related to other kinds of political institutions and movements at all levels – from the early cow-protection movements of the 1880s and 1890s in north India, or the town-based *sabha* representing sectional interests, to the early Presidency Associations and Indian National Congress. 'Community' was one of the key terrains on which such institutions started to map the constituencies for whom they would exercise power.[17]

Most of the older work on late nineteenth-century Indian politics and history discussed the period of 1870 to the 1910s in terms of this 'emergence' of Indian national politics and organisation.[18] English-educated elites and powerful non-English-educated intellectuals, spurred on by changes in communication technology and the accessibility of vernacular literatures,[19] established new political institutions. This chapter will be concerned more with popular responses to religious community mobilisation. But these publicists were important in the building of civic institutions that were to reflect, in crucial ways, on the nature of 'religious' community representation. Mostly based in the presidency capitals of Bombay, Calcutta and Madras, but also spread across smaller cities like Lucknow, Allahabad and Poona, these leaders promoted a measured critique of the colonial system, gradual Indianisation of the government services and political reform and change.[20] Organisations loyal to the British, such as

---

[17] See Anil Seal, *The Emergence of Indian Nationalism: Competition and Collaboration in the Late Nineteenth Century* (Cambridge: Cambridge University Press, 1968).

[18] However, the suggestion that 'national' institutions developed around campaigns to lobby for administrative jobs and low-level representation has been challenged by a nationalist historiography that dates national mobilisation back at least to the Indian mutiny-rebellion.

[19] Ulrike Stark, *An Empire of Books: The Naval Kishore Press and the Diffusion of the Printed Word in Colonial India, 1858–1895* (New Delhi: Permanent Black, 2007).

[20] See, for example, the work of Romesh Chander Dutt, *The Economic History of India in the Victorian Age: From the Accession of Queen Victoria in 1837 to the Commencement of the Twentieth Century* (London: Kegan Paul, 1904).

The British Indian Association, were displaced as the mouthpiece of elite public opinion by institutions that took a more overt political standpoint. For example, the Indian Association of Calcutta, headed by Surendranath Bannerji, protested against the 1878 Vernacular Press Act that had aimed at controlling the growing Indian press. In Madras, the Mahajan Sabha was founded in 1884, and in Bombay, the Bombay Presidency Association was formed in 1885. In the same year, the Indian National Congress was formed, initially under the auspices of Allan Octavian Hume – the first all-Indian organisation of its kind. Crucial too to the formation of these organisations was India's integration into the global economy via its colonial relationship with Britain and its penetration by global capital, and the increasing speed of movement of goods and information. The London exchange banks were allowed, by the Secretary of State for India over the same period, to control the circulation of capital between India and the rest of the world, around a system that favoured British capital and trade. Intensification of colonial trade with and capital investment in India were accompanied by the growing confidence of urban-educated professionals who critiqued the overall relationship between the colonial metropolis and India.[21]

The early 'political' organisations, especially those that developed with a national agenda, were almost entirely dominated by powerful middle-class professional groups – those of high status within their own communities, who were able to take advantage of the new opportunities offered by forces of gradual Indianisation. To this end, most of the earliest demands of the Indian National Congress, and organisations like it, revolved around the professional interests of these leaders and publicists. For example, a key demand of the early Congress was the opening up and reform of the Indian Civil Service.[22] In making these demands, these men also questioned anew the nature of the relationship between Indian society, and Western political organisation and institutions – a set of critiques that had their 'social reform' precursors in an earlier part of the century, in movements like the Brahmo Samaj.[23] There were also a whole new set of

---

[21] John McGuire, 'The World Economy, the Colonial State, and the Establishment of the Indian National Congress', in Mike Shepperson and Colin Simmons, eds., *The Indian National Congress and the Political Economy of India 1885–1985* (Aldershot: Avebury, 1988), pp. 40–60.

[22] For an extensive history of the early Congress, see John R. McLane, *Indian Nationalism and the Early Congress* (Princeton: Princeton University Press, 1977).

[23] For more details, see Charles H. Heimsath, *Indian Nationalism and Hindu Social Reform* (Princeton: Princeton University Press, 1964).

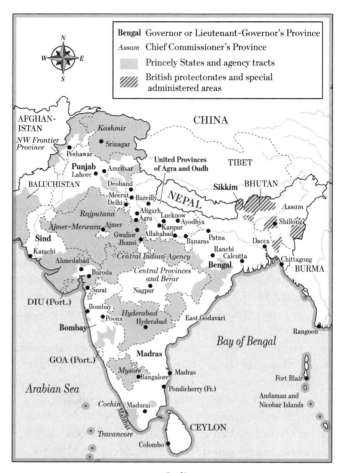

MAP 1. India, 1900

questions being raised about everyday customs, particularly around family life, law, and the status of women. Most famously, the issue of age of consent for marriage became a key point of debate and argument through our period, as we saw above. The concerns of these representatives of the larger national organisations failed to mobilise fully more than a very small section of India's vast population. Nevertheless, their representations of the politics of the 'masses' coincided with colonial stereotypes of Indian social disorganisation, and their assumptions about the essentially 'religious' sensibilities of the common man struck a chord with the colonial state.

(II) COMMUNITY MOBILISATION, REPRESENTATION AND MARGINALISATION

The early national Indian organisations, then, were both socially narrow and politically limited. They were also limited by virtue of being 'national'. From the outset, the Congress excluded social or religious issues from its debates, at least in theory – a situation that encouraged institutions like the Prarthana Samaj and the Social Conference, under the leadership of Justice Mahadev Govind Ranade and Sir Narayan Ganesh Chandavarkar in the last decades of the nineteenth and early twentieth century. This latter institution involved attempts to reform and 'modernise' Hindu traditions, by opposing excessive expenditure on rituals and rites, discouraging child marriage, and supporting widow remarriage and female education.[24] Certainly, many of the same men who joined the early political associations were also active in these social-reform movements. And in reality, religious issues lurked in the background agendas of Congress participants. A good example of this was the issue of cow slaughter in the late 1880s, which connected a range of local concerns across north India, and around which Hindu and Muslim participants often disagreed. Already by the 1870s and 1880s, then, different registers or levels of political discussion were becoming clear. First, official or formal decision making in the national and provincial institutions was based largely on a compromise about religious community and religious questions. Second, there was a growing desire at more local levels of Indian political life to discuss religious practices, and the extent to which the state might adjudicate conflicts over such practices, one way or the other. Third, the vast majority of Indians living in towns and villages, many of whom survived hand to mouth, may have connected to these national and local concerns. But their interpretations, for example, of the impact of religious practice in everyday life were often very different to official and intellectual assumptions about Indian social organisation. This will be explored in more detail below.

The tension between these different levels of political debate or concern is extremely important. From a very early stage in the development of broad political institutions like the Presidency Associations, 'secular' political activity, which avoided direct discussion of religious matters, became a norm, especially when it came to questions of governance and political

---

[24] To some extent, these men were influenced by colonial assumptions of the inherent 'decadence' of Hindu society, as illustrated in J. N. Farquhar, *Modern Religious Movements in India* (London: Macmillan, 1915).

representation. Yet the same individuals who presented this secular political stance at the level of the province or nation often stood for something
quite different in districts and cities. This spatial difference in Indian
politics continued, in a different form, right up to the end of the twentieth
century. For example, Madan Mohan Malaviya – a publicist from
Allahabad – took part in the national and largely secular Congress meetings, but also promoted Hindu revivalist organisations in his home city in
the 1910s.[25] Other leaders, even those not associated with Hindu or
Muslim revivalism, suggested that 'the masses' could only be reached via
an appeal to religion.[26] The nature of Indian National Congress secularism
was therefore, from the very beginning, compromised by this dual political
register. The duality was enhanced with the appearance of a younger/
newer generation of national publicists, whose political experiences related
a little more to forms of regional mobilisation – for example, the more
radical posturing of Bal Gangadhar Tilak and his use of the Ganpati
festival in Maharashtra, and Lala Lajpat Rai, an Arya Samajist of the
Punjab (discussed more below).

It was often during the early large-scale anti-colonial mobilisations
therefore that such leaders employed a religious rhetoric or appeal, most
notably during the protests surrounding the Viceroy's (George Nathaniel
Curzon) decision to partition Bengal in 1905. Some historians have suggested that one explanation for the rise of middle-class support for anti-
colonial protests against this partition was linked to the growing political
dissatisfaction of English-educated, high-caste Hindus in Bengal (*bhadralok*) who were unable to find professional employment or government
appointments.[27] But the partition agitations revealed much more than
just the disgruntled ambitions of urban intellectuals. Once Bengal was
divided (ostensibly and partly for administrative reasons, but also as a
means of containing Bengali criticism of the state), the nature of competition between struggling professional communities was altered. For example, in the newly created East Bengal, more Assamese and Muslims were
encouraged to compete for subordinate civil-service positions. This was
deliberate Government of India policy, to cut down to size what was seen
as a troublesome Hindu minority.[28] However, agitation around partition

[25] C. A. Bayly, *The Local Roots of Indian Politics: Allahabad 1880–1920* (Oxford: Oxford
    University Press, 1975).
[26] McLane, pp. 67–73.
[27] Sumit Sarkar, *The Swadeshi Movement in Bengal, 1903–1908* (New Delhi: People's
    Publishing House, 1973), pp. 23–8.
[28] *Ibid.*

pulled in a wide array of other movements, largely alienated from these urban elites or their concerns.

The social basis of the agitation, then, illustrates the interaction between the different registers of politics, in which support for some of the more radical leaders could be galvanised by workers' strikes or village-based movements. 'Swadeshi',[29] for the Calcutta professional and monied interests, was a means whereby boycott of English goods could be used to make constitutional demands. The swadeshi agitations launched in 1906 often based ideas about national economic development in cultural and 'religious' ideas.[30] For example, Aurobindo, a principal Bengali leader in this phase, talked of the idea of 'religious sacrifice' in the abandoning of the use of foreign goods. Swadeshi 'vows' were made in temples.[31] Temples and religious authorities were also easily persuaded to join a boycott that involved the rejection of 'foreign' materialism.[32] The anti-colonial movements of 1905–11 also branched into more direct forms of revolutionary action. The use of foreign goods was commonly argued to be 'ritually polluting' in pamphlet literature of the time – a theme that was continued in later Gandhian agitations across north India.[33] This kind of politics had a deep history. As early as 1867, a form of swadeshi had been publicised in the Calcutta Hindu mela, started largely under the auspices of the Tagore family.[34]

Sumit Sarkar has argued that, during the partition agitation, traditional Hinduism became 'the primary communication between the intelligentsia and the masses'.[35] Certainly, pandits were encouraged, at all levels, to promote swadeshi products and to apply social pressure on local communities connected to temples and religious events. Muslims were not entirely

---

[29] The term 'swadeshi' can be translated broadly as 'self-sufficiency' or 'indigenous manufactures', but it had more complex meanings, which related to ideas about homeland and individual identity. See Manu Goswami, 'From Swadeshi to Swaraj: Nation, Economy, Territory in Colonial South Asia, 1870–1907', *Comparative Studies in Society and History*, 40, 4, 1998, 609–36.

[30] *Ibid.*

[31] C. A. Bayly, 'The Origins of Swadeshi (Home Industry): Cloth and Indian Society, 1700–1930', in C. A. Bayly, ed., *Origins of Nationality in South Asia: Patriotism and Ethical Community in the Making of Modern India* (Delhi: Oxford University Press, 1998), pp. 197–9.

[32] See Gordon Johnson, 'Partition, Agitation and Congress: Bengal 1904–1908', *Modern Asian Studies*, 7, 3, 1973, 533–88.

[33] See William Gould, *Hindu Nationalism and the Language of Politics*, ch. 3.

[34] Anil Baran Ray, 'Communal Attitudes to British Policy: The Case of the Partition of Bengal 1905', *Social Scientist*, 6, 5, 1977, 39–40.

[35] Sarkar, *The Swadeshi Movement in Bengal, 1903–1908*, pp. 310–11, 421–2.

alienated from these events, and the famous Muslim agitator from Patna, Liakat Husain, addressed meetings of striking railway workers and disseminated anti-British literature between 1906 and 1907. However, more keenly remembered after the partition agitations had died down were the communal riots of the winter and spring of 1906–7. As with the broader appeals to Hindu unity, this violence was largely generated by the spreading of support for partition by particular agents among Muslims through the East Bengal countryside. Mullas – agents of the Nawab Salimulla of Dacca – increasingly promoted, via communal tracts, the boycott of Hindus. But this was not perhaps the principal factor in what culminated in riots and violence against property, principally in the Jamalpur subdivision in April and May 1907. The riots of this period illustrate the multilayered complexity of such conflicts. Behind the official accusations and nationalist counter-accusations that the violence was generated by high-status Hindu swadeshi operatives, or the reactionary Nawab of Dacca, more contingent narratives and accounts are apparent. For example, the increasing power of moulvis and petty officials now taking advantage of revivalist ideas disseminated in the seminaries of Dacca and Chittagong was crucial in the popular dissemination of anti-Hindu sentiment among Muslim lower classes. These petty preachers reminded Muslim peasants of their subordination to (predominantly Hindu) landowners and mahajans (moneylenders). Effectively, then, some of the violence of 1906–7 was a form of no-rent agitation or the withdrawal of Muslim servants and prostitutes to Hindu lords, born as much of social discontent as broad religious sentiment. Yet participants in such moments of violence could, and did, prove to be useful cannon fodder for leaders seeking political influence on a local body.[36]

More significant in this violence was the dissemination of news and rumour following the conflicts. Like a range of other movements that were publicised as having 'communal dimensions', the partition agitations were represented in the press and by officialdom in terms of community reactions and solidarities. For example, state descriptions of 'revolutionary terrorism' were juxtaposed to the supposed 'effeminacy' of Bengalis by British observers such as T. B. Macaulay and John Strachey.[37] To some extent, the symbols of mobilisation were based around the ideologies of

---

[36] *Ibid.*, pp. 444–60.

[37] Baran Ray, 'Communal Attitudes to British Policy', pp. 42–3; Mrinalini Sinha, *Colonial Masculinity: The 'Manly Englishman' and 'The Effeminate Bengali' in the Late Nineteenth Century* (Manchester: Manchester University Press, 1995).

intellectuals like Aurobindo in his pronouncements about the past glories of 'the Hindus'. Some of the main leaders of the boycotts bought into this. Surendranath Banerjea wrote that 'Swadeshi had evoked the fervour of a religious movement. It has become part of our Dharma'.[38] When it came to discussions of the violence of 1906–7, these broad images of community solidarity were important in guiding officialdom and the nationalist press to blame, principally, the 'illiterate' Muslim 'badmash' (ruffian) for the 1906–7 riots.[39]

Contrary to these accounts from the columns of papers, official reports and oratory soapboxes, participation by workers and peasants in mass movements and protests usually complicated this view of mass primordial sentiment. For example, during the partition agitations, well-organised hartals (strikes) were observed by Muslim and Sikh arsenal and railway engineering workers in Rawalpindi. Tens of thousands of Bombay workers went on strike and demonstrated when Tilak was sentenced in July 1908. Events such as these sparked the interest of international socialists and encouraged radicals such as A. K. Ghosh in his promotion of Anushilan recruits.[40] The Anushilan Samiti – a revolutionary organisation – promoted from 1905 'akharas' and militant cells across Calcutta's neighbouring towns.[41] Quasi-religious mobilisation was therefore, at one level, a form of social experiment in drawing together an idea of nationality that challenged Western conceptions of nationhood. Yet it was often largely a middle-class or high-caste interpretation of the complexities of Indian society at large, which incompletely captured the realities of most worker and peasant identities.

It was not at all the case, however, that those very varied arenas of 'mass' politics that leaders appealed to through speeches and in the press were based on either uniform or coherent religious community identities or a common set of religious practices. In fact, it was highly unlikely that any unified notion of religious community would unite the quotidian interests of the urban and rural poor, even within a single province. For many of those groups, whose agitations were ascribed to 'communal' awareness, broader changes in the colonial economy and social relationships were often important. And 'religion' served very different and specific purposes, not easily related to official discourses of religious fanaticism and common superstition. For example, in the 1870s and 1880s, the colonial state

---

[38] Baran Ray, 'Communal Attitudes to British Policy', p. 45.
[39] For details on this, see Suranjan Das, *Communal Riots in Bengal, 1905–1947*, pp. 53–4.
[40] Sumit Sarkar, *The Swadeshi Movement in Bengal*, pp. 238–48.
[41] *Ibid.*, pp. 472–5.

tightened its control of forest zones for revenue purposes – a context that created the scene for Koya tribal rebellion in Rampa in the Godavari Agency (in present-day Andhra Pradesh) in 1879–80, where new excise regulations and moneylending terms provoked a rebellion covering 5,000 square miles. In 1886, in the same region, another uprising employed the title of 'Rama's army'.[42] In these uprisings, religion served as a means for the hillsmen to effect their deliverance from oppression, or as a means of creating courage and unity in the face of materially more powerful opponents: oaths and sacrifices helped to create loyalty and solidarity.[43] Similarly, the Birsa Munda rebellion south of Ranchi in 1899–1900 protested against the erosion of the Munda's joint landholding system. Their leader, Birsa, was a Vaishnavite visionary, endowed for many of his followers with healing powers. Again, religion played a specific role here – becoming a means whereby power and solidarity could be enhanced at a moment of crisis.[44] In other areas, religious sects and groups rebelled against the domination of their 'history' by other communities and organisations: in Punjab, Sikh organisations and newspapers increasingly distanced themselves from the Arya Samaj over the 1890s and 1900s, even though its Singh Sabhas had often promoted the Aryas' *shuddhi* movements. Significant here were the attempts of the Arya Samaj to reconvert 'outcaste' Sikhs, for example from the Mazhabi and Rahtia (weaver) communities. This led to a reaction from other high-status Sikh communities, and moves from around 1905 to promote the distinctive and separate features of the Sikh faith and community.[45]

These differences between official/nationalist views of religious mobilisation and quotidian realities can be looked at in other ways. Concentration on riots themselves to some extent takes up, uncritically, official and quasi-official narratives of 'the communal problem', and places responsibility in the hands of uneducated masses and religious fanatics. Equally, a problem in using large-scale, institutionally led 'movements' of middle-class anti-colonial nationalism to define a narrative is that it tends to overlook important ideological and social trends in periods of apparent

[42] Sumit Sarkar, *Modern India 1885–1947* (London: Macmillan, 1983), pp. 45–6.

[43] For more detail on this, see David Arnold, 'Rebellious Hillmen: the Gudem-Rampa Risings 1839–1924', in R. Guha, ed., *Subaltern Studies I: Writings on South Asian Society and History* (Oxford: Oxford University Press, 1982).

[44] K. S. Singh, *Dust Storm and Hanging Mist: A Study of Birsa Munda and His Movement in Chota Nagpur 1874–1911* (Calcutta: Firma K. L. Mukhopadhyay, 1966).

[45] See Kenneth W. Jones, 'Ham Hindu Nahin: Arya-Sikh Relations, 1877–1905', *The Journal of Asian Studies*, 32, 3, 1973, 457–75.

hiatus, for example the period 1909–18.[46] Neither was it necessarily the case that ideas about strengthening the 'Hindu community' or 'service' to the community found audiences beyond the limited readership of newspapers and journals, despite their rapid rise in number of this period. Whereas between 1870 and 1900 very few publications were 'gagged' by the colonial state, by 1905, 1,359 journals and newspapers reached an estimated two million subscribers, 200 of which were considered by the British to contain potentially disloyal political commentaries.[47] While newspapers would have been disseminated beyond the literate, this readership nevertheless made up less than one per cent of India's total population in 1901.[48]

What can be seen at a more popular level in the 1910s was the importance of religious community and religious ideas in articulating social disadvantage and social grievances. For example, riots in Calcutta in September 1918 involved Muslim attacks on Marwari businessmen by communities aroused partly by pan-Islamic propaganda from itinerant 'ulama. Other movements for community assertion in this period of the 1900s and 1910s involved the promotion of social status via the formation of caste associations. In Tamilnad, for example, untouchable Nadars raised community funds for educational and social-welfare projects and as a means of claiming Kshattriya status. The 'Justice' movement in Madras from 1915–16, launched by C. N. Mudaliar, T. M. Nair and P. Tyagaraja Chettia, forged ahead in political mobilisation of intermediate caste protests against Brahmanical domination of education and the services.[49]

Some of the Christian missionary movements, too, had for a long time used religious faith as a basis for the articulation of social disadvantage and advancement. For example, the Society for the Propagation of the Gospel in Lucknow at the turn of the century directed some of its resources into the training and development of 'native Christian' women workers, whose devotion was represented as part and parcel of their social and gender advancement.[50] But it was not only those converted by Western

---

[46] Carey A. Watt, 'Education for National Efficiency: Constructive Nationalism in North India, 1909–1916', *Modern Asian Studies*, 31, 2, 1997, 339–74.

[47] N. Gerald Barrier, *Banned: Controversial Literature and Political Control in British India, 1907–1947* (Columbia: University of Missouri Press, 1974), pp. 8–10.

[48] The total Indian population, according to the 1901 census, stood at roughly 238,396,000.

[49] Sarkar, *Modern India*, pp. 156–9.

[50] See, for example, Bishop of Lucknow to H. W. Tucker, 11 November 1898, *Lucknow Letters Received* (Rhodes House Library, Oxford: The Papers of the United Society for the Propagation of the Gospel (hereafter USPG)), vol. 1.

missionaries in the late colonial period for whom religious identity became a means of reasserting new social identities. As Susan Bayly has shown, for the St. Thomas Christians of Kerala, an ancient Christian identity accorded distinctive social power, and the Portugese-converted Tamil-speaking Paravas of the Cormandel Coast adapted the power of Christian identity to their own pre-existing systems of status assertion.[51]

There were areas in which the interests of ordinary Indians and those of local leaders did connect around issues of religious community, for example in municipal government, where newly enfranchised urban leaders from the last quarter of the nineteenth century made decisions about local places of worship and religious practices that affected large numbers. It was in the control of towns that some of the most important competition between different political factions took place. At certain moments, as Chris Bayly showed for Allahabad, this competition could manifest itself along the lines of Hindu or Muslim symbols of power.[52] The municipal boards, even as early as the late 1860s and early 1870s, when the chairmen of these institutions were nominated officials, could be the centres of patronage politics, although electors to the boards from 1883 were limited to those in possession of incomes from Rs. 120 to Rs. 150. A seat on the municipal board, particularly the secretaryship, would allow elected members to build up retinues of supporters and dependents who could help in other elections, and who could ensure the selection of favoured contractors for public works. This meant that, in some periods, contractors themselves attempted to get onto the municipal board. In a more directly competitive way, the levying of indirect taxation in the municipality, particularly the 'octroi', could be 'managed' by one group of traders to challenge the interests of another.

In the area of religious observance, religious sites and their management, the local boards were crucial, so that party politics eventually linked to local religious management. The area of hygiene management around slaughterhouses or kebab shops was one issue in which Hindu and Muslim members of boards could exercise influence on behalf of their community constituencies. Most of the research in this area, however, has focussed largely on factional politics and the rise of middle-class professionals and urban businessmen in local politics. In some parts of north India – particularly western UP and parts of Punjab, for example – this resulted in

[51] Susan Bayly, *Saints, Goddesses and Kings: Muslims and Christians in South Indian Society, 1700–1900* (Cambridge: Cambridge University Press, 1989), pp. 6–9.
[52] C. A. Bayly, *The Local Roots of Indian Politics.*

competition for and exchange of land ownership, as moneylenders with a foothold in the municipality were able to purchase estates. In some cases, this competition manifested itself along the lines of religious community, especially by the 1910s.[53]

The point here is that such interests did not by necessity revolve around the broad differences between Hindus and Muslims, but that particular changes in the nature of the local state, local government, civic associations, land holding and control of urban resources and contracts could generate competition along these lines. For example, when the principle of election was introduced in municipal government, it could sharpen existing business alliances that revolved around specific religious communities. However, such competition could have also easily manifested itself along the lines of caste or faction. A closer look at the same themes in Madras and other parts of India shows that differences between religious communities were insignificant where they did not revolve around relative landed or economic power. In the South, control over local government bodies related more often to factional competitions that could interact with an emerging non-Brahman lobby. Around the turn of the century, the most powerful faction able to exert pressure within the new institutions of state in Madras, for example, was described as the 'Mylapore' group. By the 1910s, these men had, in some cases, become judges in the Madras High Court, sat in the Legislative Council or taken their places on government commissions. This powerful clique also had a presence in the religious life of the region, forming a Dharmarakshana Sabha – a society for temple reform. During the war, they used the vehicle of the Home Rule League and allied with Annie Besant to push for greater devolution of power. For most of the period up to 1916, however, they were opposed by other factions in the city, most prominently a group known as 'Egmore'. Most importantly, another loosely defined group of professionals for most of this period expressed their loyalty to the Raj during the war, and championed the cause of the non-Brahman communities. Their 'Non-Brahman Manifesto' of December 1916 argued that Brahmans (who made up only two per cent of the province's population) were over-represented in the public services, the University Senate and the High Court. This movement also formed a platform for the launching of Tamil and Telugu newspapers.[54]

---

[53] See, for example, Francis Robinson, 'Municipal Government and Muslim Separatism in the United Provinces, 1883–1916', *Modern Asian Studies*, 7, 3, 1973, 389–441.

[54] Christopher John Baker, *The Politics of South India, 1920–1937* (Cambridge: Cambridge University Press, 1976), pp. 22–9.

Once control over municipal and other bodies was not just an exercise in representation but an exercise in the control of patronage, then calls appeared for more formal protection of particular interests. Most famously, Muslim demands for secure representation on municipal boards, either through reservation of seats or forms of separate electorates, became common in north India from the 1900s. Critically, the whole affair of power being vested in elected elements of local government, limited by property and education, shaped the nature of this competition further. The property qualification for the municipalities could disqualify a large proportion of one particular community of lower economic status (as was the case in parts of western UP among Muslims). So, tied in with the calls for representation on the basis of community, the symbolism of certain castes and communities being 'disadvantaged' or 'backward' (a notion already being driven by colonial ideas of development) came into play.[55] This was reinforced by British colonial policy from 1882, in relation to education and specifically the Hunter Commission report, which assumed that the 'educational backwardness' of Bengali Muslims formed an argument for the special consideration of Muslims as a whole in India.[56] It was the extension of this politics into broader provincial and national debates that eventually led to the formation of associations designed to protect or promote the interests of religious communities – most notably the formation of the Muslim League in December 1906, out of the petition of leading Syed Muslim families to the Viceroy, calling for separate Muslim representation in elected boards and assemblies.

In 1909, the Councils Act established separate electorates for Muslims, and continued the principle of elections to the council through the municipal and district boards. Separate electorates had been called for by the Muslim League's 'Simla Deputation' on 1 October 1906, and effectively meant that the British Raj regarded the Muslim community as having the right to express separate political interests. This backed the early League's vision of colonial government as the arbiter of community interests, and their desire to shore up conservative Muslim voices, by recognising the 'historical importance' of Muslims in north Indian governance. To this end, the Viceroy, Lord Minto, also opposed the setting up of electoral colleges for creating Muslim electors, since it was feared that these might eventually be controlled by Congress leaders.[57] The issue of special representation eventually linked different levels of governance

---

[55] Robinson, 'Municipal Government and Muslim Separatism', pp. 410–15.
[56] Hardy, pp. 120–1.
[57] *Ibid.*, pp. 158–64.

directly – between the local affairs of faction, competition, town politics and land control, up to the provincial council itself. The struggles around separate representation did not of course only involve Muslim petitions. Hindu communities, particularly those associated with non-official organisations that could lobby government from a different angle (such as the Congress and more local associations), campaigned against special or separate electoral bodies. Most directly, a range of Hindu organisations began to build power and support on municipal boards across India, and their efforts increased from 1909 onwards. Separate electorates did not always result, either, in the mobilisation of political interests around irreconcilable religious community representatives. In 1916, the Lucknow Pact, involving moderate Congress leaders and the League, accepted the principle of separate electorates as a means of pressing for a jointly conceived programme for constitutional change and self-government.

Elections and the control of boards were not the only spheres in which the politics of community competition evolved as a result of separate electorates. For most Indians, which faction controlled the municipal or district board was less important than the ways in which the boards affected broader community concerns, and matters of everyday existence.[58] However, the ability of the urban and rural poor to use religious community as a means of empowerment was often limited by elites' control of channels of information. For example, across UP and Bihar, popular cow-protection movements were publicised by urban notables seeking to carve out political careers for themselves in the municipalities between 1882 and the mid-1890s.[59] It was the symbolism and mobilisation associated with cow protection too that generated political connections between the politics of the town and the countryside.[60] As we will see, powerful notables were thereby able to appropriate what might have been large-scale popular mobilisations for their own political ends.

Cow protection, then, is a theme that illustrates well the ways in which political symbolism could mean very different things at different levels of politics, between city and countryside. For urban elites, the development of economic arguments for the promotion of each *gaurakshini sabha* (cow-protection society) in western and northern India became a means of giving such activities respectability vis-à-vis the administration. Rights

---

[58] See Gyanendra Pandey, 'In Defence of the Fragment: Writing about Hindu–Muslim Riots in India Today', *Economic and Political Weekly*, 26, 11/12, 1991, 559–61.

[59] C. A. Bayly, 'Patrons and Politics in North India', *Modern Asian Studies*, 7, 3, 1973, 350.

[60] Sandria B. Freitag, 'Sacred Symbol as Mobilizing Ideology: The North Indian Search for a "Hindu" community', *Comparative Studies in Society and History*, 24, 4, 1980, 597–625.

and privileges in relation to cow slaughter (for Muslims) or cow preservation were increasingly framed with reference to formal frameworks of law.
And of course, local regulations on slaughter could be changed and interpreted through the municipalities. In 1886, Hindu organisations in
Allahabad put pressure on the municipal board to pass a bye-law prohib-
iting 'kine slaughter' within municipal limits. Disputes over the legality of
slaughter, then, reached the Allahabad High Courts in the following year,
and from there were publicised across the rest of the country.[61] This had an
effect across a range of public functions and forms of social life in north
India as a whole, contributing to what some historians have described for
the later 1920s period as the 'communalisation' of politics, at least for
urban elites.[62] In 1893, rioting and violence spread across the north in
India in relation to cow protection and slaughter, and this grew out of
protests at more popular levels, as we will see. However, cow protection
became a particularly useful rallying call for those aiming to generate
power on a local representative body. Moreover, the arguments about
Hindu physical health connected to bovine products related to other
middle-class concerns in the 1890s about Hindu communal strength.
Important, here, in the early 1890s were debates surrounding the age of
consent and the means of building powerful 'Hindu' families, insulated
from the Western colonial reformism. The Age of Consent Bill, which
raised the age of consent to marriage to twelve, also generated debate
about how far foreign rulers should intrude into the private religious
affairs of Indian subjects – a theme that connected again to formal regulations and rulings about cows.

The importance of religious community in political mobilisation for
Indian elites to a great extent, then, revolved around the mobilisation of
resources for the winning of local power in representative institutions. For
these men, the mass politics of the Indian countryside was significant only
insofar as appeals to religious sentiment might have a special relevance to
peasants, labourers and the poor. For most Indians, however, the everyday
struggles of life continued to be paramount, although political, economic
and technological change was certainly bringing ideas about religious
community more to the forefront. This was nowhere better illustrated in
the late nineteenth century than in the widespread cow-protection riots in
eastern UP (Bhojpur region) in 1893. These riots were of much more
extensive significance for the politics of mass rural mobilisation than the

[61] McLane, pp. 287–94.
[62] Robinson, 'Municipal Government and Muslim Separatism', pp. 418–19.

urban-based *gaurakshini sabha*.[63] Increasingly too, organisations and associations of the urban and rural poor challenged the appropriation of community leadership by notables on the municipal and district boards, although this process was highly differentiated across India. Another important point of contact between these different levels of politics was made through cultural institutions. And it was where such cultural institutions developed specific social campaigns that were pertinent to broader religious communities and groups that 'Hindu' and 'Muslim' mobilisation could, momentarily, connect Indians from a wide range of social backgrounds.

(III) EDUCATION AND CIVIL SOCIETY: INSTITUTION
BUILDING AND SOCIAL REFORM

Institutions of social and religious reform set up by powerful publicists to protect and promote the interests of specific religious communities often emulated the institutions of the colonial state. A key element of the colonial state's ideological dominance and legitimacy in India was the idea of colonial 'organisation', structure and rational governance, in juxtaposition with Indian social 'disorganisation' and the assumed irrationality of its pre-colonial political structures.[64] And it was in this context that late nineteenth-century movements of religious reform and revival were articulated within the framework of modern political organisation, or *sangathan*.[65] The 'Association', 'Society' or 'Committee' had its origins among the English-educated elite of the Presidency capitals. In some respects the '*sabha*', '*samaj*' and '*samiti*' emulated these structures, but they were also based in distinctively regional traditions that were not entirely influenced by European notions of association and organisation.

Where organisations formed to lobby government, it made sense for Indians to combine in movements and institutions that paid lip service to the principles of mendicancy allowed by the state. From the 1860s onwards, governments in India began to consider recruiting Indians into

---

[63] Gyanendra Pandey, 'Rallying Round The Cow: Sectarian Strife in the Bhojpuri Region, c. 1888–1917' in Ranajit Guha, ed., *Subaltern Studies II: Writings on South Asian History and Society* (Delhi: Oxford University Press, 1983), pp. 60–129. See also Anand Yang, 'Sacred Symbol and Sacred Space in Rural India', *Comparative Studies in Society and History*, 22, 1980, 576–96.

[64] For more detail on this, see William Gould, *Bureaucracy, Community and Influence: Society and the State in India* (London: Routledge, 2011), ch. 1.

[65] See John Zavos, *The Emergence of Hindu Nationalism*, pp. 34–57.

the higher echelons of the bureaucracy, although until the 1910s, 'Indianisation' of the higher services was very slow.[66] So those with professional aspirations for government service or with ambition to promote constitutional reform joined associations that could petition the Governor or Viceroy. In contrast, the *sabha* or *samiti* often combined functions that were specific to local Indian developments. For example, in the early years of the twentieth century, the notion of 'self-help' and 'service' or *seva* led to particular kinds of quasi-charitable functions for such organisations. In many cases, they represented the development of local political lobbies, which related to specific issues of reform, language, identity or locale. Where the spheres of political organisation were limited by a non-existent or restricted franchise, but the resources of intellectual debate were open (as was the case in most of British and princely India), political activity found its outlet in literary ventures and associations, which promoted political identification through culture, social communication and languages of power. For some historians and political scientists, these activities were part of a particular sphere of 'civil society', which had a very important role in communal identity mobilisation.[67] For example, the journalistic activities of the much-cited Bengali writer Bankimchandra Chattopadhyaya in the 1880s served to focus attention on the cultural roots of Indian patriotism and 'Hindu' identity via novels and satires that discussed the dangers of liberal reformism for Hinduism.[68] The literati could turn their hand to constructive work. Around the partition of Bengal agitations, Rabindranath Tagore's village reconstruction programme was implemented on the principles of *swadeshi*, particularly in Kaligram pargana (revenue or administrative unit), via a Hitaishi Sabha. These organisations sponsored schools, health centres and training centres for handloom weaving.[69]

---

[66] Indeed, the pace of Indianisation was also somewhat disappointing even through the interwar period for most Indian political institutions. See J. D Shukla, *Indianisation of All-Indian Services and Its Impact on Administration 1834–1947* (New Delhi: Allied, 1982).

[67] See, for example, Francesca Orsini, *The Hindi Public Sphere 1920–1940: Language and Literature in the Age of Nationalism* (Oxford: Oxford University Press, 2002), pp. 225–50; Sudipta Kaviraj, 'On State, Society and Discourse in India', in James Manor, ed., *Rethinking Third World Politics* (London: Longman, 1991); Ashutosh Varshney, 'Ethnic Conflict and Civil Society: India and Beyond', *World Politics*, 53, 3, 2001, 362–98.

[68] For an excellent discussion of Bankimchandra, see Tanika Sarkar, *Hindu Wife, Hindu Nation: Community, Religion and Cultural Nationalism* (Delhi: Permanent Black, 2001), ch. 4, pp. 135–62.

[69] Sarkar, *Swadeshi Movement in Bengal*, pp. 344–9.

It was in the area of education that ideas of Indian nationality and configurations of 'Hindu' or 'Muslim' identity were most fruitfully pursued by Indian intellectuals. The most well-researched institutions in this sense were the Aligarh Muslim University or Muhammedan Anglo-Oriental College movement on the one hand, pioneered by Sayyid Ahmad Khan, and the Banaras Hindu University on the other, driven by Madan Mohan Malaviya. Both of these education projects were much more than the bricks and mortar of their campuses or even the graduates they produced. They were movements in themselves, which (in very different ways) aimed to position an idealised notion of Indian citizens who could be at one and the same time Hindu/Muslim Indians and subjects of a Western/Christian colonial power. Both Aligarh and Banaras, and others like them, negotiated with the colonial government for resources and were influenced by British ideas about the content and shape of curricula. The Muhammadan Anglo-Oriental College (MAO) movement (and to a lesser extent BHU) was explicitly set up around the project of how Muslims or Hindus might negotiate their subjecthood within a colonial system while contributing to the national and global aspirations of their community.

Before looking at these sorts of institutions in more detail, it is necessary to consider the broader growth and interest in educational institution building in the late nineteenth century. Following the 1854 'Despatch on "General Education in India"', gradual efforts were made to affiliate colleges with a London University–style system.[70] From the 1860s, colonial debate revolved around the possible extent of 'anglicisation' and the desire to promote colonially defined notions of 'oriental' learning. For Muslim communities, the madrasa foundation accelerated in the late nineteenth century, and the Barelvi and Deobandi schools in Bareilly and Saharanpur set the pace from the late 1860s and continued to define in broad terms differing interpretations of Islamic education within colonial India. Private madrasas also continued to play an important role through this period. Significant too was the 'Westernisation' of educational institutions, with madrasas and other 'oriental' colleges following the examples of government-sponsored institutions by designing examination and classroom systems. Nevertheless, among the Muslim community, teachers were still drawn from among the 'ulama.

Similarly, other educational institutions were developing and changing in scope in response to the perception of European or specifically British notions of instruction. In some cases, schools established by Christian

---

[70] *The Despatch on 'General Education in India'*, Bristol Selected Pamphlets, 1880.

missions filled a space in the provision of the colonial state, and the activities of missionaries were 'used' by the state to maintain stability. For example, in the North-East in the late nineteenth century, American Baptists, Welsh Presbyterians and the Baptist Missionary Society took over government schools.[71] In educational projects for all communities, the education of women provided new approaches to instruction, which allowed urban middle-class professionals and the growing Indian bureaucracy to champion social change. The issue of Muslim women's education, in particular in the late nineteenth century, was affected by the increasing colonial control of religious property trusts that funded it – the *waqfs*. Yet at the same time, there were government projects to fund new schools on Western lines. Women were also increasingly involved in promotion and innovation in women's education. The journalists, publicists and activists Muhammadi Begam, Wahid Jahan and Rokeya Sakhawat Hussain were all involved in the establishment of girls' schools and literature promoting them.[72]

For every large-scale education project or institution, there was an array of challengers or critiques, which threw up alternative visions of what Indian education should mean. Educational debate and discussion quite closely mirrored political debate on other issues, since most education projects and institutions were driven by factional conflict and interest-group formation, as well as conflicting ideologies about regional and national identities. This can be seen through the history of perhaps the most famous Muslim reformer and educational pioneer of the final quarter of the nineteenth century, Sayed Ahmed Khan. Sayed Ahmed came from a 'loyal' background as far as the British were concerned, in a phase when the most publicised 'all Indian' technique of political mobilisation involved the petition to government. Born into a Mughal family and serving as a jurist for the Company, Khan remained loyal to the British during the 1857 uprisings. As a result of his experience of colonial service, he argued from 1870 that Muslim education in general in India was too rigid and disabled by its inability to take on what he saw as the best features of Western education.

Most Muslim commentators on education in this period continued to believe that education and religious instruction were inextricably linked.

---

[71] Frederick S. Downs, *History of Christianity in India Volume V, Part 5: North East India in the Nineteenth and Twentieth Centuries* (Bangalore: Church History Association of India, 1992), p. 53.

[72] See Gail Minault, *Secluded Scholars: Women's Education and Muslim Social Reform in Colonial India* (Oxford: Oxford University Press, 1999).

However, Sayed Ahmed Khan argued that, in reality, the prime importance of education in Persian or Arabic for most Muslims was not the requirement to read religious texts but to qualify for official employment. For Sayed Ahmed, Islamic theological education could be transformed by a new approach to education, which would bring more Muslims into contact with Western institutions and forms of education – instructing them in the traditions of their religion and simultaneously preparing them for employment in the state. As an intellectual, he was interested in squaring the scriptural authorities of Islam with what he saw as the strengths of 'Western' rationalism. This was partly about promoting the local and personal interests of individual Muslims, but more importantly about the fulfilment of Islamic society at the forefront of world civilisation: to claim for Islam the advances of science.[73] The blueprint for the Muhammadan Anglo-Oriental College was Oxford and Cambridge.

Such a project could not be established without fierce debate and disagreement, however, between Muslim intellectuals. Conservatives believed that religious instruction along traditional lines should be given continued primacy. Some educated Muslim women, on the other hand, presented alternative models for how Muslim society should respond to the project of creating citizen-subjects for the future nation. The Muhamedan Educational Conference, headed by Badruddin Tyabji in 1903, opposed the advanced plans for the organisation of a Muslim university as 'premature'. Sayyid Mumtaz Ali and Muhammad Begum founded the weekly newspaper *Tahzib un-Niswan* in 1898 in Lahore, which promoted the religious education of women – a project that in its inception had clashed with Sayed Ahmed's views. Mumtaz Ali was no straightforward Muslim modernist but a Deobandi reformer who aimed to promote the madrasa's focus on the more complete religious education of the Muslim community as a whole. Islamic 'modernism' did not necessarily tessellate completely with the promotion of women's education: issues of gender could cut across the whole debate about Muslims' position as subject-citizens.[74]

An important aspect of this debate around Muslim education lay in a new bifurcation of secular and religious scholarship, in which the worldly ambitions of Muslims in India were given a new kind of priority. This ran

---

[73] David Lelyveld, 'Disenchantment at Aligarh: Islam and the Realm of the Secular in Late Nineteenth Century India', *Die Welt des Islams*, New Series, 22, 1/4, 1982, 85–102.

[74] See Gail Minault, 'Sayyid Mumtaz Ali and "Huqquq un-Niswan": An Advocate of Women's Rights in Islam in the Late Nineteenth Century', *Modern Asian Studies*, 24, 1, 1990, 147–72.

alongside a shift from the concept of *ummah* to *qaum* – the idea of ethnic community over a community of believers – suggesting that success in worldly ambition would contribute to broader religious causes.[75] This revival of aspects of the 'spiritual' for futuristic and worldly programmes epitomised other forms of revivalism across India.[76] It was to be seen too in the range of institutions of Hindu organisations, which will be explored more below.

The eventual Anglo-Oriental College and Muslim University movement that emerged was riven by factionalism and rivalry between the 1880s and 1910s, not least between an older, more conservative generation of leaders and founders and a younger generation that took control later. However, it quickly became one of the central institutions of Muslim political mobilisation in India.[77] For some, this movement represented the attempts of an older Mughal service elite to adapt in the face of rapid political change and to champion the interests of the 'Muslim community' to the state.[78] However, Aligarh was not the only driving force of change in the Indian Islamic world. Neither should it be assumed that because Sayed Ahmed Khan was naturally placed at the epicentre of this narrative, that the story of Muslim mobilisation is one of reaction to the pressures of colonial modernisation. Changes in the many Muslim communities of India over this period also related to the reformism of the sharif 'ulama themselves in the intellectual life of Delhi and other urban centres, or the debates over institution building between shias and sunnis.[79] Also extremely important over the late nineteenth century was the development of education for the 'ulama – in particular, the Deoband *dar al-ulum*. Deoband was to educate generations of Indian 'ulama who had little to do with Muslims who negotiated or socialised directly with British administrators, and who for the most part actively opposed the decadence of Christian European culture.[80]

The MAO College, which eventually became a university movement, was designed to be a centre of learning for all Muslims in the British

---

[75] David Lelyveld, 'Disenchantment at Aligarh'.

[76] See Amiya P. Sen, *Hindu revivalism in Bengal, 1872–1905: Some Essay in Interpretation* (Delhi: Oxford University Press, 1993).

[77] David Lelyveld, 'Three Aligarh Students: Aftab Ahmad Khan, Ziauddin Ahmad and Muhammad Ali', *Modern Asian Studies*, 9, 2, 1975, 227–40.

[78] David Lelyveld, *Aligarh's First Generation: Muslim Solidarity in British India* (Princeton: Princeton University Press, 1978).

[79] See here the work of Justin Jones, which will be explored in more detail in the following chapter.

[80] Hardy, pp. 170–4.

Empire. In this sense, the projection of Muslim power in India was tied up with British colonial notions of its own subjects and the 'character' of its Empire as a whole. Higher education also became a broader political battleground. Curzon's Indian Universities Commission of 1902, and the later Muslim Universities Act, limited the total number of Indian institutions of higher education as a method of maintaining government control over a growing cradle of anti-colonial protest. Within the college itself, divisions began to emerge between different factions of older and newer generations of old boys, who competed as champions of the growing Muslim public dissatisfaction with the largely British staff of the college. The key figures in the younger group were the brothers Mohammad and Shaukat Ali, who were later to build upon their factional victories in the college to reach a much wider form of political agitation. This development reflected a broader point: educational institution building and fundraising became the building blocks for regional and national networks of political contact, for educating and preparing graduates principally for political and government careers and, in the case of Aligarh, for furthering specifically Indian Muslim political agendas.[81] By 1914–15, the 'Young Party' in the Muslim League had become the focus of colonial defensiveness. James Meston, Governor of UP, wrote to the Viceroy in March 1915 that 'Education has not affected their generous impetuosity, their lack of industry, their blind acceptance of short cuts to any goal'.[82]

Both in educational movements and other kinds of institutions for religious community mobilisation, there were of course regional and ideological differences across India in the late nineteenth and early twentieth centuries. The interests of Muslim leaders in Muslim majority provinces like Punjab and Bengal were very different to those in NWP/UP, since power revolved around consensus between more demographically balanced communities rather than the assertion of minority rights. In a similar fashion, discussion about 'Hindu' identity was broken down into a wide range of different movements. Some of these used the vehicle of religion and ethnic difference to express socio-economic and class tensions – for example, the Satyashodhak Samaj in Maharashtra[83] or the Self-Respect

---

[81] Gail Minault and David Lelyveld, 'The Campaign for an Indian Muslim University, 1898–1920', *Modern Asian Studies*, 8, 2, 1974, 145–89.
[82] James Meston to Hardinge, 25 March 1915, Hardinge Papers, File 64, University Library, Cambridge.
[83] Gail Omvedt, *Cultural Revolt in Colonial Society: The Non-Brahman Movement in Western India 1873–1930* (Bombay: Scientific Socialist Education Trust, 1976).

movements in Tamilnadu.[84] In general, there was clearly a great deal of
disagreement about what exactly was being revived or strengthened when
leaders and organisations described their project in terms of the Hindu
community.

Regional differentiation in Hindu reform and revivalism over this
period is well exemplified by the Arya Samaj, which, while initially influential in Punjab, was not so prominent outside that province and parts of
NWP/UP. The Samaj was formed by Dayananda Saraswati in 1875 as an
attempt to focus upon what he believed to be the essential texts of
Hinduism – the *Vedas* – and to oppose the later accretions of social and
religious tradition brought by Brahmanism. The early Arya Samaj that
emerged in Punjab therefore presented a unique kind of social reformism
and critique of caste, which was complicated by its continued attachment
to the fourfold divisions of *varna*. The Samaj promoted reform through
education, attempting to square Western knowledge and didactic educational practices with interpretations of 'original Hindu' ideas. It was therefore an ambitious movement, which attempted to offer a totalising
framework for Indian and specifically 'Hindu' life. It was dominated by
those very Vaishya caste groups who had been successful in taking advantage of the changes in society and education brought by colonialism –
banias, khatris and aroras. The Samaj's critique of caste offered the hope
of new kinds of social mobility to these Vaishya communities, and presented them with a compromise solution to the new world in which they
found themselves – a middle-class milieu in which they often dominated
local bureaucracies and the judiciary. They could continue to live as 'good
Hindus' while following a more modern lifestyle that criticised polytheism,
unnecessary ritual and older caste prejudices, and upheld the ideals of
individual merit.[85] This was certainly part of the appeal of the Samaj to
one of India's leading 'extremist' leaders in the Congress in Punjab, Lala
Lajpat Rai.[86]

[84] D. A. Washbrook, 'Development of Caste Organization in South India 1880–1925', in
C. J. Baker and D. A. Washbrook, eds., *South India Political Institutions and Political
Change* (Delhi: Macmillan, 1975).
[85] In this sense, the Arya Samaj was an organisation based to some extent in strategies of
'emulation' of that which it opposed in Western modernity. For more on this idea, see
Christophe Jaffrelot, *The Hindu Nationalist Movement and Indian Politics, 1925–1990s*
(London: Hurst, 1996), pp. 14–16.
[86] See Norman G. Barrier, 'The Arya Samaj and Congress Politics in the Punjab, 1894–1908',
The Journal of Asian Studies, 26, 3, 1967, 363–97.

The Arya Samaj developed into a movement that connected directly with mainstream Punjabi politics by the first decade of the twentieth century, particularly those associated with Congress. This allowed its ethno-religious mobilisation to enter the political mainstream across north India, partly because the Samaj was based on church-like institutional units at many levels – the Arya Samaj Mandir.[87] In 1906, Arya Samaj members made up almost half of the Punjab delegation to the annual Congress session, and for most of the 1900s, they made up around half of the membership of the Punjab Congress Committee.[88] By the 1920s and 1930s, this set the scene for the Arya Samaj's appearance in public political discourse as an organisation of somewhat aggressive Hindu reformism, which had targeted, in particular, converts to Islam (and low-caste communities of other faiths, for example Sikh Mazhabi and Rahtias) through the *shuddhi* or purification movement.[89] At the turn of the century, the Samaj then was seen as a regional powerhouse of Indian nationalism, which had a practical set of agendas, a form of 'constructive' programme of national rejuvenation, which foreshadowed Gandhianism, and a range of organisational drives in the area of education. For example, in 1893, the Samaj divided between the 'DAV' and 'Gurukul' sections in relation to promotion of education. The former group espoused the setting up of Anglo-Vedic institutions, which largely followed a more Western pattern, whereas the latter worked for the establishment of universities and schools on the pattern of a rejuvenated 'ancient' Hindu model.

The Arya Samaj then effectively instilled elements of its swadeshi, self-help and industrial and educational development agendas into the Congress platform, especially in the Punjab. This was assisted by the fact that, particularly at this stage, the Congress was a political shell into which could be poured ideas to capture national attention and mobilise delegates' support. In the 1900 Congress session in Lahore, Punjabis were naturally able to dominate proceedings, and so, by extension, the Arya Samaj had a relatively well-publicised national voice, perhaps for the first time, through a national-level institution. They were able to dominate the discussions of the Subjects Committee by putting education and industry-related proposals on the table. The attempts to enhance the authority of Punjabi delegates in the future Congress were overturned by a powerful Bengali

---

[87] Zavos, *Emergence of Hindu Nationalism*, p. 49.
[88] Barrier, 'The Arya Samaj and Congress Politics', p. 367.
[89] *Shuddhi* principally involved the 'reconversion' of particular communities of Muslims and Christians back to the 'fold' of Hinduism.

lobby from 1901. However, Arya Samaj involvement with the Congress certainly coloured the image of the latter institution in the eyes of Muslims in north India. From 1904–5 onwards, this position was strengthened by the growing national popularity and political influence of Lala Lajpat Rai himself. Over the period of 1905–8, Rai, through his newspaper, *Panjabee*, extended the Hindu community interests of Punjabi Arya Samajists to the national stage of political debate, publishing a range of books and articles on Indian nationalism, social reform and British imperialism.[90]

By 1923, the Arya Samaj was mired in controversies surrounding conversion to Islam and Christianity, and its forms of Hindu mobilisation were attributed with more sinister motives, as we will see in the following chapter. But distinctions between Hindu reformism and 'political' Hindu nationalism should be retained. So too should the differences between organisations like the Arya Samaj and changes in everyday religious practice. For example, over this period, cow protection, the promotion of Hindi and the identification of the 'golden age' of Hindu civilisation were all themes that were taken up by professional and trading communities and literate urban Hindus.[91] Yet despite the emergence of these symbols and common ideas, forms of 'living' Hindu traditions continued to adapt and change around regional bases or sampradayas. Beliefs and forms of worship were highly variable: low-caste practices in parts of India disparaged the rituals of vegetarian offerings and Sanskrit medium of higher castes, and could proclaim their local deities to be more powerful, offering animal sacrifices through worship in the vernacular.[92] The Arya Samaj and organisations like the Hindu Mahasabha (discussed later in this chapter and the one that follows it) evolved outside of and despite these living traditions. While not systematically 'reformist', then (there was not always a concrete notion of which specific institutions should be 'reformed' for these organisations, aside from caste itself), such organisations and institutions nevertheless fitted what John Zavos has described as a 'systematic', 'acculturative' model of institutional development in that they evolved through contact to and reaction with other religious movements and institutional/ state structures.[93] The Arya Samaj, for example, developed to a great extent

[90] Vijaya Chandra Joshi, *Lala Lajpat Rai: Writings and Speeches, Volume 1, 1888–1919* (Delhi: University Publishers, 1966).
[91] See Christopher R. King, *One Language, Two Scripts: The Hindi Movement in Nineteenth Century North India* (Bombay: Oxford University Press, 1994).
[92] Chris Fuller, *The Camphor Flame*, pp. 255–6.
[93] John Zavos, 'The Arya Samaj and the Antecedents of Hindu nationalism', *International Journal of Hindu Studies*, 3, 1, 1999, 57–81.

around reactions to Christian missionary activity in the Punjab in the final decades of the nineteenth and early twentieth centuries.[94] And this elicited a counter-reaction and response from missionary organisations working in the same province.[95]

On the matter of caste, the Arya Samaj did adopt a somewhat indirect 'reformist' stance. Dayananda himself had set out the basic principle that the notion of *jati* should be discarded in thinking about caste in favour of a merit-based notion of *varna*. Indirectly, this undermined the authority of certain living traditions based on networks of caste-sampradaya. Also important was the setting up of the Arya Samaj mandir or 'church' for each branch that was established, which indirectly critiqued the institutional functions of caste. The Samaj adopted more direct methods or practices of 'reform', which, as we will see, brought it into direct conflict with Muslim and Christian communities. The *shuddhi* campaigns of 1907 (and those set up for 1922–3) involved rituals that reclaimed Muslims, Christians and some Sikhs (and low castes or untouchables) to their 'caste', or – in the case of the Arya Samaj – *varna*, which could find a kind of physical home or space in the mandir setting. Increasingly over the late nineteenth and early twentieth centuries, with the exception of notable controversial movements, *shuddhi* ceremonies targeted untouchables and low castes. The importance of this was that it offered a real challenge to orthodox Hindu ideas about caste purity, which meant that the Samaj was not only a challenge to Muslim and Christian organisations (indirectly protecting low castes too from the possibility of conversion), but also to high-caste Hindu orthodox organisations. For example, in 1909 in Hoshiarpur, the Arya Samaj led a *shuddhi* ceremony for low castes such as Chamars, which elicited a reaction from the local Sanatan Dharma Sabha, leading to conflicts.[96]

There was a tension, then, between the radical reformist stances of some Arya Samajis, seeking to reclaim untouchables and representing them as an integral part of the Hindu community, and the espousal of a unitary Hindu community that did not grant the same status to low castes and untouchables. As we will see in Chapter 3, this tension was evident in the Hindu Mahasabha sessions of 1923. And it was true that, increasingly, the notion of unity and uniformity took precedence in the public stance of Arya Samaj leaders over reformism, particularly around caste. This

---

[94] See Kenneth W. Jones, 'Communalism in the Punjab: The Arya Samaj Contribution', *Journal of Asian Studies*, 28, 1, 1968, 39–54.
[95] See Lahore, letters received Vol. 6, USPG, Rhodes House Library, Oxford.
[96] *Ibid.*

difference between the Arya Samaj of the early phase up to the 1920s and the Arya Samaj thereafter tells the historian a great deal about how political identities relating to the idea of 'Hindus' and 'Muslims' changed dramatically after the Great War, in the period of dyarchy. In the earlier phase, espousers of social radicalism within the framework of religious tradition did not necessarily desire to represent such projects in terms of a 'national' Hindu community as an organic whole, or to describe anything specific about the cultural content of the nation. These characteristics can be seen in the limited, experimental and open-ended projects of social service, for example in the late nineteenth and early twentieth centuries. Certainly, from about 1909–10, public debate surrounding the Hindu community, constructive nationalism and social service borrowed trends from European thought, particularly around eugenics and national identity.[97] By the 1920s, however, particularly in the context of a very changed political milieu, ideas about Hindu and Muslim identity shifted to juxtapose community and nation more forcefully.

Sanatan Dharma Sabhas, orthodox institutions that were established to defend what were considered to be the crucial aspects of the 'Hindu' faith, also contributed to these debates. The Arya Samaj had stimulated discussion about what it considered to be the corrupting and erroneous aspects of high-caste culture and social practice. In the same vein, the reactions to the Samaj were not based in attempts to disaggregate Hinduism but to encourage Hindu unity in a different and defensive way. The Sanatan Dharma Sabhas championed what they considered to be 'traditional' Hinduism against reformist critiques. To a great extent, such organisations were founded with the specific aim of opposing particular pieces of reformist legislation, as well as entering the fray with other institutions. The Bharat Dharm Mahamandal, for example, opposed the Age of Consent Bill. Yet at the same time, this organisation also sought itself to promote certain social reforms, such as control over unnecessary marriage expenses.[98]

Other institutions set out deliberately to represent the Hindu community as an entity that had separate political interests, although relatively few politicians believed that it was possible to define a 'Hindu community' in this sense. The All India Hindu Sabha (precursor to the Hindu Mahasabha) was formally founded in 1915 in Hardwar, although more localised Hindu Sabhas existed from the 1880s, which linked provincially shortly thereafter in some cases. The first attempt to replicate the Hindu

[97] Carey A. Watt, 'Education for National Efficiency', pp. 339–74.
[98] Sandria Freitag, 'Sacred Symbol as Mobilizing Ideology', p. 605.

Sabha in a variety of cities across India was at a meeting in Lahore on 4 August 1906. On the whole, its objectives and those of the Sabhas that followed it were unfocussed and usually lacking a definite programme.[99] Most of these associations, particularly the more local ones, were short-lived and ephemeral, although in cities such as Allahabad and Banaras, their fortunes were better sustained, mainly due to the importance of these cities as centres of Hindu devotion and pilgrimage. From 1909, such institutions reacted more to Congress's perceived failure to promote Hindu self-assertion. The prime mover here was Lala Lal Chand, who, at the time of separate representation for Muslims in the 1909 Morley-Minto reforms, encouraged moderate communal appeals to government on the behalf of the 'Hindu community'. Colonial enumeration further provoked this communal politics. The 1911 Census challenged assumptions that the Hindu community could contain India's diverse low-caste and tribal religious traditions. The Hindu Sabha, in a different but connected way to the Arya Samaj, reacted by encouraging popular enumeration.[100]

The national network of Hindu Sabhas – under the umbrella of the Hindu Mahasabha – was given a new urgency, then, by a perception of colonial state intrusion in communal enumeration, and fears that the state would begin to 'interfere' with established religious customs. The view of Hindus as 'a dying race',[101] encouraged by this spirit of enumeration, was to influence the Samaj leader, Swami Shraddhanand, in his promotion of Hindu *sangathan* (organisation) in the late 1910s and 1920s – a central ideology of the 1920s Mahasabha. At the heart of this communal politics was a fear of an apparently organised Indian Islam. But its movement was slow and its scope limited. The first all-India Hindu Sabha of 1915, like its satellite organisations, was a middle-class organisation of educated elites, little concerned with popular politics, but it did stimulate other provincial Hindu Sabhas in UP, Bihar and Bombay. So, as was the case with the educational and institutional developments of Muslims, the key centres of institutional development around religious community were in the United Provinces and the Punjab – the latter to some extent explained by connections to the Arya Samaj. At this stage, the Hindu Sabhas were loosely organised and straggling, with intermittent meetings and inconsistent memberships. They were largely composed of leaders and publicists who

---

[99] Zavos, *Emergence of Hindu Nationalism*, p. 112.
[100] *Ibid.*, pp. 114–20.
[101] The notion of Hindus as a 'Dying Race' was most clearly articulated by U. N. Mukherji of Calcutta in a series of articles in *Bengalee* in 1909.

were associated with organisations like the Congress, or who were involved in religious and cultural revival in their home cities.[102]

The Hindu Sabhas deliberately attempted to distance themselves from issues of controversy between different sects or social-reform movements. This meant that they had to focus upon subjects and discussions that would unite as wide a community as possible: cow protection, the promotion of Hindi against Urdu and the efforts to maximise the representation of the 'Hindu community' in areas of competition with other religious communities. Rather like the Congress but in a more disorganised and less coherent way, the Hindu Sabha (and later Mahasabha) was also to act as a form of lobbying movement to government – allowing it eventually to petition government around issues such as civil-service recruitment and representation on the Indian councils. Although somewhat incoherent at this stage, this activity prepared the Hindu Mahasabha for more forceful institutional development as a political party in the 1920s. However, its politics was practically irrelevant in the south of India, where conflicts on the apparent basis of religious community were very rare, at least before the 1920s.[103]

Attempts to systematise or homogenise religious belief around a broader sense of community also occurred among Sikhs in Punjab. Controversy surrounded the decision in 1905 to remove all idols from the Golden Temple in Amritsar (and thereby dissuade Hindus from using it). After this event, the idea that Sikhism should be viewed as a faith entirely distinct from Hinduism also became a fierce debating point in the Lahore newspapers. In this debate, between writers in the *Tribune* and the *Khalsa Samachar*, the latter supported by local Sikh reformist organisations, the Singh Sabhas, discussion surrounded whether rituals around the Adi Granth should be viewed as, essentially, idol worship.[104] Reformists pushing for recognition of an autonomous Sikh community were sponsored by powerful landowners, businessmen and professionals. And in general, the institutions of community association and organisation over this period were attempts by largely middle-class urban professionals and businessmen to further their own professional and political interests. This involved lobbying and influencing local and municipal government where, as we have seen from the 1880s, Indians had more power and were

---

[102] Richard Gordon, 'The Hindu Mahasabha and the Indian National Congress, 1915–1926', *Modern Asian Studies*, 9, 2, 1975, 145–203.

[103] Baker, *The Politics of South India*, pp. 3, 193.

[104] Amrit Kaur Basra, 'The Punjab Press and the Golden Temple Controversy (1905): An Issue of Sikh Identity', *Social Scientist*, 24, 4/6, 1996, 41–61.

promoting particular social and educational projects. The Hindu Sabhas, for example, in the cities of UP/NWP, directly served the business interests of powerful urban financiers and industrialists, particularly by the inter-war period. The Muslim organisations, too, still catered largely to a social and political elite.

Relatively low-status communities continued, in many instances, to live and worship in a way that was little affected by these organisations: poorer Muslim communities in Banaras regularly took part in Hindu festivals, as well as Muslim ones, and across rural India, a range of syncretic practices mixed religious traditions and beliefs.[105] Students for the Deobandi seminary were drawn from communities who had little contact with the corridors of power or bureaucratic recruitment and whose politics critiqued European colonialism in a very different way to the publicists of the Simla Deputation. The cow-protection violence that occurred in the Bhojpuri region in 1893 and later in 1917, from the perspective of colonial officialdom, appeared to have been instigated by higher-caste agricultural communities – Rajputs, Thakurs and Brahmans. However, lower-caste Ahirs and Koeris had their own agitations. Ahirs in particular were occupationally associated with cattle tending and developed their own ideologies of cow protection. Muslim resistance to these movements, too, came not only from leading communities but also from poorer Julaha weavers. These different social standpoints on cow slaughter/protection did not lead to a clear and consolidated idea of divided Hindu and Muslim interests. In this sense, the very social complexity of 'Hindu' and 'Muslim' mobilisation in these years meant that the notion of 'communalism' could not be applied as a uniform category of explanation.[106] The institutional consolidation of religious communities, then, was a dynamic of political mobilisation, complicated and sometimes contradicted by cross-cutting social interests.

Similar patterns of social differentiation can be seen in the field of literature and language use. Debates about which languages should be used in any particular region or across India for education, commerce, the courts or administration became particularly intense just as the projects of regional and national publishing and journalism developed on a large scale. The journal, newspaper and tract made new forms of literature or debates about language possible. And those with the skills and finance to publicise literary pursuits were able to open up such debates about

---

[105] For more on this, see Nita Kumar, *The Artisans of Banaras: Popular Culture and Identity, 1880–1986* (Princeton: Princeton University Press, 1988).
[106] Pandey, 'Rallying Round The Cow', pp. 103–29.

language. Print culture was therefore at the centre of these endeavours, and, moreover, the issue of promoting vernaculars took place against the ever-present power of English as a language of rule. Colonial hierarchies were developed through the 'high' literacy associated with English, and it was in reaction to this that the literati across India promoted the vernaculars.[107] A central figure here was Syed Ahmed Khan in the debates around and promotion of Urdu. Attempts to define a clearer and dominant language in Nagri were led by figures such as Harischandra Bharatendu in his promotion of a nationwide standardised Hindi through publishing and educational endeavours. For the Banaras-based journalist, language, literature, religion and territory were all important in defining Hindu identity, and he linked Sanskritised Hindi unambiguously to the Hindu community and high-caste Vaishnavite belief.[108]

However, for most of the period up to the 1910s, the promotion of vernacular literatures, although it began to map, for example, Hindi onto the 'Hindu' community and Urdu to Muslims, did not generate lasting antagonism or controversy. It was not until the 1920s that, for example, movements for the promotion of Hindi began to be represented in earnest as communally competitive. The question as to how this came about and why such controversies appeared at all is extremely important and warrants careful consideration. Certainly, the idea that the Hindu community might be connected to the promotion of Hindi was certainly something on the horizon of some of the key political publicists and leaders of the 1900s and 1910s. And in the 1888 session of the Indian National Congress, local issues such as the prevention of cow slaughter, as they applied to cities such as Allahabad, could still create the suggestion of a potential Hindu–Muslim divide.[109] Nevertheless, none of these developments created a uniform or broad sense that the interests of populations might be defined by ideas of religious difference, or that such differences existed uniformly across the entire subcontinent.

However, over the period up the 1910s, the issue of language increasingly entered into broader political discussions about the nation. For example, Hindi and the Devanagri script was at the centre of the project of late nineteenth-century Hindu revival. Dayanand Saraswati, the founder of the Arya Samaj, shared with Keshub Chandra Sen and a range of other Bengali leaders the desire to promote Hindi as a national

---

[107] Veena Naregal, *Language Politics, Elites and the Public Sphere: Western India Under Colonialism* (London: Anthem Press, 2001), pp. 4–5.

[108] Dalmia, pp. 432–4.

[109] McLane, *Indian Nationalism and the Early Congress.*

language. Moreover, the particular form of Hindi chosen by these intellectuals was important and defined later language debates of the interwar period. Dayanand and figures like him chose to concentrate on the promotion of a highly sanskritised Hindi as part of the project for the rejuvenation of the 'true' or 'original' language of Hindus. This was despite the fact that most speakers in what came to be known as the Hindi belt would have spoken neither a standardised Hindi nor one that was entirely devoid of Persian influences.

A key element of Hindi promotion in the late nineteenth century revolved around script, particularly the use of Devanagri. Indeed, since Hindustani contained a vocabulary that connected to both sanskritised Hindi and Urdu, it was around the issue of script that some of the most important controversies of the period raged. An important institution, linked to the Arya Samaj in this project, was the Nagri Pracharini Sabha based in Banaras, whose first secretary, Shyam Sundar Das, claimed that the idea for the Sabha had come out of a meeting of the Samaj.[110] The Nagri Pracharini Sabha was a crucial institution at the end of the century in promoting Hindi as a language of the courts in UP. The Arya Samaj educational institutions, such as the DAV colleges, were also instrumental in pushing the cause of Hindi. It was through Hindi journalism and literature that perhaps some of the most important progress in publicising Hindi was made. As well as Harischandra, the journals *Brahman, Ksatriyapatrika, Hindi Pratap* (edited by Balkrishna Bhatt) and *Anandkadambini* (edited by Babu Radhakrishnadas) were important in forwarding the cause of Hindi as the language of Hindus and as a national language.[111]

The cause of the Hindi literati was also furthered by the Banaras Hindu University (BHU) project, driven by Madan Mohan Malaviya. In a manner similar to the Aligarh University, BHU started in 1905 as a project that had a wider significance than just the establishment of a university. The finance for the university was the result of fund-raising among Hindu landed interests across the Hindi belt, through north and central India. Like Aligarh, it was designed to impart a particular kind of cultural and 'national' education that brought with it qualities not to be found in other institutions. This related to the symbolic and religious significance of Banaras itself, a town considered as the heart of Hindu culture. BHU

[110] Krishna Kumar, 'Hindu Revivalism and Education in North-Central India', *Social Scientist*, 18, 10, 1990, 4–26.
[111] Dalmia, pp. 141–2.

slowly developed, too, into the centre for the development of standardised Hindi syllabi for teaching in other colleges around the country.

The politics surrounding the differences between Hindi and Urdu were only one example of a range of other language movements across India. In western India, for example, from the late 1870s, Marathi was acquiring a dominant place in high literary pursuits in Bombay presidency, led by Chitpavan Brahman intellectuals. Over our period, Marathi literature and the politics of bilingualism were furthered by voluntary associations, such as the Bombay Education Society, and the earlier Students' Literary and Scientific Society. These organisations acted as intermediaries between the local intelligentsia of urban centres and colonial officialdom in producing a corpus of printed literature in both English and the vernaculars.[112] But in Pune, the high-caste intelligentsia's intermediary position in the literary and educational sphere was challenged by the low-caste Satyashodhak Samaj, led by Jotirao Phule, which used non-literary public performances such as the *tamasha* to contest high-caste dominance of the municipalities.[113]

In writing about the development of language politics in late nineteenth- and early twentieth-century India, historians and literary scholars have frequently made use of the idea of the 'public sphere'.[114] This framework presents the idea of a hegemonic middle-class public who developed voluntary institutions and publishing enterprises that defined the idea of public space via institutions of civil society. However, most scholars have also sought to complicate the traditional model of the public sphere presented by Jurgen Habermas in looking at European society in the modern period. Francesca Orsini, for example, has argued, with reference to the Hindi literary sphere, that instead of a twofold division of 'public' and 'private', we might consider Indian society in terms of three layers: public, private and 'customary'. For Orsini, this 'customary' sphere related to cultural practices and beliefs that unevenly overlapped between both private and public matters. Certainly, the development of literary spheres in India was very different to the experience of most European states, not least because of the complication of bilingualism among the social and literary elites. The symbolic power of the English language and its association with governance in India also recreated forms of colonial hierarchy in cultural affairs and in popular media. Perhaps most significantly, as was argued in the first section, the sphere of vernacular literary pursuits was

[112] Naregal, pp. 232–5.
[113] *Ibid.*, pp. 268–70.
[114] For example, Francesca Orsini and Veena Naregal.

more commonly associated by the politically powerful in India with the politics of the disadvantaged.[115] And just as appeals to the grassroots were often made via a religious idiom, so too did the use of Hindi, Urdu, Marathi, Bengali or other regional languages presuppose a different level of political mobilisation, which was often deliberately divorced from Western notions of secular mobilisation. Finally, the promotion of particular vernaculars involved projects of standardisation and definition, which reinforced institution and organisation building as a means of asserting particular kinds of collective identities. Insofar as language movements were concerned with the future shape of state power, as well as literature, the arts and 'culture', such institutions tied into the whole process too of how different communities shaped their approach to an imagined free Indian state.

(IV) RIOTS AND 'COLLECTIVE VIOLENCE'

The 'communal riot' has been the focus of intense interest to historians, political scientists and observers of India as the archetypal manifestation of community identity. Yet, as the last chapter suggested, although instances of such violence appear to be reasonably common across South Asia, and are often very serious in terms of human cost and damage to property, they have to be treated with great care by historians. First, the apparent ubiquity and frequency of such conflicts is questionable: for the most part, and with the exception of widespread moments of intense ethnic violence, such as 1947 or Sri Lanka in the early to mid-1980s, over our period, accommodation between religious communities was the norm for most regions. Second, as we have already argued, even where such violence appears to be endemic or prolonged, the exercise of finding causes is fraught with such difficulties that even an apparently straightforward clash between Hindus and Muslims can be related to factors little connected to religious difference or belief. Finally, because such events are extreme examples of human conflict, the historian is wont to put rather too much stress on their significance. In other words, just as contemporaries who experienced such violence often took the account of the riot out of context to explain a belief in irreconcilable differences between communities, so too have

---

[115] This was a constant refrain of M. K. Gandhi in the 1910s and 1920s, who associated the gulf between India's urban educated and rural peasant communities in terms of knowledge of vernaculars and, in particular, Hindi. See 'Gandhi's Speech on Non-Cooperation in Calcutta', 13 December 1920, *Collected Works of Mahatma Gandhi* (Ahmedabad: Navajivan Publishing House, 1972), Vol. 22, No. 57, pp. 84–9.

historians and other observers lost a sense of scale in examining riots. This is as true for the period up to the 1910s as any other period, although the significance attached to riots and conflicts in the late nineteenth century is different to that for the interwar period.

Common in research into the communal riot in the late nineteenth century has been the approach to the riot as a signifier of non-elite political identity and mobilisation. In fact, the complex colonial ethnographic descriptions of communities, as we will see, were very often based in official and non-official research and reporting on riots. The most researched example of religious or 'communal' violence in the late nineteenth and early twentieth century, looking at this signifier, has been that associated with the cow-protection movements, which developed across the United Provinces from the 1880s and 1890s. Interest in this mobilisation and its attendant conflict was not only the product of its sheer scale, but importantly the ways in which cow protection could link different levels of political activity in the region – from the village to the province and even nation. This latter theme was taken up particularly by Sandria Freitag in terms of the idea of the widening of public arenas, as political identities surrounding the 'Hindu' scaled up on both a geographical and an ideological level. For Freitag, the importance of cow protection was also that it illustrated the ways in which competition and conflict between religious communities could be the result of the expansion of the boundaries around a particular community as a result of internal debate.[116] And importantly, for her, such collective action could be the means by which non-elite communities entered public arenas of debate, especially where literacy levels were low. Gyan Pandey's detailed research on the cow-protection riots in eastern UP and Bihar in 1893 and 1917 relates the conflict to specific registers of caste difference and status assertion, in a context where the popular view of cow protection from the point of view of low-caste Ahirs, Koeris and Kurmis was quite different to that of UP's urban elites.[117] For both Freitag and Pandey, cow protection became a means for relatively low-status communities to assert higher status via association with something of symbolic importance to Hinduism as a whole: in this case, the cow.

For both of these historians, then, there is an implicit and sometimes explicit connection made between the status concerns of aspirant low-caste

---

[116] Sandria Freitag, 'Sacred Symbol as Mobilising Ideology', p. 603.
[117] See Gyanendra Pandey, 'Rallying Round The Cow' and *The Construction of Communalism*, pp. 158–200.

communities and the politics of violent action. Although Pandey in particular is keen to unravel the quotidian politics of peasant resistance here, the assumption seems to be that the most serious and widespread conflicts were those involving Ahirs, Koeris and communities of similar status, so that violent confrontation typified their engagement with a broader political issue. In contrast, as we have already seen, cow protection had a more genteel side: the first *Gaurakshini Sabha* was founded in the Punjab in 1882. But the whole issue became more significant following a High Court ruling in the North-Western Province (later to become UP), in which it was ruled that the cow could not be defined as a sacred subject based on section 295 of the Penal Code. The latter set out the punishment of imprisonment for the destruction or defilement of sacred objects of any religion. It was from this point that what had begun as a largely urban phenomenon, supported by powerful Hindu notables, became something that appealed to particular rural districts of NWP – in particular Azamgarh and Gorakhpur districts. In each place through the 1890s, both Muslims and lower castes involved in the handling of cow products and skins were targeted in propaganda and clashes. And this was then associated with the reform movements of certain peasant castes, in the Gwala movement of Ahirs and Kurmis.[118] Episodes such as that of the cow-protection violence, then, suggest that religious mobilisation could be a means of critiquing the colonial state, outside the confines of elite-driven paradigms of religious identity politics.

Popular movements of religious assertion could lead to anti-colonial agitations for Muslims too, and not just through the Young Muslim party. In 1913, the destruction of part of the Machhli Bazar Mosque for the purposes of road building in Kanpur led to widespread and coordinated protests against what were seen as the colonial government's interference with religious space. The protests connected the city to the wider religious community and employed distinctive symbols of Islamic martyrdom, mourning and defeat, which emulated religious events such as Mohurram.[119] However, Shia movements in India regarded these kinds of symbolic politics with suspicion and often outright opposition, largely as a result of conservatism and the desire to position themselves more favourably vis-à-vis the colonial state.[120] Religious events and the

[118] Pandey, *The Construction of Communalism*, pp. 90–1, 155–6, 166.
[119] Sandria Freitag, 'Ambiguous Public Arenas and Coherent Personal Practice: Kanpur Muslims 1913–1931', in Katherine P. Ewing, ed., *Shari'at and Ambiguity in South Asian Islam* (Berkeley: University of California Press, 1988), pp. 147–53.
[120] See Justin Jones, 'The Shi'a Muslims of the United Provinces of India, c. 1890–1940', PhD Dissertation, University of Cambridge, 2007, pp. 176–80.

promotion of religious community could be a means of asserting loyalty in a more direct fashion in this period. In March 1915, for example, the Sanatan Dharma Sabha in Bankipore sent a petition to Viceroy Hardinge, suggesting that the Kumbh Mela at Hardwar might be an occasion in which Hindus could advance prayers to the King Sovereign, just as Muslims did to the Sultan of Turkey.[121]

Similar divisions of religious/ethnic outlook apply when looking at 'collective violence', which have dominated writing on Ceylon, although, here, there has been more of a stress on the economic frameworks for conflict. Writing on communalism in Sri Lanka has been almost entirely concentrated on the Sinhalese–Tamil conflict and the specific 'ethnic' violence that has arisen since the mid-1970s around the Tamil minority struggle for a separate homeland, the Eelam.[122] However, most writers, even anthropologists and political scientists looking at contemporary Sri Lankan society, have related their studies of 'collective violence' to deeper histories, especially where ethnic identities have been related to change in upwardly mobile social groups over time.[123] In other instances, there has been a stress on the use of Buddhist tradition and religious change.

To some extent, the religious and 'caste' composition of Sri Lanka mapped onto its geographical regions, with dominant cultivator (Goyigama) Sinhalese Buddhists in the interior, and fishing/trading, Christian and Muslim communities peopling the coastal towns, particularly around the south-western region. Some coastal villages were predominantly Roman Catholic as a result of Portugese influence in the sixteenth and seventeenth centuries. During the period of Dutch power in the 1760s, political legitimacy and support fluctuated between the colonial power and the Kandyian Kingdom, and in this scenario, political opposition to the state was localised in nature. After the British annexation of Kandy, this duality was largely ended as the colonial system formalised. For example, with British expansion, the market economy extended further inland with increasing trade in coffee, tea, coconut and rubber, encouraging new forms of social mobility particularly for the Muslim coastal populations. Taxation and trade disputes formed the backdrop to rebellions and riots

---

[121] Secretary of Sanatan Dharma Sabha to Hardinge, 15 March 1915, in Hardinge Papers, File 64, January to March 1915, University Library, Cambridge.

[122] This will be looked at in more depth in Chapters 6 and 7. Importantly, most of the interest in violence in Sri Lanka came about in the mid to late 1980s, and so to some extent predated the more sophisticated approaches to discourses of 'communalism'.

[123] For example, John D. Rogers, 'Social Mobility, Popular Ideology and Collective Violence in Modern Sri Lanka', *The Journal of Asian Studies*, 46, 3, 1987, 583–602.

in 1848 and 1866 in a system in which society and the economy were rapidly changing, and most of the riots of the late nineteenth century were concentrated in the area of the greatest market penetration – the south-western part of the island.[124] However, the key background to the more serious 1915 riots was the gradual Buddhist revival that began to take shape from the 1860s with the development of new educational institutions, newspapers and associations and construction of temples.

For writers in the 1970s and 1980s, this revival provided the means by which new upwardly mobile groups could challenge traditional elites, on the one hand, and the basis for a cultural nationalism that critiqued Western influence, on the other.[125] For those writing more in the context of the mid to late 1980s ethnic violence in Sri Lanka, greater attention was given to the ideological background to Eelam provided by changes in Buddhism.[126] It is more or less agreed that in Ceylon at least, the appearance of something approximating a 'communal' conflict took place in 1883 in clashes between Buddhists and Roman Catholics, the latter objecting to a procession in Cotahena, Colombo, in which religious images and icons were smashed, and it was rumoured that a monkey would be nailed to a cross. In response, as was the case with the 'music before mosques' controversies in north India, Buddhists stepped up the organisation of more extensive processions through Catholic areas of settlement, and significantly, outside Christian churches.[127]

As in India, this was clearly a context in which in the background of long-standing movements of revival, religious movements and associations attempted to extend sacred space. Although played down by the older literature, control of religious 'space' became important, as there was more to play for in the control of municipal politics between different groups of colonial subjects. In 1903 in Anuradhapura, Ceylon, maritime Buddhist communities reacted to local government construction on a site that was considered sacred. Very quickly, funds were raised for those accused of participation in the rioting that ensued, and a support base

[124] *Ibid.*, pp. 587–9.
[125] Gananath Obeyesekere, 'Personal Identity and Cultural Crisis: The Case of Anagarika Dharmapala of Sri Lanka', in Frank E. Reynolds and Donald Capps, eds., *The Biographical Process: Studies in the History and Psychology of Religion* (The Hague: Mouton and Co., 1976); L. A. Wickremeratne 'Religion, Nationalism and Social Change in Ceylon, 1865–1885', *Journal of the Royal Asiatic Society*, 2, 1969, 123–50.
[126] S. J. Tambiah, *Buddhism Betrayed? Religion, Politics and Violence in Sri Lanka*.
[127] Rogers, pp. 585–90.

generated by a wider Sinhalese intelligentsia.[128] Importantly, both in this case and in Kanpur in 1913, the publicity of the conflicts then spread by newspaper and report, and comparisons were made with earlier conflicts with the actions of local leaders and with religious 'struggles' in other parts of India/Ceylon.

However, for the most part, there was relatively little conflict registered as 'communal' in nature in Ceylon for most of the late colonial period, with the exception of a series of riots in the summer of 1915.[129] Here, the clash appeared to occur around competition between the Sinhalese population and Muslim immigrants from the south coast of India. Here again, as was the case in the cow-protection and urban riots in India, there were specific 'religious' triggers for the violence, but also deeper-seated economic or political contexts that allowed it to spread and multiply. Specifically, the wartime shortages created animosity towards the relatively new Muslim trading communities, many of whom as shopkeepers provided grain and credit, but also this was a period of extending cash cropping from the highland areas towards the coast. The supposedly religious triggers again bore a resemblance to some of the key triggers in India, in this case, music before mosques. In August 1912, the Buddhists from a town near Kandy, Gampola, were arranging an annual 'Perahara' or procession during the festival of Wesak, and the coastal-based Muslim trading community raised public objections to the procession passing in front of their mosques. Again, the decision of the government agent was important here: a ruling established that music should not, henceforth, be played closer than 100 yards in distance from the principal mosque of the town. The trustees of the Wallahagoda Temple successfully appealed to the district court at Kandy, where they invoked article 5 of the Kandyian Convention, in which on the assumption of power in Ceylon in 1815, the British had undertaken to protect the religious rites and institutions of the Buddhists. But their appeal was overturned by the Supreme Court.

This was the background to the conflicts around the procession of May 1915, importantly adjudicated, as was often the case in India, through state executives and the decisions of courts. As in the Kanpur mosque dispute, the legalistic framework of 'rights' and its manipulation by powerful publicists building patronage networks meant that the conflict took on a broader political significance. From the end of May, rioting spread from

---

[128] *Ibid.*, p. 589.

[129] Jayawardene Kearney and Fernando Blackton, 'The 1915 Riots in Ceylon: A Symposium', *Journal of Asian Studies*, xxix, 1969–70, 219–66.

Kandy, across five different provinces, and in the first week of June, violence was reported in Colombo. The government highlighted the importance of damage to property in this conflict, which amounted to something in the region of six million rupees.[130] But the governmental response was significant in other ways. Being almost entirely unprepared for these events, the local government and officials represented the violence in terms of resistance to colonial power, not only declaring martial law but contributing to the deaths of 63 by the armed forces and police and imprisoning key Ceylonese leaders on charges of sedition.

The key movement identified by officials as being behind the violence was the Buddhist 'Temperance' movement – part of a Buddhist revival on the island, which dated back to the mid-nineteenth century, and involved the assertion of Buddhist rejuvenation under Sinhalese power. This revivalist movement had, over the last thirty years of the nineteenth century, managed to establish two centres of learning: networks of schools and societies and the Young Men's Buddhist Association.[131] Significantly, aspirant lower- and middle-level castes, outside the elite groups and *mudaliyars* and *goyigama* castes of Sri Lankan society, were more commonly drawn to this form of revivalism. The Buddhist Temperance movement, started in 1912, was also related to opposition to government policies of regulation of liquor distilling, which, it was claimed, led to increased heavy drinking of toddy among lower socio-economic groups. This was part of a broader cultural nationalism, attractive to some of the wealthy Ceylonese nationalist leaders, who indulged in the critique of Western decadence as a way of asserting Sinhalese supremacy.

The links between the temperance movement and the violence of May 1915 are very difficult to maintain, yet the official mind certainly strove to make such connections. The pressure by Sri Lankan elites for greater representation on the legislatures partly explains this colonial paranoia. But there was another, different element here. Bands of 'English volunteers' – mainly planters and employees of commercial firms – wreaked havoc, carrying out retributive floggings and, in some cases, summary executions. A commission appointed under Sir John Anderson concluded that all of the executions had been illegal but that they had been carried out

---

[130] Colonial Office Files, PRO, 54/785, Chalmers to Bonar Law, Confidential, 14 October 1915.

[131] A. P. Kannangara, 'The Riots of 1915 in Sri Lanka: A Study in the Roots of the Communal Violence', *Past and Present*, 102, 1984, 130–65.

'... in good faith'.[132] While the offenders were punished, the scale of their punishments was considered to be very light, even by the standards of the period. Again, as in similar instances in India, there was difference of opinion between the Governor of Ceylon, Sir Robert Chalmers, and the Colonial Secretary of Ceylon, Reginald Stubbs, alongside more local officials. The former considered that the idea of rebellion coming out of the rioting was misplaced. Yet even Chalmers regarded the tough putting down of the violence to be a necessary action as 'a way of dealing with Orientals'.[133] And the idea of the 'unruly' Sinhalese became a common trope in these letters. It was Stubbs, however, who was the main convert to harsh and direct military action, believing in a Western-educated Ceylonese plot to engineer violence against colonial rule. The Secretary of State Bonar Law, along with other officials, also believed that there was a pro-German conspiracy afoot.

The general depiction of unruly 'orientals' was just one manifestation of more detailed representations, as in India, of specific ethnic and religious groups in terms of behavioural and political characteristics. The 'Coast Moors' were characterised by officialdom, both in the 1910s and interestingly as late as the early 1980s, as posing a threat to Sinhalese women because of their 'coarse' manners and largely male migration patterns.[134] These Muslim communities were, however, likely to have been influenced by pan-Islamic ideologies coming from India and because of the exile of Arabi Pasha in Ceylon. These characterisations of community linked the colonial ethnographies to nationalist depictions of 'violent communities' in interesting ways. Whereas both state and Sinhalese society identified Muslims in relation to gendered violence, rioting on the Buddhist side was lain firmly at the door of 'criminal' communities by Sinhalese leaders – 'vagrants', 'criminal classes' and 'habitual criminals'.[135] More recent depictions of the rioters are that they stood low in the hierarchy of caste – *batgama*, *salagama* (described as 'most combative) and *vahampura* castes – who were depicted in official surveys as the victims of processes of modernisation and urbanisation.[136] Members of the *batgama* community,

[132] *Report of a Commission Appointed by his Excellency the Governor to enquire into and report upon the circumstances connected with the shooting of L. Romanis Perera and nine others* (1917).
[133] 54/782 Chalmers to Bonar Law, Confidential, 18 June 1915.
[134] See A. P. Kannangara, 'The Riots of 1915 in Sri Lanka'.
[135] See P. Ramanathan, *Riots and Martial Law in Ceylon, 1915* (London: St. Martin's Press, 1915).
[136] A. P. Kannangara.

whose traditional caste occupation was soldiery, were also supposedly acting on the basis of a martial past.

The role of rumour and political construction of the aftermath of this event is also revealing. In some cases, these were linked to the international situation: one rumour around Kandy was that the Sinhalese would go unpunished for attacks on 'Coast Moors' because Britain was at war with Turkey.[137] After the event, Chalmers was dismissed from his post, and it was widely believed that this was because he had appeared relatively soft and conciliatory during the period of rioting. The new Governor, Sir John Anderson, was flooded with petitions about illegal shootings, and quickly came to the conclusion that the action in Ceylon had been unjustified in its harshness. Four of the Europeans involved in the killings were punished, even though Anderson did not have the full support of his Executive Council. Anderson was, from this point onwards, ostracised by the European community and had to base his authority on reference to the Colonial Office. However, it wanted to pass 'a sponge over the slate' on the whole affair and, despite pressure from Ceylonese leaders, was unwilling to appoint a Royal Commission of Enquiry.[138] As well as the issue of British non-official culpability in the violence itself, a factor in this whitewash was probably also the lack of official preparation. The problem of state function, in a similar way to the Kanpur violence, was key here. It is likely that most of the local administration in and around Kandy relied upon superior headmen for information about local populations. Unfortunately, part of the status marking for many of these supposed local leaders was that they should maintain as great a distance as possible from the politics of the local population, especially as most of the *mudaliyars* were Christian. This lack of contact to some extent also explains the propensity of high-caste Christian informers to lay the blame for most of the violence on collectively sometimes caste-defined 'criminal classes'.

Bearing in mind the extent to which the broader political significance of the communal riot depended upon how the violence was subsequently publicised and its outcomes disseminated, it is extremely important to look carefully and closely at how riots were reported. This is important not just as a means of examining the mechanisms of the violence themselves, which sometimes implicated official and semi-official agencies. It is

---

[137] Kannangara, p. 156.
[138] P. T. M. Fernando, 'The British Raj and the 1915 Communal Riots in Ceylon', *Modern Asian Studies*, 3, 3, 1969, 245–55.

also crucial for looking at how the significance of riots in general political discourse went well beyond, in many cases, the immediate instance of conflict itself. This is clear in the case of the series of cow-protection riots in 1893, in Kanpur in 1913 and in Ceylon in 1915. Attempts to dissect and anatomise the riots have done a great deal in uncovering the complex social bases of such disputes. But in an attempt to relate the violence of riots to popular manifestations of mobilisation, they have shifted attention away from the important mechanisms whereby local religious communities interpreted and made use of local state power. In uncovering the autonomous subaltern agent, the state has been somewhat written out. Yet it was the problems of state narration of communal violence and the anticipation or reaction to government action at these moments that played such a crucial part in allowing the riot to determine longer-term notions of religious difference in South Asia.

CONCLUSION

The half century that followed the uprisings of 1857 was one in which the development of new institutions of political representation ran alongside the establishment of organisations for the promotion of religious community. In fact, the entire basis of thinking about 'Hindu' or 'Muslim' communities in this period related to an intellectual ferment, in which thinkers related India's religious traditions to other world religions. But 'religion' did not simply feature in these discussions as a matter of belief or even social organisation. It also related to cultural production and the changing means of political communication. This was also, crucially, a period in which the politics of local patronage now overlapped with local representative institutions, which could control religious spaces and institutions, and through them, religious practices. Religious community, then, over the late nineteenth century was related to both cultural attempts to delineate the boundaries and limitations of national community and to the actions of the local state. And to this end, institutions of religious reform, revival or *sangathan* – from educational movements to the Arya Samaj or Hindu Sabhas – homogenised a public sense of what it meant to be a 'Hindu' or 'Muslim' for many Indians. In some areas, like the North East, the inability of the state to govern remote areas adequately gave opportunities (often encouraged by the administration) to Christian missionary organisations, like the Welsh Presbyterians. However, the organisations representing broad religious communities failed to mobilise fully even a small section of India's vast population. And their representations of the politics of the 'masses' coincided with colonial stereotypes of Indian social disorganisation. For most Indians, religious community served quite different purposes – the means of asserting higher status locally, the basis for rebellion or reform, or a process whereby they could seek local accommodation. These differences between the exponents of 'Hindu' or 'Muslim' mobilisation and quotidian realities appeared in other ways. The very phenomenon of the communal riot itself entailed much more than just apparent violence between two or more communities. Observers such as the state and local politicians attached other signifiers to such events, most notably publicising them as examples of how India's violent local populations needed to be controlled, educated or governed. This process certainly did not end in the period of the Great War, as the next two chapters will explore.

3

Transforming Spheres of Community

The Post–First World War Colonial World

Following the end of the Great War, the basis of British power in India changed significantly. In an attempt to appease what it considered to be new political interest groups, the British and Indian governments reformed the basis of representative politics as a result of promises of 'gradual realisation of responsible government' during the war. Crucially, some Indian subjects were given more powers at the provincial level. The financial and fiscal basis of the Raj shifted in tandem, with more focus on the flexible revenues of income tax, rather than land revenues, which brought different middle-class publicists into negotiation in the reformed legislatures. The 1920s was also a time of dramatic change for 'communal' politics, particularly from the point of view of public discussions about the prevalence of riots and more minor clashes across north India. Historians have tended to chart the occurrence of communal violence in waves. Whereas, following non-cooperation from 1922, there were more 'riots' in absolute terms (particularly in north India), following the end of Civil Disobedience in 1934, this violence appeared to decline until the 1940s. Again, by the early 1950s, for three decades, mobilisation around religious community declined dramatically again, it seems, at least in terms of the occurrence of conflicts and riots. However, charting the ebb and flow of the politics of 'communalism' according to the prevalence of riots is problematic. First of all, there were, and continue to be, often very local and contingent reasons for such conflicts. Moreover, the reason for such violence is rarely as straightforward as government reports and the media set out. What is significant, however, is how the notion and discussion of 'communalism' changed in the interwar period. And here, riots and conflicts were important in informing a public sense of religious antagonism.

This chapter will look at how this process was linked to specific changes in the relationship between the state at all levels and power brokers in Indian society who sometimes worked through civic institutions, and it will be followed in the next chapter by a consideration of the deeper social bases of religious mobilisation. One of its main arguments will be that the 1920s was a period in which the legitimacy of the colonial state was questioned in new and more radical ways than ever before by a range of institutions, leaders and publicists. This led to the setting up of a range of parallel quasi-state organisations and bodies. These revolved around local structures of mobilisation and power, generated by heightened competition and new claims to political recognition by community and caste organisations. The changing significance of class and other ethnic identities, as the state attempted to redefine minority and special interests, was also important, and these themes will be taken up in Chapter 4.

Nearly all researchers and writers on the subject of 'communalism' agree that there is a gulf between religious practice, on the one hand, and communal identity, on the other. It is important not to lose sight of this distinction. However, all too often, academics and the media have assumed that there is a direct line of causality between the two, particularly for the post–Great War period, in which violence on the basis of 'community' appeared to become more common across India. This and the next chapter will argue that religious sensibility and belief is so heterogeneous in India that, even within the main religious traditions, it cannot ever fully explain the extent to which the idea of a united and combative sense of religious *community* came into being. Second, religious beliefs are subject to change, but are unlikely to shift dramatically in the short term, in relation to political context, institution building and transformations in state power and authority. Identification with 'community', however – which is different to individual religious belief – does adapt and change in a very close relationship to political context. Here, the work of Gyanendra Pandey, in its description of discourses of 'communalism', is useful in that it presents the idea of community organisation in terms of representation and interpretation by those writing and speaking about riots and conflicts (for more detail on this, see Chapter 1). Nevertheless, it is still necessary to find explanations for why, despite the disconnections between lived religion and 'community', direct violence and other kinds of conflicts between erstwhile religious communities increased after 1918. The problem with over-emphasis on the idea of discourse and representation is, after all, the point that violence that emerged out of 'communal' riots in the 1920s to 1930s (and today) killed people in larger numbers than ever before. Its effects were therefore not just connected to a shift in political culture, but related to tangible political events and to how ordinary Indians experienced politics and the state.

(1) THE GREAT WAR AND ITS AFTERMATH

India's contribution to the British war effort between 1914 and 1918 has been well documented, particularly in its effects on the rapidly changing politics of anti-colonial protest from 1918–19.[1] What is perhaps less well researched (beyond the work on north Indian Muslims and the Khilafat agitations) is the extent to which these global changes affected the political representations of religious community. Without doubt, the war years and the following period of repression, constitutional reform and economic slump redefined the relationship between Indian subjects, political and cultural organisations and the colonial state when compared to the period up to 1914. The war also made the experiences of co-religionists overseas more apparent than ever before – something particularly evident in the causes championed by the Muslim League and Shia Political Conference in relation to the Middle Eastern states and communities.

This section of the chapter will argue that the political changes of the interwar period presaged a new or sharpened sense for a range of parties, of the political importance of religious community. The stress here is on redefinition rather than transformation, since for most of the 1910s at least, Indian politics largely revolved around the existing webs of local and low-level institutional/factional alliances that related to local boards, educational institutions and religious foundations, as we saw in the last chapter. There were other kinds of political association that paralleled the obvious 'national' movements like the Congress, reflecting continuity from earlier phases too: local caste associations, city-based cultural institutions and societies[2] and rural-based farmers' movements.[3] This was a differentiated interaction of new and old political institutions and agencies, then, which, as the multitude of regional case studies has shown, varied across the subcontinent. Yet the issue of religious controversy and conflict

[1] For example, John Gallagher and Anil Seal, 'India Between the Wars', *Modern Asian Studies*, 15, 3, 1981, 387–414; David Omissi, *Indian voices of the Great War: Soldiers' Letters, 1914–1918* (London: Palgrave Macmillan, 1999).

[2] See, for example, C. A. Bayly, *The Local Roots of Indian Politics*.

[3] See Gyanendra Pandey, 'Peasant Revolt and Indian Nationalism: The Peasant Movement in Awadh, 1919–1922', in Ranajit Guha, ed., *Subaltern Studies I: Writings on South Asian History and Society* (New Delhi: Oxford University Press, 1982), pp. 143–97.

seemed to cut across provincial boundaries, being represented officially and in the press, importantly, as an 'Indian' issue, even when its manifestation in riots could be related to very specific local circumstances. The public and media responses to moments of apparent religious controversy or antagonism was more apparent than ever before, partly because of the rapid development of political journalism, examined later in this chapter. This section will examine these processes, relating them to changes in India's political economy, and the effects of political and economic change on the meaning of the state and mobilisation on the ground.

For imperial historians, the Great War created a kind of 'bargain basement' for empire builders, with Ottoman and Russian spheres of interest now available for exploitation, and the British taking control of German East Africa, Mesopotamia and Palestine.[4] The apparent 'crisis of Empire' in the period of 1919–20, in which uprisings occurred across the areas of formal and informal Empire, took place against the backdrop of a new kind of imperial expansion. British imperial administrators were now obliged to think more clearly in terms of minorities and minority politics in their colonial territories. Ideas of 'self-determination', sometimes on a national basis, were inflected by the break up of the Ottoman and Habsburg empires. And the gradual delegitimisation of colonial systems forced their regimes to rely increasingly on new, defined minority interests for reasons of state power. In Mesopotamia, Egypt, Africa, Malaya and India, the British propped up the interests of specific 'loyal' communities as a means of restoring or reinforcing the increasingly fragile basis of their power. Simultaneously, newly formed political parties championed these minority interests and used the languages of self-determination to push forward their agendas. Finally, the period shortly following the Great War was one in which an older cultural pessimism was rejuvenated, giving rise to new critiques of Western modernity and the assertion of broadly based cultural and religious identities.

But for most Indian administrators in this phase, there were more palpable concerns. In the aftermath of the war, it was increasingly evident that the old British confidence about India's place within the Empire was shifting. Whereas India had contributed massively to the war effort itself, leaving it with a national debt of £370 million, it had long been British policy to ensure that it did not become a defence liability or a burden on the British taxpayer and that it should remain peaceful. To this end, the colonial state needed to find new, more efficient ways of extracting revenue

[4] John Gallagher and Anil Seal, 'India Between the Wars', p. 395.

from India, without incurring political risks. The view from the Government of India itself was that the base of support from the colonial regime would need to be reconsidered after the war. In official thinking, although there was some variation, this generally meant efforts to 'rally' moderates as a way of diluting or marginalising more radical anti-colonial threats to British authority. But it also meant bringing urban professionals and monied communities into consideration, especially since the fiscal basis of the colonial state could no longer depend upon the important, but inflexible, land revenues. For example, the basis of Indian defence was changed, since Indian politicians enfranchised under the system of dyarchy after the first elections of the 1920s naturally viewed such expenditure as a diversion from internal funding of the new political system (after 1921, the Indian army could no longer, as a rule, be used outside spheres of Indian defence, at the cost of the Indian taxpayer).[5]

Also, from 1917, India was allowed to impose a tariff on foreign cloth imports (even those from Britain, although the British government attempted to promote imperial preference too throughout this period), as a means of alleviating her financial difficulties. India's tariff autonomy was extended in October 1921, signalling the beginning of the end of the dominance of the Lancashire lobby in Indian trade, as India could begin, theoretically, to protect its own manufacturing, and Bombay interests could be accommodated more easily.[6] In reality, tariff autonomy allowed the British government to resist pressure from the Lancashire lobby, when its trading competitiveness was declining, and instead to focus on the financial benefits of remittances from India. These changes made sense in the context of a British–Indian relationship that was rapidly shifting, as British exports dipped and London no longer held the position of financial centre that it once had. Fear among Britain's conservative political elites about the possibility of a Labour electoral victory, once the electorate had been extended in Britain after 1918, led to higher levels of social spending at the expense of defence.[7] Most important of all for India were the Montagu–Chelmsford Reforms, resulting in the Government of India Act 1919, which will be explored in more detail in the second section. This new constitution granted the provinces a certain level of autonomy

[5] Keith Jefferey, '"An English Barrack in the Oriental Seas"? – India in the Aftermath of the First World War', *Indian Economic and Social History Review*, XII, 4, 367–84.

[6] Clive Dewey, 'The End of the Imperialism of Free Trade', in Clive Dewey and A. G. Hopkins, eds., *The Imperial Impact: Studies in the Imperial History of India and Africa* (London, Athlone Press, 1978).

[7] John Gallagher and Anil Seal, 'India Between the Wars'.

from the centre in both financial and legislative matters, but divided each provincial government into elected and non-elected, officially controlled ministerial portfolios. This was not yet full provincial autonomy but gave some substance (and certainly the appearance) to Indian demands for inclusion in legislative matters. The provinces were given control over land revenue, irrigation, excise and stamps, and the centre continued to control income tax, salt, opium and customs.

One of the classic episodes in histories of Indian nationalism between the wars is the 'Western-educated' Indian response to the end of and aftermath of the Great War, in particular, in reactions to the Rowlatt legislation, extending the wartime measures of repression and control in India.[8] The Rowlatt Bills laid down that, for a period of three years, suspected terrorists could be arrested, detained and interned without warrant, charge or trial. The continuation of these wartime emergency provisions, previously existent in the 1915 Defence of India Act, were significant in their ideological impact on the faith of Indian professionals in the notion of 'British justice'. Importantly, the outspoken critics of the Bills (e.g. the Bombay Muslim lawyer and future leader of the Muslim League, M. A. Jinnah) pointed out that this was hardly the kind of reward that India might have expected in response to India's wartime contribution. For the prophetic Jinnah, in the context of the highly awaited constitutional reforms, it was likely now that public reaction and rejection would be swift across the country.[9]

However, Rowlatt, despite its extreme implications for the chattering classes of urban India, was only likely to affect the vast majority of the Indian population infrequently, and for most, interest in the finer details of such Gandhian protests were inconsistent, unpredictable, or even based in indifference or hostility.[10] What the Rowlatt Bills and reactions to them did expose, though, was the multilayered nature of colonial decision making and the sense of deep uncertainty about state power from the point of view of a section of the British ruling class in India. There was no uniformity of approach when it came to the extension of wartime emergency powers. Whereas the Viceroy Chelmsford and some of the provincial Governors supported the Bills and particularly their tough application in

---

[8] The most obvious example of this can be seen in Judith M. Brown, *Gandhi's Rise to Power: Indian Politics 1915–1922* (Cambridge: Cambridge University Press, 1972).

[9] M. H. Saiyid, *Mohammad Ali Jinnah* (Lahore: Elite Publishers, 1945), p. 238.

[10] See M. K. Gandhi, *An Autobiography or The Story of My Experiments with Truth* (London: Penguin, 1982), p. 423.

Punjab, which elicited strong Congress condemnation,[11] there were many administrators, particularly at more local district levels, who offered strong critiques.[12] The massive loss of life in the trenches had affected the world view of postwar ICS entrants, and some of them were critical of 'the atavistic values which gave an authoritarian establishment its license to rule'.[13] There was also a clear lack of confidence that the proposed constitutional reforms, eventually implemented in 1919–20, would tide over what appeared to be rising opposition to and publicity against the British presence.

This uncertainty, appearing as inconsistency for many in India, was perceived by much larger groups than those directly affected by Rowlatt. Regional-language newspapers in India's old presidency areas, and Hindi and Urdu newspapers in the United Provinces, for example, discussed the sense of confusion and disappointment of returning Indian troops at the end of the war and the destroyed hopes of a wide range of political agencies, especially Muslims disappointed by British policy in the Middle East. For example, *Young India* at the beginning of 1919 reported on M. M. Malaviya's speech to the Delhi Congress session about how movements towards self-government did not seem to be any closer with the termination of the war. Over the same week, newspapers also reported on the speech of Dr. Ansari, Chairman of the Reception Committee of the Muslim League, which expressed concern about the future of the Muslim holy places at the end of the war.[14] The *Mufid-e-Rozgar*, on 19 January, reported in more detail on the British occupation of the holy places and the need for Muslims alone to settle the Caliphate.[15]

These newspapers had been expanding rapidly in number from the end of the war and into the 1920s. In UP alone, ninety-seven newspapers and periodicals were published by 1924, varying in circulation from smaller Urdu weeklies like *Al Bashir*, with around 500 readers, to Hindi papers like *Pratap* and the English-language *Pioneer*, with circulations of between 6,500 and 8,000.[16] Between 1921 and 1922, the total number of

---

[11] See 'Congress Report on the Punjab Disorders', *Collected Works of Mahatma Gandhi*, 20, 1, 25–38.

[12] See, for example, Michael Carritt, *A Mole in the Crown* (Hove: Author, 1985).

[13] Clive Dewey, *Anglo-Indian Attitudes: The Mind of the Indian Civil Service* (London: Hambledon Press, 1993), pp. 218–19.

[14] *Report on the Newspapers Published in the Bombay Presidency for the week ending 4 January 1919*, p. 17, 25, L/R/5/175, OIOC.

[15] *Report on the Newspapers Published in the Bombay Presidency for the week ending 11 January 1919*, p. 27, L/R/5/175, OIOC.

[16] 'Statement of Newspapers and Periodical Published in U.P. 1924', Home Political, F. 204/IV/25 NAI.

publications 'proscribed' by the state also increased dramatically.[17] This broadening publicity about the questionable legitimacy of a colonial system that promised reform but was tardy in its delivery was to have a knock-on effect, as state agencies attempted to adjudicate what they saw as 'communal' conflicts. In particular, it will be seen that these questions of legitimacy informed those lobbying government in the interests of their own particular communities.

As we have already seen, the colonial system granted authority to local power brokers in different contexts, albeit in a situation in which the significant power of state coercion lay firmly in the hands of the coloniser. In the administration of revenue, for example, not only was a degree of latitude given to powerful landholding interests in parts of India, but also an extensive lower bureaucracy was employed to administer its collection and lower-level court disputes.[18] In the towns and cities too, municipal politics, as we saw in the last chapter, had become an arena for competition between different political factions well before the interwar period. Historians writing from what came to be known as the 'Cambridge school' in the 1970s and 1980s suggested that these networks of political organisation and competition meant that ideology was relatively unimportant for institutions of political mobilisation.[19] However, there was a range of other popular movements across the subcontinent for whom municipal/ district boards or assemblies were relatively insignificant, as we saw in the last chapter. These expanded in number and complexity in the interwar period, particularly as the economic slump of 1919 began to affect rural incomes in a new way. Also important was the wider and deeper impact of the state in some areas. For example, following the war, land-revenue demands shot up for certain rural communities, for example the Adivasi communities in Surat district in the Bombay Presidency. In their Devi movement from 1922, these communities began to react against local officials, particularly those involved in the administration of excise revenues. The movement caught the attention of Congress leaders, who, as in other areas, attempted to link the movement to broader agitations and anti-colonial postures. But the growing power of a richer and more

---

[17] 'Publications etc. proscribed under sect. 12 (1) of the Indian Press Act 1910, and since its repeal, under section 99-A of the Code of Criminal Procedure, 1920 to 1924', Home Political 33/35 1925, NAI.

[18] See William Gould, *Bureaucracy, Community and Influence: Society and the State in India, 1930–1960s* (London: Routledge, 2011).

[19] One of the classic later examples of this is David Page, *Prelude to Partition*.

independent Adivasi peasantry was the key development.[20] Also connected to this process of institutional diversification was the widening significance of organisations representing 'Hindu' and 'Muslim' interests, as we will see.

The economic instability experienced after the war, following the rapid rise in commodity prices and the subsequent worldwide slump of 1920, encouraged organisations of self-help and informal association. An even greater crisis came at the end of the decade. The indices for the retail price of food dropped by almost a hundred per cent between 1928 and 1933, and credit severely contracted over the period of the depression.[21] The effects of economic crisis also fuelled opposition to colonialism in a range of different contexts across Asia and north Africa, creating the context for uprisings in Egypt, Iraq and Syria. But more directly, the economic climate probably helped to create a keener sense among increasingly large sections of urban and rural India of the meaning of their Indian subjecthood. This manifested itself in the reaction to the slump following the war. By 1922, the slackening markets for cotton in India and increasing competition from Japan meant that mill owners sought to solve the problem of declining profits by lowering wages. One result in Bombay was the development of general strikes in 1924 and 1925, and following attempts at workforce reorganisation, further strikes in 1928–9.[22] The effect of the economic slump in these latter years in the countryside was, in instances where peasants paid revenue directly to the colonial state (such as in the *ryotwari* area of Kheda district in Gujarat), to generate support for Gandhian nationalism among cultivators in some parts.[23]

The relationship between price rises and popular discontent was not always so direct or even evident at all. For example, in the winter of 1921–2 in Bengal, crops were recovering and there was a relative absence of economic distress in the countryside. But it was precisely in this period that countryside agitations were at their height. Non-cooperation in India

---

[20] David Hardiman, 'Adivasi Assertion in South Gujarat: The Devi Movement of 1922–3', in Ranajit Guha, ed., *Subaltern Studies III: Writings on South Asian History and Society* (New Delhi: Oxford University Press, 1984), pp. 196–230.

[21] B. R. Tomlinson, *The Political Economy of the Raj 1914–1947: The Economics of Decolonzation in India* (London: Palgrave, 1979), pp. 35–6.

[22] Morris David Morris, 'Labor Discipline, Trade Unions and the State in India', *The Journal of Political Economy*, 63, 4, 1955, 296.

[23] See David Hardiman, *Peasant Nationalists of Gujarat: Kheda District 1917–1934* (Delhi: Oxford University Press, 1984).

between 1920 and 1922 also worried the colonial state more because of the unpredictability of movements below the level of the main leaders.[24] However, more and more Indians, despite the limited nature of the Government of India Act, were being brought into contact with forms of political mobilisation and opposition and organs of political publicity. It was no coincidence that in drafting the new constitution for the Indian National Congress, presented in Nagpur in December 1920, Gandhi lowered the membership fee to two *annas*. The time was certainly ripe for the introduction of a wider sense of Indian citizenship to broader constituencies, many of them more directly affected by the government's closeted decisions than ever before.

Close studies of the changing political economy of India's northern cities shows how the interwar period pushed many economically disadvantaged communities, especially those of *sudra* castes, into the cities for work. This movement had an important effect on low-caste political mobilisation, particularly around markers of religious identity, and their attempt to replicate local state agencies – a theme to which we will return in the next chapter. In general terms, however, it is clear that the relatively fast rise of India's urban populations in the interwar period must have brought larger numbers of India's poor into contact with a new variety of political agencies. The average number of people employed in factories in the towns and cities of UP, for example, rose by 33.2% between 1921 and 1931, although these increases were gendered – over the same period, the number of female industrial workers rose by only 15.9%.[25] The mode of recruitment of industrial workers in cities like Kanpur, through *mistris*, reinforced caste and community ties within the city, as workers were brought together around rituals and festivals. This tended to lead to the concentration of particular communities in different mohallas (with a division between Muslim and Hindu regions of some cities). Factory jobs could also be divided along caste and community lines, particularly in activities that involved the handling of animal products. Workers were also not unaffected by revivalist activity promoted by the Arya Samaj and *tanzim*, for example, especially as in cities like

---

[24] Sumit Sarkar, 'The Conditions and Nature of Subaltern Militancy: Bengal from Swadeshi to Non-Cooperation, c. 1905–1922', in Ranajit Guha, ed., *Subaltern Studies III: Writings on South Asian History and Society* (New Delhi: Oxford University Press, 1984), pp. 271–320.
[25] *Census of India, 1931, The United Provinces, Part I Report* (Allahabad: Government of India Press, 1932), pp. 53–4.

Kanpur and Bombay, industrial employment tended to increase worker sectionalism.[26]

The blatant exercise of arbitrary state power around the end of the Great War (epitomised in the massacre at Jallianwallah Bagh in Amritsar on 13 April 1919) also made the limited rights of Indian subjects more apparent, and the creation of new forms of political publicity and political association accelerated over the interwar period. For example, the first Indian workers' unions were formed in the immediate postwar period – the All India Trade Union's Congress was formed in 1919 and the Bombay Textile Labour Union (BTLU) was formed in 1926 following the 1925 general strike. The political press detailed the formation of factions and sub-factions of principal parties, who had been given a taste of power at the provincial level, and to some extent, this politicking took place irrespective of the concerns of workers. For example, around the 1926 elections in UP, political leaders manoeuvred around the relative merits of factions connected to Motilal Nehru and Madan Mohan Malaviya, and between the Swarajists and other groups connected to the Congress organisation. By mid-1927, Dr. Ansari described the latter as 'hopelessly divided into political camps which are mutually distrustful and antagonistic'.[27] However, just as state agencies increasingly sought to map and quantify Indian populations, so Indians themselves became aware of such official interventions and keenly entered into debates about these factional struggles. Precisely because industrial workers in India's big cities were required to reconstitute their identities in relation to the village, and in terms of the often casual nature of their employment, it made sense for them to engage forcefully at times with political movements. This political action was then fertilised with sectional rivalries, often on the basis of caste and religion, which meant that workers, too, could seek out a powerful party leader at a provincial or municipal level at a time of crisis such as a strike and could involve themselves in some of the Congress protests.[28]

The 'class' or 'communal' characteristics of most political societies and movements and those who populated them was not often easily fixed or categorised, as India's highly mobile population could move in and out of movements generated to meet particular contingencies. However, when it came to 'Hindu' or 'Muslim' organisations, perceptions of the

---

[26] Chitra Joshi, 'Bonds of Community, Ties of Religion: Kanpur Textile Workers in the Early Twentieth Century', *The Indian Economic and Social History Review*, 22, 3, 1985, 251–80. See also Rajnarayan Chandavarkar, *Origins of Industrial Capitalism* (Cambridge: Cambridge University Press, 1994), pp. 397–8.

[27] See *The Leader*, January 1926 and 26 August 1927.

[28] Chandavarkar, *Origins of Industrial Capitalism*, pp. 400–2; 414–7.

vulnerability of the community were crucial, often being expressed in the language of political rights, as framed by an official and constitutional discourse of representation. Both the Hindu Mahasabha, as it was rejuvenated in 1923, and the Muslim League were popularised around ideas of community decline and threat, particularly in relation to census figures.[29] Other organisations discussed the need to promote Hindu or Muslim physical strength and fertility. The Arya Samaj *shuddhi* campaign of 1923 aimed to win back the Muslim Malkana Rajputs to Hinduism in the wake of Hindu reactions to the Mappila rebellion. The latter, in the first months of 1921, involved Muslims of the Keralan region rising up against a British-sponsored Hindu landlord, but the uprising deteriorated into general rioting, leading to the killing and forcible conversion of Hindus of the region, as we will see later in the chapter. Samaj Sewak Dals were encouraged on the back of the Bharatiya Hindu Shuddhi Sabha, led by Swami Shraddhanand, as a way to encourage physical culture.[30] Throughout the same period, Muslims in UP towns also organised *tanzim* (organisation) and *tabligh* (religious proselytisation) movements to promote communal prayer, physical organisation and physical culture. These ideas of decline or crisis were importantly tied to community defence and organisation, and increasingly articulated in terms of forms of religious community through the 1920s.[31]

At the heart of efforts to build up community strength, through population increase, physical culture and moral regeneration or reform, was the notion of *sangathan* or organisation. Forms of religious *sangathan*, sometimes emulated state-driven ideas of institutional organisation, via civic institutions. The nature of the Indian state and political system was becoming increasingly apparent to ordinary Indians, as forms of political publicity and economic opportunities became more complex. This was fuelled partly by constitutional reform and partly by a rapidly expanding vernacular press.[32] Local variation in colonial authority and the unevenness of power, as experienced by Indians in different contexts across India,

---

[29] For example, the first meeting of the Hindu Mahasabha in Banaras in UP discussed the need to respond to the possible decline of the Hindu community, supposedly evident in the census operation. See *The Leader* (Allahabad), 29 July, 17 August and 22 August 1923.

[30] *The Leader*, 5 April 1923; Charu Gupta, 'Articulating Hindu Masculinity and Femininity. Shuddhi and Sangathan Movements in United Provinces in the 1920s', *Economic and Political Weekly*, 33, 13, 1998, 727–35.

[31] For more on the groups who promoted tanzim, see Gail Minault, *The Khilafat Movement: Religious Symbolism and Political Mobilization in India* (New York: Columbia University Press, 1982), pp. 193–4.

[32] John Zavos, *The Emergence of Hindu Nationalism in India*.

also meant that official toleration of political institutions was variable: one feature of the colonial state and political system was its inconsistency and its arbitrary fluctuations of authority.[33] Whereas a local government in one region might strictly tow the line of the central Government of India, in other places there were significant variations in colonial state action, particularly in reacting to Indian parties and movements.

This is well illustrated in one of Gandhi's early *satyagraha* protests during the war period, in Champaran, where the decisions of the district and provincial governments for a hardline against the agitation went against the more cautious policy of the Government of India itself.[34] Similarly, in Punjab, the hardliner O'Dwyer ensured that the Montagu–Chelmsford Reforms worked in the favour of the martial lobby by cutting down the size of urban constituencies.[35] Such episodes seemed to contradict a powerful discourse of universal *ma-bap* governance, based on order, the maintenance of the rule of law and colonial justice. In reality, government servants at different levels now had to take the spheres of urban political mobilisation much more seriously – a situation increasingly publicised by the vernacular press. However, since few had the means at their disposal to influence or exploit state agencies directly through the bureaucracy and local organisations of political representation, other means had to be found. It was in this context that hastily and temporarily constructed organisations of community pressure became important.

For example, in the immediate aftermath of the Mappila rebellion, a range of Hindu and Muslim defence organisations sprang up, which did not last more than a few years in most cases, usually declining as the political context shifted. The Samaj Sewak Dals and *shuddhi*-related organisations came about in response to the perceived threat created by the rebellion and the drive to reconvert the Malkana Rajputs back to Hinduism as part of an Arya Samaj project. Looking at the journal literature that promoted these organisations, their conception of *sangathan* could also be an indirect response to Gandhi's galvanising influence on the Congress from 1919–20. Just as the constitution of the Congress had been rewritten to create different levels of committees and to widen its membership, so too, these tracts and papers argued, should other specifically Hindu organisations set themselves up to have maximum political and

[33] See, for example, the commentaries of M. K. Gandhi in *An Autobiography, or The Story of My Experiments with Truth*.

[34] M. K. Gandhi, *An Autobiography, or The Story of My Experiments with Truth*, pp. 370–3, 382–6.

[35] Dewey, *Anglo-Indian Attitudes*, p. 217.

administrative impact. For example, one of the leading supporters of Hindu sangathan in the UP press, *Abhudaya*, throughout the period from 1922–4, discussed the need to organise committees at all levels, which would connect different levels of Hindu Sabha organisation. It also contained articles that directly critiqued the *ahimsa* of Gandhian politics.[36] Throughout the mid-1920s, organisations like the Mahabir Dal were hastily put together based around the city-based *akhara* (gymnasium) of north India. Most of these bodies fluctuated in relation to the perceived threat of communal violence or conflict. The *shuddhi* and Hindu sangathan movements were therefore not only related to the fear of declining numbers, thrown up by readings of the censuses of 1911 and 1921,[37] but also a reaction to more general forms of political organisation and mobilisation, which the new political system had encouraged. The formation of competitive 'communal organisations' also occurred among Muslim groups. In the aftermath of the reforms, Shi'a political organisations in UP argued that they had been muscled out of the seats reserved for Muslims in the new legislatures by the Sunni community. Against this background, the All India Shi'a Political Conference was formed in 1925, eventually with its own newspaper *Sarfaraz*, largely in opposition to the perceived Sunni dominance of the Muslim League.[38]

The interwar period was undoubtedly a phase of rapid political change, in which the actions of the state became more tangible for most Indians, more readily mediated via rapidly formed political and community organisations and apparently more intrusive in everyday matters. Increased circulation of newspapers, a rapid increase in the number of political institutions and the growing power of Indian representatives at municipal and district levels did mean that even all-Indian affairs could be experienced by those in the most remote rural areas. However, neither the mass publicity surrounding Congress's mass protest movements in 1920–2 and 1930–4, nor the vaunted constitutional changes in 1919–20 and 1935, made a direct impact on the lives of most Indians. The vast majority of India's population was still disenfranchised – as we will see, the Raj sought to reform India's constitution as a means of controlling its populations and extracting its resources. The rhetoric of responsible government was, for the most part, simply that. In this context of political promise, debate and

[36] Gupta, 'Articulating Hindu Masculinity', p. 729.
[37] For more detail on the ways in which religious communities reacted to the censuses, see K. W. Jones, 'Religious Identity and Indian Census', in N. G. Barrier, ed., *The Census of British India: New Perspectives* (Delhi: Manohar, 1980).
[38] Justin Jones, pp. 210–11.

engagement, religious community organisation and mobilisation became one crucial means of indirectly influencing local administrations. Since the petitions of communal organisations were written in a period of rapid political change, in which representative government was a future possibility, their appeals were largely about controlling a share of state power: demands about jobs in the bureaucracy or seats on boards and assemblies. In this situation, religious community organisations encouraged the rapid establishment and evolution of competitive movements, set up to 'defend' particular interests. The following section will explore this dynamic process in more detail, against the specific background of the system of dyarchy.

(II) POLITICAL CHANGE IN THE 1920S: COMMUNITY ORGANISATIONS AND THE STATE

The most important imperial decisions to affect Indian politics after 1918 were two constitutional reforms, which fundamentally altered the structure of political organisation, mobilisation and power. The Government of India Act 1919, following the Montagu–Chelmsford Reforms proposals, introduced a system (known as 'dyarchy') in which greater legislative and financial autonomy was granted to the thirteen provinces. Following a series of Round Table talks in London in the early 1930s, the next round of constitutional reforms resulted in the 1935 Government of India Act, which developed further the federal principle and granted full provincial autonomy, allowing Indian ministers to control entire provinces under a slightly less limited electorate. Under the first set of reforms of 1919, provincial governments were divided so that the provincial ministerial portfolios were shared out between officially nominated ministers, on the one hand, and an Indian elected element, on the other. Roughly three-quarters of each new legislature were elected and the remaining quarter were nominated. Clearly, this system, which effectively came into full operation after the first elections under the new system from the end of 1921, altered the focus of high-level political mobilisation. In particular, political leaders were now able to extend networks of power and influence over larger areas of Indian politics and could make clearer connections between different districts and towns across larger administrative areas. However, these reforms should in no sense be viewed as a retreat by the colonial power in India, and were effectively limited in the amount of real political power and 'responsibility' they granted to most Indians, despite the liberal rhetoric surrounding them.

It was no surprise, then, that not only the Indian National Congress but also an array of religious and communal organisations structured their institution building and reorganisation around the provinces too. Very quickly after the passage of the 1919 Act, the Congress altered its constitution to build committees that reflected the administrative structures of the colonial system. Other political parties and organisations followed suit, among them religious organisations, like the Arya Samaj and Sanatan Dharma. It is beyond doubt that the constitution led to the 'provincialisation' of politics in India at a formal level, but this had a varied purchase, not least because the cohesiveness of provincial identities was extremely varied across India.[39] The 1919 Government of India Act extended the electorate to a minor degree, with the electorates for the Imperial (central) Assembly varying in size from 20,000 in Assam to more than 180,000 in Bengal. For the Provincial Assemblies, around 1.5 million were enfranchised, for example, in UP, one million in Madras and Bengal and about 500,000 in Bombay and Punjab. This roughly corresponded to between three and five per cent of the total populations of these provinces.[40]

Although the Act effectively refocussed the attention of the political press on the electoral politics of the new Assemblies, for most Indians, the reforms made little direct impact and were a disappointment. Indian elected ministers were able to control the provincial ministerial portfolios of health, education and local government. Nominated officials, under the control of the provincial Governor, held onto the reserved portfolios of police, finance and justice. The contrast with the shift to universal male suffrage in the UK from 1918 was stark, and certainly exposed British colonial claims that India was truly leading towards responsible self-government. This was especially tangible for those who sensed that the British were to continue to use repression alongside conciliation, according to political circumstances.[41] Some of the crucial areas of governance were reserved, yet there was now a little more for career politicians to aim for in the provincial arena. Perhaps most important as far as the colonial state

---

[39] For example, there was a vast difference between the 'provincial arena' of Bengal, with its rich tradition of socio-political reform and intellectual debate, and linguistic particularity, compared to the more artificial provincial identity of UP.

[40] P. G. Robb, *The Government of India and Reform: Policies Towards Politics and the Constitution 1916–1921* (Oxford: Oxford University Press, 1976), pp. 112–3. The electorate was extended again on the basis of a property qualification in 1935, to about 35 million in total, or roughly ten per cent of the total population, and included women.

[41] *Ibid.*, p. 121.

was concerned was the reorganisation of colonial finance, pushing more autonomy to the provincial level and shifting the fiscal base more to items such as income tax. This reorganisation of the revenue base was also linked to colonial calculations of political risk at the end of the Great War and the need to placate what it saw as some of the most powerful Indian monied interest groups. It was significant in this respect that tariff autonomy (albeit very limited in its actual implications for Indian business and industry) accompanied the reforms.[42]

Since the reforms essentially changed the context of party political mobilisation, they also had an effect on the formation and activities of organisations representing religious and caste communities. Studies of this process show how parties based in a focus on religious community, on a broad although largely artificial basis, developed in the 1920s.[43] The key sources used for much of this work are contained in the official record, which led some historians to downplay the significance of ideology in the formation of religio-political movements in favour of the examination of political factionalism.[44] The archetypal institution here was the Hindu Mahasabha, which lurks behind most general accounts of the rise of 'communal politics', yet which is rarely unpacked as an organisation in detail. What is remarkable is that even where detailed research has been done (e.g. by Richard Gordon), the Hindu Mahasabha appears to be little more than a loosely affiliated collection of politicians who, for one reason or another, was discontented with the direction of the Congress or who combined affiliation with both. Many of its members probably cared little for the more explicit ideology of Hindu *sangathan*, as espoused by some associated organisations like the Rashtriya Swayamsevak Sangh (founded in 1923), or the local movements of religio-political mobilisation such as *shuddhi* of the Arya Samaj. Indeed, there was probably a very wide array of interpretations of what 'Hindu' India actually meant within this organisation, albeit most coming from a high-caste perspective.[45]

---

[42] See Clive Dewey, 'The End of the Imperialism of Free Trade'.

[43] David Page, *Prelude to Partition*; Richard Gordon, 'The Hindu Mahasabha and the Indian National Congress, 1915–1926'.

[44] This seems to characterise the work of Gordon and Page in the 1970s and 1980s. For a searing critique of David Page's work, see review by David Lelyveld, *The American Historical Review*, 89, 2, 1984, 505–6.

[45] See Gordon, pp. 147–8: 'The groups working in close co-operation with the communal associations, no less than the Congress in its Swarajist guise, represented a confused medley of interests ... The relationship between the causes politicians were prepared to espouse and their immediate or even long term political objectives was by no means as direct or obvious as historians are inclined to infer'.

However, the looseness of ideological commitment to Hindu nationalism in the Mahasabha in the 1920s probably tells us as much about the requirements of mobilisation at a provincial level under the new reforms as it does about the nature of 'Hindu' or 'Muslim' organisations themselves. The system of dyarchy meant that leaders had to work out political deals and alliances that often diluted party political programmes. Below the level of the new provincial councils, things were different. Older forms of institutional political mobilisation around patron–client networks, which might have involved local bodies such as the municipalities, district boards or powerful educational institutions, now became the power bases for wider political opportunities. In other words, in certain municipalities, 'Hindu' and 'Muslim' parties or groups based around specific caste coalitions formed. For example, the Kanpur municipal board, from the late 1920s into the 1940s, saw the formation of a 'Hindu' party, which overlapped with membership of the local Hindu Sabha.[46] In Aligarh, municipal board politics coalesced with the caste coalition that dominated district political mobilisation, with competition between caste-based groups.[47] In Madras, members of the Justice Party, on a non-Brahman platform, consistently battled with groups such as the Mylapore groups for the control of the Madras Corporation, and eventually the control of the Provincial Council.[48] The politics of south India was largely isolated from the type of Hindu–Muslim competition seen in the north, and, to a great extent, there was little ideological difference between some of the main political groupings in the early to mid-1920s. However, by 1925, E. V. Ramaswami Naicker's Self-Respect Movement, publicised through his weekly *Kudi Arasu*, more clearly laid down the ideological principles of non-Brahmanism – the abolition of untouchability, access to temples and wells, protests against Brahmanical control of religious rites and rituals and the uplift of women.[49] And in the north, central and western parts of India, it appeared that these networks of political power continued to serve, at important moments, the idea of the mobilisation of specific religious communities, in particular the Hindu and Muslim. Despite the uniform pattern of provincial autonomy, then, there were wide variations in how this mobilisation took place across India.

[46] *Citizen Weekly* (Kanpur), 11 October 1941, 12 July 1941.
[47] Zoya Hasan, *Dominance and Mobilisation: Rural Politics in Western Uttar Pradesh 1930–1980* (New Delhi: Sage, 1989).
[48] Baker, *The Politics of South India*, pp. 64–7.
[49] *Ibid.*, p. 83.

These patterns encourage the historian to look well beyond the obvious institutions of anti-colonial political mobilisation or the debates of the legislative councils to understand why there was so much discussion of the 1920s as a decade of 'communal' conflict. Obviously, as David Page, Richard Gordon, Peter Reeves and Gyanendra Pandey have shown, the occasion of elections, for example those of 1926, meant that high-level electoral appeals to religious community in political mobilisation were used in a new way – for example, between M. M. Malaviya and Motilal Nehru in the Congress/Hindu Mahasabha political competition in UP.[50] But the emergence of new arenas of provincial party political competition does not provide a full answer for why the politics of religious community seemed to grow in importance across India in the 1920s. Gyanendra Pandey in his influential work *The Construction of Communalism in Colonial North India* looks at the changing purchase of the idea and discourse of 'communalism' over this very period, and points out that the changing significance of 'communalism' as an idea accompanied ideological developments in Indian nationalism.[51] But this study still raises a number of unanswered questions. For example, how was it possible for a range of religious-mobilisational ideologies to have such an impact at certain moments, apparently on communities of Indians for whom they had little direct relevance? Why did it suit the purposes of politicians across India to adopt, even temporarily, symbols of religious or communal mobilisation?

An alternative way to tackle these questions is to reconsider the nature of political *practice* in India in general, and to relate it to the specific decade of the 1920s. The work of Paul R. Brass and Harold Gould in the 1960s and 1970s and Zoya Hasan in the 1980s showed how political mobilisation around a 'Congress system' of politics in the 1950s and early 1960s was based, to a great extent, around clientelist factions. Local Congress leaders would mobilise specific followings not, or at least not predominantly, around ideological issues, but around personal leadership and electoral contingency. These contingencies required rapid identification of causes of popular significance in any particular locality, which meant that such leaders were not always in control of mobilisations, when an appeal to religion was made. Such appeals might have engaged wider

---

[50] See *The Leader* (Allahabad), 21 January 1926. Work on the connections between elections and communal violence has also been carried through to the contemporary period in Steven I. Wilkinson, *Votes and Violence*.

[51] Pandey, *Construction of Communalism*, ch. 7.

networks of supporters. Often quite personal rivalries defined the nature of political competition, and factional power blocs were formed around specific leaders based on linkages and alliances at different levels of the polity – district, province and sometimes all-Indian. However, the building of faction also interlinked with temporary community building around issues that might be of mainly local significance. For example, in UP, Ram Ratan Gupta in Kanpur was involved in the promotion of city-based Hindu Sabha activities, but his political ambitions were also developed through connection with a Congress factional leader with influence across central and eastern UP – Algu Rai Shastri.[52]

The 'Congress system' was in a process of infancy and formation during the 1920s: the Congress organisation itself only took on the characteristics of a modern political party after the broadening of its political membership and the experience of electoral politics in a limited form in the late colonial period. However, the work of Paul R. Brass, Harold Gould and Mushirul Hasan are useful in looking at how, as significant local power blocs formed, hastily constructed bases of mobilisation become significant. Brass and, to a lesser extent, Gould suggest that although caste and some-times religious community defined the boundaries of political cliques and factions (especially in regions like Aligarh district in western UP), these could shift and alter very easily.[53] There was therefore rarely anything concrete or definite about how caste and religion played into political mobilisation in this kind of scenario. If it served the interests of a local leader to highlight the idea of a caste or religious constituency as a way of building a power base, then such communal divisions could matter, but of course, there often had to be underlying reasons for competition between the constituencies that were being mobilised. This certainly appeared to be the case around the 1926 elections in north India. In early 1926, for example, riots around a Ramlila procession in Aligarh the previous September were subsequently used by a leading political figure in the city, Jwala Prasad Jigyasu, to build political support around the issue of music

---

[52] See 'Representations against Sri Ram Ratan Gupta for Hardoi District (North) in the State Assembly Elections', AICC Papers, File no. 4674 1951, NMML.

[53] For example, whereas the political influence of Ch. Charan Singh in Meerut was based on the promotion of the Jat community, it was also necessary for him to mobilise support and influence at many different levels of the administrative and political apparatus, and this cut across the politics of caste or community. See Paul R. Brass, *Factional Politics in an Indian State: The Congress Party in Uttar Pradesh* (Berkeley: University of California Press, 1965), pp. 147–50.

before mosques.[54] In other places, for most of the decade, local political mobilisation was based on cross-communal factional alliances and cooperation, particularly in areas where religious community cooperation was vital, such as interwar Bengal and Punjab.

Caste and/or religious community, therefore, under the right kind of circumstances, could very easily become the bases for division and mobilisation, especially where groups needed to be mobilised quickly in the absence of other pre-existing political issues. The point about the factional political system was that, operationally, it was ideologically empty to a large extent. It could adapt and shift around issues that might suit a particular moment. In the early 1920s, a range of immediate contexts made religious community and caste mobilisation (often for the assertion of religious status) relevant and useful as an ideological justification for an emerging factional system. This and later sections will explore a range of such contextual factors, and suggest how and why, in the 1920s, religious community could become important in mainstream politics for a time and then seem to disappear again in the mid-1930s. It was to appear again in the latter part of that decade and then disappear largely for India as a whole in the early 1950s for a number of years, as a theme taken up by the popular media and political commentary.

Important to this entire process for the 1920s was, first, the *temporary* nature of the system of dyarchy. The 1919 Government of India Act had a deliberately limited shelf life – a situation that allowed the colonial state to maintain the shifting bases of its authority. Dyarchy assisted the rapid formation of Indian institutions and associations, not just because it provincialised politics or that it represented a new phase in the widening spheres of political mobilisation, but because it was a deliberately temporary stage of constitutional change. At the time of the 1919 Government of India Act, it was known that the reforms would be reviewed in ten years' time. The very term 'progressive realisation' of responsible self-government also meant that political leaders had to be prepared to adapt quickly. For example, the principle of separate electorates for Muslims, extended in the 1919 Government of India Act, was a mechanism that had been the subject of highly changeable negotiation, agreement, disagreement and redefinition – from the initial phase of Muslim League lobbying in 1906–7, to the Lucknow Pact negotiations of 1916 and the alliances between Hindu Congress leaders and Khilafatists in 1918–19. The politics of separate representation changed again after the All Parties conferences

---

[54] 'Aligarh Ramlila Disturbance Case', *The Leader* (Allahabad), 20 January 1926.

in 1928, and once again in the early 1930s with the Communal Award proposals. Uncertainties also surrounded political commitments to anti-colonial mobilisation. Leaders associated with Gandhi's Non-Cooperation movement in the early 1920s, or Civil Disobedience between 1930 and 1934, could quickly shift towards a position of contesting the elections of 1921–2, 1926 or 1937, since what served their particular interests at any particular moment was usually of a temporary nature.[55] Such shifts could be justified by the argument that the councils would be 'wrecked from within', since it was known that, in any case, a new constitutional system would, in time, replace them.

Around the elections of the 1920s, then, it is perhaps not at all surprising that political alliances and divisions were fragile. The classic example of this was the entrance of the symbolically powerful but organisationally insubstantial Hindu Mahasabha of 1925–6. Academic and popular interest in this organisation relates to the contemporary rise of the Hindu right, and in particular the BJP's own account of its 'nationalist' history. The Mahasabha has been seen as the forerunner to some of the key organisations and parties of Hindu nationalism in late twentieth-century India. Importantly, it is highlighted as the 'true' organisation of Indian nationalism by a range of parties on the Hindu right, and in this sense has allowed such organisations to construct their own legitimate 'nationalist' histories. The most important ideological facet of these organisations, however, was not the degree of their popular support, which in relative terms was quite weak. More significant was their rationale for attempting to draw out and construct a sense of the 'Hindu' community, despite the very problematic nature of that project. This was a project that, at different times and in different places across India, could be taken up by a range of different parties, including those that were professedly 'secular'. There were often instrumental political reasons for this, as we have already explored, but the idea of a consolidated and united 'Hindu' community was also adopted by largely urban-based professional groups.

Institution building around the Muslim community is less problematic to explore in the sense that organisations like the Muslim League, although centred on a fragile coalition of interests among regionally, socially and linguistically divided communities, nevertheless were usually driven by clearer community-oriented rationales. The most influential Muslim organisations were based in north India where there were powerful

---

[55] See Richard Gordon, 'Non-Cooperation and Council Entry, 1919–1920', *Modern Asian Studies*, 7, 3, 1973.

traditions of Indo-Islamic culture and where Muslim communities were in significant minorities. For the Muslim League, one of the key problems for the presentation of a Muslim front in India, even one based clearly on the assertion of minority political rights, was the balancing out of the very different kinds of social interests of Muslims on the basis of region and lifestyle. The League's stress on issues such as separate representation, Muslim share of government jobs and administration was not likely to strike a chord with the vast majority of poorer Muslims: most would not have qualified for the franchise, have much influence in local political institutions or have the necessary qualifications for government service. These social distinctions were extremely important in setting out the conceptual battlegrounds between different institutions attempting to define their constituencies.

The idea of the 'Hindu community' or 'Hindu nation' also had a differential purchase in different parts of India and at different levels of politics. For most of north India – UP, Bengal and Punjab – the political institutions of Hindu nationalism shared some common features and concerns, although in the last two cases, these were very much coloured by a sense of Hindu minority status.[56] There were important (and often locally quite specific) manifestations of political support for notions of a consolidated Hindu community. In western India – Bombay and Maharashtra – a broad sense of Hindu community could be built around a 'sons of the soil' Maratha mythology, or by the specific mobilising strategies of Chitpavan Brahmans within the Hindu Mahasabha. In the south, in contrast with the north and west, outside areas such as Hyderabad, where the Hindu Mahasabha promoted forms of Hindu defence as a protest against the actions of Muslim-dominated administrations, Hindu organisations along the lines of the Mahasabha were relatively few or weak, as there was no particular rationale for mobilisation along such lines.

Ideas of Hindu unity, as has been suggested in a range of works on Hindu nationalism, also related to a desire by north Indian publicists to emulate colonial organisational structures.[57] As the colonial state sought to delineate the boundaries of social organisation, to quantify and organise Indian populations and to set up institutions for their representation, so some parallel Indian organisations started to base mobilisation around the rationale of *sangathan*. As will be explored in the following section, this

---

[56] See Joya Chatterji, *Bengal Divided: Hindu Communalism and Partition, 1932–1947* (Cambridge: Cambridge University Press, 1994).
[57] John Zavos, *The Emergence of Hindu Nationalism.*

was apparently the case for organisations, parties and movements relating to Hindu, Muslim and Sikh communitiies. Part of the rationale for 'Hindu *sangathan*', then, was largely functional and pragmatic – the need to create sabhas and parties to reflect the emergent colonial structures of political response. As the last chapter suggested, it was no surprise that such organisations (e.g. the early Hindu Sabhas, the Muslim League, Singh Sabha and the Shia Political Conference) should have come about around the early twentieth century, sometimes in anticipation of or reaction to colonial projects such as the decennial census and local government reforms. Organisations like the Hindu Mahasabha were rejuvenated in the early 1920s, just as the framework of colonial institution building shifted around the ostensible framework of 'responsible self-government'. There were crucial political transformations, particularly around provincial mobilisation and electoral conduct, which affected the view of 'communal politics' in the interwar period too, which have been dealt with in the previous chapter. To a great extent, these changes in the context of colonial governance and the emergence of a discourse of political organisation also coincided in many ways with internal debates about the limits and borders of religious community, which had much to do with religious reform and theological discussion.[58]

As far as the Hindu Sabhas are concerned, there are other ways of looking at this discourse of communal unity, however: many of its members were from high-caste communities anxious to retain privileges and social advantage. This came about via the promotion of Indian cultural and national unity – something common to a range of manifestations of Indian nationalism. In these ideological constructions, there was little space for notions of plurality, either social or religious, and so evidence of fissiparous tendencies along those lines could not be easily accommodated. Organisations like the Hindu Mahasabha, then, and parts of the Congress organisation were therefore reactive rather than proactive in responding to the emergence of caste organisations or the appearance of forms of regional separatism. For example, in its reorganised meeting in 1923 at Banaras, the Hindu Mahasabha made a point of reacting to the initiatives of the Arya Samaj in publicising forms of 'caste' unity. In contrast, by the 1930s, the outspokenly secular Congress Working Committee (which was of course very different to provincial manifestations of the Congress) strongly attempted to accommodate and subsume what it perceived as threats to 'Indian unity' by ostensibly celebrating the

---

[58] For more on this, see Justin Jones's work on the Shi'a organisations in UP.

idea of cultural diversity. As we have already seen in the last chapter, a range of 'Hindu Sabha'–style organisations had been forming for a few decades across north India. But they could not easily be formed into a coherent political movement, not least because there was clearly no natural consensus about the nature of the 'Hindu community' itself. Similarly, in the late 1920s and 1930s, right through to the war period, a range of 'communal' organisations formed around the local *akhara* (gymnasium), caste-based institutions and voluntary drilling movements. But these movements, although promising a sense of continued mobilisation and political engagement, came and went like the monsoon. For example, in the late 1930s, a range of 'Hindu' volunteer organisations were hastily formed and then dissolved again but used by factional leaders. They included the Arya Vir Dal, the Mahabir Dal and Hanuman Dal, which appeared in some of the more remote districts and towns of UP.[59]

The temporary nature of dyarchy, and the fact that it empowered more moderate wings of the largest Indian political parties, served the purposes of those political leaders who benefitted from sudden local manifestations of support. Under a limited electorate, political publicists had to manage quickly and sometimes manufacture organic, simple ideologies that bore little relation to anything programmatic in a political sense. It did not even particularly matter that most of the communities being 'mobilised' had their own agendas as far as religious community or political aims were concerned. Because electoral politics was limited, both in terms of those enfranchised and in terms of the longevity of dyarchy itself, leaders and agencies were encouraged to build largely informal 'mass' followings that rarely had to be based on *political* issues of common interest or electoral promises. To create the appearance of a mass popular support was therefore valuable. And appeal to pre-existing religious identities or indeed to invented ideas of community became appealing in this transitional period, since religious community revivalism could be pertinent to the strengthening of bonds between otherwise divided populations, for example urban and rural workers.[60]

The actions and reactions of the colonial state at all levels also shifted over this phase of rapid constitutional and political transition, and this can be seen at an obvious level through the changing emphases of the decennial census. Whereas in the period from 1881 to 1911, the science of

---

[59] This process will be examined in more detail in Chapter 5. See also 'Report on Volunteer Organisations covering the first half of 1939', L/PJ/8/678 OIOC.

[60] Chitra Joshi, 'Bonds of Community, Ties of Religion'.

ethnography made a confident mark on representations of community, firmly establishing a sense of European knowledge about Indian society, by the 1931 census, doubts and insecurities about this process from the British side had clearly arisen. Writing in the report of the 1931 census, A. C. Turner noted that

> ... the caste return has been impugned by some who contend that it is likely to perpetuate by official action what they consider to be undesirable, viz, caste differentiation, and by others who think the returns are vitiated for demographic purposes by the attempts of the lower castes to return themselves as belonging to groups of higher status.[61]

Perhaps most significant here was a sense of uncertainty that the colonial system was really capable of containing or mediating rapidly expanding and changing caste and community organisations. Turner's comment above suggested that the meaning of community was being transformed by local movements, which would use the basic frameworks of communal definition for parochial purposes.

However, this sense of uncertainty in the context of rapid political change also meant that over the medium term it suited colonial officialdom to consider India's constitutional development in terms of manageable constituencies. It made sense, then, for the Raj to present itself as 'protector' of beleaguered minorities – a situation that tended to identify Muslims (particularly in north India) as 'historically important'. The official view of Muslims in most parts of India was that they formed a distinct political interest group, to the extent that their whole political culture and ways of living could be marked out, in official surveys, as different. Lord Ronaldshay, Governor of Bengal, for example, suggested that the two main communities had 'a profoundly different outlook on life, resulting in social systems which are the very antithesis of one another'. But Islam in India was heterogenous at every level, particularly that of political organisation: Montagu and Chelmsford received forty-four deputations from different Muslim groups/organisations claiming to speak for the community, leading up to the postwar reforms.[62] The most obvious example of colonial promotion of Muslim separateness was in the extension of separate electorates in the 1919 Government of India Act – an idea that not only suggested that Muslims needed protecting in legislative bodies (and therefore forms of reservation), but also that the very articulation of their

[61] *Census of India 1931, Report*, p. 533.
[62] Quoted in Zoya Hasan, 'Communalism and Communal Violence in India', *Social Scientist*, 10, 2, 1982, 26–7.

political interests via electorates was entirely separate. This was not just down to the Muslim perception of political disadvantage. Many powerful Muslim communities harboured a profound scepticism about the assumptions behind European notions of political representation. However, to some extent, the idea that Muslims should be seen as a separate political community was the product of an outlook based on the norms of *sharif* culture and Mughal tradition, drawn upon by north Indian Muslim elites. In these calculations, social status could also be seen as a basis of representation.[63]

Importantly, the contemporary vogue of describing religious communities as primordially irreconcilable, yet fitting them into a liberal, European model of minority rights and representation, was also taken up by organisations like the Congress. The Lucknow Pact of 1916, in which the Congress agreed to the principle of separate electorates for Muslims, attempted to present a united front to the Government of India. But it presupposed that Hindu and Muslim political interests could be seen as different. Some of the main leaders of the Congress also tended to discuss all-Indian politics in terms of the different political traditions of Hindus and Muslims. Gandhi, for example, spent a large proportion of the mid-1920s, after the collapse of the non-cooperation movement, building campaigns to oppose Hindu–Muslim antagonism. His rhetoric revealed that he too believed the communities could be seen as separate entities. In an article in which he responded to various charges that he had 'encouraged' Muslim separatism by backing the Khilafat movement, Gandhi admitted that 'the Malabar happenings undoubtedly disquieted the Hindu mind'. Later in the same article, he placed an even more definitive characterisation on the two communities as possessing specific characteristics.[64] Common was a powerful colonial trope of the 'muscular Muslim' versus the 'cowardly' Hindu – for example, local British representations of Muslims often represented them as an embattled though tough minority, driven by strong faith and carnivorous diet.[65]

These structures created contexts for the broad communal appeals that mobilised large numbers for political purposes. Yet a look at the instances

[63] Farzana Shaikh, *Community and Consensus in Islam*, pp. 120, 234–6.
[64] 'Hindu–Muslim Tension: Its Cause and Cure', 29 May 1924. In M. K. Gandhi, *Collected Works*, Vol. 28. p. 49. Available at http://www.gandhiserve.org/cwmg/VOL028.PDF
[65] See, for example, the account of William Chaning Pearce about the riots of 1947 in Mathura District, in which he describes the Muslim Meos as a tough, resolute and independent community – W. A. Chaning Pearce, IPS, UP, 1947. MSS.EUR.F/161/144 OIOC.

of direct conflict between communities was not simply a matter of political mobilisation. By the interwar period, such confrontations certainly seemed to be more common than in earlier years, and often related to moments of political change or mobilisation – elections, protests and political processions. When we look at the catalogue of official reports on communal violence from the early 1920s, some interesting patterns emerge, not least an official preoccupation with the control and policing of religious custom and space. And in these surveys of communal violence, it is clear that often quite localised disputes were categorised under broader, politically significant 'causal' themes. In Bombay province, there were eleven major riots described as 'Hindu–Muslim'. Of the six conflicts in 1928, two (in Sholapur and Surat) involved the making of music by Hindu processions in front of mosques – often shortened in files to 'music before mosques', and the remaining four, in Godhra, Nasik and Bombay and environs, were apparently related to local religious processions. In Bengal, while there were only five officially recorded cases of Hindu–Muslim conflict in 1919 (and none in 1920–1), there were twenty-five in 1923. A good proportion of these moments were also recorded as being related to 'music before mosques', with the term becoming almost a standardised term of reference for a wide array of different local confrontations.[66] In UP, there were ninety-one reported 'serious' Hindu–Muslim clashes between 1923 and 1927 inclusive. Again, the majority of these conflicts were related to music before mosques and cow-slaughter controversies.[67]

Importantly, these moments of conflict were not simply treated as routine moments of 'disorder' that were disconnected examples of everyday religious controversy. By 1925–6, 'communal' violence in north India became a political issue that exercised the minds of legislators, colonial officials and nationalist ideologues in a completely new way. In late August 1926, resolutions were passed in the Indian Legislative Assembly regarding the regulation of religious festivals, in which, on the one side, accusations were directed against government for wilful neglect and, on the other, reflections of the newly 'political' nature of Hindu–Muslim quarrels were discussed. In these debates, Alex Muddiman suggested that what used to be 'particular' disputes now seemed to have significance and importance all over India. Importantly, official opinion focussed on the culpability of the press and religious/local leaderships in stirring up the otherwise passive urban and rural masses. In contrast, leaders associated with the Congress

---

[66] 'Hindu Muslim Tension and Riots', MSS.Eur.F.161/142 OIOC.
[67] 'Statement of Communal Riots in the UP Between 1922 and 1927', L/PJ/6/1890 OIOC.

suggested that the bases for Hindu–Muslim conflict would disappear once India was free – that the events involved 'three parties'.[68] The idea that 'leaders' were deliberately stirring up religious animosities was also used as an explanation by officials investigating a riot that surrounded an *Arti* ceremony during Muslim prayer time in Aminabad Park, Lucknow, in September 1924. Similarly, in a riot during *Chehlum* in Allahabad in October 1924, the Commissioner pointed out that the 'community' leaders perpetuated the violence, and suggested that 'as soon as quiet was restored, recriminations broke out, and both parties devoted themselves to doing as much harm as possible to each other. The Malaviya family was especially virulent against both the Muhammadans and the authorities'. For this Commissioner,

The masses quarrel about such matters as the sacrifice of cows, the blowing of sankhs, music in front of mosques and a hundred other details, but these are merely surface manifestations of what is at bottom a struggle for political power and place under the new constitution.[69]

The idea of deliberate communal conspiracies involving key religious leaders also characterised reports on rioting and violence in Bengal – in a report on violence in Kankinara, near Calcutta, in mid-October 1924, Hindu police officers helped to protect a Hindu procession that had never before passed through a Muslim area.[70]

The next chapter will explore the ways in which these colonial and nationalist representations of communal conflict obscured much more complex realities, particularly in the relationships between poorer Indians and state agencies. There are also unanswered questions about how and why community concerns and anxieties might have led individuals and groups to take part in moments of violent public activity, for reasons that cannot be simply related to the activities of broader 'community' organisations, explored in this section. In this connection, the significance of religious community should be analysed at the level of the family and individual, as well as the broader society, as a means of complicating what has all too often been presented as a uniform picture of sectarian conflict. In this analysis, the intersection between family, broader society and state, then, is highly significant – a theme explored in the final section of this chapter.

[68] Legislative Assembly Resolutions regarding the regulation of religious festivals 24 August 1926 to 1 September 1926, in 'Communal Disorders', L/PJ/6/1890, OIOC.
[69] Report of the Allahabad Commissioner, 'Communal Disorders', L/PJ/6/1890, OIOC.
[70] 'Rioting between Hindus and Muslims at Kankinara nr. Calcutta', L/PJ/6/1889, OIOC.

(III) COMMUNITY, FAMILY AND 'NATION'

Alongside political and institutional contexts and public representations of community in interwar India, ideas about religious community also changed in relation to the family and domestic space. With the development of public debates about social and religious reform especially from the 1870s, attention had been drawn to customs and rituals linked to rites of passage and, in particular, the political and civic rights of women. The symbolism of the normative Indian family – Indian father, daughter, son and especially mother figure – was, in the interwar period, painted vividly in the nationalist literature and the press in terms of a national ideal and in relation to ideas of public service. As many scholars have pointed out, the symbolism of the Indian woman, especially as 'mother' figure, was firmly knitted to nationalist allegories surrounding the nation itself. Throughout our period and well into post-independent India, Indian nationalist ideologues evoked motherhood as a kind of metaphor: from the writing of Bankimchandra to the cow-protection movements (see Chapter 2).[71] Propriety and service were exemplifiers of ideal womanly attributes in a context where women were objects of reformist analysis within the 'woman's question'.

Women's access to and engagement with public political debates in this period was a difficult one, then, since any kind of economic freedom would not be compatible, to a large extent, with the traditionally ascribed 'duties' of Indian women.[72] But there were of course important variations across India in terms of how issues such as 'women's education' were implemented and approached, as we will see. The Indian journalist's delineation of the ideal Indian family showed an increasingly sharp boundary between the idea of a Hindu or Muslim family. This section will look at the latter process in relation to the definition and redefinition of the legal rights of men and women in the sphere of 'private law'. It will also explore the pathologies of sexual representation, in particular resurgent concerns in

---

[71] See Sandhya Shetty, '(Dis)figuring the Nation: Mother, Metaphor, Metonymy', *Differences: A Journal of Feminist Cultural Criticism*, 7, 3, 1995; Partha Chatterjee, 'The Nationalist Resolution of the Women's Question', in Kumkum Sangari and Sudesh Vaid, eds., *Recasting Women: Essays in Colonial History* (New Brunswick: Rutgers University Press, 1990), pp. 233–53; and Aamir R. Mufti, 'A Greater Story-Writer than God: Genre, Gender and Minority in Late Colonial India', in Partha Chatterjee and Pradeep Jeganathan, eds., *Subaltern Studies XI: Community, Gender and Violence* (Delhi: Permanent Black, 2000), pp. 13–36.

[72] Orsini, pp. 244–5.

the interwar period about the masculinity of Hindu or Muslim identity and the need to preserve the honour of the Hindu or Muslim woman.

In *The Nation and its Fragments*, Partha Chatterjee set out the now well-known argument that before the advent of a coherent institutionally based Indian 'nationalist' movement, Hindu reformers aimed to create a domain of 'sovereignty' aside from and in reaction to the colonial state in the domestic sphere itself. For Chatterjee, this project had far-reaching implications for definitions of the political role of women, reinforcing a new form of patriarchy in the later nineteenth and early twentieth century, and setting out bourgeois virtues in the domestic sphere.[73] This domain of sovereignty required middle-class Indian women to be different to Western women by maintaining family cohesion and spiritual purity – a situation that allowed social reform to go so far but no further.[74] Life under colonialism generated a range of debates about the roles of women among Indian social reformers and religious revivalists, which connected to national political debates. Within and across these debates, there was a tension between the promotion of 'modernisation' of Indian society and the desire to either preserve distinctive Indian traditions or find the 'modern' within such traditions.[75] Writers and ideologues discussing the normative roles of Indian women and how they reflected other issues surrounding social reform in society might, then, mobilise around self-consciously 'Western' and largely secular views about gender or find solutions to colonial critiques about Indian women within existing religious traditions.

Importantly, in India it was possible to achieve both of these things at once, since the notion of the 'secular' and the modern in India, as discussed in Chapter 1, was wedded by many ideologues to the revival of religious tradition. For some historians, the late nineteenth century represented a stalling of liberal modernist thinking, since many forms of Indian nationalism promoted social conservatism, particularly in relation to the family. However, Indian nationalism had always been characterised by the ideological mixing of selected elements of both liberal and revivalist thought, precisely because of India's distinctive colonial context for political debate. Chatterjee has expressed this idea in terms of the nationalist discourse separating the outer from the inner world – where the outer, material circumstances of 'Western' modernity might be embraced for pragmatic

[73] Partha Chatterjee, *The Nation and its Fragments: Colonial and Postcolonial Histories* (Princeton: Princeton University Press, 1996), pp. 6, 129–30.
[74] *Ibid.*, p. 128.
[75] Sen, *Hindu Revivalism*.

reasons, while the inner, spiritual and unique nature of Indian life might be retained. Through this, notions of the 'home' and 'world' were constructed by nationalist ideologues, the former being female and the latter essentially male. Importantly, the inner domain was one of sovereignty, away from the outer realities of conflict with a foreign power.[76] Consistent in all of these arguments about social reform was the critique of the colonial state's championing of the public sphere of reform.

These distinctive ideological formulations about reform and the 'women's question' developed in new ways as ideas surrounding 'religion' as an inner, sovereign spiritual world spilled out into the public domain more forcefully and as the political stakes were raised in the 1920s. The arguments about who controlled the reins of progressive reform became particularly intense when struggles for political representation became more acute in the interwar period. Chatterjee suggests that the status of women in Indian society was largely isolated by nationalists from the colonial state as a sphere of autonomy effectively right up to the end of the colonial period.[77] However, more recent research on the debates about personal law reform have shown how, from the 1920s at least, serious discussions were already emerging in private members' bills to the new legislatures, around possible future legislation on the legal rights of women to inheritance and divorce.[78] With the rapid expansion of membership of political institutions and organisations after the war, and the upsurge in circulation of social reform journals (particularly women's magazines – 'stri upyogi' literature), attention was increasingly drawn to the roles of community and family in the idea of the nation. The idea of a distinctive and normative Indian *family*, as well as just the creation of the ideal Indian woman, was hardened in interwar public discussions about the relationship between the private and public lives of Indians. Crucially, publications such as *Stri Darpan*, edited by the Nehru family, began to link discussion of women's domestic lives to political matters more clearly after 1920. Most significantly, *Chamd*, founded in 1922 in Allahabad, located women's roles squarely in the centre of national political development.[79]

Key to this expansion in 'women's' literature were changing modes of communication, patterns of consumption and contact with the wider world. Obviously, the massive and rapid expansion in membership of

---

[76] Partha Chatterjee, 'The Nationalist Resolution of the Women's Question', pp. 238–9.
[77] *Ibid.*, pp. 249–50.
[78] See Eleanor Newbigin, 'The Hindu Code Bill and the Making of the Modern Indian State', PhD dissertation, University of Cambridge, 2008.
[79] Orsini, pp. 262–9.

organisations like the Congress, with its new 2 anna membership effected with the Nagpur constitution of 1920, brought not just workers and peasants clearly into a national movement, but also many more women. This was indicative not just of a changed Congress, but also of a changed political world in which the promise of universal suffrage and the political rights of women were brought onto the agenda more persistently than ever before. The widening and rationalising of the Congress organisation, for example, as a mass party in the 1920s, also provided space for the strand of Gandhian constructive nationalism, which focussed explicitly on the domestic family economy. The simplicity of khadi and spinning within that programme was deliberately evoked as a means of building on the symbolism of the distinctively Indian family, which might cut across other class, caste and religious divisions. This too was the most obvious manifestation of a larger and more complex set of processes surrounding reactions to changes in middle-class consumption, urban life, fashion, technological change and cultural pessimism. Such changes can be particularly seen in the means whereby khadi was propagadated as a project for household and women's reform in northern and western India.[80]

The interwar period was also a time in which a largely secular and 'universal' notion of women's rights within the Indian family emerged for perhaps the first time via the Child Marriage Restraint Act or Sarda Bill, passed in October 1929. One of the leading scholars in this field has argued that the struggle for a bill to raise the age of consent in India was the first time that a cross-communal notion of Indian, secular and universalised sense of women's rights was championed across the political spectrum.[81] Katherine Mayo's book, *Mother India*, published in 1927, had contained searing critiques of the patriarchal social practices of Hindu men towards their women folk, and feminists in England were quick to call for colonial trusteeship of the reform process. The supposedly modernising stance of the colonial state was thrown into question directly when it became blatantly apparent that it sought to defeat or at the very least throw up obstacles to the passage of the proposed Child Marriage Restraint Act. Allowing the passage of social legislation of this kind, British administrators felt, could place the carefully developed networks of conservative collaboration in jeopardy. Not for the first time, but in very stark terms,

---

[80] See Lisa Trivedi, *Clothing Gandhi's Nation: Homespun and Modern India* (Bloomington: Indiana University Press, 2007).

[81] Mrinalini Sinha, *Specters of Mother India: The Global Restructuring of an Empire* (Durham: Duke University Press, 2006), pp. 152–4.

the moral high ground of social and religious reform had been effectively wrested away from the colonial state, as Indian social reformers and writers of a more radical hue critiqued both Mayo's book and the colonial stance. According to Sinha, support for the Sarda Bill (although it was in the end quite a toothless Act) represented a 'turning point in a revised national political imagination in India'. Most importantly, the episode revealed the importance of the constituency of Indian women as a key political force in its own right, a constituency with its own new collective identity in the public realm.[82]

However, around the apparent strength of the universal and normative Indian ideal here, a more complex and subtle series of debates related to the on-going legal rights of women to divorce and family property. Moreover, the controversy around *Mother India* and the Sarda Bill also helped to publicise and in some respects strengthen the position of both Hindu and Muslim religious conservatives. For example, in Uttar Pradesh at the end of the 1920s and in the early 1930s, conservatives from both communities opposed the implications of the Sarda Act. In December 1929 and January 1930 across UP, organisations such as the Jamiat-ul-Ulema organised meetings and circulated pamphlets instructing Muslims to oppose the Act and to protect Sharia. On 13 December 1929, Deobandi Muslims even formed a suicide corps to protest against the legislation.[83] By mid-January 1930, hartals and black-flag processions were taking place against the Act, and in Shajahanpur, one Muslim leader called on his co-religionists to join Hindu Congressmen, as 'Hindus too' were against the legislation.[84]

This was critical at a time in which some of the most important parts of north India had experienced an apparent upsurge in 'communal conflict' too. In 1928, it also appeared, at least at the level of constitutional negotiation, that although a new generation of key political figures were pushing the Congress organisation in a more radical direction, the Hindu Mahasabha had made important gains in inter-party negotiations. The Nehru Report, produced in 1928 in response to the Simon Commission, had allowed lobbyists sympathetic to the Mahasabha to push Congress to backtrack on its support for, among other concessions, separate electorates for Muslims. Alongside one stream of universal secular radicalism, identified by Sinha, were other strands of renewed religious conservatism, most of which backed the political directions of Hindu conservatism or

---

[82] *Ibid.*, p. 153.
[83] Police Abstract of Intelligence (PAI), 11 January 1930, No. 1, CIDL.
[84] PAI 25 January 1930, No. 3, CIDL.

Muslim separatism. Some of these lobbies, especially those connected to the Arya Samaj in north India, explicitly took up the issue of social and religious reform. For example, the meeting of the rejuvenated Hindu Mahasabha in 1923 in Banaras discussed its relationship with the Arya Samaj and considered the issue of social and religious reform.[85] In 1934, the growing desire of publicists to start the process of considering social reforms that impinged upon religious matters was illustrated in the proposals for an Untouchable Abolition Bill. Here, leading Congress figures in UP came head to head with Hindu sanatanists and Muslim conservatives, and were largely represented by the conservative Urdu press as attempting to rejunvenate and modernise Hinduism in a communal way.[86]

New political opportunities arose for women to mobilise in their own right in the 1920s and 1930s, and radical secularists supported universal 'modern' values for the Indian state. However, this was also a time in which forms of Hindu and Muslim patriarchy were reinforced in political organisations and popular journal literature. As the following discussion will suggest, moments of community insecurity bolstered the claims of men to dominate and protect women in all spheres of life. This was a totalising paternalism, which often devalued the ostensible political gains of women. This position becomes clearer when we look at how the Sarda Bill was related to broader and deeper debates about personal law reform, in which a project in the redefinition of the roles of Hindu and Muslim women was taking place. As one historian has convincingly argued, from the 1920s to the 1950s with the eventual passage of the Hindu Code Bill, debates about personal law reform were configured to enhance the power of particular Hindu men in a context of community-based insecurities. For example, the actions of M. R. Jayakar in promoting the Hindu Gains of Learning Act of 1930 furthered urban Hindu middle-class male ambitions to break free from the shackles of customary law as part of a larger attempt to assert the individual power of the new male head of the household in the late colonial period.[87] This also had the knock-on effect in some cases of marginalising Christian minorities in South India, who were multi-vocal in their continued attachment to customary law and therefore not easily categorised by

---

[85] *The Leader* (Allahabad), 17 August and 22 August 1923.
[86] See William Gould, *Hindu Nationalism*, pp. 124–5.
[87] Eleanor Newbigin, 'The Hindu Code Bill', Conculsion; see also Flavia Agnes, 'Women, Marriage and the Subordination of Rights, in Chatterjee and Jaganathan, eds., *Community Gender and Violence*, p. 121.

either jurists or politicians, who increasingly sought to define the legal and political definitions of different religious communities.[88]

The family and the scope of laws governing it, then, was an extremely important arena that was woven into public representations of religious community power. Religion became more than just about belief and practice, but also a symbolic terrain that connected these overlapping sovereignties in a way made particularly sharp by the often contradictory colonial stance surrounding religious identities and reforms. In this sense, in order to understand the meaning and purchase of 'communalism' in the interwar period, the historian needs to reach down to the level of how the public and domestic interacted, especially in north India. Here, representations of the 'duties' of women are significant, but so too are those of men and masculinity. Research on the pathologies of sexual identity has shown that 'communalism' also had a strongly gendered aspect to it in the 1920s and 1930s, and continues to do so to the present day, as we will see in the next chapter. Research on the political economy of late twentieth-century India has also demonstrated a correlation between the mobilisation of women's social capital (in the form of educational attainment and literacy for example) and the prevention or control of 'communal' violence.[89]

Recent work on the social and cultural history of north India has shown how male anxieties about sexuality and domestic control in the late colonial period contributed to the assertion of communal identities. According to these arguments, the appearance of projects to promote Hindu *sangathan* were related to a desire to level out differences of caste within middle-class urban society and the need to control aspects of the domestic sphere. A rhetoric of middle-class respectability and communal identity enclosed women in an idealised representation of the domestic sphere and laid bare anxieties of Hindu men – a theme that will be explored in more detail in the next chapter.[90] The apparent publicity of strengthened communal identities in the interwar period, then, was as much about the content of this rhetoric and anxiety as it was about the manifestation of violence itself. The deep-seated desires to prevent contacts between Hindu women and Muslim men, to control the circulation of obscene publications and to promote the masculinity and control of Hindu men all fed into this ideological promotion of middle-class respectability.

---

[88] Chandra Mallampalli, *Christians and Public Life in Colonial South India, 1863–1937: Contending with Marginality* (London: Routledge, 2004), pp. 83–4.

[89] Amartya Sen, *Development as Freedom* (Oxford: Oxford Paperbacks, 2001).

[90] Charu Gupta, *Sexuality, Obscenity, Community: Women, Muslims, and the Hindu Public in Colonial India* (Delhi: Permanent Black, 2001), pp. 321–3.

Connected to these movements to project and control domestic spaces were concerns over health, which distinctively engaged literate communities, via Hindi journal literature. Some of the main household journals promoted a range of indigenous practices that aimed to lessen 'degenerative' tendencies associated with Western modernity. Importantly, these cures also linked to ideas for enhancing or improving male sexual potency. One Swami Ratnagiri, *Chamd* claimed, had been dispensing medicines to people in Mathura. The Swami, feeling sorry for an old man who had been working for him, gave him some of his special 'healing medicines', with the result that 'the old man took all the tablets in one go and, having acquired too much energy, had to marry thrice'. Other claims behind this particular cure were that 'in seven days the blood can be increased in the body. In twenty-one days, the face can become as shiny as an apple. In 40 days, homosexuality, diabetes and weakness can be treated. Ladies can become fertile and the heart strong'.[91] Print culture therefore became a vehicle for middle-class consumption and aspiration raising, but also forms of pessimism about the 'decline' of the Hindu community. Common in the north Indian newspapers were treatments to induce or enhance virility. 'Otogen' was commonly advertised in papers in 1940s UP, and gave 'a surprising increase in vitality and energy within the first 24 hours', and claimed to make a man or woman look and feel fifteen to twenty years younger than the actual age, increase height by from two to four inches and weight by from five to ten pounds.[92]

New forms of Hindu masculinity were perhaps as important, then, as the delineation of women's roles in these publications. The exponents of *shuddhi* and *sangathan*, particularly in the popular north Indian press, persistently described the effeminate and cowardly decline of 'Hindu' manhood. This was of course, as Charu Gupta has pointed out, a response to colonial stereotypes examined in the previous chapter and a challenge to aspects of Gandhian *ahimsa* at an ideological level.[93] However, the notion of the 'cowardly' Hindu was powerful enough to enter into Gandhi's own representation of Hindu–Muslim difference. The apparent polarisation here was over the means rather than the end. Both Gandhians and Hindu nationalists wanted to promote a form of community strength, but whereas the Hindu Mahasabha privileged the akhara, Gandhi

[91] 'Wonder of Ratnagiri: One who amazed the whole world'. *Chamd*, December 1931, p. 160.
[92] *National Herald*, 10 April 1948, p. 7.
[93] Charu Gupta, *Sexuality, Obscenity, Community*, pp. 232–4.

represented strength in terms of courage and self-control in the face of external brutality. In this formula, Muslims were still represented stereotypically as active aggressors:

There is no doubt in my mind that in the majority of quarrels, the Hindus come out second best. My own experience but confirms the opinion that the Mussalman as a rule is a bully, and the Hindu as a rule is a coward ... as a Hindu I am more ashamed of Hindu cowardice than I am angry at the Mussalman bullying.[94]

The central communal stereotypes, traditionally related to the hard-line position of the Arya Samaj and Hindu Mahasabha, therefore had a purchase in political discourse between the wars that moved beyond the limitations of such organisations and institutions.

CONCLUSION

The political and constitutional changes of the interwar period had a dramatic effect on both old and newly formed religious community organisations, at all levels of the Indian polity. Principally, the 1920s and 1930s were decades in which organisations claimed to represent 'Hindu', 'Muslim' and to a lesser extent 'Sikh' and 'Christian' communities in ways that were not attempted before. To an extent, this was the result of the dissemination of political information around riots and conflicts. The increased circulation of newspapers and the growing power of Indian representatives at municipal and district levels meant that many more formally disenfranchised Indians came into contact with All-Indian political movements. The anticipation of constitutional and political change in this period, too, meant that local conflicts, many of them around religious disputes, were mobilised quickly and temporarily by aspirant political leaders. In the absence of real political power, religious community organisations became a means of promoting particular agendas, demonstrating muscle power and influencing local administrations. Many of the communal organisations that emerged or grew in the 1920s were also defensive in the sense that their concerns were focussed around competition with other religious communities.

However, as the next chapter will explore in more detail, growing interest in the phenomenon of communalism and the appearance of communal organisations was not just of instrumental significance. Neither were the obvious institutions the only (or even in many cases the principal)

---

[94] M. K. Gandhi, 'Hindu–Muslim Conflict, Its Causes and Cure', *Young India*, 29 May 1924.

manifestations of a growing public interest in the politics of religion. First, organisations like the Hindu Mahasabha (perhaps even the Arya Samaj) and Muslim League, as defensive movements, can be viewed as projects for the protection of particular regional or national social interests, which were sometimes only tangentially related to religious practice or identity. A range of other forms of religious community mobilisation was the result of organic attempts to find common ground between vulnerable communities, particularly those making sense of new economic challenges. Second, focus on ideas of religious identity could result from cultural conformism or rebellion. Here, the politics of the family and debates about its place in Indian society and the nation were crucial. And here too, the relative roles of men and women within the 'community' became a central point of debate, highlighting in different ways discussions about the supposed differences between 'Hindus' and 'Muslims' in Indian society.

4

Defining Spheres of Community

Society, Religious Mobilisation and Anti-colonialism

As well as being an era of great political change, the 1920s and 1930s was also a time of urbanisation, steady development of industrial activity and changes in the social lives of Indian workers and peasants. The great industrial city of Kanpur, for example, in the United Provinces (Uttar Pradesh) in the interwar period, became one of the key centres in north India for rural–urban migration to cotton mill and factory work. Here, immediately following the Great War, three new mills were set up. The slump did not create serious setbacks in this steady growth, and in the period of 1930–7, the total number of millworkers in the city increased by 31.2%.[1] The *bastis* and neighbourhoods of the city were largely organised around caste and religious community differences – a situation that was enhanced as a wider array of peasant communities made their way to the city.

These (largely) male sojourners sought the proximity of caste and community fellows as a means of mediating and surviving the often unfamiliar urban environment. The struggle for employment in the mills also strengthened many of these bonds. This was partly about ritual distance: in the Elgin Mill, many Brahman workers would not eat in the dining shed for fear of ritual pollution by other castes or Muslims. *Mistris* or jobbers – the fixers of recruitment into the mills and factories – generally worked in the favour of their own communities too. This enabled control over particular groups of workers, so community affinity became a dynamic of social authority, as well as association, with the *mistri* often

[1] Chitra Joshi, 'Kanpur Textile Labour: Some Structural Features of Formative Years', *Economic and Political Weekly*, 16, 44/46, 1981, 1823.

accepting dasturi (a bribe) for work. The existence of reserve (termed as *badli*) workers was also a dynamic of this relationship, and a fact that made it difficult for those in employment to bargain for better conditions and wages for most of the interwar period.[2] However, community and caste association was not just a means of maintaining social dominance, but also provided the basis of opposition to overbearing bosses and *mistris*. Kanpur's workers, in many cases, used the politics of Hindu mobilisation to assert higher status in the urban environment. Religious community and caste, then, interacted in complex ways with other kinds of class and occupational identities when we look at this level of politics, and it is this theme that will form the central focus of this chapter.

(1) CLASS, CASTE AND COMMUNITY SOLIDARITY

In previous chapters, we have argued that a sense of 'community' around the idea of being Hindu, Muslim or Sikh cannot be consistently or solely related to commonalities of religious belief. We are left therefore with the question of how far other kinds of solidarities help to reinforce the idea of religious community. It is important to distinguish between social being and social consciousness here, and how historians describe collective interests did not necessarily correspond to actually existing identities. This is especially the case when we take into account the dynamic uses of 'caste' and 'class' identity in the early part of the twentieth century. The meaning of 'caste', as we will see, shifted dramatically over the late colonial period, as Indians formed associations to rewrite the histories of their communities and assert enhanced social status. But this was usually a localised process in which the modern representations of the caste community in question corresponded to specific local publicists. The 'Mahasabha' of a particular caste might have significance in the district or region of one particular province/state but be irrelevant to members of the corresponding or comparable 'caste' community in another region. In addition, the issue of social status and political authority in connection to caste identity was in any case highly differentiated across India, even where members of a comparable *jati* could be found in different regions.

Examinations of 'class' in the pre-independence period have commonly related its dynamics to Western notions of capitalist development: the penetration of capitalism into India was described by some historians in the 1960s as 'imperfect', largely as a result of the financial and political

---

[2] *Ibid.*, 1827–9, 1831–5.

dominance of colonial interests. Instead, what might have emerged as a mercantile middle class in the nineteenth century were thought of as communities engaged more in comprador or 'middleman' activities in an Indian economy, where business interests operated from the top down.[3] For related reasons linked to the nature of the colonial economy, an urban working class in India's big cities is said to have not developed fully as a result of incomplete industrial development.[4] These older interpretations of class in India are still quite powerful in academia, and have certainly assisted social scientists in writing about the 'rise' of the middle classes in contemporary India: high-status urban dwellers who have benefitted in the late twentieth century from the eventual opening up of the Indian economy and the explosion in a range of technical and service industries. Generalisations about class on the basis of structural factors have not just taken place on the plane of capitalist development, but also on that of education and political mobilisation. Another level of middle-class development outlined by historians was that of the 'Western-educated' intelligentsia, which made up members of the professions, arts and, importantly, politics and who dominated institutions of 'civil society'.[5] In analyses of these groups, there is something of a stress on the creation of a dominant English-speaking or 'Western-educated' middle class who benefitted from the limited educational opportunities and transnational connections created by colonialism.[6]

Viewing the dynamics of 'class' in India in terms of a stage of economic development along Western lines of the progress of capital's penetration is therefore problematic.[7] Also, the assumption that Indian anti-colonial protest or the political process itself was dominated by a relatively homogenous Western-educated elite across the subcontinent is rather too convenient to be entirely useful without significant qualification. One of the earliest critiques of this notion of a dominant Western-educated middle class, which was powerfully argued for up to the early 1930s, was that of David Washbrook in a review of Judith M. Brown's work on Gandhi in the early

---

[3] B. B. Misra, *The Indian Middle Classes. Their Growth in Modern Times* (Oxford: Oxford University Press, 1961).

[4] M. D. Morris, 'The Effects of Industrialisation on "Race Relations" in India', in G. Hunter, ed., *Industrialization and Race Relations: A Symposium* (London: Oxford University Press, 1965), p. 160.

[5] Michelguglielmo Torri, '"Westernised Middle Class", Intellectuals and Society in Late Colonial India', *Economic and Political Weekly*, 25, 4, 1990, PE2–PE11.

[6] See Modhumita Roy, '"Englishing" India: Reinstituting Class and Social Privilege', *Social Text*, 39, 1994, 83–109.

[7] For elaboration of this idea, see Rajnarayan Chandavarkar, *The Origins of Industrial Capitalism*.

1970s, which outlined the multifarious and multifaceted social and political institutions around which influential political leaders built up influence.[8] In the same period, the academic fashion was to depict Indian politics in terms of vertical patron–client relationships, in which the interests of the supposedly dominant Western-educated middle classes were in fact largely dependent on linkages with significant institutions and individuals above and below them.[9] Some have argued that this requires a reorientation of the notion of 'middle class' in India in relation to region, since communities, simply by virtue of being highly educated or 'intellectual', did not necessarily share autonomous class interests.[10]

However, once we relate the notion of class to real (and changing) contexts of state power or political and economic opportunity in non-static environments, some kind of purchase can be made in comparing different kinds of class and community solidarities. In rural areas of north India, the economic slump following the end of the Great War highlighted perhaps more starkly than ever the differences between subsistence smallholders and landless labourers, on the one hand, and an increasingly powerful rich peasantry, on the other, who, by the 1930s, formed the backbone of rural governance and support for anti-colonial politics. Increasing commercialisation in agriculture also probably consolidated quasi-class interests for those rural communities who were able to finance agriculture. State action over land revenue, tenancy and agricultural investment, some have argued, assisted specific groups in India's agrarian economy, who were later to make up a national 'bourgeoisie' of dominant agrarians.[11] In many of the structural analyses of agrarian society, a common theme is how colonial circumstances reinforced certain forms of social dominance. And in these accounts, the interwar period is crucial.[12] In the towns and cities of India too, the interwar period was one of increasing work opportunities in the industrial sector, with a complex pattern of migration from the rural hinterland into towns and cities. Class formation among these workers was complicated, as we saw at the beginning of this chapter, by connections to pre-existing community ties that went back to the village, but was also heavily influenced by the specific

---

[8] David Washbrook, 'Gandhian Politics', *Modern Asian Studies*, 7, 1, 1973, 107–14.
[9] See, for example, Christopher John Baker, *The Politics of South India*.
[10] Torri, p. PE6.
[11] For an exploration of the literature surrounding these class formations, see B. R. Tomlinson, 'The Historical Roots of Indian Poverty: Issues in the Economic and Social History of South Asia', *Modern Asian Studies*, 22, 1, 1988, 123–40.
[12] *Ibid.*

contexts of the urban mohalla, the jobber recruitment system and the networks of support found in the city.[13]

Urban professionals' participation in political and voluntary activities had been growing since the last few decades of the nineteenth century, as we have seen in Chapter 2, but outside the readership of early journals and newspapers, it was perhaps not altogether self-consciously class based. The institutions these professionals formed, however, across India did relate to an array of trading communities, particularly in provinces like Punjab and areas like Gujarat. For example, Vaishya communities were able to take advantage of changes in communication and transport across India, to form wider networks of contact to other cities and overseas, and such solidarities could be strengthened during slump periods. Finally, for many of these groups, the means for development of quasi-class solidarities were created by social institution building – the caste association, religious organisation or educational endeavour. This applied particularly to those urban communities with high aspirations for social improvement, in an era of extreme competition and paucity of resources. In the interwar period, there is no doubt that the scramble for government jobs and positions on municipal boards took place within a specific high-caste/high-status section of the professional and business population of most Indian towns and cities.[14]

Another significant area for highlighting 'class' aspirations, then, was government service. Throughout the colonial period, Indian governments depended upon state-defined communities and reliable 'families' whose education was geared towards gaining government employment to staff the subordinate (and in some cases upper) bureaucracy. For example, during the 1920s, the India Office began to review the process of Indianisation in the Indian Civil Services and the nature of the examination process. In these files and others like them, comments on individual candidates continued to relate quality to family background. In the 1926 batch, for example, one S. S. Bajpai was described as belonging 'to a family which had done well in Government service', and it was noted that the father of Khurshed Ahmad Khan, another candidate, was also a prominent official.[15] Across India, the culture of the ICS was to rely largely upon the local knowledge of deputy collectors, tahsildars and even more subordinate staff – a situation that also carried across to an extent into the Indian

---

[13] See, for example, Chitra Joshi, 'Bonds of Community'.
[14] Charu Gupta, *Sexuality, Obscenity, Community*, pp. 22–3.
[15] 'Comparative merits of candidates recruited to ICS in London and Allahabad exams'. Appointments Box 153, File 660/1926, Uttar Pradesh State Archives, Lucknow.

police. There was a recognition that a range of subordinate officers, particularly in revenue departments, would seek to establish political power bases and, in some cases, enhance income through official rank.[16] As with other communities of mutual support, here was another form of solidarity, which very much linked to status aspirations and social expectations. This was not least because such employment was linked to family histories going back, in some cases, a few generations. In both the interwar and late twentieth-century periods, permanent and strategic symbols of status and wealth could be literally constructed to create a more concrete sense of shared community. Shrine and temple building was promoted by wealthy industrialists, largely drawn from the same mercantile communities traditionally associated with the urban middle classes of both north and south India.[17]

Crucially, the demographic characteristics of the Indian bureaucracy often overlapped with well-to-do support for political protest, suggesting that their 'class' or community solidarities often made sense largely in the context of state power or protest against it. These were professionals that could maintain links between different levels of the Indian polity, but at other moments, they could use the very same class and professional identities to forward a defensive and anti-colonial 'cultural' politics, often through institutions of civil society. Evidence for this is provided by the careful scrutiny of candidates for all levels of government service (but particularly the ICS) in terms of candidates' political activities.[18] There were huge variations across British India, particularly once we look into the specific nature of institution building, issues of social reform and dynamics of political competition. However, some common patterns are also apparent. In late colonial Punjab, one historian describes how powerful urban middle classes, particularly Vaishyas who supported Hindu reformism/revivalism as a reaction to British influence, were partly driven by the same kind of status aspirations as those aiming for government and bureaucratic employment.[19] In central and western UP, Muslim

---

[16] See William Gould, '"The Dual State: The Unruly Subordinate", Caste, Community and Civil Service Recruitment in North India, 1930–1955', *Journal of Historical Sociology*, 20, 1–2, 2007, 13–43.

[17] John Stratton Hawley, 'Modern India and the Question of Middle-Class Religion', *International Journal of Hindu Studies*, 5, 3, 2001, 217–25.

[18] See, for example, 'Notes on Political Activities of Indian Candidates', L/SG/7/185 coll 3/42/ C/A, Service and General Files, Oriental and India Office Collections.

[19] Richard Fox, 'Urban Class and Communal Consciousness in Punjab: The Genesis of India's Intermediate Regime', *Modern Asian Studies*, 18, 3, 1984, 459–89.

dominance of the revenue and police administrations generated urban competition between quasi-nationalist institutions that in the inter-war years increasingly took notice of government employment.[20] In Tamilnad, the Indian National Congress was a largely conservative and elitist organisation, which in social terms related quite closely to those communities recruited into government service or those who controlled local representative institutions. Here, party politics under a limited elec-torate was therefore related to the leverage that could be exercised on local governments.[21] For example, in the 1920s, the local board system in Madras 'relied on recruiting a few powerful men who, in return for the grant of a position of considerable status and power and the opportunity to manipulate the system to personal advantage, would collaborate with the rulers and carry out many of the functions of government in their stead'.[22]

It is therefore very difficult to talk about class in India, especially in relation to religious activity and mobilisation, without considering a host of other cross-cutting identities, particularly approaches to *jati*. Here, the discipline of anthropology has provided the more detailed studies of the relationship between class and caste. In some cases, this has been the result of a move in ethnography and anthropology away from village-based studies, which has allowed social scientists and historians to think a little more in terms of broader social structures.[23] It is also linked to a shift in such studies to look at the material basis of caste, which was something touched upon but not prioritised by the older structural approaches of Louis Dumont and Srinivas in the 1960s and 1970s.[24] Clearly, there is no simple correlation between class and caste identities, with the former cutting across and complicating the latter. For some scholars, one effect of the impact of modern capitalist relations in colonial India has been the reproduction of caste in different forms with, for example, new relation-ships between different *jati* reflecting forms of exploitation.[25] Critical, here, is the way in which class and caste become the means by which

[20] Paul R. Brass, 'Muslim Separatism in United Provinces: Social Context and Political Strategy before Partition', *Economic and Political Weekly*, 5, 3/5, 1970, 173.
[21] For more detail on this, see David Arnold, *The Congress in Tamilnad: Nationalist Politics in South India, 1919–1937* (London: Curzon Press, 1977).
[22] Christopher Baker, *The Politics of South India, 1920–1947*, pp. 124–5.
[23] Chris Fuller and John Spencer, 'South Asian Anthropology in the 1980s', *South Asia Research*, 10, 1990, 85–105.
[24] Louis Dumont, *Homo Hierarchicus: An Essay on the Caste System* (London: Weidenfeld and Nicolson, 1970); M. N. Srinivas, *Caste in Modern India and Other Essays* (London: Asia Publishing House, 1962).
[25] C. Meillassoux, 'Are There Castes in India?', *Economy and Society*, 2, 1, 85–211.

Indians make or become a part of 'communities' under specific kinds of conditions.[26] Importantly, forms of solidarity were not the natural out-growth of either class or caste (or any other form of natural association), but were often strategic, related to context and justified or filled out with meaning in relation to class and caste. The nature of working-class politics in Bombay is perhaps best captured by Rajnarayan Chandavarkar:

> Between subordinate and dominant groups were complex layers of intermediaries who, in changing situations, facilitated the processes of both exploitation and resistance. Their relationship was mediated by institutions which were driven by their own logic and subject to pressures not simply reflective of the prevailing sets of production relations and attendant effects.[27]

This all leads the historian to a sense of hesitancy in ascribing concrete characteristics surrounding any kind of natural identity or presupposing that it generated certain kinds of behaviour or collective action. In this sense, Chandavarkar's ideas about class solidarity – its contingent nature – can also be related to religious or community solidarity. Moreover, class as an idea originating in Marx's reflection on early nineteenth-century European society is not at all easily transposed to contexts like India, and yet a whole range of radical movements in India have, since the early twentieth century, used the idea of class struggle to promote radical political change. In a similar fashion, the idea of an all-encompassing 'Hindu' identity certainly does not fit the reality of the various religious practices, beliefs and associations of those described by the state as 'Hindus'. Yet, under certain political conditions, the mobilisation of large groups of people under the banner of 'Hindu', 'Muslim' or 'Christian' rights still occurred. And, as the final section of this chapter will explore, sometimes ideas about religious community 'disadvantage' were framed in terms of 'class' backwardness.

As we also saw in the last chapter, communal representation developed in an increasingly urgent manner in the interwar period. Wartime and postwar conditions, for example, created the right conditions for the 'capture' of important institutions for those groups with the wherewithal to do so. For example, in Surat, western India, 'Western-educated' anti-colonial politicians managed to get control of the municipality in the 1920s. Rapidly rising prices and the inflationary pressures linked to the final year of the war, coupled with greater income tax demands, encouraged more forthright attempts to influence local affairs in the municipalities.

[26] Balmurli Natrajan, 'Caste, Class, and Community in India: An Ethnographic Approach', *Ethnology*, 44, 3, 2005, 227–41.

[27] Chandavarkar, pp. 14–15.

High-caste merchant families (known in western India as sheths) felt hard hit by this rapidly changed situation and were less able to influence the colonial authorities as their institutions (such as the Samast Vanik Mahajan) collapsed. With the rise of Gandhian politics in western India, those from different backgrounds were able to assert their status and build new kinds of solidarities, especially the urban-based professionals and petty traders of the city, and rural communities such as Kanbis (Patidars). Alongside the assertion of political power in the locality as a result of political and economic changes, leaders among these groups also established new public organisations, reform movements and journals, with the specific purpose of enhancing the social status of their 'community' through caste associations. Forms of Sanskritization relating to the inward-looking issues of *jati* were framed in the language of public reform. Since this process involved notions of spiritual purification and religious reorientiation around forms of neo-Vaishnavism, there were also implications for the religious identity of these groups. This was particularly the case, as Gandhian forms of mobilisation also employed forms of sacred metaphor, with 'dharma' or sacred duty providing one of the central motifs.[28] Such a specific focus on the sacred content of political mobilisation meant that as well as class and caste, religious community easily became a solidarity that had purchase by the 1920s. But it did so in a particularly urgent and competitive way in places like Surat, precisely because the advocates of this political symbolism were the arrivés of the city – those who had benefitted from the changed economic circumstances and the rise of a new form of anti-colonial politics. These groups were particularly anxious to take advantage of the new benefits of a limited electoral system, the loaves and fishes of patronage that went with municipal power, and the mobilisation of local resources. And the politics of religious solidarity, in this phase, became a 'common-sense' approach, even though it militated against the complex social realities of the city.[29]

A comparable process can be seen in interwar UP cities. But in this case, by the 1920s, it was apparent that the increasing prominence of urban poor in the larger industrial centres was having a new kind of impact on ideas about community solidarity. Lower-caste *sudra* labourers in particular began to champion some of the causes of Hindu mobilisation,

[28] Douglas Haynes, *Rhetoric and Ritual in Colonial India: The Shaping of a Public Culture in Surat City 1852–1928* (Berkeley: University of California Press, 1991), pp. 180–226; William Gould, *Hindu Nationalism and the Language of Politics*.
[29] Haynes, pp. 273–81.

somewhat on their own terms, but not necessarily with any kind of reference to older rural traditions and practices.[30] Higher-caste merchant communities had already made their mark via the patronage of religious institutions and caste reform, which linked piety, prosperity and political authority. By the 1920s, more independent organisations, like the Adi Hindu Backward Classes Association, were claiming warrior ancestry. Stress on virility and power in the protection of Hindu processions was then used as a lever for promoting their work interests in the bazaars. They also linked to specific caste uplift movements aimed at the promotion of higher social status.[31] A rapid proliferation of caste associations in the 1920s and 1930s also made their mark in colonial census operations in 1930–1 and 1940–1, with those of lower castes (such as the Yadav Mahasabha) often promoting kshattriya status.[32] But the religious ideologies of groups such as the Adi Hindu Mahasabha did not always set up a coherent challenge to high-caste leadership of the Hindu community, not least because of their association, often, with heterodox devotional bhakti traditions. And efforts at caste uplift, even where they were based in Sanskritisation (emulation of rituals and practices of upper castes), often served to reconstruct cultures of social inferiority or the need to emulate higher-status communities.[33]

In periods of rapid political and constitutional change, like that of 1918–40, new forms of solidarity emerged in ways that involved rich and variable discussions of pre-existing ideas about 'community'. These naturally overlapped with notions of class difference and solidarity, since both forms of loyalty were contingent upon institutional action and context. Importantly, both caste and class or professional identities could be reinforced or strategically employed, by reference to broader religious community concerns: low-caste migrants to north Indian cities championed the causes of Hindu mobilisation in the 1920s as a means of asserting local status and power; western India's trading communities championed public and religious reform as part of the complex agenda of municipal domination and professional solidarity. This is not to suggest that a sense of 'community' was entirely functional. 'Hindu' movements in particular operated at many different levels of Indian politics, from the all-Indian arena down to village organisations. And at each level, the motivations for those who associated with such organisations could of course relate to

[30] Joshi, 'Bonds of Community, Ties of Religion'.
[31] Nandini Gooptu, *The Politics of the Urban Poor in Early Twentieth Century India* (Cambridge: Cambridge University Press, 2001), pp. 185–204.
[32] Gould, *Hindu Nationalism*, p. 27.
[33] Fuller, *The Camphor Flame*, p. 256.

shared beliefs and values. But at the level of political debate, competition and mobilisation, men and women could be more than one thing at once. What really mattered was who they communicated with and who they decided to fight against at moments of rapid change and political crisis.

(II) THE SOCIAL BASES OF RELIGIOUS COMMUNITY ORGANISATIONS

As we saw in Chapter 3, publicists from all backgrounds who established religious community-based organisations built up their consideration of what made 'Hindus' or 'Muslims' a single community with reference to the political future and a future Indian state. Most resolutions of the Muslim League and Hindu Mahasabha meetings in the interwar period were concerned with maximising political representation along the lines of religious community – a form of jostling for position in the light of future political and constitutional change. In particular, populations across the subcontinent, encouraged by gradual Indianisation of the public services and by new representative institutions, were beginning to question the survival of older aristocratic and landed power bases, on the one hand, and the attempts of the colonial state to maintain the hierarchies of rural India, on the other. To some extent, this was related to the changing structure of the family and the desire to control property in the different context of the urban sphere. At another level, it could be about the desire to gain access to the resources of the state itself, particularly through employment in the civil services. In some parts of India, this struggle drew in those defining Sikh and united Christian interests too. The culture of the subordinate and provincial civil services, as well as systems of city governance like the municipalities, made it easy for those competing for jobs to think in terms of how the resources of the state could be used (through their employment) to the benefit of their own particular community or locality.[34]

Since broad-based community organisations were often concerned with control of state agencies and government recruitment, on the surface at least, it appeared that they largely catered for the interests of elites. For example, the apparent elitist nature of the Muslim League (which represented itself as the premier Muslim organisation for Muslims across India)

---

[34] Francis Robinson, 'Municipal Government'. See also William Gould, '"The Dual State: The Unruly Subordinate"'.

was used by some non-Muslim organisations to suggest that low-status Muslims did not subscribe to the broad religious community identities set out by the League.[35] In fact, there was a range of other local organisations, in which poorer Muslims did take part, probably even more explicitly concerned with assertion of religious identity but which sometimes created further divisions between Muslims as a whole. These included the *tanzim* and *tabligh* movements of the 1920s in UP, especially those of the Shi'a community, which through the 1910s, 1920s and 1930s increasingly distanced Shi'a politics from Sunni.[36] The Khaksars and the volunteer movements that became active from the late 1930s, and particularly in response to the context of world war, also involved a broad social cross-section of Muslims, but were only unevenly supported by organisations like the League.[37] Likewise, Christian organisations shared this sense of minority status and the need to represent their interests in a coherent way to the colonial state. Because of the predominance of the community in the south (in the early 1930s, India's 6.2 million Christians were most numerous in Madras Province, Travancore Orissa, Bihar and Assam), separate representation was only granted in Madras. The politics of Indian Christian representation and communal lobbying was also compli-cated by the fact that so many converts had come from the 'Depressed Classes', that is, low-caste and Dalit communities, and so any measure of separate recognition for the community tended to antagonise Hindu reformist organisations. In the 1931 census, for example, pressure was brought to bear on low-caste converts to return themselves as Hindus.[38]

By the 1920s and 1930s, a range of different community spokesmen attempted to represent their interests in relation to recruitment across subordinate and all-India services. For example, in 1935, the Hindu Sabha in Delhi petitioned the government about the need to maximise Hindu recruitment in the railway services, with a particular reference to the Punjab. The Sabha suggested that Hindus have always had a greater influence in the services than Muslims.[39] Similar petitions and demands

---

[35] This was in fact one of the main rationales for the Congress's decision to launch a 'Muslim Mass Contacts' campaign in the late 1930s as a means of winning over popular Muslim support in opposition to the Muslim League. See Gould, *Hindu Nationalism*, pp. 223–32.

[36] See Justin Jones, pp. 180–5.

[37] Gould, *Hindu Nationalism*, ch. 7.

[38] See J. H. Beaglehole, 'Indian Christians – A Study of a Minority', *Modern Asian Studies*, 1, 1, 1967, 59–80.

[39] J. B. Sharma to S of S of India – resolution of meeting of Hindu Sabha, 30 June 1935, 'Communal Representation in the Services, including railways and increased representa-tion of Muslims in the Public Services', L/SG/7/30, NAI.

came, by the mid-1930s, from 'depressed classes' organisations.[40] The issue here was not just one of middle-class career aspirations, but also a sense in which local administrative posts could become platforms for the mobilisation of the interests of local factions and communities. Yet at the same time, it was a peculiarly middle-class and status-driven preoccupation to target government employment, as was suggested in the first section of the chapter and as will be discussed in the pages that follow.

Jawaharlal Nehru, who had by the early 1930s risen to a position of authority within the Congress, attempted to position the party in a way that was completely at odds with what he described as 'communal' organisations. His view of organisations like the Hindu Mahasabha and Muslim League was based on the principle that they were politically reactionary as a result of their limited social bases. By the 1940s, he was to claim that the League largely only stood for the interests of larger landholders. Similarly, the Mahasabha for him represented none but the interests of powerful Hindu business lobbies and conservative landed communities. Nehru's view of the limited social appeal of these organisations is difficult to contest. Certainly, both organisations were dominated by those of high status, and Nehru was probably also correct in his assumption that such powerful figures feared the emergence of new social and political challenges in those periods. For example, in the interwar period, civic organisations emerged that petitioned the relatively young municipal boards in north Indian cities to remedy the problems of insanitary conditions and what they saw as the associated problems of urban poor pavement squatters and hawkers. In some cases, these concerns about environment and urban overcrowding linked to the 'national' agendas of religio-political movements, which sought to reform the 'backward habits' of lower castes.[41] This is not to argue that supporters of communal organisations were exclusively middle class. Certainly, the power of the discourse of Hindu or Muslim mobilisation meant that lower castes could (and did) also play the status card by making reference to their position as 'defenders of Hinduism'.[42] But for many involved in such movements, community

[margin handwritten note: *Nehru's views of communal groups*]

---

[40] 'Representation of Scheduled Castes in Public Services', Appointment (B) Box 28, file 159/1952, UPSA.

[41] For a survey of this process in Ahmedabad, see, for example, K. L. Gillion, *Ahmedabad: A Study in Indian Urban History* (Berkeley: University of California Press, 1968). For UP, see Nandini Gooptu, 'The "Problem" of the Urban Poor Policy and Discourse of Local Administration: A Study in Uttar Pradesh in the Interwar Period', *Economic and Political Weekly*, 31, 50, 1996, 3245–54.

[42] *Ibid.*

mobilisation related to a range of fears about the state and its control and about social and cultural change.

In the interwar years, as was explored in the last chapter, calls to mobilise on the basis of 'Hindu' or 'Muslim' identity were related to complex concerns within well-educated urban populations about the maintenance of public morality and the power of the middle-class urban high-caste male. Indeed, cultural signifiers for both *ashraf* Muslim communities and high-caste Hindu men depended upon assertions of patriarchy, control of women's entry into the public, and through these mechanisms, the preservation of a 'sacred geography' of the household.[43] The definition of the private and religious spaces in these patriarchal ideologies was also a means of positioning men in public spheres, particularly in relation to political organisation and governance. But this meant that the resources of family status had a bearing in public matters too.

These status aspirations were related to economic changes in the urban context in the 1920s and 1930s and the rapidly changing conditions of public employment. When we look at attempts to gain employment in the civil services and professions and the behaviour of civil servants, for example, attempts to bolster the status resources of families is clearly evident. This happened through the linking of political interest groups to community organisations, through employment or more directly in the mobilisation of resources for status raising (by marriage, property acquisition or investment). For example, those attempting to apply for the Provincial Civil Service went to the extent of proclaiming their background status, its importance and how government service had traditionally assisted them in maintaining their significance to the British Raj. This continued well into the 1940s. One memorial on behalf of an officiating SDO, Maharaj Singh, to the UP government argued that he belonged to 'a most respectable and loyal Jat zamindar family of Muzaffarnagar district. The family has an excellent record of military and social services rendered to Government. They helped the Government during the last Great War and have rendered substantial help during this War ... they are paying Rs30 a month towards the war fund to the end'.[44] This middle-class preoccupation with the use of government office also informed a powerful Muslim lobby to the Government of India, which suggested that the

[43] For a discussion of this process among north Indian Muslims, see Ayesha Jalal, *Self and Sovereignty: Individual and Community in South Asian Islam Since 1850* (London: Routledge, 2000), pp. 69–73.

[44] CB Rao, DM, Ballia to Christie, 15 Nov 1944, 'Recruitment to the UPC (Executive) Service in 1945, Appointments, box 254, file 8/1944, UPSA.

reasons for the preponderance of Anglo-Indians and Europeans in the Railway Services and the paucity of Muslims there was that those already working in 'Establishments' became aware of vacancies quickly, preventing their advertisement, so that they would instead go to members of their own communities. On leave, promotion, transfer and so on, Establishments clerks could

> ... exercise a certain measure of influence ... the possibilities are greater with less experienced officers. Even experienced officers have on occasions (ie. During the rush of work) to depend on Establishments clerks to a certain extent in such matters ... and it will be admitted that a competent clerk conversant with the rules of procedure can present a case so as to increase or reduce the chances of a particular decision by giving undue prominence to a certain point of view.[45]

In an era of political uncertainty and rapid change in the interwar period, these status aspirations and concerns were enhanced. And added to them was an important anticipation that one of the great threats to middle-class and high-caste power was the resurgence of internal social challenges from two specific angles (which in the discourse of Hindu nationalist organisations were often conflated). The first of these was the appearance of more upwardly mobile low-caste working-class communities, migrating more readily between countryside and town. Urban readers were getting access, of course, to more information via newspapers about their movement. As we saw at the start of this chapter, in order to protect their interests in the town or city, factory workers and skilled or semi-skilled artisans naturally leaned upon pre-existing caste and community networks. At the same time, professionals and government employees appeared to show much more interest in issues of public health and urban order. We see the emergence of 'self-help' organisations, civic bodies to discuss the problems of city dirt and support for the quasi-reformist agendas of organisations like the Arya Samaj.[46] A key ideological agenda that offered a solution to the perceived social chaos that middle-class fear generated in the face of these social changes was of course that offered by the Hindu right: an authoritarian, centrist and broadly community-based set of institutions, explored in the last chapter, which challenged pluralist ideas about the Hindu community.

Second, this urban Hindu sense of social challenge was also a reaction to Muslim communities, particularly in north India and especially at

[45] *Report on the Representation of Muslims and other minority communities in the Subordinate Railway Services. Vol. 1 Report* (New Delhi, 1932), p. 417.
[46] See, for example, *Citizen Weekly* (Kanpur), a civic newspaper that detailed the preoccupations of middle-class dwellers of the big north Indian city.

important moments surrounding public controversies and riots. Charu
Gupta has discussed the moral fears of Hindu middle classes in relation
to the supposed advances of the Muslim male. This set of fears related, on
the one hand, to the questions surrounding Indian (and particularly
Hindu) notions of masculinity derived from colonial ethnographic
accounts. On the other hand, it related to ideas of the sexualised identity
of the Indian Muslim. In the 1920s, it is clear that there were attempts in
the journal literature and in public speeches and institutions (in Uttar
Pradesh and other parts of the Hindi-speaking north at least) to represent
the specifically masculine traits of Hindu men. Common in these representations were the depictions of Hindu men as protectors of women, specifically from the idea of Muslim abduction. Central to this process was the
depiction in popular literature of the Khilafat movement and the Moplah
rebellion in Malabar as examples of Muslim extremism and danger, with a
plethora of very specific publications brought out to bring this home to
readers.[47] A range of Hindu organisations, including caste movements like
Kshattriya Upakarini Mahasabha (a movement designed to unite Rajput
clans) and the Gujar Conference, supported the aggressive *Shuddhi* movements of the Arya Samaj, which aimed to reconvert Malkana Rajput
Muslims in the area of Agra, Mathura and Aligarh back to Hinduism.
The movement was also extended into other arenas. A key aspect of this
kind of Arya Samaj activity in north India was the representation of
masculine heroic prowess in a way that drew upon Rajput and Maratha
legends.[48] Muslim efforts at defence against the threats of Samaj conversions also invoked assertions of male power: in Punjab, local *maulvis* told
their congregationists not to let their women go to the bazaars for fear of
molestation.[49]

These stresses on Hindu and Muslim masculinity had effects that went
beyond the several thousand or so reconversions that actually took place in
western UP. They were extremely important for the decisions of organisations like the Hindu Mahasabha and Muslim League to sponsor or encourage volunteer corps and militant organisations. They also, as will be seen in
the next chapter, encouraged other institutions to link public political
protest to largely masculine shows of strength and authority. Very common in the conflicts across north India during the mid-1920s, which were
described as 'Hindu–Muslim', was the public display of male strength by

[47] Gupta, pp. 224–7.
[48] *Ibid.*, pp. 229–39.
[49] Jalal, *Self and Sovereignty*, p. 251.

different urban groups. This was particularly evident in the controversies about taking out processions with music in front of mosques. For example, in August 1926, a 'Dadhkando' procession resulted in rioting in Allahabad, and the following year, although the procession was restricted in its route, Hindu akharas joined the Dadhkando Committee in setting up a hartal in the city.[50] In a conflict in Saharanpur in August 1923, Muslim akharas developed around Muharram in competition with Hindu akharas, and rivalry between the Muslim groups led to a competition to build the longest 'jhanda' or bamboo pole for the procession, which would have to pass beneath sacred peepul trees.[51] But perhaps most critical of all was the way in which such conflicts were re-publicised in newspapers and tracts or mentioned in speeches by leading politicians, thereby creating a kind of temporary folk lore of rumour and speculation about broad (and sometimes exaggerated) communal differences. In Allahabad again in September 1926, the Ramlila processions became a moment for press speculation and government concern, as local government attempts were made to create a compromise between Hindu and Muslim leaders about music before mosques. In these deliberations, discussions about the 'essential' aspects of religious observance were central, as was the fear of spreading publicity about rioting and violence: for some Hindu leaders in the city, the issue of music before mosques was quickly becoming 'all Indian', and the government sought replies from all other districts about the 'practice' of music before mosques in each region.[52]

In literary and political representations of Hindu masculinity, advertent double standards were applied to the issue of female abduction. Hindu men managing to win the heart of Muslim women were depicted in novels and legends as heroic and selfless. The reverse was represented as abduction and a form of violence. This fitted well with depictions of Muslim debauchery and immorality in how Islamic rulers were represented by the Hindi press;[53] in popular Arya Samaj depictions of Muslim decadence and licentiousness, such as the famous *Rangila Rasul* (Merry Prophet); and in specific attacks on Muslim government servants (such as the case of Raza Ali, accused of abduction in 1924) as a means of making a challenge for

[50] See *The Leader* (Allahabad), 28 and 29 August 1927.
[51] G. B. Lambert 'Movements of missionary or proselytizing character', 'Communal Disorders', L/PJ/6/1890, OIOC.
[52] 'Ramlila, Allahabad', General Administration Department (GAD), file 613/1926 UPSA.
[53] For example, see the journal *Stri Darpan* in the period of 1923–4, which frequently carries stories of the excess of Muslim rulers.

local power.[54] Colonial monitoring of the press noted that '...another common thread runs through the great majority of the vernacular papers, namely communal prejudice, and all too frequently incitement to inter-communal antagonism' and went on to comment how this often related to the publication of inflammatory pamphlets.[55] The delineation of women's private roles and public image by men via these communalised pamphlet and newspaper debates related to what Partha Chatterjee has described as the 'new' patriarchy of Indian nationalism. On the one hand, women's place in the home was contrasted to both Western practice and indigenous tradition in creating a new bourgeois moral order.[56] However, the women of the 'other' community could be imagined via other more sexualised fantasies of male domination, which cut across themes of middle-class respectability.

The question still remains as to how, beyond the mechanisms of the media and rapidly developing institutions of civil society, such representations of Muslims had a particular purchase for so many, particularly in urban areas, and what it was about this period, in social and political terms, that permitted such forms of publicity to be so popular. Part of the answer exists indirectly in the literature. Alongside negative depictions in Hindi pamphlets and literature of Muslim men were campaigns to segregate communities and to boycott goods. For example, in the 1920s, the Arya Samaj and Hindu Mahasabha continually promoted the need to encourage Hindu traders, businesses and job opportunities. In 1930–1, this could manifest itself in large-scale contests between traders in particular goods, for example in Allahabad over the sale of cloth.[57] There are many possible explanations for these developments, which go beyond the issue of how violence was reproduced for political reasons. Some of the most convincing relate to the changing political economy of the urban dweller, the changing social circumstances of those living in small- to medium-sized towns and how that impacted upon rural hinterlands. Within this, changing ideas about the family were crucial, especially the ways in which India's professional and mercantile communities attempted to represent status in relation to the respective roles of men and women. This was a situation in which individuals and institutions sought order and uniformity, in a context in which the private beliefs of so many were

[54] Gupta, pp. 243–59.
[55] Irwin to Lambert 23 March 1929, 'Note about the Indian press', Hailey Papers, MSS.EUR. E220/15A.
[56] Partha Chatterjee, 'The Nationalist Resolution of the Women's Question'.
[57] Gould, *Hindu Nationalism*, pp. 101–11.

rapidly becoming public knowledge; hence, the drives of Hindu reform and revivalist organisations to regulate and prescribe the correct forms of worship and lifestyle choices. For example, attacks were made on *Pir* worship by Hindu nationalists as debased. It was also a time of renewed opportunity and competition in which the power of older urban and rural elites was being eroded by new political circumstances.

Looking at more general popular support for Hindu and Muslim mobilisation is more difficult still. Official reporting on the roles of workers and peasants in moments of communal conflict was a means of defining class hierarchies, setting out the differences between the educated and uneducated or those of high status and low. This often makes the use of riots reports and the like problematic as sources. Clearly, popular and/or religious consciousness had a part to play in the formation of what onlookers described as 'communalism'. But the religiosity of individuals or groups does not sufficiently explain 'communal' or religious violence or that the 'natural' political tendency of the main cannon fodder of such conflicts (i.e. workers and peasants or the unemployed) was religious mobilisation. This, too, was a middle-class and colonial fiction, and very much formed a part of the justification for communal mobilisation itself by political leaders. In this sense, the documenting of communal conflict – the discussions and commentaries that surrounded it – was also a politically motivated means of delineating the politics of the urban and rural poor.

As we have already seen in Chapters 1 and 2, from the early 1980s, there was a powerful move to record anew the 'popular consciousness' of disempowered Indians in terms of their local or regional religious cultures. In some cases, this work has reinforced elite representations of theological and religious controversy.[58] Or it has led to the conclusion that the essential political 'voice' of 'lower classes' was community mobilisation, thereby reiterating late colonial arguments about the primordial nature of Indian political consciousness and class identity. However, some of the most successful research on popular politics and the mobilisation of the poor has suggested that religious mobilisation was one of many different kinds of strategies used by Indians in rural and urban contexts – sometimes being, for example, a social survival strategy. Importantly, there was no clear popular 'consciousness' that could be easily defined here, but a disaggregated formation of extremely variable local stances, which often

---

[58] Rafiuddin Ahmed, *The Bengal Muslims, 1871–1906: A Quest for Identity* (Delhi: Oxford University Press, 1981).

related to the workplace, and different layers of political control or suppression.

In particular, it is in the history of labour, the politics of labour organisation and the struggles of ordinary Indians with the local state that we begin to get a more nuanced view of how religious community intersected with political mobilisation for most poor Indians, both men and women. Obviously, it is impossible in the framework of this book to do full justice to this subject. But when looking briefly and comparatively at the cities and districts of UP, Bombay and Bengal, some crucial themes and differences become apparent. In Bengal, the politics of working-class protest and unionisation was subsumed under a leftist leadership in the interwar period, which moulded its authority around older markers of social/religious status and the division between 'coolie' and 'babu'.[59] In Bengal and UP, religious community affinity could also form the basis for social boycott of officials at moments of anti-colonial protest, such as those of 1921–2 in Midnapur district. Or it could be a means of identifying 'miracle' workers who subverted normal patterns of social power (e.g. the reception of Gandhi as a saintly 'mahatma' among the rural poor of Gorakhpur district).[60] In Bombay too, the politics of workers' protest often revolved around caste and religious community as a means of challenging the everyday impositions of the local state.[61] In contrast, in the cities of UP such as Kanpur, low-caste mill workers asserted their ritual status as a means of championing their claims to leadership of the Hindu community in instances of urban conflict and competition.[62] Religious community, then, in different ways, was a practical means to exercise collective defence or pressure against quotidian forms of suppression and repression.

In other ways, religious community could form a means of psychologically lifting the community's moral power above adversaries through the magical power of particular religious rituals. In the early 1920s, for example, Santal rebels engaged the colonial state on the basis of a belief in a 'golden age' in which forest land was free. Important in these moments of community action are ideas and rumours of outsider influence or political change, which are felt to alter materially the well-being of the

[59] Dipesh Chakrabarty, 'Trade Unions in a Hierarchical Culture: The Jute Workers of Calcutta 1920–1960', in Ranajit Guha, ed., *Subaltern Studies III: Writings on South Asian History and Society* (Delhi: Oxford University Press, 1984), pp. 151–2.

[60] See Shahid Amin, 'Gandhi as Mahatma: Gorakhpur District, Eastern UP, 1921', in Ranajit Guha, ed., *Subaltern Studies III: Writings on South Asian Society and History* (Delhi: Oxford University Press, 1984), pp. 1–61.

[61] Raj Chandavarkar, *Origins of Industrial Capitalism*.

[62] Nandini Gooptu, *The Politics of the Urban Poor*.

community as a whole. Religious practice, then, becomes a means for removing the ills of a community, sometimes allowing key leaders to be endowed with miracle powers, which subvert existing hierarchies of social power. In 1922, for example, Santal rebels in Jalpaiguri believed they were immune to police bullets, as they were wearing 'Gandhi Maharaj caps'.[63] In UP, similarly, local 'saintly' leaders, akin to Gandhi, were imbued in popular movements with ritualistic power – for example, the figure of Baba Ramchandra who toured UP in the 1920s and 1930s, performing the *Ramayana* and interspersing its recitation with political appeals. Another figure, Ragho Das, fulfilled a similar role in the eastern districts of the province in the 1930s.[64] These movements may or may not have connected to 'Hindu–Muslim' conflict, but they were mostly concerned with the positioning of disadvantaged communities in relation to local political power holders. Christianity played this role too for important low-status communities. For example, in the region of Jharkhand, people's movements pushing for tribal rights have been encouraged by the (proportionally) small Adivasi Christian community of the region since the early 1930s.[65]

Importantly, however, these varied practices of popular resistance were easily drawn into larger narratives of communal mobilisation in the 1920s and 1930s. And as political observers everywhere lost sight of everyday complexities, notions of a broad Hindu–Muslim political division were reinforced in this period. As Kancha Ilaih has argued, important sections of India's populations – the 'Dalitbahujan' – have been described officially and by political elites as 'Hindus', even though their rites and religious practices, as well as their everyday lives, are markedly different to those of most high-caste Hindus.[66] As we will see in the following section, these myths about the unity of different religious communities were part of other, cultural projects, which were not simply concerned with the direct business of politics and political representation. The idea of community also entered movements that set out to standardise and publicise the nature of 'Hindu' and 'Muslim' literature and music.

[63] Sumit Sarkar, 'The Conditions and Nature of Subaltern Militancy', pp. 298, 305–11.
[64] Gould, *Hindu Nationalism*, pp. 51–3.
[65] See Sushil J. Aaron, 'Contrarian Lives: Christians and Contemporary Protest in Jharkhand', *Asia Research Centre Working Paper No. 18* (London: London School of Economics, 2007).
[66] Kancha Ilaih, 'Productive Labour, Consciousness and History: The Dalitbahujan Alternative', in Shahid Amin and Dipesh Chakrabarty, eds., *Subaltern Studies IX: Writings on South Asian History and Society* (Delhi: Oxford University Press, 1996), pp. 165–200.

(III) COMMUNITY AND THE PUBLIC SPHERES
OF LANGUAGE, LITERATURE AND MUSIC

As well as being a product of specifically political developments, mobilisations around religious community in India were also often movements of
cultural production: the creation of a sense of Hindu or Muslim solidarity
overlapped with efforts in the interwar period to delineate 'national' arts,
particularly in literature and music. The framing of culture in relation to
religious community involved active, modern projects of standardisation
and artistic consolidation. And in this, it came up against a range of
challengers – artists who rejected the idea that cultural output should be
confined by association with communities or nations. This struggle over
culture and the arts served to sharpen the attempts of Hindu nationalists,
for example, to appropriate or lead what they saw as 'national' culture.
This section of the chapter will explore how the social support for Hindu
nationalism can be traced through literature and music, and tied to the
growing aspirations of urban middle-class communities, especially in
north India.

During the 1920s, debates about language, particularly around the
promotion of a 'national' language, intensified, as the language medium
for governance and justice became more important in the context of
dyarchy. The focal point of debate in the north in this respect was the
position of Hindi. As discussed in Chapter 2, there had already been a
series of debates around language from the late nineteenth century, particularly in relation to educational institutions and the journalistic activities
of the likes of Harischandra Bharatendu. The difference by the 1920s was
that these debates now more clearly involved national rather than provincial organisations and movements, being, for example, publicised by
Gandhi and organisations like the Hindi Sahitya Sammelan. Over this
period too, efforts were made in Hindi-speaking provinces and districts
to establish Hindi as the official language of local boards, educational
institutions and assemblies. Like the late nineteenth century, but in a
more expansive way, the 1920s saw the establishment of new publishing
projects, some of them focussed upon literature or upon domestic and
'women's' issues, such as *Chamd* (1922), *Madhuri* (1922) and *Sudha*
(1927). Publications changed in scope in this period too, with the appearance of political weeklies and dailies, some of which concentrated on
factional conflicts and sometimes came about in reaction to local conflicts
such as 'Hindu–Muslim' riots. These were low-price newspapers whose
editors sought to appeal to a broader popular audience than the literary

and highbrow journals. Papers such as *Aj* (1920), *Vartaman* (1920) and *Pratap* (1920) were all founded in UP and were edited by some of the leading provincial Congress figures. Crucially, these journalistic developments, as Francesca Orsini has argued, related to a newly developed awareness about the difference between Hindi- and English-speaking readerships.[67]

By the 1920s, language debates in other regions appeared to become more sharply competitive. This occurred, for example, in south India over the relative merits of Tamil and Hindi or English (Madras/Tamilnadu), and in the North East of India in a highly complex manner through competition between a wide array of regional languages. In the case of Tamil, this was a contest between a regional notion of Tamil as mother tongue with nationalist aspirations and the centralising tendencies of English or Hindi. In the late nineteenth- and early twentieth-century promotion of Tamil, importantly, the celebration of language involved for some a process of deification and devotion. For others, such as E. V. Ramasami Naicker, Justice Party leader in the late 1930s, it was about the promotion of a socially repressed Dravidian culture.[68] In contrast, in the North East, the main language conflict was between Bengali and Assamiya, a problem heightened by colonial policy in suppressing the latter during the second half of the nineteenth century. However, in this region too, 209 'scheduled' tribes and a range of other ethnic groups each promoted their own languages and, in some cases, forms of regionalism.[69]

The most elucidated debate in the literature was the struggle between advocates of Hindi and Urdu. This was not a straightforward issue of a polarisation of two camps around competing languages. There was a great deal of discussion, through language-promoting organisations like the Hindi Sahitya Sammelan (founded in 1910 out of the Nagri Pracharini Sabha), about the possibilities of promoting different registers of Hindi or 'Hindustani'. Its members discussed questions of language structure and content: should Hindi be dominated by Sanskrit words or should its connections to Urdu be encouraged? Should the Devanagri script be used or should Hindi users adopt the Roman alphabet? This took place among a new institutional commitment to anti-colonialism, with the Sammelan being composed in large part of Congress sympathisers. There was no

[67] Francesca Orsini, pp. 36–7; 63–6.
[68] Sumathi Ramaswamy, *Passions of the Tongue: Language Devotion in Tamil India, 1891–1970* (Berkeley: University of California Press, 1997).
[69] John Samuel, 'Language and Nationality in North-East India', *Economic and Political Weekly* 28, 3/4, 1993, pp. 91–2.

natural division between religious communities in the use of Hindi and Urdu any more than there was always a clear delineation between the languages themselves. In fact, the form of language was itself being worked out through processes of standardisation and accommodation to local and regional trends through our period. Among the old Urdu-speaking 'elites' of north India, for example, there were very many Hindu members of the literati, and vast populations of Muslims were literate in Hindi. Nevertheless, the issue of Hindi as a national language began to take on 'communal' implications by the late 1920s.

The very process of standardisation in a range of cultural spheres, including literature and language, went hand in hand with discussions about signifiers of nationality. And the delineation of what constituted Indian national culture related to competing symbols of community power. Mahavir Prasad Dvivedi was one of the first successful editors of Hindi journals that attempted to promote a sense of Hindi standardisa-tion, for example through projects like *Sarasvati* (1903–20). For Dvivedi, the Hindi journal was promoted as an educational medium through which carefully selected cultural products might be publicised and developed. At the same time, there was an attempt to enrich the different forms of literary output through the medium of languages like Hindi, appealing to the tastes of interwar middle-class readers.[70] Such projects were also linked to the promotion of new kinds of commercial enterprise – something that partic-ularly appealed to urban, high-caste, middle-class Hindu communities.

As literary consumerism developed in the interwar period and a range of newspapers appeared to fuel it, specific issues of community competition drove debates in print. The papers *Arti* and *Anand* only came into publication in 1924 after a Hindu–Muslim riot in Lucknow in 1924 surrounding the 'Arti' ceremony in Aminabad park. The Hindi and Urdu newspapers of UP in the early 1930s also lined up around 'communal' controversies through the interwar period: for example, around Bakr 'Id riots in Ayodhya in early April 1934, Urdu papers like *Hamdam, Sadaqat and Sarfaraz* criticised Hindu actions and urged Muslims to organise for defence. The Hindi *Anand* and *Surya*, by contrast, defended Hindus in the dispute.[71] Since the promotion of Hindi journals was also part of the project of competing with what were seen as the influences of English elitism, this cultural competition was given a distinctive anti-colonial

---

[70] Orsini, pp. 54–7.
[71] *Report on the Newspapers in the United Provinces for the week ending 14 April 1934*, L/R/5/101 OIOC.

edge, in which the promotion of Hindi had implications for forms of social conflict. For example, these periodicals, journals and papers were keen to chart the 'progress' of their respective languages in terms of its use in the courts, administration and education. Since many of the Hindi publications were aimed against what were seen as the detrimental cultural influences of English, it was easy to transform anti-English fervour into a critique, too, of the languages that the British had promoted in the past. Clearly, for the Hindi press and figures like Mahavir Prasad Dvivedi, Urdu was one such language.

Hindi was also juxtaposed to Urdu and English in terms of the latter two languages' 'foreignness'. As we saw in Chapter 2, the promotion of Hindi could run alongside the idea of the history of the 'Hindu nation', especially for organisations like the Nagri Pracharini Sabha. Complex debates in the interwar period surrounded the origins and development of Hindi and Urdu in terms of deeper literary and linguistic influences. In these debates, questions were raised about the 'national' legitimacy of past regimes, particularly Muslim courts and kingdoms. For example, the journal *Chamd* celebrated the ways in which Muslim poets from Akbar's time used Hindi as a court language and contrasted this history to the attitude of contemporary Muslim communities.[72] Throughout the 1930s, the Arya Samaj in north India published pamphlets criticising the erroneous nature of Islamic belief and the tyranny of Muslim Empires and promoting Hindi.[73] A flourishing Hindi pamphlet literature, much of it 'proscribed' by the state, juxtaposed anti-colonial struggles with notions of religious sacrifice.[74] In these debates, there were of course proponents of a hybrid language, which combined Hindi and Urdu – supporters of what came to be known as Hindustani. The government-sponsored Hindustani Academy was the centre for these views, which included those of Gandhi and Premchand. Hindi would 'become' a truly national language once it had assimilated and combined with other linguistic influences like Urdu. In contrast, the more hardline promoters of Hindi in UP, such as Malaviya, Tandon and Sampurnanand, suggested that the Indian polity had once known, in the past, a national language that had to be recovered. Hindi was therefore, for these thinkers,

---

[72] *Chamd*, Pt. 1, 2, December 1931, p. 275.
[73] See, for example, Mahashay Nandlal Arya, *Devotional Songs of a National Complexion, Kranti Bhajnavali* (Ghazipur: Arya Bhajnopadeshak, 1937), PIB 77/2 OIOC.
[74] See, for example, pamphlets in the 'Proscribed Publications' sections of the India Office collections, such as Jagnath Prasad Arora, *Beriyom ki Jhankar* (Banaras: Sangrakantra Va Prakashak, 1930), PP.Hin.B.298 OIOC.

deeply rooted in a national historical narrative, which largely defined both Indianness and what it was to be a 'Hindu'.[75]

It was also the most explicit exponents of a broad 'Hindu' identity in the 1920s who were among the most forceful exponents of Hindi as a national language. For example, the Arya Samaj made the promotion of Hindi one of its 'rules'. The early Hindu Sabhas, discussed in Chapter 2, was quick to take it into its programme, as was the rejuvenated Hindu Mahasabha in 1923. Equally forceful in their objections were a range of Muslim organisations who sensed the potential communal implications of the promotion of Hindi at a national level. Importantly too, these protests often happened in the context of an appeal to the colonial state at critical moments of political and constitution reform, such as the UP Muslim response to the Indian Statutory Commission in 1928.[76] The issue of script was largely at the root of these squabbles, with Urdu written in the Persian script and Hindi in Devanagri. In the mid to late 1920s and throughout the 1930s, the Muslim League had objected to the use of Hindi in the latter script on the grounds that many less well-educated co-religionists would not be able to use it. In the Punjab, this opposition to Hindi and the promotion of Urdu had been used to oppose the influence of Gandhi on the Khilafat movement: Maulvi Abdul Hakim's pamphlets, for example, claimed that Gandhi was hurting Muslim interests most specifically by undermining Urdu.[77] These kinds of reactions to the proponents of Hindi continued into the 1930s. The Wardha scheme of education, promoted by the Congress in the late 1930s, elicited criticisms of the anti-Urdu bias of Sampurnanand, the Education Minister in UP, by the Muslim League.[78]

It was not just organisations representing religious interest groups that objected to the more aggressive promotion of Hindi. South Indian organisations also began to campaign against its position as a potential national language in the interwar period too, in particular the Self-Respect movement in Tamil Nadu. The issue of language was therefore not merely a pragmatic consideration of which language should be adopted for administration. Concerns about the educational and professional advancement of one's community were part and parcel of a larger debate about how

[75] For more discussion on this, see Orsini, pp. 134–5.
[76] *Representation of the Muslims of the United Provinces (India) to the Indian Statutory Commission*, July 1928 (Allahabad), pp. 30–1.
[77] Jalal, *Self and Sovereignty*, p. 230.
[78] 'Report of the Committee appointed by the Council of the All-India Muslim League to examine the Wardha Scheme', in K. K. Aziz, ed., *Muslims under Congress Rule, 1937–1939: A Documentary Record* (Islamabad: NIHCR, 1978), pp. 175–90.

composite/homogenous or explicitly diverse the Indian nation could be. Because this was about a future Indian state, the issue of language and identity was easily related to status aspirations for communities anticipating the future infrastructures of state power and how those structures might be controlled. The very language of power was still, to some extent, ready to be defined.

But debates about language also took place in a context in which English was still a pre-eminent language of elites who built political connections across the whole of India. The tenor of the arguments about language in this period was therefore also about how far Hindi might actually be able to replace English as a link language, which would forge contact between communities rather than serve as a force for divisiveness. Not surprisingly, then, even the most vociferous champions of Hindi found themselves constructing claims for the expansive, historical breadth of the language – a language that could accommodate and assimilate. It could only do so legitimately for the likes of Tandon and Malaviya, though, by being related to something equally essential and all embracing (at least in their eyes) in India's deep past. Crucially, these kinds of arguments often actively sought to mask internal divisions or to relegate them to a later date, a little like the delineation of the 'communal problem' itself, which would (for many Congress leaders) be resolved in a future democratic constitution. The frustration of minority religious groups and the vast areas of non-Hindi-speaking south India was often as much about the assumption of agreement and uniformity on the part of the north Indian Hindi (and Hindu) proponents, as though the core identity of India had already been resolved. For Tamil speakers in the south in the early twentieth century, particularly those associated with the Dravidian movements, Tamil could represent a form of historically derived national identity, divinity, purity and 'motherness' much better than Hindi.[79] Regional language disputes also cut across these controversies, for example, the competition between proponents of Telugu and Tamil in the south.

Historical debate around language was therefore critical to the ideological formation of Indianness and the Indian nation. Here, Indian intellectuals were informed by western orientalist periodisation of Indian history: theories of origin were central to many nineteenth-century British commentaries, travelogues and ethnographies. In an attempt to place India's multiple linguistic and cultural features into their world view, British

[79] Sumathi Ramaswamy, 'En/Gendering Language: The Poetics of Tamil Identity', *Comparative Studies in Society and History*, 35, 4, 1993, 683–725.

observers on India related its populations to notions of progress and development. The chief institutions in this process were the Asiatic Society and the Archaeological Survey, but historical scholarship also went into the district gazetteers, which charted the physical and human geographies of each Indian district. Nationalist historical writing of the early twentieth century adopted these European narratives but challenged their conclusions of British modernisation. Such histories juxtaposed British with Muslim 'rule' in a way that emphasised each as 'foreign'. Important in much of this writing was the motif of the Aryan 'golden age' as a point of reference between institutions like the Arya Samaj and scholars of the Vedas, Sastras and epics. This is clearly evident in the writings of Gaurishankar Hirachand Ojha (1863–1947). An age of decadence in which this ancient civilisation succumbed to Muslim invaders neatly dovetailed with British views of Muslim despotism and misrule.[80] The division of India's history into phases of Muslim invasion and the development of a self-confident, resistant Hindu society was also reflected in the work of one of the key educational ideologies of the Congress, Sampurnanand.[81]

Such simplifications of the past ignored the complex web of alliance and counter-alliance that cut across religious community and different forms of polity through the medieval period. Crucially, the (homogenously presented) Hindu communities in these histories always retained a level of social and cultural autonomy from Muslim rulers. This did not mean that there were not attempts (notably through Gandhian initiatives and institutions like the Hindustani Academy) to ensure the production of histories that celebrated aspects of Indo-Islamic civilisation. However, the focus on conquest and defence against Muslim/British despotism certainly appeared to influence the growth of martial traditions among communities aspiring to higher-caste status. A range of caste organisations, as we will see later in this chapter, developed their own caste histories, which mirrored the mainstream 'national' accounts appearing in Hindi journals like *Chamd* and *Madhuri*. Such histories, through the Hindi journals, were also related to middle-class lifestyle concerns in north India. In *Chamd* in October 1931, the connection between the promotion of Hindi and critiques of the Muslim community was made explicit. Importantly, as suggested above, this linked very strongly to a middle-class concern about status aspirations and government employment:

---

[80] Orsini, pp. 183–6.
[81] See Gould, *Hindu Nationalism*, pp. 175–6.

Hindi language was given a great importance in the Muslim Raj and Muslim poets have given it a high place ... But now Hindi is losing its place. People are trying to remove Hindi from official work. Apart from government officials, there are quite a few Muslims who are against Hindi.[82]

Cultural change resulting from a new focus in politics on questions of religious identity and national belonging can also clearly be seen in music, particularly in western and northern India. In some cases, this involved high-caste reform of public cultural practices. The practice of Rashtriya Kirtan in the area of Maharashtra, promoted by Bal Gangadhar Tilak in the early part of the century as a form of Brahmanical devotionalism to national precepts, is important here. The performers of kirtan, a form of devotional song and speech, known as kirtankars, were able to subsume political messages into a form of audience-based devotionalism, which appealed to early exponents of the 'Hindu' nation. For example, in the early 1930s, kirtankars could be used to promote forms of anti-British swadeshi.[83] However, in other parts of India, religious songs or musical performance at the time of important ceremonies was not always entirely controlled by the patriarchal and 'national' reforming spirit of high-caste ideologues. Women in north India sang in public spaces during melas (e.g. Kajalis), and jocular wedding songs – garis, or galis – were sung by women of the bride's side and often contained illicit messages.[84] Equally, during festivals such as Holi in cities like Banaras, women often sang licentious songs in public spaces as part of the license to abuse men.[85]

Nevertheless, the nationalist drives for standardisation in all spheres of life, particularly the search for origins of a possible 'national' language, were also to be found in the field of music. This was, in the first instance, about the formalisation of music education, which found some of its early inspiration in princely states, such as Baroda, with Moulabaksh Ghissenkhan setting up a school there.[86] In the early 1920s, Vishna Narayan Bhatkhande, a musician and academic from Bombay, sought to institutionalise, centralise and systematise Indian classical music. Just as educational 'reformers' and Hindi/Urdu promoters attempted to create a standardised system of education and language to meet the needs of a future Indian nation by presenting particular readings of India's past, so

---

[82] *Chamd*, October 1931, p. 178.

[83] Anna Schultz, 'Hindu Nationalism, Music and Embodiment in Marathi Rashtriya Kirtan', *Ethnomusicology*, 46, 2, 2002, pp. 307–22.

[84] Charu Gupta, pp. 86–7.

[85] *Ibid.*, pp. 89–90.

[86] Vamanrao H. Deshpande, *Indian Musical Traditions: An Aesthetic Study of the Gharanas in Hindustani Music* (Mumbai: Popular Prakashan, 2001), p. 148.

Bhatkhande attempted to define a future project by selecting particular kinds of cultural roots. At the heart of his arguments with other composers, teachers and academics was the question of how far music should be connected to the sacred, and in this sense the debates very much connected to the 'religious' content of Indian cultural traditions. For Bhatkhande, the idea that Indian classical music could be related back to the Vedas was little more than a mythology, and that in fact music as it was practiced across the subcontinent was relatively modern with links to traditions that were more likely to be only a couple of hundred years old. Yet there were other powerful figures in the study and practice of classical music who sought to maintain the idea that music should be related to a more distant Vedic past, even if the textual evidence for such claims was non-existent. Other reformers, like Vishnu Digambar Paluskar, a musician from southern Maharashtra, attempted to rid music of what he saw as its worldly association with courtly decadence to bring it back to a pristine association with Hindu devotionalism.[87] Both Paluskar and Bhatkande were involved, too, in setting up educational institutions – the former in Maharashtra and the latter in Gwalior (the Madhav Sangeet Vidyalaya) and Lucknow (the Marris College of Music).[88]

Both of these promoters of Indian music outlined agendas that defined how Indians *ought* to enjoy or participate in music. For both, music was to have an instructive purpose in public, which fitted with overarching concepts of national culture. Important in this project were European critiques of Indian music in relation to Western as culturally 'half awakened', and in other areas, such as south India, the quest for 'modernity' was associated in particular with use of the violin – an instrument with social cachet.[89] In the attempt to define national musical traditions, both Bhatkande and Paluskar had to set out the boundaries of acceptable musical performance and content. In this, both criticised what they saw as the long-standing control of music by Muslim courtly culture and *gharanas* (musicians' guilds) and the lack of 'understanding' therein of its essential historical roots. For both, Muslim musicians and music, because of the context in which Mughal sponsorship had moulded performance, had corrupted a 'true' Indian classical tradition. For Paluskar, there was, however, a more direct attempt not only to establish a national tradition in musical

---

[87] Janaki Bakhle, *Two Men and Music: Nationalism in the Making of an Indian Classical Tradition* (Oxford: Oxford University Press, 2005), pp. 96–125.

[88] Deshpande, p. 148.

[89] See Amanda J. Weidman, *Singing the Classical, Voicing the Modern: The Postcolonial Politics of Music in South India* (Durham: Duke University Press, 2006), pp. 26–46.

performance, but also to ensure that it was closely tied to the Hindu reform agendas of western India. He established a Gandharva Mahavidyalaya for the promotion of a distinctly Hindu reformist form of musical education, which was explicitly linked to Vedic learning. Such institutions linked music to a culture of sacrality, with religious rituals and devotional singing institutionalised as part of a musical curriculum.[90]

It was not simply that musicians like Paluskar were closely linked to the religious rhetoric surrounding both Gandhian mobilisation (Paluskar was a stong advocate in the early 1920s) and Arya Samaj or Sanatan Dharm publicity, that allowed these projects to tie into broader competition between religious communities. The projects themselves, in a similar way to the language disputes, helped to define the boundaries of Indian subject-hood/citizenship in relation to an imagined Indian past – a past marked by ages of 'Muslim' dominance, or 'Hindu' subordination. In these constructions too, minority voices were subordinated to a sense of a greater 'Hindu' tradition – in the case of the Gandharva Mahavidyalaya and Paluskar's schools of music, a form of paternalistic Brahmanism. Women, although involved in his musical projects, were encouraged, as in many of the Hindi journals of the period, to be (in Gandhi's words) 'queens of the household'[91] and to uphold an ancient burden of cultural and religious purity in the domestic sphere against ideas of Western degradation.[92] There were no Muslims in Paluskar's music schools, perhaps partly because of their associations with the Arya Samaj and its aggressive *shuddhi* movements. More widely, Muslim musicians who had traditionally taken part in Hindu processions, such as those around Ramlila, were increasingly removed as a result of the music before mosques controversies.[93]

According to Janaki Bakhle, Muslim music in these national projects of music standardisation was deliberately hidden from view, even though in earlier phases there was little clear distinction in the performance of music between Hindus and Muslims.[94] Indeed, the interwar period saw an increased sacralisation of music, as with other forms of cultural production such as poetry and literature. Sound had been associated with divine

---

[90] Janaki Bakhle, pp. 137–64.
[91] Parel, *Gandhi: Hind Swaraj*.
[92] Tanika Sarkar, *Hindu Wife*, p. 41.
[93] 'Muhs. Were not employed to play music in the processions this year, for fear they should stop playing of their own accord in front of mosques', Crosthwaite to Lambert, 10 October 1926, Ramlila, Allahabad', General Administration Department (GAD), file 613/1926 UPSA.
[94] Bakhle, pp. 174–5.

energies in a range of Hindu traditions, particularly the devotional religion of *bhakti*, which allowed its inherent spirituality to be defined in 'Hindu' terms to popular audiences.[95] Temple music had therefore provided a root for musicians reforging the idea of 'national' music alongside Mughal courtly music. Piety and ritual was, via popular religious practice, brought into everyday life in new ways.

Despite these movements in standardisation and renewed sacralisation of music in the late colonial period, it is important not to lose sight of the vigorous creativity in popular folk music and in the Sufi traditions, which complicated and sometimes directly challenged national projects of standardisation. In southern Tamil Nadu, bow songs were used in rituals of worship for the dead, and have been described as ritual languages used to summon gods.[96] In the North East, the Mizo Christian converts indigenised religious music, transforming hymns with their own musical traditions, often against the standardising efforts of missionary movements.[97] Baul singers in Bengal tended to reject the orthodoxies of both religious traditions. They could be either Hindu or Muslim, and although often of low-status background, used ideas of religious renunciation to critique the whole basis of fixed community identities, as they moved between different social contexts.[98] Qawwali music was developed around sufi rituals, which promoted forms of Islamic mysticism, experiential closeness to God and religious universalism, that responded to orthodox Islam in India.[99] However, as with other forms of cultural nationalism, music and theatre involved communal exclusions, and this was also marked in the gendered politics of music and performance. Although Paluskar's schools allowed women to become performers, their roles were very much limited to those prescribed by men and related to devotion and maintaining morality. In theatre, particularly in western India, women performers were either excluded entirely or given particularly limited roles in relation to moral expectations. For many directors, this involved

[95] Selina Thielemann, *Singing the Praises Divine: Music in the Hindu Tradition* (New Delhi: A. P. H. Publishing Corporation, 2000), pp. 4–9.
[96] See Stuart H. Blackburn, *Singing of Birth and Death: Texts in Performance* (Philadelphia: University of Pennsylvania Press, 1988).
[97] Downs, pp. 98–100.
[98] This is set out in detail in relation to the 'anti-identity' of bartaman identity (meaning the ascertaining of knowledge through one's own senses rather than that of others), in Jeanne Openshaw, *Seeking Bauls of Bengal* (Cambridge: Cambridge University Press, 2004), pp. 242–52.
[99] Regula Burckhardt Qureshi, *Sufi Music of India and Pakistan: Sound, Context and Meaning in Qawwali* (Cambridge: Cambridge University Press, 1986), pp. 79–83.

the use of male actors for female roles. Some of the concerns in the 1920s and 1930s, as more educated women were beginning to enter the acting profession, revolved around the issue of whether shows should stop during women's menstruation every month, since contact with them would be ritually polluting.[100]

These trends towards standardisation in literature and music represented only one, albeit powerful, strand in the cultural world of India's middle classes. In some respects, it helped to reinforce what Tanika Sarkar has described as forms of 'Hindu nationalism', which reached back to the first phases of print development in mid to late nineteenth-century Bengal. Here, the arts were related to the depiction of relationships between the domestic and public spheres, in which reading, listening and performance were increasingly set out as functional projects in nation building and community consolidation. However, by the 1930s, other artistic movements were already challenging this trend in literary and musical revivalism. The All-India Progressive Writers' Association and the Indian People's Theatre Association boldly presented a secular and leftist alternative to the paternalistic traditionalism of Hindu/Muslim organisations and movements.[101] Their deliberately cross-communal projects completely rejected what they described as the 'communalist' agendas of the more traditionalist promoters of Hindi, and instead they furthered the cause of 'Hindustani'. What was clear by the last two decades of British power was how the battlefield between this 'secular' and its opposite 'communal' outlook on the arts was more vividly depicted. Secularism was not the only issue at stake. The delineation of 'community' in relation to politics and literature was not only confined to religious communities, but also those of caste in our period, as the next section will explore.

(IV) CASTE, RELIGION AND 'MINORITY' STATUS

In the early 1930s, the first serious proposals for special representation for low castes in the civil services and in representative institutions defined 'depressed classes'. This was most obvious in two areas: the All India Census of 1931, which will be examined more below, and the proposed Communal Award. The Communal Award of 1932 associated religious

---

[100] Neera Adarkar, 'In Search of Women in History of Marathi Theatre, 1843–1933', *Economic and Political Weekly*, 26, 43, 1991, WS87–WS90.

[101] See Talat Ahmed, *Literature and Politics in the Age of Nationalism: The Progressive Episode in South Asia, 1932–1956* (London: Routledge, 2008).

and caste solidarities anew by suggesting that separate electorates might be extended to 'depressed classes'. In the Award, the constitutional notion of 'minority' was extended to these 'depressed classes' – effectively a list of low-caste communities. And the state was encouraged to consider the possibility that these disadvantaged communities, defined on the basis of caste, could make claims for special consideration or even political representation in a comparable way to religious minorities. Muslim, Christian and low-caste claims, then, for special consideration in constitutional proposals related to a discourse of 'backwardness' defined in terms of 'class', as well as ethnicity. In September 1932, Gandhi made a vociferous protest and launched a fast against the principle of separate electorates for untouchables contained in the Communal Award. Eventually, an agreement was reached between Gandhi and the untouchable leader, B. R. Ambedkar, known as the Poona Pact. This established that untouchables would be granted reservation of seats out of the general electorates (i.e. those pertaining to caste Hindus) under a joint electorate system, but with the provision of special electoral colleges for the selection of candidates.

In political and electoral terms, the most important immediate implications of the Communal Award were in provinces like Bengal, where the proposal to distribute seats in central and provincial assemblies under the new reforms on the basis of weightage to religious minorities did not effectively benefit Hindus. Because of the reservation of twenty seats for 'depressed classes', not only were the 'caste Hindus' seriously underrepresented in terms of seats, but so too (although to a lesser extent) were Muslims. However, the latter still had separate electorates, even though in Punjab and Bengal they enjoyed bare majorities.[102] What followed was jockeying from all parties in Bengal to discuss, in a new way, the contribution of their community to the wealth or political status of the province. Therefore, whereas in some periods it paid to highlight the 'backwardness' of one's community, at critical moments like that of 1931–2, in the midst of the Communal Award negotiations, another tactic was to highlight political power and significance. This had happened in the past in the 'Representation of Muslims of the United Provinces' to the Indian Statutory Commission in 1928.[103] In Bengal, the process was led by,

---

[102] Bidyut Chakrabarty, 'The Communal Award of 1932 and Its Implications in Bengal', *Modern Asian Studies*, 23, 3, 1989, 493–523.
[103] *Representation of the Muslims of the United Provinces (India) to the Indian Statutory Commission*, July 1928, Allahabad.

among others, P. C. Mitter, a member of the Bengal government, who argued that Hindus disproportionately contributed to excise revenues, made up a large proportion of the landed interest in the province and were the largest contributors of court fees.[104]

Madras Presidency Catholics, too, had made claims throughout the 1920s for recognition in government services. But Protestant spokesmen in the All India Conference of Indian Christians, such as Augustine Ralla Ram, opposed separate electorates for Christians (even though one was granted in Madras in 1932) and attempted to advance a different kind of non-sectarian patriotism. In doing so, organisations such as the Central Conference of the Methodist Church represented Hindu and Muslim communities as stereotypically 'caste-ist' and 'fanatic' and attempted to celebrate their own anti-communalism. However, some Catholic leaders attempted to nurture a common Catholic consciousness through the Communal Award. Seven hundred thousand of India's three million Catholic population in 1921 resided in Madras Presidency. The Catholic Mangalore Conference of August 1930, while pushing for the annulment of the definition of their property and institutions as 'alien bodies' vested in the Pope, was also concerned that only Protestants would represent the 'Christian' position at the Round Table Conferences. The Mangalore delegates too, therefore, promoted separate electorates for 'Indian Christians', and in doing so, forged a tactical alliance with Protestants. However, there were key disagreements within this manufactured community. Bombay Catholics opposed separate electorates, and Dalit Adi Catholic organisations continued to critique casteism within the Church: in December 1936, Adi-Catholics demanded the right to sit with caste Catholics during prayer in St. Mary's Cathedral in Kumbakonam and, when this caused caste reaction, launched a province wide protest.[105]

The Congress Working Committee was forced into a difficult position by the Communal Award of 1932. By rejecting the Award, it threatened the position of parties (particularly Muslims) on whom it relied to protest against the reform proposals as a whole. On the other hand, it would be difficult to justify the acceptance of the award as a secular nationalist party. In the end, the Congress resolved to neither accept nor reject the Award, leading to the setting up of a breakaway group from the Congress, under the leadership of Madan Mohan Malaviya, the Congress Nationalist Party. The latter set opposition to the Communal Award as its agenda, especially from the perspective of Hindus in Bengal and Punjab.

[104] Chakrabarty, 'The Communal Award', p. 505.
[105] Mallampalli, pp. 135–48, 172–80.

These developments demonstrated how the more conservative high-caste Hindu voices were a powerful force to be reckoned with within a range of Congress organisations across India.

The Award therefore sharpened the debates about what 'minority' actually meant in electoral terms in India. It reopened discussions about whether separate electorates should be retained for Muslims, and how far special representation and reservation, which had hitherto been connected to religious community, ought to be extended to other kinds of community. One of the problems this laid bare was the extent to which untouchables should be considered as part of what contemporaries described as 'the Hindu fold'. As was seen in previous chapters, discussions about the social composition of the Hindu community had, for many years up to the 1930s, revolved around the issue of lower-caste 'uplift' and the reform of customs relating to divisions between castes. But perhaps one of the most palpable ways in which the relationship between untouchables and other Hindus came to the fore was in the support for Gandhi's fast against separate electorates for untouchables in September 1932. During this period, Gandhi's protests were backed (although in a way that was never fully intended) by organisations promoting Hindu *sangathan* – the very organisations that had, from the 1910s, attempted to maximise the demographic representation of Hindus vis-à-vis other communities. A range of Muslim organisations across India also dramatically opposed Gandhi's fasts to the extent of forms of social boycott. For example, in parts of western UP, members of the local Khilafat Committees voted to boycott Hindu shops that had promoted the social uplift of Chamars.[106]

In other respects, these developments in the 1930s transformed the ways in which caste and community-based organisations represented their interests to the state. In the case of low castes or untouchables, this was most obviously illustrated in the developing career or Bhimrao Ramji Ambedkar – the foremost proponent of separate electorates for untouchables from 1931–2. Ambedkar's family was from Ratnagiri district in Maharashtra, and his Mahar caste background created a context in which he was effectively treated as an 'untouchable', suffering segregation in schools and public spaces and general discrimination on the basis of caste taboos and ideas of ritual pollution.[107] Even before being elected to

---

[106] For a more detailed account of this process in UP, see William Gould, 'The U.P. Congress and "Hindu Unity": Untouchables and the Minority Question in the 1930s', *Modern Asian Studies*, 39, 4, 2005, pp. 845–60.

[107] Christophe Jaffrelot, *Dr. Ambedkar and Untouchability: Analyzing and Fighting Caste* (New York: Columbia University Press, 2005).

the Bombay Legislative Council in 1926, Ambedkar had campaigned for the extension of the principle of separate electorates to 'untouchables'. Perhaps most significantly, from the mid to late 1930s, partly through his journal debates with Gandhi, Ambedkar provided the leading intellectual basis for low-caste critiques of high-caste dominance of the political system. His main publications, including *Annihilation of Caste* and *What Congress and Gandhi have done to the Untouchables*, presented a searing indictment of the religious bases of caste in India. For Ambedkar, caste could not be seen simply as an Asian form of division of labour, but a hierarchical division of labourers, which was closely related to the theological precepts of Hinduism itself – a situation that completely obliterated individual freedoms.[108] These arguments obviously presented problems not only to high-caste Hindus promoting orthodoxy or gradual social reform, but also to Hindu ideologues who used religion for mobilisation, such as Gandhi. Ambedkar's ideas effectively undermined the entire premise that a modern national identity could be based around the idea of a 'Hindu community'.

Interventions such as those of Ambedkar, and the responses to them over India as a whole, illustrated a changed political and official context in the consideration of caste and religious community in the mid to late 1930s. First, the nature of institution building around community changed in its scope and nature. For most of the period up to the 1920s, organisations that claimed to speak for broadly defined religious communities focussed as much on questions of social and religious reform as those of political mobilisation. By the 1930s, there was more of a drive, particularly in movements like the Hindu Mahasabha, Muslim League and Akali Dal, to frame resolutions in terms of the wider political proposals thrown up by the colonial state. This is not to argue that the older issues had lost their champions in such organisations, but that questions of political representation and weightage became more pressing.

Second, following the 1935 Government of India Act and a decade of dyarchical government, it was clear that the colonial state was not ready to let go of the principle that representation should be based around community (see Chapter 3). The notion of 'religious minority' related more closely to electoral arithmetic than ever before. This affected not only 'Hindu' and caste organisations but also Muslim movements. For example, the Shia Political Conference and other associated local Shi'a

[108] B. R. Ambedkar, *Annihilation of Caste* and *The Untouchables: A Thesis on the Origins of Untouchability* (Jullundur: Bheem Patrika Publications, 1971).

organisations began to frame demands for special recognition of the Shi'a community within Indian Islam along lines that resembled, sometimes even emulated, similar claims among low castes in relation to caste Hindus.[109] This changed with context. In the early 1920s, the newly formed 'Shi'a League' opposed the Sunni-dominated Muslim League's domination of Muslim seats in the new legislatures. In the mid-1930s, the Shi'a Political Conference actually opposed separate electorates for Muslims for a time.[110] Similar concerns were also evident in colonial discussions about the question of weightage, percentages of reservations for communities in different kinds of institutions and the need to maintain particular special privileges. This was a politics of numbers, an application of communal surveys to the distribution of political power that had never been so fully pushed through before.

We should, however, be wary not to overemphasise the significance of constitutionalism in these processes to avoid simplification of fluid and contingent political/ideological appeals to community and caste.[111] More complex responses to state action, including a redefinition of community in terms of 'minority', can be seen in the flurry of petitions to government around the All India Census. The census in India provided the basis for colonial ethnography and anthropology in such a way that India itself became a kind of human laboratory for competing academic theories and claims.[112] Central to the European academic fascination with India was the intersection between religion and ethnicity, and such projects of research had complex and often decisive implications for governance. Although, to some extent, the range of different European views of Indian society over the twentieth century, from the racial theories of the likes of H. H Risley to the cultural studies of Denzil Ibbetson, were very much entrenched in the academic fields of Europe,[113] Indian responses to the studies in the census (and the census itself) helped to shape the nature of the politics of 'minority' claims, particularly in north India. When the transformations between the census of 1931 and that of 1941 are viewed

---

[109] Gould, 'The U.P. Congress and "Hindu Unity"'.
[110] See Justin Jones, 'The Shi'a Muslims of the United Provinces of India', ch. 5.
[111] For a critique of David Page's constitutional approach to the politics of communalism, see David Lelyveld, Review of David Page, *Prelude to Partition*, in *The American Historical Review*, 89, 2, 1984, 505–6.
[112] Christopher Pinney, 'Colonial Anthropology in the "Laboratory of Mankind"', in C. A. Bayly, ed., *The Raj: India and the British, 1600–1947* (London: National Portrait Gallery, 1990), pp. 278–304.
[113] For an excellent analysis of European ideas about race and ethnicity as part of the academy, see Susan Bayly, 'Caste and Race in the Colonial Ethnography of India'.

in relation to the political context, it becomes clear that ideas about caste were increasingly related to older claims about religious community. In particular, by 1941, the concept of religious minority, particularly vis-à-vis a notion of a unified Hinduism, took on board the cultural implications of ethnic separateness created by caste division. Also pertinent, right up to the 1930s, was the European ethnographer's desire to frame European racial superiority in the context of Indian division.

The authors of the 1931 census report, perhaps even more than those before them, framed most of their demographic analysis around ethnic and religious divisions in the population. Rates of urbanisation, gender and age distributions, literacy, fecundity, fertility, customs and occupations all became opportunities to compare different religious communities and castes. For example, the Census Commissioner noted of UP that in Najibad municipality, a race for enumeration had created competition between the main religious communities: 'With a view to influencing respective representation on the municipal board each side imported large crowds of its own community from the neighbouring rural areas on census night, so that the population of the municipality rose by some 6,000 in a night'.[114] It was also noted that 'Vaishyas' as a group were more fertile than either 'Brahmans' or 'Rajputs', and that both 'Kayasthas' and 'Jats' were more fertile still. Muslims as a whole were more fertile than most of the high-caste Hindu groups.[115] Clearly, caste organisations attempted to approach the census by representing community claims, some of which entailed a reorientation of status and local power. This was well recognised in the UP, where the report remarked how the whole practice of the census had effectively led to the hardening of caste identities.[116]

By 1941, as the following chapter will show, the context of a new kind of religio-political mobilisation under the auspices of the Muslim League meant that the census operations became a much more direct fight between advocates of Hindu and Muslim enumeration. Specific institutions and new methods were adopted to tie the context of institutional and electoral politics to the whole enumeration effort. Petitions to the Census commissioners about the conduct of the census operations came from organisations such as the Hindu Census Committee based in Ludhiana. Even before the census had taken place, a range of organisations had already decided that they should take a defensive stance and claim that the whole project would be riddled with irregularities in such a way that their community

---

[114] *Census of India 1931 – Part I Report*, Allahabad, 1932, ch. II, p. 124.
[115] *Ibid.*, p. 228.
[116] See Gould, *Hindu Nationalism*, p. 112.

would suffer. Much more so than in 1931, direct claims of corruption among census officers formed the basis of petitions and representations to government. From the Hindu side, particularly organisations linked to the Hindu Sabhas, the claim was made that Hindus were being deliberately underrepresented: the president of the Bengal Hindu Mahasabha complained that the Chief Minister of Bengal, Fazlul Huq, was deliberately interfering with the census work. The most intense controversy, in which the president of the Hindu Mahasabha, Veer Savarkar, played a part, occurred in Assam. Here, colonisation schemes were allegedly being controlled by Muslim immigrants, and the overall Hindu population was enumerated thirteen per cent lower than in the 1931 census. Veer Savarkar threw in his support to the local Hindu Sabha, writing a statement entitled 'Hindu Assam in Danger', which vaguely attempted to inflame communal sentiment with the dubious claims of a conspiracy to convert Assam into a Muslim majority province. At the heart of Savarkar's report was again the accusation against Muslim colonists in the land-development scheme. But in his usual purple prose, Savarkar also dwelt upon the 'ancient and glorious past of the Hindus of Assam – the home of the Ahoms'.[117]

But the most interesting representations came from communities and caste organisations now more squarely associating themselves with the concept of political 'minority'. The Government of India was inundated with representations and petitions from a wide range of organisations from as early as late 1939, even more so than a decade earlier. In November and December 1939, the All India Jamiatul Momineen requested that its community be recorded as Momins in the census; the Jagrid Brahman Mahasabha and the All India Koli Rajput Mahasabha petitioned to be represented separately. Over the next year, similar requests came into the Government of India from the Jain Terapanthi Sabha, the All India Yadhava Mahasabha, the All India Jatav Youth League, the All India Kashyup Rajput Mahasabha, the Perika Mahasangham, the Sri Sayana Association, the All India Khangar Kshatriya Youth League, the UP Teli Mahasabha, the All India Chandravanshiya Kshatriya Mahasabha, the All India Vaishnao Brahman Mahasabha (who wanted to be recorded as Vaishnoo Brahmans), the Hindu Backward Classes League (who requested that the specific caste

---

[117] Statement of Savarkar, Dadar, Bombay, 8 July 1941 in 'Complaints or representations from organisations representing different communities about matters of communal interest arising in regard to the census enumeration' Home Dept. File No. 45/11/41 – Public, NAI.

of each representative be allowed), the All India Kurmi Kshatriya Association, the All India Sainik Kshatriya Mahasabha (who wanted all Malis and Rajput Malis to be recorded as Sainik Kshattriyas), The All India Meo Panchayat and a range of other caste and sectarian groups from across the country.[118] Each state government received even more specific claims for representation in the census.

The response of Muslim organisations, such as the Muslim League, and the Hindu organisations, such as the International Aryan League, and the various regional Hindu Sabhas revealed different trends. The high-caste Hindu organisations were at pains to point out the long-standing erroneous basis of colonial ethnographies, particularly in their apparent desire to set out the separate religious and ethnic identities of tribal and low-caste groups. A letter from the president of the Bengal Brahman Sabha, the Calcutta Pandit Sabha, and professors of the Government Sanskrit College, Calcutta, all set out on a richly stylised typeset, argued:

We beg to submit that, really speaking, there are no such people as 'aborigines' which is a name coined by some modern antiquarians who have based their conclusions on the mere hypothesis that the Aryan Hindus came to India from the outside. As a matter of fact, the accepted orthodox Hindu view is that the Aryan Hindus are natives of India and have not come from outside. The so-called aborigines are Hindus 'fallen' from their original status owing to some misdeeds, as recorded in many of our Shastras...

... As Brahmins who have dedicated their lives to the study of subjects relating to Hindu religion and society, we are regarded as authorities on those subjects and our word should be regarded as final in these matters. We claim to know the details of the Indian society more than any outsider.[119]

The Muslim League, particularly in Bengal, launched a counter-attack. Fazlul Huq, Chief Minister of Bengal, organised a monster meeting in the town hall of Calcutta on the 9 March 1941 and also launched a one-day protest. The meeting saw the uniting of Muslim leaders in Bengal with representatives of the All India Scheduled Castes Association, the Kidderpore Scheduled Castes Association, the Sri Rabidas Nanjawan

[118] 'List of the complaints or representations from organisations representing different communities about matters of communal interest arising in regard to the census enumeration', in 'Complaints or representations from organisations representing different communities about matters of communal interest arising in regard to the census enumeration' Home Dept. File No. 45/11/41 – Public, NAI.

[119] Chandidas Nyaya-Tarkatirtha, president of the Bengal Brahman sabha; Durgacharan Sankhya-Vedantatirtha, Pres of the Bengal Varnashram Swarajya Sangh and Calcutta Pandit Sabha; and two other profs of Gov Sanskrit College, Calcutta, 15 April 1941 to the Census Officer, Gov of India, in *Ibid.*

Sabha of Tiljala, the Mirzapore Scheduled Castes Association, the Shambazar Scheduled Castes Association and the Howrah Scheduled Castes Association. Also making speeches from the dais of the town hall were leaders from some of the principal tribal organisations – Babu Lal Soren, the leader of the Santhal Village Improvement Society of Bankura, and Vishnu Hazda Adibasi. Rather like the Hindu organisations, this meeting made accusations about the corruption involved in the census operations, but this time the culprits were Hindu officials who apparently dominated the project and who forced all Scheduled Caste and tribal groups to return themselves as Hindus very much against their interests. Fazlul Huq and other Muslim League leaders made speeches in which the Scheduled Caste groups and tribals were depicted as being in a struggle against the caste thraldom of the upper castes, represented in the Hindu Sabha. As such, like the Muslims across India, they were invited to assert their specific minority interests as separate political communities. The League leaders also mobilised the support of the European Planters' Association, which apparently had asserted in the early 1930s that since most of its labour was 'tribal', it should be recorded as such. In some cases, organisations went to great lengths to point out, in ethnographic terms that reflected the tenor of the census itself, how they were culturally separate from high-caste Hindus. For example, the president of the All India Adibasi Mahasabha sent a message to the meeting saying that Adibasis had their own religion, that they did not worship in temples and that many of them ate beef.[120]

The political positioning of religious 'minorities' gathered pace then through the 1930s and early 1940s and through battles around representation such as those of the census. Caste-based and religious community organisations, to an extent, responded to the new frameworks of constitutional proposals. But the 'representations' of community groups that flooded into government surrounding the census also demonstrated that the framing of colonial policies or constitutions was not paramount in defining the shape of religious and caste 'minority' politics. This was perhaps most clearly seen through the developing organisations that cut across the broader religious community interests, such as the Shia Political Conference, or the low-caste organisations that challenged high-caste representations of Hindu unity. Institution building around caste or religious community was, nevertheless, by the 1940s, often more directly

---

[120] Memorial of the Calcutta District Muslim League, 5.3.41 to Sir Reginald Maxwell, on Tribal Religion in Census, in *Ibid*.

concerned with the issue of political representation when compared with the early 1920s. What responses to the census show was that by the late 1930s and early 1940s, the struggle to use caste and ethnic identity to critique other forms of identity politics (e.g. around religious community) was linked to broader, national political debates. The politics of community had no doubt broadened, as the technologies of the state and of communication changed, but most importantly as the political stakes were raised, as Chapter 5 will go on to explore.

CONCLUSION

This chapter has argued that popular ideas about caste, class or occupation became more tangible in reference to broader religious community concerns, and that ideas about religious community were shaped by other solidarities: low-caste migrants to north Indian cities championed forms of Hindu mobilisation and revivalism in the 1920s and 1930s as a means of asserting local status and power; western India's urban traders were at the forefront of public and religious reform as part of the complex agenda of municipal domination and professional solidarity. Political discussion of 'minorities' or the nature of 'minority status' transformed through the 1930s and early 1940s too, as caste and community organisations responded to new constitutional proposals. But religious 'community' also complicated other social structures and, in particular, cut across the potential solidarity of occupational groups between different regions, cities or even neighbourhoods. Neither was the role of religious community in this process entirely functional. In each particular locality, the importance of intermediaries at all levels of the Indian economy and workplace meant that patterns of domination and subordination worked according to their own forms of internal logic. In a similar way, the struggles to assert a unified sense of Hindu or Muslim community identity were complicated and challenged by local networks of power, ritual and social hierarchies or other contingent associations.

It was perhaps because the notion of a broad Hindu community, for example, was so easily challenged and broken down at so many levels that Hindu nationalists appropriated cultural projects in attempts to define the essence of the community. This involved active, modern projects of standardisation and artistic consolidation. In the area of language and literature, as in music, this could include attempts to essentialise and 'purify' art of 'foreign' influences. But here again, such projects came up against a range of challengers – proponents of artistic traditions that rejected the idea that cultural output should be confined by association with a sense of community or nation. These developments could only have taken place, however, with a growing audience and population for whom the enjoyment of culture really mattered. As literary consumerism developed in the interwar period and a range of newspapers appeared to fuel it, specific issues of community competition drove debates in print. Reading, listening and performance were increasingly set out as functional projects in nation building and community consolidation. And in this sense, they appealed to a deeper, emotive sense of community engagement, which went beyond the pragmatic considerations of local political power.

5

State Transformation, Democracy and Conflict

High Politics and the Everyday in the 1940s

Between 1948 and 1950, Mridula Sarabhai, a Gujarati Congress leader, sent a series of reports to Jawaharlal Nehru on the violence following India's partition in the summer of 1947, the fate of refugees in camps, the problem of housing in Muslim areas of Delhi and, most importantly, the problem of female abduction. Her letters and reports illustrated, often in graphic detail, the involvement of not only civilians but also of specific government servants, policemen, army personnel and local politicians in the perpetuation and encouragement of violence. In late October 1948, she conducted a fact-finding tour of the Agra area in western UP and Dholepur State (in present-day eastern Rajasthan) – an area close to some of the worst instances of violence and with a considerable urban Muslim population – with Inspector Hans Raj of the Intelligence Bureau. Sarabhai and Hans Raj met the Principal of the Holman Institute in Agra, who passed on some information about the alleged location of women abducted from across the border. According to Sarabhai's informant, at Deeg, twenty-five miles from Bharatpur, it was rumoured that there were two or three abducted Muslim women in every house. In Dholepur, in Bari, abducted women were also allegedly being kept in a big forest called Dang. A headman of fifty villages in Bari, said to be 'working against the Congress', also allegedly knew about them. Sarabhai's information was that a gang of people, including policemen – thanedars and a city kotwal – were reportedly abducting Muslim women who had taken refuge from violence or who had been previously kidnapped from villages all over Dholepur state. These women were brought to Delhi and sold. Sarabhai's informant went on to suggest that 'Delhi people should be used' to conduct an enquiry because the state people and police would be of no use.[1]

This episode illustrated how, around India's partition, reporting on Hindu–Muslim conflict was highly dependent on local context, but also that state acquiescence or the involvement of government servants and policemen often formed a part of the rumour surrounding such events. Sarabhai had her doubts about the veracity of the reports in this case and many others, and suggested herself that speculation about the actions of individuals in positions of authority was also part of the continuing 'atmosphere of violence'. Also significant were the national and parliamentary debates underpinning Sarabhai's fact-finding tours. The issue of 'abducted' women and their recovery was highly emotive and, as we will see, entered national debates about religion, Indian secularism and the role of state institutions in legislating for the Indian family.[2] The image of the abducted Hindu woman took on a heightened symbolic significance around partition, which simplified and homogenised much more complex realities. In other reports, Sarabhai expressed surprise that women 'reclaimed' from abduction often had no intention of returning to their families and sought instead to start a new life on their own. These episodes also illustrated, crucially, that the implications of the partition violence stretched well beyond the moments of independence and the political concerns of the main political parties involved: the displacement or division of families or the loss of relatives caused long-term damage, with extremely complex implications for the social lives of those involved. And the violence of partition, particularly in its effects on those whose new national identity or sense of belonging was in doubt, extended into the early 1950s and beyond.

(I) THE 1940S, 'COMMUNALISM' AND THE POLITICS OF INDIA'S PARTITION

Despite the long-term effects of the partition violence attending Indian independence and its lasting effects on millions of families, 1947 has

---

[1] 'Report of my visit to Agra on 21 October 1948', 'Correspondence of Mridula Sarabhai relating to the recovery of abducted women in UP', Mridula Sarabhai Papers, reel 9, F. No. R/UP/13 – 1948–53, NMML.

[2] For a complex discussion of female abduction and the debates around legislation that dealt with this issue, see Rita Menon and Kamla Bhasin, 'Recovery, Rupture, Resistance: Indian State and Abduction of Women during Partition', *Economic and Political Weekly*, 28, 17, 1993, WS2–WS11.

become an almost fixed ending or starting point for the vast literature on the history and politics of late colonial or early independent India. The implications of this approach have been to underplay somewhat the crucial continuities in systems of politics and governance between the two phases. It also suggests that the predominant experience of the post-1947 citizens of the independent states was permeated by a new sense of democratic freedom – a state of being delivered by a triumphant nationalist movement. Emphasis on 1947 has also meant that much of the writing on religious mobilisation or communalism in India has examined the late colonial phase in the context of the events of partition. In other words, 'problems' of increasing communal mobilisation are 'read back' from 1947 and explained in the light of India's partition. The classic example of this is the interpretation of the Lahore Resolution of 1940 as the first example of the 'Pakistan Demand', and the interpretation of Jinnah's politics from that date as unequivocally driving for a separate sovereign state.[3] Although it is easily argued that 1947 represented a clear chronological break in terms of the politics of South Asia, these approaches tend to underestimate the degree to which there were important continuities, not least in state structures and the politics of religious mobilisation, over the entire period of the 1920s to the 1950s and beyond. Equally, however, the specific circumstances of India's partition certainly need to be borne in mind, not least because the creation of two entirely separate states in 1947 was the result of very specific decisions made at the top level of politics in the few months leading up to independence.

The narrative of the 'high politics' of India and Pakistan's independence has been well covered elsewhere, and it is not the intention to revisit it in detail here. What has been less well researched is the gulf between these high-level decisions, involving the main parties at the centre – namely, Congress, Muslim League and representatives of the British Raj – and everyday experiences of the partition. As we will see in this chapter, relatively recent research has explored the latter, particularly in terms of 'historical memory', but the broader significance of these social histories to the larger issues of state change, independence and partition have only

---

[3] See, for example, Stanley Wolpert, *Jinnah of Pakistan* (New York: Oxford University Press, 1984); R. J. Moore, 'Jinnah and the Pakistan Demand', *Modern Asian Studies*, 17, 4 (1983), pp. 529–61; and Anita Inder Singh, *The Origins of the Partition of India* (Delhi: Oxford University Press, 1990). The clearest and most thorough critique of this kind of argument can be found in Ayesha Jalal, *The Sole Spokesman: Jinnah, the Muslim League and the Demand for Pakistan* (Cambridge: Cambridge University Press, 1985).

recently been explored in any detail.[4] There are other problems of historical analysis of the phenomenon of 'communalism' around independence. Because of the significance attached to the 1947 dividing point by those doing research on India, relatively few historical studies have looked at how forms of religious community or 'ethnic' mobilisation straddled independence. And few have looked at how such mobilisations connected to instances of apparent communal violence, under rapidly changing political regimes. Studies of 'communalism' in contemporary India have also not generally taken enough account of the detailed analyses of historians of the late colonial period, many of which have produced valuable frameworks for thinking about 'communalism' over longer periods. To some extent, the problem is one of disciplines. The archival research and training of the historian is of quite a different order to that of the field-working political scientist or sociologist. Yet curiously, some of the most interesting analyses of 'communalism' have pertinence to different temporal contexts, which largely encourages cross-fertilisation between disciplines.

As Chapter 1 explored, 'communalism' can be examined in terms of representation and discourse. It was an idea with a wide array of political applications, and rarely, by itself, explained the complex causes of mass violence in India. This is not to downplay the horrors of the multifaceted violence described by contemporaries as 'communalism'. The events surrounding 1947 provide a cautionary note to historians to avoid complacency about the realities of murderous attacks between those espousing different religious identities. But in many cases, getting to the bottom of the subsequent meanings, outcomes and 'products' of such moments of violence is often as important to those studying political events, as is unravelling the concrete causes of conflicts in any particular situation. The reasons for this become clear to any scholar who attempts to look at a particular conflict in any real depth: as we have already seen, the texts surrounding moments of religious violence are often extremely rich. They are nearly always contested, and there are invariably a range of narratives and counter-narratives, not just about the riots or events themselves but also about the surrounding circumstances. In some cases, even the roles of

[4] The best examples of this can be found in Vazira Zamindar, *The Long Partition and the Making of Modern South Asia: Refugees, Boundaries, Histories* (New York: Columbia University Press, 2007); Yasmin Khan, *The Great Partition: The Making of India and Pakistan* (London: Yale University Press, 2007); and Sarah Ansari, *Life after Partition*. See also Taylor C. Sherman, William Gould and Sarah Ansari, 'From Subjects to Citizens: Society and the Everyday State in India and Pakistan', *Modern Asian Studies*, 45, 1, 2011.

'religion' or 'community' are questionable in these events. Indeed, in the drawn-out moments of extensive violence, attempts to locate specific explanations for events are often fruitless, since the preconditions and background factors are themselves subject to multiple contestations. Yet, as this book has suggested throughout, there are some frameworks for better exploring and making sense of this complexity.

These problems in studying religious community conflict apply to the 1940s, even though it might appear that the reasons for the violence of partition are obviously about the creation of two separate independent states. And at this stage, the problems of oversimplification largely relate to historical assumptions about the uniform nature of the state (or state 'idea') itself and the implication of those states or their agents in such violence. Chapter 1 looked at how the writing on 'communalism' has been largely based on a uniform set of assumptions about how the state acted in India, and has subsequently divided its analyses into separate considerations of 'colonial' and 'post-independent' forms of communal conflict. For example, the difference between Gyanendra Pandey and Chris Bayly about whether or not 'communalism' can be seen to be a distinctively 'colonial' phenomenon illustrates the ways in which the exercise of state power in such conflicts can be taken as a uniform 'given' for any particular period of history.[5] This book attempts to present the state (and state power) in India over our entire period not as a background entity but as something composed of powerful social actors, contested in its authority and porous in its interaction with societal forces. In this sense, state 'actions' were largely the varied and contingent actions of local authorities, which usually had only ambiguous connections to the aims of statesmen and governments at the centre. As the following sections will explore, these ambiguous state functions affected the nature of violence between communities and parties too in the 1940s. Because state power was particularly fractured in this way, over the period from 1946 to 1950, failing formal mechanisms often gave way to quasi-state mobilisations, on the one hand (through volunteer organisations, for example, based around 'community') or to the direct control by political leaders of bureaucrats and policemen, on the other. Mobilisation around the symbols of religious community provided one clear organisational answer to the weaknesses exposed by state agents, and at times served to influence or affect Indian governance and at other times sought to challenge or replace it.

---

[5] See Chapter 1.

A re-examination of the final phase of Congress–Muslim League competition and the complex institutions and pressures informing those parties provides a means of introducing this idea and giving it shape. As will be discussed in more detail in the following sections, the formal political structures of the Muslim League, the Congress and the rhetoric with which they represented the idea of the nation and its people should be distinguished from the means whereby political power was exercised (or experienced) at the ground level. In most accounts, the high politics of India's partition involved a three-way negotiation between the Congress, League and British producing a series of attempted agreements, which take us through the Cripps Mission of 1942, the Cabinet Mission of 1946 and the final negotiations between the main parties with the final Viceroy, Mountbatten, from March 1947. In this narrative, the League leader, M. A. Jinnah, is backed into a corner by the Congress whose interests increasingly dovetailed with those of British negotiators eager to decolonise swiftly and as painlessly as possible from around July 1945 and who acquiesced in the partition of India in March 1947. By agreeing to partition, Congress effectively neutralised Jinnah's demands for 'parity' (an equal share) in the central government, which specified the League's exclusive right to represent Muslims in any future government.

Jinnah's apparently intransigent demands, based on the claims that Muslims represented a separate nation, however, concealed a much more complex set of political desires. First, there is some doubt about whether Jinnah ever really aimed for an entirely separate sovereign state for Muslims. Second, and even more importantly, the process of the 'high politics' narrative illustrates how Jinnah's demands regarding 'Pakistan' related to the changing dynamics of Muslim League power in Bengal and Punjab. Negotiations at the centre were tempered by events in the provinces. After the 1945–6 elections, the League formed ministries in these most important Muslim majority provinces, and it was from this point that Jinnah could negotiate from a position of relative strength. Third, and perhaps most importantly of all, the meaning of 'Pakistan' for most of north India's Muslims was never transparent before Mountbatten's announcement of 3 June 1947 to divide and quit India, and even after that there was no clear idea where the boundary would lie. Neither were the national identities of Hindus or Muslims who found themselves on the 'wrong' side of the border entirely clear for a number of years after August 1947. Conflicts between religious communities in this period, then, whether they centred around 'Pakistan' or not, were rarely likely to be based on a uniform set of ideologies about what it would mean to be 'Pakistani' or 'Indian'.

In many ways, there was nothing new in this disjunction between high politics and everyday political competitions and conflicts. It has been shown in different ways elsewhere that the Congress Working Committee's formal resolutions were not uniformly adhered to at district or town levels in the interwar period, for example during Civil Disobedience.[6] The same could be said for the other powerful regional parties of our period, such as the Justice Party in South India, the Punjab Unionist Party and the Krishak Praja Party in Bengal, for example. In a related way, the common disconnection between the decisions of politicians at the centre/province and the quotidian realities of Indian politics for the masses created variation in the purchase of 'communalism', secularism and religious mobilisation. Whereas a provincial-level government might espouse a certain approach to religious neutrality, the inability or reluctance of local bureaucrats and policemen to act along similar lines shaped the actual performance of violence. The outcomes of this disjunction in the early to mid-1940s were, however, somewhat different, as the following sections will explore. The gap between rhetoric and reality of political organisations, on the one hand, and the lack of cohesiveness in state structures, on the other, created fertile conditions for the development of rapidly formed organisations of communal mobilisation. These organisations not only usurped the rhetorical and political authority of political parties, they also exercised quasi–state power, particularly in relation to the right to violent force and action.

(II) MILITARISM AND VIOLENCE IN 1940S UTTAR PRADESH

This process was perhaps nowhere more clearly illustrated than in the sudden expansion in the number of quasi-militaristic organisations of 'community protection' during the war years in India. Looking more closely at the nature of the violence itself in north India around the period of 1945–9 and comparing it to other phases of apparent 'communal violence' in India both before then and afterwards, some specific characteristics to its organised nature become clear. For most of the late colonial period, a good proportion of reported violence appeared around what officials frequently defined as 'riots', reportedly generated by specific trigger

---

[6] Gould, *Hindu Nationalism*, pp. 9–10.

factors, and foreshadowed by local preconditions, such as the clashing of festivals or religious spaces. Other late colonial conflicts were clearly related to moments of direct political competition, as we saw around the elections of the 1920s. Evidence from a range of different sources suggests that in the phase of anticipated political transition of the mid-1940s, the character of violence described as 'communal' also changed. This section will examine these processes with specific reference to the growing militarism surrounding community mobilisation in Uttar Pradesh, or UP. This is a particularly important state in this respect, not least because of the ambiguities surrounding the meanings of 'Pakistan' and the two-nation theory for the significant Muslim minority of the region.

As we saw in the last two chapters, there were often specific political contexts for conflicts between different religious communities, and sometimes such violence served particular political/electoral purposes, especially as representative institutions developed. By the 1940s, these pragmatic purposes of violence sometimes appeared to be clearer, being connected in many instances to the notion of 'Pakistan' or its opposition. However, this too created a self-serving justification for conflict between communities, which ultimately obscured the concrete bases for sectarian quarrels. In this period, specific 'volunteer' organisations (albeit hastily organised and unstable) championed the techniques of military organisation and drilling. Such movements allowed a broader range of political agencies to engage simultaneously with the larger political questions of the time (popularised by the Congress and League). This overlap and interrelationship between movements at different levels created new stresses and patterns, which either fed into or cut across the broad Congress–Muslim League split in UP. The activities of volunteer movements tended to subvert other broad understandings of communal solidarity. And very often, their involvement in conflicts illustrated the fluid nature of political allegiances in urban contexts – with parties moving in and out of relationships with other volunteer bodies. Sometimes there were quite unexpected allegiances and unusual agreements, which clearly cut across Hindu–Muslim divides and perhaps more clearly reflected pragmatic political choices of the moment. Yet the violence between these groups was still presented by the media and sometimes by the state as broadly Hindu–Muslim. The reasons for this, I will argue, are that even though volunteer organisations dipped in and out of involvement with other political parties, they nevertheless brought new concepts and practices of violence (and latent violence) into Indian party politics.

Community 'defence' and the building up of resources for possible future conflict created the means for a range of organisations to enhance their local power bases. It also affected public discussions of communalism itself. A sense of this process, albeit from the angle of colonial agencies, can be seen in the fortnightly reports of Henry James Frampton in the UP who, by 1945, was reporting on the increasing militarisation of local 'communal' organisations.[7] Important, here, were new public discussions of the international situation of world war, the emulation of volunteer activity in other contexts and the emergency mobilisation of resources for the conduct of war in India itself. There were often factors, then, somewhat external to immediate Indian political circumstances that had an impact on militaristic community mobilisation: the context of an imperial power at war and the extent to which the 'Pakistan Demand' tied into it; the introduction of wartime controls and rationing; the enhanced focus on security and law and order; and the emergency recruitment into the Indian civil services. For example, the 'communal' riot took on a still different meaning with colonial concerns about 'drilling movements' in this period.

The rapidly changing circumstances of the 1940s also involved the difficult relationship between Gandhian nonviolence in Congress volunteer movements and the more directly militant organisations that promoted drilling. Key to this ideological debate were colonial and nationalist (including Gandhian) assumptions about natural tendencies of different religious communities. For example, the powerful colonial assumption that the Muslim community was more 'violent' foreshadowed cultural understandings about the ethnography of violence in north India. Hindu *sangathan* was also based around the notion of the communal strength, unity and 'organisation' of the Muslim community as a whole.[8] For the Bengali essayist, Saratchandra Chattopadhyay, Hindus possessed a quality of mind not accessible to the Muslim community whose strength was rather described in terms of 'virility', using images such as rape and the kidnap of women.[9] This notion of the relative physical fitness and activity of different communities had a key impact on colonial discourses about communal difference and formed an important part of how volunteer movements represented themselves: Hindu organisations, for example, explicitly sought to challenge long-standing colonial (and nationalist)

---

[7] See Frampton Papers, Fortnightly Reports, Centre of South Asian Studies, University of Cambridge.

[8] 'Hindu Sangathan Ka Dhong', *Chamd*, VI, 1, 4, 1928, 438–40.

[9] These ideas are taken from 'Bartaman Hindu-Mussulman Samasya', explored in Joya Chatterji, *Bengal Divided: Hindu Communalism and Partition 1932–1947*, pp. 168–80.

assumptions about Hindu 'weakness', particularly in relation to diet and bodily discipline. As such, the culture of the *akhara* shaped many volunteer organisations by suggesting that bodily power had an otherworldly dimension relating to self-discipline and control.[10]

Discussions about the tendency of different communities to promote violence had an important effect in a number of localities: workers and middle-class publicists in urban north India were actively involved, in some areas, in militaristic activity and organisation and drilling movements. Although separate from the traditional *akhara* (gymnasium) culture of the towns and cities, which drew upon traditional practices of physical culture, there was an important link between modern drilling and gymnasia. Joseph Alter has shown how the activities of the *akhara* were popularised amongst middle- and lower middle-class small-town dwellers and appealed to the specific political world views of that section of north India's population. Lower-caste movements in UP cities such as Kanpur, Agra and Allahabad also made claims to be the genuine 'defenders' of Hinduism, as we saw in the last chapter.[11] Gooptu clearly shows how aspirant *sudra* communities who had entered urban centres in the interwar period used the symbolism of Hindu community defence to defend against marginalisation and to reinforce traditional claims to *kshattriya* status. For example, in 1923–4 in Allahabad, low-caste participants at the Ramlila formed a *Khuni Dal* or Suicidal Corps in glorification of Ram.[12] To some extent, these movements were encouraged by Hindu Sabhas who attempted to recruit Ahirs into their volunteer movement the 'Hindu Sewak Dal' in north Indian cities in 1924–5.[13]

However, these were not the only communities promoting forms of militaristic volunteer activity in the interwar period. First, there were many situations in which local party bosses would mobilise teams of relatively low-caste retainers to flex some political muscle, sometimes through the administration and police itself.[14] Second, looking at the kinds of audiences attracted by some of the key north Indian Hindu

---

[10] See Joseph S. Alter, 'Indian Clubs and Colonialism: Hindu Masculinity and Muscular Christianity', *Comparative Studies in Society and History*, 46, 3, 2004, 497–534; Joseph S. Alter, 'Gandhi's Truth: Nonviolence and the Bimoral Imperative of Public Health', *The Journal of Asian Studies*, 55, 2, 1996, 301–22.

[11] Nandini Gooptu, 'The Urban Poor and Militant Hinduism in Early Twentieth-Century Uttar Pradesh', *Modern Asian Studies*, 31, 4, 1997, 879–918.

[12] *Ibid.*, pp. 898–9.

[13] 'Note from G. B. Lambert on movements of a missionary or proselytising character', in H. R. Roe to DIG Police, UP, 2 January 1925, 'Communal Disorders', L/PJ/6/1890, OIOC.

[14] For examples of this, see William Gould, *Bureaucracy, Community and Influence*, ch. 4.

Congress leaders – P. D. Tandon, Mahabir Tyagi and Algu Rai Shastri, who were also involved in volunteer activity – it seems that the support for Congress-driven efforts also involved urban middle classes. There were often strong ideological factors in the development of movements for physical culture, which might appeal across different socio-economic groups.[15] Volunteer movements associated with the Congress incorporated ideas and rituals of individual discipline, which connected in some cases to powerful representations of the male body and broader socio-sexual identities.[16] Volunteering and movements for promoting physical fitness were also powerful dimensions of late colonial Congress nationalism via some of north India's key leaders, albeit in very different ways: Gandhi, Bhagwan Das, Sri Prakash and Mahabir Tyagi all related their own physical well-being to religion, juxtaposing physical with spiritual fitness.[17] These ideas were derived from concepts of individual spiritual strength drawn from an array of sources – the most mainstream being Gandhian 'swaraj', Tilakite philosophies of action and the physical organisation and discipline connected with militant Hindu and Muslim organisations.

Physical culture, fitness and bodily control were subjects of interest and concern for a range of nationalist ideologues and were perhaps most commonly related to Gandhian ideas of state violence. In particular, the work of Purushottam Das Tandon over this period shows how easily ideas of Hindu defence and militaristic organisation could be legitimised and publicised by the very organisations that had traditionally adopted Gandhian nonviolence. In 1947, Tandon was involved in the organisation of various Hindu defence projects and most famously set up the *Hind Rakshak Dal*. His speeches and political posturing about Hindu defence across north India up to and around independence caused considerable embarrassment for the Congress organisation as a whole, but demonstrated the widespread support for semi-military organisation.[18] Clearly, the

[15] Physical fitness and discipline in Indian wrestling has a long history in cities like Banaras combining physical well-being with spiritualism. Joseph A. Alter, *The Wrestler's Body: Identity and Ideology in North India* (Berkeley: University of California Press, 1992).
[16] Joseph S. Alter, 'Gandhi's Truth: Nonviolence and the Bimoral Imperative of Public Health'.
[17] Correspondence with Bhagwan Das, 31 March 1940–6 December 1942 Sri Prakash Papers NMML; Sampurnanand Papers NAI; Narendra Dev Papers, NMML; Letter to Parasram Mehrotra, 9 June 1932 *The Collected Works of Mahatma Gandhi Vol. L*, p. 25; Mahabir Tyagi, *Meri Kaun Sunega*.
[18] For more detail on this, see William Gould, 'Congress Radicals and Hindu Militancy: Sampurnanand and Purushottam Das Tandon in the Politics of the United Provinces', *Modern Asian Studies*, 36, 3, 2002, pp. 619–56.

Gandhian notion of Hinduism as a peaceful, essentially tolerant and all-embracing force in Indian politics was not uncontested in public debates about community organisation. Similarly, in Bengal in this period, questions of culture, religion and identity for the Hindu bhadralok merged into a wider preoccupation with nationhood on the basis of increasing anxiety.[19] If we look at the writings and views of some leading UP figures, this shift can be identified in the writings of Tandon and Sampurnanand, as well as in the more obvious views of Savarkar.[20] Some leaders, especially Congressmen, who had been ardent opponents of 'communalism' in the mid-1930s, seemed to accept the inevitability of a political world in which communal identity would serve a short-term purpose in the face of the League's propaganda. There was a good response from some district Congress Committees and other organisations across north and western India to Tandon's explicit opposition to Gandhian ahimsa and the need to organise a Hindu defence corps, which would protect nation, community and language.[21] This shift in the 1940s had important effects on the everyday contacts between ordinary citizens and the state across India. Even avowedly 'non-political' societies and cultural journals began to discuss the importance of community mobilisation and defence.[22]

The approach of war in Europe and Asia from the late 1930s encouraged the formation of volunteer movements in India, and such organisations made more obvious moves to adopt forms of military training, especially drilling. There was much more to this process, however, than simply the anticipation of Indian defence. As we will see, the formation of volunteer organisations promoted new kinds of political conflicts and new forms of comparisons between the physical culture and territorial ambitions of communities. Training camps for 'officers' were established by a

[19] Chatterji, *Bengal Divided*, pp. 166–85.
[20] Sampurnanand demonstrated a greater concern for the protection of Hinduism's cultural and philosophical purity in his later writings from the 1960s. Sampurnanand, *Evolution of the Hindu Pantheon* (Bombay: 1963), pp. 80–102.
[21] Tandon Papers, file 93, 3 August 1947 NAI. Well before the organisation of the Hind Rakshak Dal, Tandon had been advocating the abandonment of ahimsa. Fortnightly Reports for the first half of April 1945, 19 April 1945; first half of October 1945, 22 October 1945; second half of November 1945, 6 December 1945; second half of January 1946, 5 February 1946. Frampton Papers, 'Confidential Report on Political and other Conditions in the United Provinces, from March 1945 to November 1946' SAS.
[22] The journals *Madhuri, Cand* and *Vishwa Bharat Samachar* all exhibited a definite shift towards the interpretation of literature and culture in terms of religious community by 1946.

range of parties, and 'physical culture' sessions became common in educational institutions.[23] Although the Congress dominated volunteer organisation and mobilisation with its relatively extensive resources and personnel, the existence of a wide range of other movements and organisations, particularly 'Hindu', often overlapped with the mainstream cadres.

Semi-formal militaristic organisation in India in this period was, crucially, encouraged by the anticipation of territorial conflict and notions of defence of 'homeland'. And in these representations of homeland, again, the issue of the supposed extra-territorial loyalties of Indian Muslims was important. This was most clearly illustrated in the correspondence sent by two presidents of the Hindu Mahasabha, B. S. Moonje and Veer Savarkar, to the Viceroy over the early 1940s, pledging Hindu support for the war effort via particular projects in militarisation. For Moonje, writing to the Viceroy in September 1940, 'The Hindus will be in a position to give immensely large help both in men, material and intellect ... in organising the defence of India'. This claim was juxtaposed to what Moonje represented as the questionable loyalty of the Muslim League, who had loyalties to countries who might oppose Britain in the war: 'In contrast ... the loyalty of the Hindus to their own Sacred Land, Hindusthan, surrounding as it is on the Western and North-Western Frontier by its traditional enemies of the last more than one thousand years, is the more stable factor its choice of its allies'.[24] The following year, Savarkar made similar approaches to the Viceroy, making the point more specific. For the Mahasabha president, subjugation and annexation of the 'lawless' tribal tracts was essential – 'these treacherous and turbulent Muslim tribes are sure to swell the ranks of any invader who marches on India to conquer her'.[25]

Clearly, the Mahasabha leaders used here the idea of the 'territorial' threat of Islam to promote projects of Hindu defence and to lobby the Government of India at war simultaneously. But its militaristic ethnographies had a broader social significance. Like other nationalist organisations, the Mahasabha mobilised colonial representations of the physical characteristics of different classes and castes. On 15 and 16 September, the

---

[23] *General Report on the Administration of the United Provinces, 1939* (Lucknow: Government of India Press, 1941).
[24] Moonje to Viceroy, 26 September 1940, 'Hindu Mahasabha 1938–1946', L/PJ/8/683, OIOC.
[25] Savarkar to Viceroy, 27 March 1941, 'Hindu Mahasabha 1938–1946', L/PJ/8/683, OIOC.

Mahasabha decided that the propaganda drive should be carried into the rural areas, 'particularly those inhabited by the martial classes'.[26] Savarkar reported in a statement to the Viceroy that Mahasabha leaders were touring India to set up 'Hindu Militarization Mandals' as a means of contributing to the 'militarization of our Hindu race'. Savarkar also admitted that if Hindus helped Britain militarily, they would also be doing a service to 'Hindudom' – to 'defend our hearths in an internal anti-Hindu anarchy'. The statement concluded aptly, 'Let Hindus measure their swords with the bravest races of the world today'.[27]

The Mahasabha's pledges had little behind them in a practical sense, since the proposed Hindu volunteer organisations were not fully formal, being rarely controlled in a consistent way by a single party and therefore relatively unstable in their activities and allegiances. This point was important, since it affected the ways in which such organisations could be employed by political interest groups. The same problems applied to the Congress organisations. 'Semi-military training' was started by the Congress in Ayodhya with the intention of forming an All-India volunteer corps. The UP Congress Committee issued circulars to all other provincial committees informing them of the inauguration of an All-Indian Central Training Camp at Fyzabad late in 1938, under the organisation of Nand Kumar Deo Vashishta. At Banaras, Vashishta argued for the need to build up military capability to take power in the eventuality of a political crisis or even the need to engineer such a situation.[28] However, the blueprints for an All-India organisation remained just that. Different groups with a range of interests in specific districts, even if they shared institutional names, followed locally specific policies and political leaders. This generally undermined any centralised control on the part of the Provincial Congress Committee, allowing organisations in some districts to share resources with obviously communal organisations like the Mahabir Dal and Arya Vir Dal. For example, at the beginning of September 1938, in Tulsipur, Gonda district, the Hindu Sabha and a selection of Congressmen joined to form a Mahabir Dal and Hanuman Dal.[29] Official surveillance of volunteer movements in June 1939 suggested that the disorganisation and proliferation of volunteer activity could connect to other political allegiances. Most significantly, the temporary nature of volunteer movements

---

[26] *Prakash*, 18 September 1941.
[27] 'Statement of V. D. Savarkar Regarding Hindu Militarization', 7 October 1941 L/PJ/8/683 OIOC.
[28] 'Note on Volunteer Movements in India (II)', December 1938 L/PJ/8/678 OIOC.
[29] PAI 3 September 1938.

clearly suggested that, in some important cases, they operated along the lines of local private armies, often made up of retainers for a local political boss:

> The country is full of mushroom organizations, created to meet the exigencies of the moment and then forgotten, seldom properly organized or systematically developed, without central control or financial backing . . . owing allegiance to nobody, or what is worse, to a local faction.[30]

Bearing in mind the common evidence of pre-preparation in the stockpiling of weapons and collective organisation during so-called 'riots' or 'Hindu–Muslim' clashes, this dispersed pattern of volunteer organisation is very revealing. As will be seen, in the immediate aftermath of partition, observers discussed the apparent pre-organised nature of particular moments of violence, the moments of individual advantage derived by members of particular communities and the complicated interplay of local interests. Yet, at the same time, during the 1940s as well as at other times, violence appeared to occur not so much along the straightforward lines of clear party or communal polarity. Instead, powerful local factional leaders, as Paul R. Brass has demonstrated for the 1950s and 1960s, mobilised temporary muscle power based on existing volunteer movements.

Despite the intermittent rise and fall of these organisations and their pragmatic motivations, broader patterns of community mobilisation still seemed to reflect the relative growth of Congress or Muslim League-affiliated movements. Organisations affiliated with a particular leader could and did share resources with other parties. The suggestion that, at the district levels, Congress volunteer activity overlapped with Hindu organisations is, for example, supported by the corresponding growth of the Muslim League volunteer corps across UP in the second half of 1938.[31] In the early years of 1940, there was also a correlation between the success of 'Congress's volunteer organisations and the popularity of Muslim League corps'.[32] The figures of membership for volunteer movements in different parts of north India illustrated a kind of semi-military arms race, with a correlation between high memberships for Congress and Muslim-affiliated movements. Clearly, these organisations were facing off, although their intentions were not simply to demonstrate the political strength of their respective parties.[33] Over the year 1941, the Congress

---

[30] 'Report covering the first half of 1939' L/PJ/8/678, OIOC.
[31] *Ibid.*
[32] APS March 1940. These reports repeatedly state the correspondence between the growth in Hindu volunteer activity and that of Muslim communal defence movements.
[33] Special Branch quarterly report to government on the volunteer situation in UP, 8 May 1941. Police CID Box 82 file 1240/1941 UPSA.

and Hindu communal bodies in north India shared resources and personnel, policed each other's meetings and opposed each other's political com-
petitors.[34] Similar collaborations occurred between the Bengal Congress
organisation and Hindu movements and bodies, who effectively served to
'hold' bhadralok Hindus for the Congress.[35] When it came to semi-
military movements, this meant that there was often confusion about the
culpability of different volunteer movements in moments of conflict and
violence.[36] Cooperation was often linked to key religious processions and
festivals, and functioned to an extent as a demonstration or display of
power. Examples are numerous, but interesting is the technique of 'policing' and cooperative action. For example, in Etah on 16 September 1938,
the Congress Swayam Sevak Dal joined with the Mahabir Dal to escort the
Ramlila Jhanda procession through the city. By the beginning of October,
the two volunteer organisations were jointly policing processions. In
Dehra Dun too, Congress volunteers had worked with Mahabir Dal
members in October 1939, which resulted in a controversy about proces-
sional music in front of a mosque.[37]

Official assessments of volunteer activity in 1939 also supported the
idea that Congress and outwardly 'Hindu' movements overlapped or were
interrelated in their memberships: 'In the United Provinces Hindu communal organisations are gaining in popularity to the detriment of recruitment
to the Congress Volunteer Corps'.[38] We also see around the time of the
Quit India in August 1942, movement of a number of volunteers from the
Congress to the RSS. This was the motivation of Lal Krishna Advani, from
Hyderabad in Sindh, who felt, in 1942, that the Congress response to what
he perceived as Muslim militarisation was not direct enough.[39] In other
places, these and similar organisations provided muscle power for specific
political purposes, which fed into broader community-based conflicts. For
example, when the Muslim League's success in the elections in Punjab in
1946 failed to result in a League ministry, the Muslim National Guards
took part in anti-government protests, facing off against volunteer movements among Sikhs and Hindus. The result was large-scale and organised

---

[34] Special Branch report, October 1941 Police CID Box 82 file 1240/1941 UPSA.
[35] Joya Chatterji, *Bengal Divided*, pp. 144–8.
[36] PAI 27 January; 27 July 1940; 27 June 1941.
[37] PAI 8 October; 15 October; 19 November 1938; 14 October 1939.
[38] Minute of W. C. Wallis, 11 March 1940 L/PJ/8/678, OIOC.
[39] Christophe Jaffrelot, *The Hindu Nationalist Movement and Indian Politics: 1925 to the 1990s*, p. 72.

violence leading up to the partition.[40] In parts of the south, in the region of Malabar in Madras Province, the situation was different. Some of the most powerful volunteer organisations developed over the years 1938–9 and continued into the 1940s were established to strengthen peasant unions in their actions against landowners and local courts where there were disputes over land. In this case, the volunteer bodies faced off against local police forces as a means of setting up alternative judicial authorities to look into disputes against landlords. By the end of 1940, in north Malabar, around 2,500 volunteers were trained to fight with lathis and swelled the muscle power of peasant unions.[41]

At district and town/city levels of politics (and to some extent at the level of the province), it was clear that ostensibly secular organisations like the Congress, via its leaders, could ally with 'Hindu' or 'Muslim' volunteer organisations. The meaning of secularism, even in relation to the Indian National Congress, became ambivalent at these levels and, as will be argued a little later, constrained the all-India negotiations between key parties up to and beyond independence. Such alliances and combinations of (factionally derived) volunteer movements were possible in the first place largely because of the necessary amorphousness of 'national' parties and regional political combinations. The UP Congress organisation, for example, was based upon a very broad array of political leaders, many of whom could not be relied upon to toe any kind of party line beyond their own factional interests of the moment. This situation was amply demonstrated again in the lead up to the first democratic elections in free India of 1951–2, when controversies arose as to the credentials and background of many supposed Congress leaders seeking tickets.[42] As a result, when it reached up to larger public meetings or the media, the radical rejection of Pakistan by militaristic communal organisations, for example, was often confused with more obviously secularist Congress activity. This has been documented in Joya Chatterji's study of the Hindu bhadralok in Bengali politics in the early 1940s. It was also clear in UP: meetings of the Arya Samaj in Lucknow in early 1943 pledged support for Gandhi but also involved violent denunciations of Pakistan and claimed the need to 'fight a civil war' to prevent it. Cultural movements were not immune to these trends. Under Tandon's chairmanship of the Thirty-First Hindi Sahitya Sammelan

[40] Robin Jeffrey, 'The Punjab Boundary Force and the Problem of Order, August 1947', *Modern Asian Studies*, 8, 4, 1974, 493–4.
[41] Dilip Menon, *Caste, Nationalism and Communism in South India: Malabar 1900–1948* (Cambridge: Cambridge University Press, 1994), pp. 152, 166.
[42] See UP Congress Committee papers, and Papers of G. B. Pant, NMML.

between 17 and 19 May 1943, representatives of the Mahabir Dal and Rashtriya Swayamsevak Sangh (RSS) attended.[43] Bhadralok cultural movements in Bengal, which involved literary constructions of historical Hindu patriotism against Muslim 'tyranny', also took on a new meaning in this era of the early 1940s.[44]

There were, however, instances where organisations mobilised with a less ambiguous and more direct communal agenda. A body that also clearly fell into this category and one more closely watched by colonial officials and leading secularists was the RSS. Despite the discussion in the historical literature of this organisation's tightly bound and secretive bases and powerful exclusive ideology,[45] the political advantages in some localities of linking to local Congress party bosses were too attractive to ignore. Across the provinces of UP and Punjab in the mid-1940s, this organisation appeared from the reports of policemen to be developing rapidly. For example, in May 1943, ten training camps had been set up in Budaun and Aligarh. Officer training camps were organised for the summer in Moradabad and Banaras. Muzaffarnagar and Lucknow districts quickly developed as strongholds.[46] Membership of the RSS also related to aforementioned middle-class urban concerns about public health and stress on bodily fitness. For political extremist groups like the RSS, these concerns were taken up to promote what was described as 'physical culture' – combining a notion of defence of Indian/Hindu culture with a promotion of physicality.

The recruitment of the RSS in north India is something that is still worthy of much more in-depth research, not least because, by 1948, it was evident that members of the Sangh had gained jobs in areas that had positioned members centrally in the retributive partition violence. In reports prepared for the Government of India on officers dismissed for misconduct, there were series of railwaymen who had joined the RSS. These men had been serving, often in large blocks of posts in particular areas/departments, along some of the main lines covering western UP and Punjab.[47] And it was on the trains moving across the border that some of

---

[43]   APS 12 February; 21 May 1943.
[44]   Chatterji, *Bengal Divided*, pp. 160–6
[45]   See, for example, Walter K. Andersen and Shridhar D. Damle, *The Brotherhood in Saffron: The Rashtriya Swayamsevak Sangh and Hindu Revivalism* (Boulder: Westview Press, 1987); Christophe Jaffrelot, *The Hindu Nationalist Movement*.
[46]   Fortnightly Report for U.P. for the first half of June 1944. Home Political, (I) file 18/6/44 NAI.
[47]   'List of persons debarred by the Central Government or a State Government Service from government service, during the half year ending June 30, 1950', 'Exclusion from Government Service of persons on account of misconduct', PWD (B), file 9EG/1948, UPSA.

the most extensive and indiscriminate killing took place over 1947–8. The RSS was also involved in this region, in one of the worst instances of pre-partition violence at Garmukhtesar fair between 6 and 12 November 1946, and here we have an example of how the involvement of volunteer organisations allowed attacks to be carefully 'planned'. Muslim casualties ran into the hundreds, as Hindus (who, according to official and Congress reports, were mostly Jats) returned from the Garhmuktesar fair in Meerut district. Little action was taken against what reporters believed were these organised attacks, as the Sub-Inspectors of Police in charge of the town and mela kotwalis were both Jats.[48] Witnesses suggested that the RSS were at the core of the action.[49]

The rapid rise, development and decline of military-style organisations often meant that there was little systematic about their overall organisation, however, even though their activities during moments of conflict meant that they could operate as quasi-military forces.[50] There were national and province-wide organisations like the Mahabir Dal, Khaksars, Qaumi Seva Dal and Hanuman Dal, but their activities and organisation depended upon the specific political context of their district or locality. For example, figures for the Mahabir Dal fluctuated greatly between districts in UP from 597 members in Bahraich to only thirteen in Saharanpur for the first half of 1941.[51] Even the relatively centralised Congress-related organisations were fluid and contingent in membership and organisation across districts. The membership figures for all Congress-related volunteer bodies in Gorakhpur district came to 8,835. In Moradabad, the total membership figure was only 445.[52] This again supports other evidence that the mobilisation of these movements depended to a great extent on the whim or power of a local factional leader, or group of leaders, for whom such movements could provide particularistic support. The classic example of this, although working at different levels of politics, was the movements initiated by P. D. Tandon. This connection to local affairs also meant that during moments of violence, Congress volunteer bodies were inevitably confused or allied with directly communal (usually Hindu) organisations. It was not just the Hindu organisations, however, that linked back to the Congress. The

[48] F. W. W. Baynes, Commissioner Meerut Division, to F. V. Wylie, 18 November 1946, 'United Provinces – Ministerial and Political Affairs', L/PJ/8/650 OIOC.
[49] Statement of Major General Shah Nawaz Khan, AICC Papers, file 20/1946 NMML.
[50] 'Note on the Volunteer Movements in India (II) December 1938' L/PJ/8/678 OIOC.
[51] Special Branch quarterly report, 8 May 1941 Police CID Box 82 file 1240/1941 UPSA.
[52] *Ibid.*

volunteer movements associated with the Khaksars[53] fluctuated in their allegiances between the Congress and the Muslim League and the Muslim Ahrar organisation allied with Congress volunteer movements over the period of the war. However, the powerful relationship between the Muslim National Guard and the Muslim League made it more likely that Hindu organisations would be associated, at least in public discourse about volunteer activity, with the Congress movements.

The sense that the main political parties were lining up with communal volunteer organisations was reinforced by newspaper reports, but there was a gap between media representation and political realities. It was easy for the print media to report on the mobilisation of joint Hindu–Congress drilling movements and processions, since this appeared to be the case on the surface, especially around religious festivals. However, more detailed scrutiny of these movements suggested that there were also very specific, often factional agencies involved in their promotion. This representational gap between media reports and political realities resembles the multilayered representation of 'communal violence' itself. Volunteer activity could be at once specific to a local political rivalry and pertinent to broader political conflict. In a similar way, apparent Hindu–Muslim conflict could appear to be about broad religious cleavage in some representations but knitted to local factional conflict at another. This situation suggests the many ways in which communalism, violence and the riot was, as a form of representation, used as a symbolic agenda in local political disputes: often quite localised and specific forms of communal mobilisation through their publicity more broadly fed into wider agendas of conflict and reprisal. As we will see in the next section looking at the immediate aftermath of India's partition, this was to be repeated in the violence following August 1947.

Crucial, too, is the question of how such organisations managed to exercise so much power at certain moments and contexts. We can explore this in terms of the areas where state sovereignty could be mobilised or captured. Thomas Blom Hansen has written extensively about the ambiguous nature of state sovereignty at the level of the local state, particularly with reference to the right to violence. For Blom Hansen, working on the Shiv Sena (far-right Hindu party) in contemporary Mumbai, there is an ambiguity around the nature and purchase of sovereignty when it comes to the right to violence and its exercise. Instead, we see the 'vernacularisation'

---

[53] The Khaksars were a Lahore-based organisation that expanded across north India. The organisation was founded in 1930 by Allama Mashraqi, and its initial aims involved social reform and 'uplift' of poorer Muslim communities of Punjab.

of democratic culture at the locality.[54] Blom Hansen's approach to Bombay would appear to be pertinent, although in a different way, to parts of north India, where the political future of key regions and subject/ citizens was in doubt or at least in a rapid process of transformation. In the situation of mid-1940s India, the high stakes of incipient or promised political power pushed local leaders to take advantage of existing drilling movements to protect their political interests or further local agendas. The principles of democratic mobilisation were compromised here, too, around the specific requirements of factional politics, patronage and, in some cases, the power of local community agendas. For example, in Aligarh, the politics of the University affected the nature of factional political mobilisation in the city.[55]

The response of government servants and officers was important too. Often denied access to the formal mechanisms for approaching the state (and as civil servants and policemen struggled to contain the claims and demands of rapidly changing political agencies), many factional leaders sought more informal means. They did this by turning towards informal structures of organisation – the local volunteer organisation, the factional leader and, through those, the symbolism of religious community. The local bodies – municipalities and district boards in particular – and district/ city Congress committees were important in allowing powerful men in each urban centre or district to influence and, in some cases, control the increasingly Indianised subordinate cadres of the civil services.[56] However, after the outbreak of war, when the ad hoc arrangements for rationing changed the nature of state power distribution, and especially by the mid-1940s when British departure seemed imminent, some of these formal mechanisms could no longer be relied upon to deliver stable political alliances. In these circumstances, not only could local militias be used to put pressure on political opponents, but also ad hoc symbolic messages became more relevant. As British authority weakened in India in the mid-1940s, competition for a range of bureaucratic and police posts changed to reflect the broad political divisions between Congress and League in many states.[57] To mobilise local militias in the period of political uncertainty, appeal to community or religious identity became increasingly attractive as a means for gathering temporary physical force and as the means to local

---

[54] Thomas Blom Hansen, *Wages of Violence: Naming and Identity in Postcolonial Bombay* (Princeton: Princeton University Press, 2001).
[55] See Zoya Hasan, *Dominance and Mobilisation*.
[56] For more details on this, see William Gould, *Bureaucracy, Community and Influence*.
[57] *Ibid.*

intimidation. For example, around the 1946 elections, policemen and bureaucrats in a range of constituencies across UP and Punjab were accused of political partisanship, particularly in connection with the Muslim League.[58] And where the future shape of 'Pakistan' seemed to be so unclear, possibly implying the incorporation of pockets of Muslim state autonomy within a broader Indian Union, the symbolism of community defence took on greater significance than it had ever had in the preceding decades.

(III) STATE TRANSFORMATION AND RELIGIOUS VIOLENCE

The events of India's partition, as the beginning of this chapter suggested, are often described as the key turning point in the political and social histories of South Asia. The high politics of India's partition have generated a thorough historical debate around the intentions of leading figures in the Muslim League and Congress, which question the extent to which there was any certainty about what 'Pakistan' would entail for most of the 1940s, or indeed whether partition itself was a favoured option, even for those apparently calling for it.[59] There is general agreement that the strongest support for 'Pakistan', in whatever form it might take in the 1940s, came from the Muslim minority areas of north India – namely, UP – where the historical power of the community was threatened. In contrast, in the Muslim majority areas of the North East and North West, Muslim elites had been well represented in the provincial governments between 1937 and 1939 and had formed political alliances with Hindu and Sikh politicians. They 'would gain little or nothing from Pakistan'.[60] This was to have significant implications for the future of provincial/linguistic groups in the future Pakistan, since, in order to get Punjabi and Bengali Muslims on side, the League needed to make concessions around provincial autonomy. The purpose of this section of the chapter is not to revisit that well-worn territory but to question the extent to which the historical accounts surrounding 1947 as an event really help us to explain the varied and contingent experiences of violence, displacement and 'religious' identity for the vast majority of Indians and Pakistanis. Moreover, it will look

---

[58] *Ibid.*, ch. 3.
[59] The fullest and most influential argument in this vein can be seen in Ayesha Jalal, *The Sole Spokesman*.
[60] Wavell to Pethick Lawrence, 20 August 1945, R/3/1/105, OIOC.

at how far a focus on 1947 as the key to examining 'communal' conflict can be unhelpful in that it places stress on the cataclysmic violence and displacement in very particular circumstances. Instead, this section will explore the processes of state transformation and their meaning for ordinary subject/citizens over the whole period of the mid to late 1940s.

As well as delineating the key debates over the political intentions of the Congress, League and British colonial administration, the mainstream accounts of India's partition discuss the issue of mass migration (estimated to have affected around fifteen to twenty million people) and the killings of between 600,000 and one million or more. The very uncertainty of these figures points to the importance of social and oral histories pursued both before and during 2007 (to mark the anniversary of Indian and Pakistani independence).[61] They also suggest the great difficulties in pinning down a collective narrative of these events. Whereas many would see the role of the historian to be charting a route through the complicated interlacing of narratives of any particular event, it appears that, here, the very voices of ordinary people make such a journey so contingent, so wrapped up with individual and family trauma spread over time and space that the quest for even smaller corroborating collective narratives becomes problematic.[62] This has resulted in a search for alternative sources to explore the histories of individual experience. Writers and commentators on India's partition, whatever discipline they hail from, make frequent reference to cultural production and output: fiction can represent emotion such as fear and anger in a more direct and nuanced way, often, than the bare historical record itself. Also significant has been the emphasis on women and women's accounts and the point that it has taken a long time for communities to wish to revisit, in the cold light of historical reflection, such painful experiences. Finally, a further problem in writing this history relates to the transitory

---

[61] See, for example, Rita Menon and Kamla Bhasin, *Borders and Boundaries: Women in India's partition* (New Brunswick: Rutgers University Press, 1998); and Urvashi Butalia, *The Other Side of Silence: Voices from the Partition of India* (London: Hurst, 2000). See also Yasmin Khan, *The Great Partition*; Vazira Yacoobali Zamindar, *The Long Partition and the Making of Modern South Asia*; Joya Chatterji, *The Spoils of Partition: Bengal and India 1947–1967* (Cambridge: Cambridge University Press, 2007).

[62] Although some historians think that the voices of 'ordinary' people are complementary to the mainstream political accounts of partition – see Bidyut Chakrabarty, 'Fluidity or Compartments: Hindus, Muslims and Partition', in Bidyut Chakrabarty, ed., *Communal Identity in India: Its Construction and Articulation in the Twentieth Century* (New Delhi: Oxford University Press, 2003) pp. 78–105.

nature of certain departments and their record keeping. For example, the Ministry of Relief and Rehabilitation records were dispersed in different areas, and where they reached state archives are very often incomplete.[63] Perhaps even more telling is the imbalance in partition narratives. Whereas there has been an outpouring of material from the Indian side, particularly in recent years, the same cannot be said for Pakistan, leading the historian to the conclusion that there are key narratives that have never been uncovered.[64]

As was argued in the last section, the violence leading up to partition, represented as 'communal', was often organised in its nature and took place around local power disputes, as the structures of state access became more uncertain. This is particularly clear in the period of extreme mass violence and migration in the months preceding and following August 1947. Yet, as was shown at the beginning, the context for this violence and the fact that state agents were often implicated carries the historian well beyond the immediate aftermath of partition and the first wave of refugees across the border in either direction. This is important because the context for what appeared as Hindu–Muslim violence over the mid-1940s was not unique to the specific phase of state transformation surrounding Indian independence, but was also part of a longer-term situation of state permeability and uncertain sovereignty. In this phase, the problem of 'communalism' was represented by contemporaries of one of a general range of 'crisis' factors, including food control and supply, rationing, refugees and their status as 'citizens' and, perhaps most importantly, the desire in government to assert authority and control over the 'law and order' apparatus. Whereas the explanations for violence could be varied and contingent, the representation of violence was clearly used by governments at all levels to justify state coercion and the perpetuation of older colonial enactments to ensure 'public order'. For example, in early 1948, following the assassination of Mahatma Gandhi, members of the RSS were arrested, and the Maintenance of Public Order (Temporary) Act was extended as a means of also controlling Muslim organisations and communists. It also justified the need for many Congress leaders at the Centre for a strong centralised state system and the continuation of older bureaucratic and police structures.

---

[63] For example, the UP Ministry of Relief and Rehabilitation records, although available in part in the UP State archives, are thin.
[64] An exception here would be Sarah Ansari, *Life After Partition: Migration, Community and Strife in Sindh, 1947–1962* (Oxford: Oxford University Press, 2005).

This view of 'communalism' as one of many threats to the nation state was associated, too, with concerns about the conduct of electoral politics over the late 1940s and early 1950s. Jawaharlal Nehru reported a conversation during the 1951 Congress Working Committee meeting with Sampurnanand and Rafi Ahmed Kidwai, in which discussion turned to the 'general situation … and more especially, the deteriorating law and order situation in various parts of the country as well as the food situation, which, bad in itself, must necessarily add to the difficulties of the law and order situation'. Nehru's concern, in looking back over the two years previous, was that the general elections might lead to 'disorder on a large scale'.[65] This note of pessimism was not just the product of his recent battle to gain control of the Congress organisation, against P. D. Tandon and Hindu conservatives in the Congress (including Patel).[66] It was also interconnected with a series of events in which the central government had taken upon itself the task of enhancing its sovereignty and control over a range of different 'challenges'. Bringing Hyderabad into line, struggling to harness conflict in Kashmir was in the background, but of even more direct concern to the Congress regime across India was the spectre of political opposition from different ends of the ideological spectrum – from communism to the Hindu right. The newspapers of 1948–50 discussed in detail the on-going police battle against 'communists' and the RSS in a way that strongly resembled the colonial fight against 'revolutionary terrorism'. Indeed, some of the same structures of government authority were mobilised to deal with these threats to Congress power.

Threats to the political mainstream in the form of communal mobilisation was easily transposed in political discussion to 'threat to the state'. And such problems connected internal communal organisations to the uncertain 'Indian' status (in the eyes of some Congress and Hindu organisations) of north India's Muslims and their supposed relationship to Pakistan. For example, in a speech on 21 January in Jhansi, G. B. Pant, the UP premier, suggested at a public meeting that the government would punish anyone who worked against the integrity or independence of the country.

---

[65] Nehru to Pant, 13 April 1951, Papers of G. B. Pant, File III, Reel 1 – 'Correspondence with Nehru', NMML.

[66] For a discussion of this struggle, see Bruce Graham, *Hindu Nationalism and Indian Politics: The Origins and Development of the Bharatiya Jana Sangh* (Cambridge: Cambridge University Press, 1990), pp. 18–32.

Many of those who believed in separatism and looked for inspiration and guidance to other quarters have already quitted this country and those who have remained will be closely watched and dealt with. They shall have no place in the country and if they do not desist from their anti-national activities, they will make their position difficult.[67]

Pant continued in the same vein: that India was many times militarily and politically stonger than Pakistan and that, in defence, the Home Guards and the Prantiya Raksha Dals were springing up around and about and the armed police had increased in strength. Finally, Pant spoke strongly against the RSS: the talk of a theocratic state was foolish and, for Pant, in any case Hindus are in the majority, so politics would reflect their beliefs.[68] As we will see in later chapters, this focus on the potential 'communalism' of the minority as a means of buttressing state power was common among other regimes in South Asia, notably Sri Lanka.

This was a phase of uncertainty in state power at all levels, articulated most obviously from the centre. At an everyday level, the print media and citizens' organisations asked what independence actually now meant when citizens' identities could be ambivalent and when the resources needed to access an ever-expanding state largesse were becoming increasingly important. Nehru's comment about the likelihood of castes and communities using their spokespersons to mobilise their interests was very much connected to this transforming situation and the anticipation that parallel structures of authority had marked the 1940s and would continue to do so. This concern manifested itself, too, in a perception of corruption, especially around rationing and food control, which once again seemed to justify the need for the exercise of powerful state control mechanisms in all spheres. Throughout the 1940s, but particularly towards the end of the decade when the promise of an independent, developmental state seemed already to be somewhat empty, newspapers reported cases of local schemes to control the rationing machinery. In files of officers in charge of this administration, this too linked to the fear of Muslim control in India of some of the key posts. The food and civil supply administrators were generally given other tasks of relief and rehabilitation of refugees. In many cases, refugee organisations came into north India with tales of Muslim violence, and the existing Muslim administrators came into the spotlight. For example, notions of corruption in food supply

---

[67] 'Give Unstinted Loyalty to Government: UP Alone can repel any enemy attack, says Premier' *National Herald* (Lucknow), 22 January 1948, p. 7.
[68] *Ibid.*

were elaborated, in some cases, with charges of 'communalism' in the press.[69] Accusations against Muslim officers continued into the early 1950s, and the idea that such officers were effectively agents of the Muslim League became a means of suggesting that they were favouring Muslim businessmen and political interests. Such accusations, for example, were made against a Town Rationing Officer of Banaras.[70] In some cases, the failures of particular departments were blamed on Muslim evacuees. And in the 'efficiency drive' in the civil services and police of the early 1950s, supposed links to Pakistan were used in other departments as a pretext for rooting out useless officers.[71]

Because of the interplay of representational communal politics and local state authorities, much of the violence shortly after independence also implicated government servants and policemen. Some of the most insightful and direct reporting in this respect on the partition violence before and shortly after independence can be found in Mridula Sarabhai's reports introduced at the front of this chapter. Her letters from Amritsar in November 1947, for example, detailed the involvement of police and politicians in looting and organised attacks. After the arrest of one police inspector at Taran Taran, Rs 30,000 worth of property was recovered. Another sub-inspector, Gur Dayal Singh, was found in possession of Rs 60,000 of property in his own house. He had conducted a hunger strike in protest, since he claimed to be working under the instructions of political leaders – passing to Sarabhai the names of some of the Punjab ministers. Sub-inspector Jagendra Singh was reported as being responsible for organising attacks on Muslims in the Beas Area, including the looting of the goods train there.[72]

The involvement of officials was also clearly evident in the Muslim areas of Old Delhi. Sarabhai was told that at 9:00 P.M. on the evening of 21 July 1948, a group calling themselves workers of the Social Services League had

---

[69] 'Members of DSO staff – complaint' 14 May 1955, 'Personal File of Sri Syed Ahmed', Food and Civil Supply, Box 21, File 791/45 UPSA.

[70] Jagnnath Prasad Srivastava, to Minister for Food and Supplies, 13 September 1950; 11 October, 'Mr Mohammad Izharul Haq (personal file)', Food and Civil Supply, Box 20, File 734/45 UPSA.

[71] For more detail on the politics of Muslim supply officers, see William Gould, 'From Subjects to Citizens? Rationing, Refugees and the Publicity of Corruption over Independence in UP', *Modern Asian Studies*, 42, 6 (2011), pp. 33–56.

[72] 'Situation Report of Amritsar', 10 November 1947, Sarabhai to Nehru and Gopalswamiji. Mridula Sarabhai Papers, File no. JN/1, 1947–8 'Communications to Pandit Jawaharlal Nehru (Prime Minister of India) by Mridula Sarabhai'. Reel no. 1, NMML.

come to the Muslim residential areas accompanying the Custodian Representatives and the police. They reportedly formed themselves into four batches and started to survey the houses and indiscriminately looted those that they considered to be empty. They also pushed out remaining occupants on the grounds that they were bogus occupants. Mostly women remained in this area and they could not resist the pressure. Shanti Dal workers came to know about this and tried to persuade the groups to stop. They asked for authorisation and it appeared that they had received the permission to proceed from the Minister of Relief and Rehabilitation.[73]

Behind this activity was often a politics of tit for tat, which related to a sense of masculine and communal pride. This did not, however, mean that displaced women were powerless in the face of these cases of violence and abduction. Recent research looking at displacement of populations of Bengal has argued that unattached women could still exercise some authority and were relatively reluctant in some cases to give up their independence by being returned to families. This was despite the fact that the 'rehabilitation' policies of the state did not allow for the distribution of refugee land to families with female heads.[74] Nevertheless, at the level of high politics, the issue of female abduction did become one of quid pro quo – a situation that, in general, affected the everyday problems of evacuees and the displaced. The issue of violence against 'Hindu' women, for example, was writ large in assembly debates at the end of the 1940s and in the early 1950s around the policies of rehabilitation themselves and also debates on the Hindu Code Bill.[75]

For Sarabhai, the very violence and uncertainty of the partition violence, in many areas, was caused by specific measures such as the Evacuee Property Ordinance. The havoc created by this ordinance, she claimed, was justified by officers on the plea that it was government policy and therefore had to be backed up to the maximum. In an interview with the Relief and Rehabilitation Officer, 'both the governments are at war with one another as far as the evacuee property question is concerned'. The ordinance was being used as a pretext to take advantage of confiscating

[73] 'Predominantly Muslim Area Survey Incidents', 22 July 1948, Mridula Sarabhai Papers, File no. JN/1, 1947–8 'Communications to Pandit Jawaharlal Nehru (Prime Minister of India) by Mridula Sarabhai'. Reel no. 1, NMML.
[74] See Uditi Sen, 'Refugees and the Politics of Nation Building in India', PhD Dissertation, University of Cambridge, 2009, pp. 242–7.
[75] For more detail on this process, see Eleanor Newbigin, 'The Hindu Code Bill'.

Muslim property, even if they had left for just a short period.[76] Sarabhai went on to suggest that the new ordinance proposed would only worsen the situation because of the way in which it would be implemented by those with very wide powers. It effectively led to the harassment of Muslims in general in north India without distinguishing them from the evacuee Muslims. This bolstered the Pakistani claim that India was losing the support and cooperation of Muslims in general. Sarabhai's informants pointed out that some members of particular families did not migrate as a matter of principle and therefore had a right to use family property. To oust them on the claim that a family member had gone to Pakistan only strengthened 'communal parties'. She concluded: 'Today, whenever a house or shop is sealed, a crowd collects and jeers and claps. "Phir hamara kya hua" Sanghites are heard telling the refugees. "We saved you from Pakistan, we saved Delhi for you and we are now getting your houses"'.[77]

In this period, there was a tendency for the 'refugee' problem to become part of the political arsenal of the conservative Hindu right in Indian politics at all levels and something that even the most moderate and leftist leaders found it difficult to ignore. For example, the crucial all-India battle for power in the immediate aftermath of partition pitched Nehru against P. D. Tandon. The private papers of the latter are littered with correspondence from refugee organisations, often framing their appeals in terms of 'Hindu' defence. But also important here was the sense in which the generation of the 'Hindu refugee' problem was wrapped up with concerns over property and local power. This implicated local governments too, and thereby added an alternative view of the problems of a broken-down state to the Sarabhai accounts. One UP Hindu correspondent helping Punjabi refugees moving into India wrote to Tandon expressing a sense of insecurity in relation to local police and administrators:

One Hindu was stabbed by some Muslim goondas … near the Devi Mandir. He with his party went to the police station to report and to the Civil Hospital for his medical certificate. Both the incharges of the police station and that of the civil hospital being Muslims created lots of troubles in his way to even record the report.[78]

---

[76] Note on the Evacuee Property Ordinance, 8 September 1949, Mridula Sarabhai Papers, File no. JN/1, 1947–8 'Communications to Pandit Jawaharlal Nehru (Prime Minister of India) by Mridula Sarabhai'. Reel no. 1, NMML.

[77] *Ibid.*

[78] Anoop Sundar Lal to P. D. Tandon 1.9.47, from Ghaziabad (lawyer), Tandon Papers, File 301, NAI.

The correspondent went on to suggest that Hindus should be swiftly militarised and armed, and that all key posts should be given to those who were not suspected of extra territorial loyalty. In case of conflict with Pakistan, he continued, the Muslim community should be treated with suspicion, all Muslims holding key posts throughout the province should be transferred to unimportant posts and all Muslims should be disbanded from the police.[79] Representatives from the Hindu refugee panchayat in Jaipur sent an array of letters to Tandon requesting assistance and representation at 'Question Time' in the Assembly. Again, many of these letters pointed the finger at the supposed Muslim bias in the administration, especially in relation to vacated Muslim properties. Refugees based in Saharanpur complained that the properties of Muslim merchants were being protected in the state, while their owners collected rent from Pakistan.[80] Representatives of Sindhi Hindu Refugee Panchayat actually provided the names of Muslim officials who they claimed had acted indiscriminately in favour of absentee Muslim landlords.[81]

If the partition violence is examined in a longer perspective, which takes into account the complex situation of violence against property, eviction and the long aftermath of migration or displacement, it becomes much more than just killing over a border between two communities. Indeed, as Chapter 1 argued, explorations of communalism in South Asia, in terms of its human impact, are perhaps more fruitful where they consider the aftermath of violence over the medium to longer term. How communities deal with the trauma of displacement and family loss and how those subjected to such events become objects of state scrutiny tell the historian a great deal about the implications of violence and the mechanisms whereby one set of historical conflicts leads to others. Often quite localised and specific forms of communal mobilisation through their publicity more broadly fed into wider agendas of conflict and reprisal. The specific reasons for extreme acts of violence could have as much to do with specific local circumstances as with the broader context of independence and partition. However, in nearly all cases, the mechanisms of the state – its personnel and coercive powers – regularly appeared as an integral facet of

---

[79] *Ibid.*
[80] Refugees at Saharanpur, Mangal Sen, Chimman Lal Sharma, Bhagwan Das, Vali Ram, Divan Chand – Punjabis to PDT, 9 Nov. 1947, No. 184, Tandon Collection, File 301, NAI.
[81] Representative of the Sindhi Hindu Refugee Panchayat, Jaipur, Durgapur Camp, Gopaldas H. Ladhani, Congress Social Worker. To P. D. Tandon, 29 January 1950. Tandon Collection, File 301, NAI.

such conflict. As we will see in later chapters, this complex interconnection between the broader mechanisms of state power and local authority continued to characterise violence between erstwhile religious communities in democratic India and Pakistan.

CONCLUSION

Indian independence brought about the end of one of world history's most ambitious colonial projects and the beginning of the world's largest democracy. Behind the speaker's podium and beyond the assemblies, the rhetoric and power of the newly independent states that were carved out of colonial India, there was considerable confusion about what freedom from colonial rule would really mean. And there was equally great uncertainty about the chances that unitary states could be maintained against, on the one hand, a holocaust of violence and, on the other, a stand-off between two national rivals based in diametrically opposing political ideologies. While the circumstances surrounding Indian and Pakistani independence highlighted the contingent nature of how individual subject/citizens experienced violence and political freedom, the combination of colonial retreat and sectarian conflict was not unique to South Asia. Indian leaders were not alone in grappling with the need to maintain secularism in the political superstructure, while religious community mobilisation continued right down the polity.

In India and Pakistan, citizens were faced with new boundaries that had both a physical and a conceptual significance. Many found themselves in a liminal space of not belonging entirely to either nation state. The rapid creation of lines on a map did not therefore just signal the physical delineation of possible new nation states. It also contributed to the ambiguities of national identity and the practical challenges for governments of matching national rhetoric with uneven state authority. These ambiguities surrounding the boundaries and borders of the state and its accompanying identities were, importantly, lasting. As the following chapters will explore, the problems of 'communalism', their connection to larger processes of national consolidation or territorial division continued to bear a relation to the basic colonial structures that had been forced to change so rapidly in the mid to late 1940s.

Kashmir provides the most concrete and obvious example of how the events around the mid to late 1940s would repeatedly come back to haunt relations between states and between different levels of the polity in South Asia. Kashmir brought into sharp focus the obsessive need of all Indian and Pakistani governments to promote national integration, and at the same time encapsulated the whole meaning of India and Pakistan as entities themselves. On the one side, the (undivided) Muslim majority state of Kashmir theoretically belonged to a state that was based on the ideological assertion of Muslims' separate political identities. On the other side, a secular state in which all religious communities were equally entitled to civic rights could also accommodate a state dominated by a religious community that was in a minority at the national level. On the back of this territorial dispute and the internal insecurities it generated, the partition also encouraged an arms race between India and Pakistan. And this ongoing international conflict has meant that families divided across the border are not easily able to visit one another, and consulates in big cities on each side of the divide quickly closed.[82]

Also important for India were the problems of setting up a secular state when the rhetoric of state power at the centre was often dramatically different to base realities in districts, towns and villages. And the debates concerning how 'secular' India was or how Islamic Pakistan should be were conditioned by 'the cathartic experience of partition'.[83] Partition, then, had a significance that extended beyond the physical lines on a map, for ordinary citizens for each country. Its effects and how those effects were remembered were also significant in the long-term state-consensus ideology of each of the new nations. It was a significance, crucially, that reached well beyond the specific events of the 1945–7 period. For example, the Indian National Congress's secularism was consistently ambivalent at local levels of political mobilisation. And importantly, this constrained its attempts (where leaders chose to champion such attempts) to neutralise more direct and extreme forms of 'communal' mobilisation in the remainder of the twentieth century.

[82] Bapsi Sidhwa, Urvashi Butalia and Andrew Whitehead, *History Workshop Journal*, 50, 2000, 230–8.
[83] *Ibid.*

6

Forging National Consensus and Containing Pluralism

South Asian States between 1947 and 1967

The dramatic events of India's partition in 1947 accompanied the carving up of old British India and presaged what was to become one of the world's most bitter and intractable international conflicts. This chapter will look at how this history, and the end of colonial power in South Asia, transformed the nature of religious and ethnic conflict. Public and media discussions of 'communalism' and its attendant violence were not suddenly different after 1947, but the terms of debate and discussion certainly shifted. Now, most Indians and Pakistanis were theoretically defined by the state as 'citizens' rather than 'subjects'. Rights were defined by democratic conventions and (rapidly in the case of India) a written constitution. This was a gradual process, not least because the basic frameworks of the administration and police remained as in the late colonial period. But now, the electoral politics that was beginning to develop through provincial autonomy from the late 1930s became a reality for all Indians. Local political rivalries had already mapped onto existing state structures, and one of the weapons in factional conflict was accusations of 'communal' partisanship.[1] A similar situation evolved in Ceylon (to become Sri Lanka in 1972) from 1948 under the United National Party, which dominated the island until 1956, although here, as we will see, tension between different ethnic communities became more pronounced. In Pakistan, power was more centralised, and the legislatures had much less authority. The domination of Punjabis and

---

[1] See more in the next chapter and, for example, 'Representations against Algu Rai Shastri, Azamgarh district (East), cum Ballia district (West)' AICC Papers, Election files, file 4617A 1951, NMML.

migrants from UP in Pakistan also created specific, cross-cutting ethnic tensions that went to the root of state power. Based on an entirely different idea of national identity, Pakistan's ethnic and religious conflicts were not analysed by observers in terms of a fragile 'secularism' as in India.

Communalism, ethnic conflict and sectarianism in both India and Pakistan often related to the specific nature of the relationship between the two states. First, the experiences of partition violence became a frame of reference for future conflict, even if sometimes only in a symbolic way. This created uncertainty not only for Hindu minorities in Pakistan, most of whom eventually opted for India, but also for many Indian Muslims who were forced to move, in the first instance, to Pakistan, but then took the option to return and found that their status as 'Indian' citizens was ambiguous.[2] The position of many Muslims in India was now quite fragile. Formally, the partition had helped to justify the establishment of a secular state in India: the country's accommodation of all religious communities with full citizenship rights acted as a theoretical counterpoise to the idea of 'Pakistan', as we saw in the last chapter. However, the essential fragility of secularism in India quickly exposed Nehruvian rhetoric as an unstable representation of Indian realities. First, the memories of 1947 had helped conservatives to limit the pace of social reform. This was evident, for example, in the watering down of the Hindu Code Bill, which aimed to empower women in matters of inheritance and divorce. Second, tension and war between India and Pakistan completely transformed the position of Muslims in India and Hindus in Pakistan. In India, though the secular constitution protected the interests and rights of minorities, Muslims, particularly government servants and policemen, were immediately placed under suspicion if they joined religious movements or parties. Most famously, Vallabhbhai Patel, India's first Home Minister, made it clear that Muslims in India would have to 'prove' their loyalty. Third, following independence, the ambiguities of national identity for India's Muslims were reinforced by India's forced integration of Hyderabad and Junagadh and the war created over Kashmir. And the centralising tendencies of governments over this period presupposed a majoritarian Indian identity that did not sit comfortably with other regional/ethnic identities. Finally, and perhaps most importantly of all, the letter of constitutional rights set out in 1950 did not prevent the continued reference to religious

---

[2] For a detailed study of this over the Punjab border, see Vazira Zamindar, *The Long Partition*.

community in everyday political mobilisation – a situation that, by the early 1980s, allowed parties of the Hindu right to re-enter more forcefully the political frame in key regions across India.

(1) NATIONAL INTEGRITY, REGIONAL SEPARATISM AND THE POLITICS OF MINORITIES

Following independence, 'national integrity' and unity were central concerns for governments of all of the South Asian states – concerns that governments felt the need to resolve through either force or accommodation. Management and containment of religious and ethnic minorities and the control of regional separatism were the general approaches in all cases, but means and ends varied. To differing degrees, governments had to present a form of 'unity in diversity', which balanced forces pulling in two different directions. On the one hand, the new rulers of India, Pakistan and Ceylon/Sri Lanka paid lip service to the idea of minority rights and the liberal constitutional rhetoric of the postwar international consensus, promoted further by anti-colonial nationalist parties. On the other hand, governments' commitments to the idea of 'diversity' were usually shallow. As ruling parties presented the façade of national integration in a range of public postures, this was often accompanied by party attempts to promote a dominant national identity. The latter could promote exclusive rather than inclusive ideologies. Agents of the state and political leaders took the lead in shaping or defining national culture and identity, even though some powerful forms of Indian nationalism had been based in ideas that essentially critiqued the 'state'.[3] In all cases, officially sponsored 'national' identities and cultural practices tended to be associated (sometimes in subtle ways) with a particular ethnic or religious group or coalition of dominant interests: Hindu 'majoritarianism' in India,[4] Punjabi–UP Muhajir dominance in West Pakistan and Sinhali control and dominance in Ceylon/Sri Lanka. In the case of India, Hindu 'majoritarianism' was more of a political posture than a discrete coalition of interests, and was to be associated with the rise of the Hindu right from the early 1980s. As such, it was concealed in the years immediately following independence and was extremely varied in its purchase at the level of state governments.

---

[3] See, for example, the exploration of the political thought of M. K. Gandhi in Anthony Parel, *Gandhi: Hind Swaraj and Other Writings* (Cambridge: Cambridge University Press, 1997).
[4] See Prakash Chandra Upadhyaya, 'The Politics of Indian Secularism', *Modern Asian Studies*, 26, 4, 1992.

In Pakistan and Ceylon, by contrast, the dynamics of ethnic conflict in the shaping of national culture and politics was less subtle. In the former, dominance of national political structures was much more about an all-out conflict between East and West Pakistan, on the one hand, and regional/ethnic rivalries, on the other. In the latter, a basic division between the majority Sinhali and minority Tamil populations led to Sinhalese Buddhists' attempted domination and appropriation of the symbols of national culture.

In the case of India, the tension between the realities of social heterogeneity and the centralising/homogenising interests of a dominant majority was illustrated within the successor regime to the Raj itself. Based around a single dominant 'national' party, the Congress claimed to represent all Indians. Being broadly based, it was a composite of wide-ranging political views, especially in the early years of its operation as a political party in the 1920s and 1930s. After independence too, it had to contain and accommodate a range of political, regional, linguistic, ethnic and religious tensions and differences.[5] The All India Congress Committee had made critical decisions in the mid-1940s leading up to independence, not least accepting partition, as a way of asserting the power of the centre over the states and regions. For this reason, it was already committed to the restraint of regionalism. At critical moments, the exponents of cultural majoritarianism, who believed in the importance of a strong central government, were exposed: during the debates surrounding the Hindu Code Bill from 1949 to the mid-1950s, the customary systems of personal law across India were lightly reformed, and it was clear that a high-caste northern Hindu agenda had triumphed.[6] In the years following independence, political organisations of the left and right and those associated with the old Muslim League were also suppressed.

It was figures such as P. D. Tandon, K. M. Munshi, Syama Prasad Mukherjee (leader of the Hindu Mahasabha in the late 1940s) and Vallabhbhai Patel who were strongest in their opposition of minority or regional separatism and the promotion of a unitary Indian culture. This was a culture many of whose exponents would not tolerate divergence from the promotion of Hindi as a national language. For example, K. M. Munshi, Governor of UP between 1952 and 1957, was rebuked by

---

[5] Paul R. Brass has, for example, shown how Congress became a party of 'consensus' by the early 1950s, for example, through the departure of Congress Socialists in 1948 and the accommodation of the others. Paul Brass, *Factional Politics in an Indian State*, pp. 40–4.

[6] For more detail on this, see Eleanor Newbigin, 'The Hindu Code Bill'.

Nehru for publicly suggesting that Urdu should only be promoted if in the Nagri script.[7] In its answer to the apparent threat of linguistic and regional separatism immediately following independence, the Congress High Command appointed a Linguistic Provinces Commission to look into the formation of the provinces of Andhra, Kerala, Karnataka and Maharashtra, and again pushed for a unitary solution in the first instance. The Linguistic Provinces Committee that followed the Commission included Vallabhbhai Patel, Pattabhi Sitaramayya and Nehru, and concluded that 'The first consideration must be the security, unity and economic prosperity of India and every separatist and disruptive tendency should be rigorously discouraged'.[8]

The concerns of the Congress regime about national integrity in India in the early 1950s through to the late 1960s were of course related to the experience of partition and its immediate aftermath. Independent India had come into being, as it were, on the back of an argument about the unity of India. The resultant cold war, involving actual conflicts in 1947–8 (known as the First Kashmir War), 1965, 1971 (around the Bangladesh liberation movement) and 1999, defined both the foreign and 'security' policy of both states. Importantly, all but one of the specific conflicts with Pakistan involved Kashmir, which, although part of the Indian Union, was given a special semi-autonomy under the Indian constitution in article 370. Modification of the constitutional status of Kashmir was one of the rallying cries of the right in Indian politics, and since independence, resistance to all forms of ethnic, religious or linguistic recognition has generally been associated with political conservatism. The conservative reactions to 'separatism', principally in Jammu and Kashmir, have been reinforced by on-going secessionist movements in the region. Conservative reaction was also contained within the Congress movement, which had always accommodated a wide array of ideological positions. In fact, those championing the idea of Indian integrity (from any ideological standpoint) have been able to claim, by opposing forms of special recognition for minorities and regions, that they espouse the 'true' secular principles of the Indian nation.

Nevertheless, Indian governments did have to take the issue of state reorganisation more seriously from the 1950s, and in setting up the States Reorganisation Commission (SRC) in December 1953, the central

---

[7] Jawaharlal Nehru to K. M. Munshi, 22 December 1955, Munshi papers. File 153, Reel 59, NMML.
[8] *Report of the Linguistic Provinces Committee, Appointed by the Jaipur Congress, December, 1948* (New Delhi: Government of India Press, 1949), p. 15.

Religion and Conflict in Modern South Asia

government attempted to diffuse growing demands for the creation of separate states in the south and west. The first manifestation of this came in the movement to create a Telugu-speaking state out of Madras. However, Nehru and other members of the government consistently stressed the importance of unilinguism and, in the case of Nehru himself, suggested that 'development' depended upon a strong centre, especially in the light of the first Five Years Plan (1951–6). The States Reorganisation Act of 1956, while redrawing the boundaries of states on a linguistic basis, nevertheless simplified the constitutional basis of states to create (with the exception of Jammu and Kashmir) a greater degree of uniformity between states. For the most part, however, central governments did not tend to react to regional movements until it was politically expedient to do so. The separate state of Maharashtra was formed after Congress's relatively poor showing in the region in the 1957 general elections, and in by-elections leading up to the formation of the state in 1960.[9] In the Punjab, the Sikh Akali Dal, which maintained close links to Sikh religious organisations, came to power at a regional level in 1966, which allowed them to successfully establish a 'Punjabi Suba' (land where Punjabi is spoken), leading to the drawing of Punjab's current boundaries. In this case, the accommodation of the Akali Dal's demands did not lead to the longer-term placation of Sikh ethno-religious mobilisation, since Sikhs were only a bare majority in the state and therefore electorally not secure. This resulted in the on-going recourse by the Akali Dal to more direct forms of mobilisation, especially in the 1980s, as the next chapter will explore.[10]

In some cases, attempts at direct secession from the Indian Union were involved (as in the case of Hyderabad and Junagadh), and in these areas, the central government stressed, usually in aggressive terms, the need to maintain the Union's integrity. The princely states of both Hyderabad and Junagadh (in the modern state of Gujarat) were 'resolved' by the Union government with the use of force and economic sanctions. In the case of Hyderabad, the Nizam's desire either to remain independent or to accede to Pakistan was accompanied by a large-scale agrarian rebellion – the communist Telangana movement – which fought against the landlord exploitation of the poorer Hyderabadi peasantry. In September 1948,

---

[9] Oliver Godsmark, 'The Mobilisation of Regional Identities in Post-Colonial Maharashtra: Responses to the Centre's Construction of a Nationalist Hegemony', Unpublished MA dissertation, University of Leeds, 2008.

[10] Atul Kohli, 'Can Democracies Accommodate Ethnic Nationalism?', in Amrita Basu and Atul Kohli, eds., *Community Conflicts and the State in India* (New Delhi: Oxford University Press, 1998), pp. 20–2.

the Indian army invaded the state in 'Operation Polo', forcing it to accede to the Union. Action against the communists followed, shifting between British-style military action and agrarian development policies. The state was eventually divided between the new linguistic provinces in the mid to late 1950s, but the Congress regime had shown as few scruples as the colonial state in using force and bypassing the normal criminal judicial system when it felt it was necessary.[11] In Junagadh, the central government used the bogey of 'Muslim communalism' to force the Muslim ruler to back down on his push to accede to Pakistan. In other areas, though, the challenge to Congress definitions of a united India did not involve secessionism but the presentation of an alternative vision or championing of 'Indianness'. For example, in Maharashtra, the Samyukta Maharashtra movement pushed for the recognition of Marathi speakers and for the formation of a separate state of Maharashtra over the period of states reorganisation by evoking the symbolism of Maratha power. The particular focus here was the cult of Sivaji, the seventeenth-century Maratha leader, traditionally championed by high-caste leaders in the tradition of Bal Gangadhar Tilak, but also, as shown in Chapter 2, by low-caste movements such as those led by Jotirao Phule at the end of the nineteenth century and non-Brahman movements in western India.[12] The Samyukta Maharashtra Samiti of the mid-1950s cut across class and caste divisions in an unprecedented way to present a Maratha vision of Indian unity that put a modern gloss on the older cults of Sivaji.[13]

In these administrative and political struggles to contain Indian regions and ex-princely states in a composite Indian nation, a common establishment view was that threats to national integrity represented a form of 'communalism' or were framed in terms of older colonial notions of 'law and order' – to be put down using the authoritative structures of the state.[14] In these arguments, communalism was no longer simply about Hindu–Muslim conflict in any particular locality or even just about a more

---

[11] Taylor C. Sherman, *State Violence and Punishment in India* (London: Routledge, 2010), pp. 168–9.

[12] Polly O'Hanlon, 'Acts of Appropriation: Non-Brahman Radicals and the Congress in Early Twentieth Century Maharashtra', in Mike Shepperdson and Colins Simmons, eds., *The Indian National Congress and the Political Economy of India 1885–1985* (Aldershot: Avebury, 1988), pp. 102–46.

[13] Godsmark, pp. 3–4.

[14] This can be seen in the early Congress government's easy adoption of the older colonial structures of policing. See David Arnold, 'The Congress and the Police', in Mike Shepperdson and Colin Simmons, eds., *The Indian National Congress and the Political Economy of India, 1885–1985* (Aldershot: Avebury, 1988), 208–30, especially pp. 218–19.

global idea of religious conflict. It became as much about opposition to an ideal of the Indian state and a composite Indian identity associated with it. Opponents of 'India', as envisaged by leaders in India's political main-stream, were fissiparous challenges comparable to that presented in the early to mid-1940s by the Muslim League. A similar kind of rhetoric surrounding the bogey of communalism emerged from regional move-ments like the Samyukta Maharashtra Samiti in the mid to late 1960s. In this case, the 'communalism' was generated by Gujarati opposition to the creation of Maharashtra and the need to include Bombay within it. The Gujarati Shethjis were presented in the Samiti's tracts as the 'alien' other. But here, ire was also directed at certain moments at the centralising drives of the central government.[15] Within Maharashtra, a regional form of ethnic exclusivism, which opposed the influence of 'outsiders' and tenden-cies towards separation (e.g. the claims for autonomy in the Vidharba and Marathwada regions of the state) was championed by the Shiv Sena. The Sena was formed in 1966 and concentrated on Maharashtra-centric pos-turing, violence against South Indians coming into the state and opposi-tion to Muslims and the left.[16]

During the 1950s and 1960s too, Tamil leaders also challenged the idea that all regions should be unambiguously incorporated into the Indian Union. These demands, which argued at the very least for greater autonomy from the centre, were based to a great extent on the promotion of the Tamil language and the idea that Tamils are racially and culturally separate. This 'Dravidian' identity presented Brahman dominance as an example of northern Indian cultural and political domination. The Congress's traditional power in this state was, however, based in the communities of Brahmans, and the Justice Party was formed partly in reaction, championing Dravidian interests, as we saw in an earlier chapter. Self-determination of non-Brahman communities in the region, then, was also based in party political opposition to Congress dominance. Although the creation of Madras state (later Tamilnadu) following states reorgan-isation in 1956 allowed the Centre to somewhat placate Dravidian leaders, the Dravida Munnetra Kazagham (DMK) continued to present an anti-

---

[15] Y. D. Phadke, *Politics and Language* (Bombay: Himalaya Publishing House, 1979); Ram Joshi, 'Politics in Maharashtra – An Overview', in Usha Thakkar and Mangesh Kulkarni, eds., *Politics in Mahashtra* (Delhi: Himalaya, 1995).

[16] Mary Fainsod Katzenstein, Uday Singh Mehta and Usha Thakkar, 'The Rebirth of Shiv Sena in Maharashtra: The Symbiosis of Discursive and Institutional Power', in Amrita Basu and Atul Kohli, eds., *Community Conflicts and the State* (New Delhi: Oxford University Press, 1998), pp. 215–38.

Congress, anti-high-caste, ethnicised political front. This involved the use of movies as a means of demonising high castes and promoting the glories of Tamil history. Following Nehru's death in 1964, attempts to reimpose Hindi as a national language led to riots and violent demonstrations in Tamilnadu and the eventual victory of the DMK in the 1967 elections in the state. Once Congress was ousted from power, though, the strong ethnic tone of the party was diluted.[17]

Centralising tendencies also characterised Ceylon/Sri Lanka's early post-independence history. Here, the same constitution on which independence was granted in 1948 was maintained up until 1972. According to the Census of 1981, seventy-four per cent of the population of Sri Lanka was Sinhalese, the majority of whom were Buddhist. The Tamil population was divided into Sri Lankan Tamils and Indian Tamils, constituting 12.6% and 5.6% of the population respectively in this period. The remaining minorities were varied, and there were significant Christian (8%) and Muslim (7.4%) communities that cut across the other ethnic groupings.[18] The main concentration of Tamil settlement is in the Jaffna peninsula to the north, and, as we will see below and in later chapters, regional distributions were crucial in the dynamics of ethnic conflict and minorities' mobilisation over the entire period. Ceylon's post-independence politics was based in a multi-party democracy dominated by two parties – the centre-right United National Party (UNP) and the centre-left Sri Lanka Freedom Party (SLFP), founded in 1951, which alternated in government between 1956 and 1977.[19] In symbolic form, this meant the immediate domination of the Sinhalese majority in controlling the images of national independence – the flag contained the historical symbol of the Sinhalese, the lion; a Citizenship Act passed in November 1948 deliberately excluded Indian Tamils from Sri Lankan citizenship and thereby the franchise (although Indian Tamils had been able to vote in the 1931, 1936 and 1947 elections).[20] And the Sinhalese-Buddhist slogan of *Rata, Jatiya, Aagama* ('Country, race, religion') originally evoked by the Sinhalese Buddhist nationalist, Anagarika Dharmapala, became a powerful slogan of the Sinhalese political majority by the mid-1950s.[21] The relationship

[17] Atul Kohli, 'Can Democracies Accommodate Ethnic Nationalism?', pp. 17–20.
[18] S. J. Tambiah, *Sri Lanka: Ethnic Fratricide and the Dismantling of Democracy* (London: I. B. Taurus, 1986), pp. 4–5.
[19] James Manor, ed., *Sri Lanka in Change and Crisis* (London: Croom Helm, 1984), p. 2.
[20] Satchi Ponnambalam, *Sri Lanka: The National Question and the Tamil Liberation Struggle* (London: Zed Books, 1983), pp. 72–9.
[21] *Ibid.*, pp. 88–92.

between 'race' and Buddhism was an important one here, with the latter religious tradition frequently depicted as a 'protector' of the Sinhalese and the key to the 'ancient civilization' of Sinhalese culture and the Sinhalese 'race'.[22]

As discussed in Chapter 2, some of the most important writing about 'communal conflict' in Sri Lanka relates the emergence of the post-independence ethnic conflict to particular social and economic changes. Most important here were the turn-of-the-century Buddhist revival, the pressures of market orientation and economic depression between the wars. Over the first three decades of the twentieth century, Sinhalese identity, this work argues, has been moulded by the increasing ways in which the Tamil minority has been viewed as 'foreign' against the backdrop of a gradually strengthening Sinhalese cultural nationalism.[23] At the root of this majoritarianism is a collective insecurity among revivalists that the Sinhalese 'race' is and has always been under threat from the hundreds of millions of Hindus in India, from which the Tamil minority is derived.[24] These arguments, although useful in their delineation of the symbols of national dominance among the Sinhalese communities, tend to result in a somewhat primordialist view of ethnic/religious difference in Sri Lanka. As we will see, there were often contingent and highly complex reasons for conflict and violence on the island, particularly from the late 1970s.

However, the commonly cited grievances of Tamil minorities are uncontested in the literature. Made scapegoats for the rural depression of the 1930s, for example, Indian Tamils were also deprived of full political rights after independence in 1948. The 1948 constitution for Ceylon, drawn up by Lord Soulbury, rejected from the outset the Ceylon Tamil demand for communal representation in the legislature. Effectively, as in India in relation to the Muslim communities, this placed the rights and demands of the Tamil minority in the hands of the Sinhalese and the extent of their goodwill. Extremely significant has been the relative neglect of Jaffna, with the region largely left out in the allocation of development funds sponsored by foreign aid, slow agricultural development and no benefits from the harnessing of the Mahaweli river. The implementation of development and the contracts that went with it also operated along the

---

[22] See Kumari Jayawardena, 'Ethnic Consciousness in Sri Lanka: Continuity and Change', in *Sri Lanka The Ethnic Conflict: Myths, Realities and Perspectives* (New Delhi: Navrang, 1984), pp. 116–7.

[23] John D. Rogers, 'Social Mobility, Popular Ideology and Collective Violence', pp. 594–5.

[24] James Manor, 'Introduction', in James Manor, ed., *Sri Lanka in Change and Crisis*, pp. 8–9.

lines of political patronage in which the Sinhalese majority were able to exert the most political leverage: patron–client linkages were made between applicants for the bureaucracy and local politicians at the centre. Tamil leaders, usually representing regional interests in Sri Lanka, did not have the same influence in the central government.[25] Academic writing has often, via these contexts, depicted historical comparisons between the earlier, relatively minor clashes such as that of 1915 and the much more serious conflicts that emerged from 1958 as manifestations of 'spates' or specific periods of violence.[26] Investigation of 'ideology' was key to this research. For example, the literature on 'communalism' and violence in Sri Lanka since the late 1950s has generally been concerned with the construction of 'myths of nationhood', on the one hand, and the link between violence and Buddhism as a religion, on the other.[27] This kind of research became particularly popular from the mid-1980s in response to the widespread rioting and violence – a theme that will be explored in the following chapter – and it should certainly be treated cautiously for examining the multifaceted and multilayered nature of the conflicts in Sri Lanka.[28]

However, some of the earliest free elections in Sri Lanka did involve the relatively uncomplicated assertion of Sinhalese majoritarianism. In the 1956 elections in Sri Lanka, both of the major parties adopted a 'Sinhalese only' policy as a means of encouraging an indigenous and consolidated national identity that critiqued English influence. In a situation that compares to the promotion of Hindi in north India, this cultural nationalism, espoused in the context of democratic mobilisation, served to marginalise minorities – in this case, the Ceylonese and Indian Tamil communities. But in other respects, this was very different to the situation surrounding Hindi in India. Part of the appeal of the 'Sinhalese only' policy in 1956 was the suggestion that the Tamil minority had taken a lion's share of government jobs.[29] The appeal to a cultural nationalism that linked language, race and religion (Buddhism), then, was clearly articulated around struggles for state power at multiple levels, in which Sinhalese saw themselves as

[25] Newton Gunasinghe, 'The Open Economy and Its Impact on Ethnic Relations in Sri Lanka', *The Ethnic Conflict*, pp. 198–200.
[26] *Ibid.*, pp. 197–8.
[27] See, for example, Stanley Jeyaraja Tambiah, *Buddhism Betrayed? Religion, Politics, and Violence in Sri Lanka* (Chicago: University of Chicago Press, 1992).
[28] For a critique of these approaches, particularly the writing of Bruce Kapferer, see Jonathan Spencer, 'Collective Violence and Everyday Practice in Sri Lanka', *Modern Asian Studies*, 24, 3, 1990.
[29] For a discussion of these concerns, see Tambiah, *Ethnic Fratricide*, pp. 78–9.

disadvantaged in the past: it took place through elections to legislatures, but also appeared at a more everyday level of government employment and opportunity. Bandaranaike's Sri Lanka Freedom Party (SLFP), formed in 1951, won the elections largely on the basis of its 'Sinhalese only' credentials and enshrined the 'Sinhalese only' approach in legislation.[30] Over time, this was to have a dramatic effect in promoting the interests of Sinhalese in the, until then, Tamil-dominated civil services. In 1956 and again more seriously in 1958, rioting and violence broke out between Ceylon Tamils and Sinhalese.[31] Significantly, throughout the 1960s in Sri Lanka, even the leftist and Marxist parties abandoned the notion of a composite multilingual state/national identity.[32]

In the face of the 'Sinhala only' Act of 1956, representatives of the Tamil minority were indirectly encouraged to promote a different kind of identity politics. In 1957, the Ceylon Tamil leader, S. J. V. Chelvanayakam, entered into a pact with the Prime Minister S. W. R. D. Bandaranaike to recognise Tamil as the language of administration in the north and east of the country and to afford these regions a measure of autonomy. The agreement was part of a deal in which Chelvanayakam's Tamil Federal Party (FP) would help to defeat the minority government of Dudley Senanayake, and was therefore carried out largely as a deal to further political rivalries. In September 1958, the Tamil Language (Special Provisions) Act was passed, which allowed Tamil to be used as a medium of instruction and administration in the Northern and Eastern provinces (the regions of Tamil population concentration). The deal and a later agreement made in 1965 were not in the end honoured. For most of the late 1950s and 1960s, the FP was the principal constitutional representative of Tamil political rights, attempting to carve out deals for the Tamil minority through legislation and political negotatiation. It was only from the mid to late 1970s that Tamil militants started to turn more towards extra-parliamentary methods. The background to this shift was the growing legitimacy of the claims for the Tamil state of 'Eelam' from around May 1972 with the formation of the Tamil United Front (TUF).

[30] Rogers, p. 595. The 'Sinhala Only Act' or The Official Language Act made Sinhala the sole official language in Ceylon. Some leftist parties, the Communist Party of Ceylon and the Tamil National parties all opposed the Act.
[31] James Manor, *The Expedient Utopian: Bandaranaike and Ceylon* (Princeton: Princeton University Press, 1988).
[32] Robert N. Kearney, *Communalism and Language in the Politics of Ceylon* (Durham: Duke University Press, 1967).

There were other ideological bases for this link between national and ethnic politics. Stanley Tambiah's work has been at the forefront of approaches to Buddhism and violence, critiquing the Western assumptions that automatically relate its traditions to modern nonviolent ideologies. One problem with this approach is that it tends to assume that a pristine Buddhist tradition, divorced from secular violence and essentially 'betrayed', actually exists outside this context of conflict. It is difficult to argue that such a tradition ever existed in Ceylon/Sri Lanka. However, through the late colonial and early independence period, the monasteries of Ceylon increasingly and more overtly aligned themselves with state power. For Tambiah, the most significant changes in the politicisation of the monasteries subsequently took place in the mid to late 1970s, as monks increasingly sought to have a direct stake in that power. This represented the weakening of doctrinal Buddhism on the island, or its distortion, and the growing power of movements to protect Buddhism, by associating it with territory and secular power. For example, political factionalism over this period began to find its way into monastic life, as Buddhism was popularised, simplified in catechistic terms and disseminated using the modern media. This has resulted in a collectivist conception of Buddhist 'nationalism' or Buddhist 'democracy' – in other words, a kind of political Buddhism. The concrete results have been that, ideologically, the monasteries have been instrumental in pushing forward romanticised notions of the Sinhalese 'noble' peasantry – an organic ideology of Sri Lankan nationhood that has militated against the idea of a composite multi-ethnic nation. By the 1970s, the monks of all sects and temples divided to support one or more of the two main parties in Sri Lanka.[33]

There have also been more complex ideological developments in which the monasteries have contributed to state authoritarianism. One significant tradition in modern Sinhalese Buddhist nationalism links violence to the state to violence to the body. This has effectively allowed violence to be a rational response, according to specific everyday cultural practices, to violence against the state. Such configurations fitted with the Buddhist text *Mahavamsa*, in which the island of Sri Lanka was granted to the Sinhalese with the Tamils as latecomers who threatened the stability of the island.[34] Using these texts as an explanation for everyday violence in Sri Lanka has also been critiqued by other work explored later. However, it is true that

---

[33] Tambiah, *Buddhism Betrayed*, pp. 58–61.
[34] Bruce Kapferer, *Legends of People, Myths of State: Violence, Intolerance and Political Culture in Sri Lanka and Australia* (Washington DC: Smithsonian Institution Press, 1986).

such texts and traditions also demonised the Tamil community, relating it to images of hell and pernicious evil spirits – a theme that also very much reflected north Indian high-caste Hindu representations of the British, on the one hand, and Muslims, on the other.[35]

These ideological approaches to violence have other kinds of implications when we look at the actual experience of violence on a day-to-day level, which often complicate 'constructivist' ideas about ethnic identity (namely, that ethnicities are socially constructed).[36] The connections between socially constructed ethnic identities and the exercise of violence have been very difficult if not impossible to tease out, as earlier chapters have suggested. However, some research on 'everyday' politics has made some inroads. In work on the everyday and violence in Sri Lanka, Jonathan Spencer has argued that there is a kind of fascination with 'vicarious violence' – the desire to witness road accidents, killings, film violence or cartoon-style violence. This manifests itself in the form of violence that is seen in Buddhist representations of hell, but also in violence in Sri Lankan (and Indian) riots – burning, cutting and dismemberment. Spencer also plays with the notion of *lajja*, which roughly corresponds to 'shame' – an everyday cultural behaviour in rural Sri Lanka. This in turn is linked to the cultural practice of public humiliation, which Spencer has also seen as an important part of the violence that reached its height in the early 1980s, linking such rituals of shame to ragging at universities and gloating during elections or sports matches. Violence in this construction is described as the loss of the necessary modicum of *lajja* or 'shame'. Importantly, there are class (caste) and gender dynamics to this, since those of lowly social or ritual status are considered to have relatively little *lajja* to lose. Overt violence, anthropologists have argued, is very much patterned in terms of gender. Violence is also about male esteem or loss of esteem or challenges to masculine status.[37] However, whereas everyday violence is usually a clumsy affair, there is, according to Spencer, a way in which collective violence has strong ritualistic elements, which involve elements such as public humiliation.

A related but different approach to everyday violence in Sri Lanka (and India) has involved investigations of how it becomes 'institutionalised'

---

[35] See, for example, the idea of the extirpation of 'evil' foreign rulers in Acharya Vithal Chaturvedi, *Rajyakranti aur Bharatiy* (Saharanpur, 1932), PIB 27/24 OIOC.

[36] For a discussion of a range of theoretical approaches to 'ethnic violence' see James D. Fearon and David D. Laitin, 'Violence and the Social Construction of Ethnic Identity', *International Organization*, 54, 4, 2000, 845–77.

[37] Jonathan Spencer, 'Collective Violence and Everyday Practice in Sri Lanka', p. 617.

around local political concerns, which 'mobilise' ideas of broader ethnic/ religious conflict. In Sri Lanka since independence, the large majority of 'civil disturbances' and riots have taken place in the areas of colonisation schemes in which MPs bring political supporters to irrigated areas, or market towns where business competition is fierce, or the capital itself. Local political leaders, some have argued, have taken advantage of the existence of urban dissatisfaction and business rivalry to provide their networks with muscle. This has also, since the 1960s, drawn in the police. After the 1977 elections, another institution linked to the main political parties promoted the idea of Sinhalese majoritarianism in the workplace – the Jatika Sevaka Sangamaya (National Workers Organisation, JSS) under the presidency of Cyril Matthews. The latter drew upon Malaysia's official policy in the protection of the 'racial' interests of the Malay majority in the workplace in his promotion of Sinhalese workers' rights. The JSS has also been mobilised for the purposes of maintaining electoral support, and has been drawn into instances of urban violence, often in routine ways in the workplace.[38] In India too, the routine operation of political violence has implicated ethnic and 'communal' conflict, often through state institutions, on the one hand, and in some areas like Maharashtra and Mumbai, workers' organisations and unions dominated by the Shiv Sena, on the other. Here too, a regional notion of 'sons of the soil' becomes a political rallying cry during elections, and a justification for the victimisation of outsiders from southern (and more recently northern) India in the develop-ment of a 'plebeian' political culture.[39]

Collective violence in Sri Lanka therefore, in combination with work on India, provides some answers to the question of how ethnic identities and violence are related, and how far the promotion of particular ideas of religious or ethnic community create conflict. In Sri Lanka, violence was often methodical in nature – as will be seen in the next chapter, the 1980s violence between Tamils and Sinhalese was very often focussed on specific areas and organised by small groups of men according to defined plans. As in the other South Asian states, this organisation took place with the complicit assistance of party leaders and security forces, who in some cases either did nothing to prevent the violence (apart from warning some residents to leave the area in advance) or actively collaborated so

---

[38] Gananath Obeyesekere, 'The Origins and Institutionalisation of Political Violence', in James Manor, ed., *Sri Lanka in Change and Crisis* (London: Croom Helm, 1984), pp. 152–66.

[39] For more detail on this process in western India, see Thomas Blom Hansen, *Wages of Violence*.

that 'politically powerful figures controlled illegal operations in the shadow of the state'.[40] The use of the administrative services and criminal gangs to prop up local and factional power has also been an element of political mobilisation in India since the 1930s.[41] Importantly, as in India too, these instances of collective violence have been facilitated by the mobilising of bands of what are described as *goondas*. But the justification for their violence and its support by state agents is very much informed by a majoritarian cultural construction of the Tamil population as being naturally inclined towards support for radical and violent anti-state resistance. This allowed much of the violence in the south of Sri Lanka to be politically justified to national and international audiences in terms of 'self-defence'.

The 'institutionalisation' of political violence is common to all of the states of South Asia. In Pakistan, as we will see in more detail, the bureaucracy, police, and Inter-Services Intelligence (ISI) have been involved in the strengthening of routine political violence between different religious sects. However, while the structures of political rivalry are important in explanations of violence, particularly in everyday affairs, these structures only become important in a broader sense at times when the grounds for competition are translated along the lines of ethnicity or religion. Crucial to this process in all of our case studies is the parallel development of the idea of 'political religion' – the interface of changing ideas about religious community and belonging and the definition of national community. In India, one form this has taken is that of Hindu majoritarianism, which has formed a complex relationship with the longer-term championing of national integrity. In the case of Ceylon/Sri Lanka, it was the development of 'political Buddhism' that allowed for the popularisation and dissemination of a 'mass' understanding of national, political religion. In all of these processes, the nature of the state and how it changed was crucial. In the development of these connections between political ideology and religious change, there were of course a range of important economic and social developments in each of our South Asian states – most importantly India, to which we now turn.

(II) THE POLITICS OF 'COMMUNITY' IN 1950S AND 1960S INDIA

By and large, writers and researchers looking at the first four decades after independence in India have created a narrative of Congress dominance and

---

[40] Spencer, p. 617.
[41] See William Gould, *Bureaucracy, Community and Influence*.

power, examining in detail the nature of the 'Congress system'. Particular focus on Congress dominance has looked at relationships between national, state and local spheres of political mobilisation, the politics of 'development' and the winning of state licenses and permits for production.[42] In this writing, forms of clientelist politics are writ large in the formation of Congress authority at all levels of the polity, but particularly in the rural hinterlands.[43] Such research on post-independence Indian politics, most prominently based on the work of anthropologists and political scientists working around the 1960s, developed the notion of the political intermediary: local-level leaders who linked national Congress decisions and mobilisations to the lower levels of Indian politics via caste affinities and factional loyalties. One of the implications of this was the existence of a gap between the political ideals and rhetoric of an older English-speaking Indian political elite, surrounding political rights and institutions, and a more vernacular political culture.[44] An Indian establishment view was that communal mobilisation after independence resulted partly from the failure of the upper-level, secular ideals of the Nehruvian Congress to link down to the grassroots of political mobilisation. Nehru himself, throughout the term of his office as Prime Minister, reiterated his fear that patterns of local politics threatened to shatter the ostensibly secular and unitary ideals of the Congress. In writing about the first Indian general elections of 1951, for example, Nehru expressed a fear to G. B. Pant that they could lead to disorder on a large scale. 'A very large number of persons will be elected from constituencies which are relatively small in area and where probably narrow communal and caste considerations will be dominant. Each caste group will insist on its own candidate. Already there are indications of this'. For Nehru, this would lead to the collapse of democracy as parochial feelings prevailed.[45]

[42] Pranab Bardhan, *The Political Economy of Development in India* (Oxford: Oxford University Press, 1984); Rajni Kothari, 'The Congress System', in Zoya Hasan, ed., *Parties and Party Politics in India* (New Delhi: Oxford University Press, 2004), pp. 39–55. The literature is however much older, going back to Stanley Kochanek, *The Congress Party of India: The Dynamics of One-Party Democracy* (Princeton: Princeton University Press, 1968), and Stanley Kochanek, *Business and Politics in India* (Princeton: Princeton University Press, 1974).
[43] Paul R. Brass, *Factional Politics in an Indian State.*
[44] For a summary of the work that developed this theory of the intermediary, see Stuart Corbridge and John Harriss, *Reinventing India: Liberalization, Hindu Nationalism and Popular Democracy* (Malden: Polity, 2000), pp. 50–1.
[45] Jawaharlal Nehru to G. B. Pant, 13 April 1951. Papers of G. B. Pant, File III, Reel 1, Correspondence with Jawaharlal Nehru. NMML.

However, it was certainly the case for those writing about the politics of early independent India that the apparent communal competition that seemed ubiquitous in the late colonial period had now given way to an atmosphere of political accommodation across most of South Asia. Whereas historians examining the late colonial period across India examined the implications of 'Muslim separatism', the Congress–Muslim League divide, or the politics of communal identity, an uninitiated reader could be forgiven for thinking that sectarian and religious controversies had been wiped off India's political horizons by the early 1950s. Instead, work looking at the 1950s and 1960s charted the problems of working a secular democracy around issues of class interest politics, the Five Year Plans, agricultural reform and Nehruvian ideals of state-driven industrial expansion and national integration. This reflected the world view of Nehru himself, who, as the quotation above suggests, was actively opposed to any form of ethnic, caste or religious mobilisation in politics.[46] It also clearly suited those in positions of power throughout India to downplay the initial state rhetoric of social redistribution at the local levels of political mobilisation. Nevertheless, caste became the main basis for affirmative action, and the strategic mobilisation of key communities continued (as suggested above) to be one of the bases of grassroots Congress support, despite the combination of the Nehruvian ideals of secularism and the apparent control of state resources by dominant castes. For most of the first two decades after 1947, more than fifty per cent of MPs coming from the Hindi belt to the Lok Sabha were high caste.[47] Yet these powerful groups in Indian politics were never able to distance themselves entirely from the specific interest politics of what came to be officially defined as the 'Backward Castes' and increasingly 'Other Backward Castes'.

There were, then, other ways in which an older politics of community and identity played out in this period too, ways that, as will be seen in Chapter 7, would have implications for the resurgence of politicians mobilising religious communities by the 1980s. Vast new electorates still needed to be mobilised and captured at election times in a context in which issues-centred political choices and parties could not be easily established in a context of one-party dominance. The large bulk of research and

---

[46] This links squarely to the priorities of 'area studies' and social sciences too in the 1960s, which viewed Nehruvian India very much in terms of a successful liberal democracy, albeit hindered by sluggish economic growth. See, for example, Gunnar Myrdal, *Asian Drama: An Enquiry into the Poverty of Nations* (Harmondsworth: Penguin, 1968).

[47] Christophe Jaffrelot, 'The Rise of the Other Backward Classes in the Hindi Belt', *The Journal of Asian Studies*, 59, 1, 2000, 86–108.

writing on 1950s and 1960s India that has come out of the social sciences has been concerned with the detailed applications of Indian democracy and the development of the welfare state, forms of local government organisation and representation. Of central importance to these studies have been the mechanisms of voter behaviour, vote mobilisation and 'vote-bank' capture. One of the key features of the older Political Science literature, for example, has been the analysis of specific localities from the mid-1960s in terms of factional politics or forms of personal politics that could, where conditions permitted, revolve around caste or religious identities.[48] More recent work has examined how electoral incentives at the town and state levels created the conditions for ethnic and religious violence itself, so that violence was in general more likely to occur where party competition was polarised rather than fractionalised (since, in the latter, electoral appeals were more readily made to minorities).[49] These practices took place in quite different ways in different parts of India. In the Hindi belt – Uttar Pradesh, Bihar and parts of Madhya Pradesh – dominant high-caste communities continued to control land and local power even after zamindar abolition, and thereby formed the key bases for Congress power in the first decades after independence. In contrast, in southern areas like Tamil Nadu, coalitions of lower castes more rapidly edged out the Congress or created very different political constellations and alliances.[50]

But behind the obvious issues of voter mobilisation, electoral politics involved other disputes – something illustrated by the number of election results that were contested across India over the 1950s and 1960s, which contained mutual accusations of 'communalism'. Up to 1966, the Election Commission appointed tribunals to hear petitions against election results. In 1952, there were thirty-eight election petitions in the Lok Sabha (parliamentary) elections and 276 to the Vidhan Sabhas (state assemblies). This pattern increased over the next two general elections, with the figures rising to fifty-six and 414 petitions for the Lok Sabha and Vidhan Sabhas respectively in 1957. In the 1962 elections, nearly fifty per cent of tribunal decisions were challenged in the high courts. A disproportionately high number of petitions came from the states of Punjab,

---

[48] The classic work looking at this in the 1960s is Paul R. Brass, *Factional Politics in an Indian State*.

[49] See Steven I. Wilkinson, *Votes and Violence: Electoral Competition and Ethnic Riots in India*.

[50] For detail on these differences, see Christophe Jaffrelot, *India's Silent Revolution: The Rise of the Lower Castes in North India* (London: Hurst and Co., 2003).

Madhya Pradesh and Uttar Pradesh. The large majority of these petitions concerned complaints about 'corruption' – bribery, intimidation of voters, promotion of 'hatred between different social classes', incurring expenditure on elections beyond the legal limits, government officers acting for candidates, breaches of official duty and so on. Extremely important in these elections, then, was not just the mobilisation of votes but the use of 'influence' around election petitions, and in all of this, the exercising of political pressure on government servants was paramount.[51] This use of influence and pressure by politicians often related to the arithmetic of caste and community alliances, since government officials involved in elections were increasingly recruited on the basis of caste considerations.[52]

In north India, as in the south, political strategies evolved that attempted to challenge the high-caste dominance of the Congress, especially in areas like Uttar Pradesh, and these were to have implications for the politics of religious community in later years. One of the most successful of these strategies in the 1960s was the mobilisation around 'kisan' identities or new forms of peasant politics. Parties such as the 'Socialists' and figures like Charan Singh formed the backbone of these movements there, eventually emerging as the Janata Dal. Integral to many of these mobilisations was the politics of affirmative action and reservation within state structures. This manifested itself in direct lobbying of national and state-level governments and resembled the tactics of communal organisations in the late colonial period but now in a very different electoral context.[53] In particular, the first Backward Classes Commission of 1955 stressed the extent to which particular leaders and representatives of caste communities considered the state, as in periods before independence, to be an edifice in which power would be shared between different proscribed community interests: 'They argued that as government service carried prestige, power and influence, the backward too should have their due share in it'. Even more explicitly, the Commission declared: 'The scale of pay in government service, security of employment, power and prestige and the scope to distribute patronage, all have combined to make government services

[51] R. Chandidas, 'Electoral Adjudication in India', *Economic and Political Weekly*, 3, 24, 1968, 901–11.

[52] For more details on this process through the late colonial period and early 1950s, see William Gould, *Bureaucracy, Community and Influence*, chs. 3 and 6.

[53] For a study of how this played out in the case of civil service recruitment in Uttar Pradesh, see William Gould, '"The Dual State: The Unruly Subordinate", Caste, Community and Civil Service Recruitment in North India, 1930–1955'.

highly attractive and consequently greatly desired'.[54] In its research, the Commission also found that there was a range of other disadvantaged castes not catered for under the existing systems of affirmative action – communities that were to be later known as 'Backward Castes'.

The first Backward Classes Commission, however, failed to develop the principle of reservations beyond what already existed for Scheduled Castes and Tribes, with the head of the Commission itself, Kaka Kalelkar, opposing the proposals. In general, the government's rejection was that, according to figures like G. B. Pant, in any case Indian society was gradually establishing itself along socialist lines and that such caste distinctions would disappear over time. Other objections were based around the idea that in distinguishing Backward Castes or Other Backward Castes, the very institution of caste would be reinforced.[55] High-caste opposition to the idea of affirmative action on the basis of caste came from both the right and the left of the political spectrum. One of the key proponents of affirmative action for Backward Castes (rather than simply 'untouchables' or 'Scheduled Castes') was Rammanohar Lohia – a Bania, who formed his own Socialist Party in 1956, which eventually emerged following mergers and splits as the Praja Socialist Party (PSP) in 1965. Despite the drives of Rammanohar Lohia to present caste as essentially more deep-rooted than 'class' prejudice in Indian society, for most of this period, party politics and the entrenched Congress bosses across the country would not entertain the idea of the extension of affirmative action.

The arguments used to resist the Backward Classes Commission reveal a range of fundamental intellectual approaches to caste and community that form the backdrop to the later emergence of Hindu mobilisation. When Lohia described caste in terms of 'vested interests' of high castes, he identified an important dynamic of north Indian high-caste social conservatism, which was, throughout this period, able to present itself as liberal and reformist, while opposing concrete change around caste disability. Liberal reformism and the promotion of merit was particularly advantageous when your particular community had enjoyed long-term historical advantages. As Lohia put it:

... the intelligentsia of India, which is overwhelmingly the high caste, abhors all talk of a mental and social revolution of a radical change in respect of language or

[54] *Report of the Backward Classes Commission* (Simla: Government of India Press, 1955), vol. I; 'Representation of Backward Classes in Government Services, Central and State', pp. 125–45.
[55] Christophe Jaffrelot, 'The Rise of the Other Backward Classes in the Hindi Belt', p. 88.

caste or the bases of thought. It talks generally and in principle against caste. In fact, it can be most vociferous in its theoretical condemnation of caste, so long as it can be allowed to be equally vociferous in raising the banner of merit and equal opportunity . . . Five thousand years have gone into the building of this undisputed merit.[56]

There was another important correspondence here, however, between the unspoken assumption of high-caste reformism and the idea of the inherent 'Hindu' nature of Indian citizen identity. Despite the rhetoric of Nehruvian secularism, the association of Indianness with Hinduness lingered, and not just within the obvious organisations of the Hindu right. One area in which this was particularly evident was in the predicament of some north Indian Muslim citizens. The suggestions by V. Patel, P. D. Tandon and G. B. Pant (in different ways and on different public platforms) that Muslims would have to 'prove' their loyalty to the Indian nation set the scene for a very new situation in which the existence of Pakistan now coloured all instances of 'communal' controversy. This was most clearly evident, at an everyday level, in public reactions to those Muslims who had remained in positions of local authority within the Indian state machinery, as the last chapter explored.

As with caste disadvantage, secularism was championed by the Congress regime to suggest that the political marking of religious difference no longer had a place in Indian society; that, indeed, the state had no right to interfere in the private religious matters of citizens. Nehruvian socialism was thereby trumpeted to signal the defeat of old Muslim League and Hindu Mahasabha style 'communalism'. Yet members of the very organisations that spread the rhetoric of religious harmony continued to promote some of the older themes of high-caste Hindu mobilisation. Throughout the 1950s and particularly into the 1960s, for example, the banning of cow slaughter became a theme not just for BJS but also some significant Congress figures. Here too, the rhetoric of development, science and modernisation were used as a kind of encapsulating discourse within which cow protection was superficially shorn of its religious trappings. Arguments for the banning of cow slaughter were tied up with the science of agricultural development.[57] The promotion of Hindi and the concurrent decline of Urdu was also touted as a 'national' and secular project, without any reference to the sensitive and loaded politics that had surrounded

---

[56] Quoted in Jaffrelot, 'The Rise of the Other Backward Classes', p. 89.
[57] For more detail on this, see William Gould, 'Contesting "Secularism" in Colonial and Postcolonial North India between 1930 and 1950s', *Contemporary South Asia*, 14, 4, 2005, 481–94.

language in the 1930s and 1940s. In UP, despite being home to the bastion of Urdu – Aligarh – in the years immediately following independence, there was a curious interpretation of the central government's 'three language' formula,[58] by declaring Urdu a modern language and discontinuing the teaching of Urdu in schools.[59]

Alongside obstruction of caste reservations at the national level was another tension at state levels of government. At the very heart of the local administrations, it was assumed that care would need to be exercised in allowing any administrative division to be dominated by a particular community. In discussions around the amendment of the Revenue Manual in UP in 1952 (which set out rules for revenue officers in the civil services), the Revenue Department suggested that government might remove old colonial instructions guarding against 'the preponderance of the persons of any one caste in tahsils'. Commentators in this file suggested that 'in the spirit of the new constitution of India, the discrimination of caste has altogether been eliminated in matters of appointment to public services. Accordingly, it has been proposed that the above provision should be deleted'.[60] Instead, it was suggested that 'any class of backward' citizen should be adequately represented. Here, the suggested application of constitutional proposals was that fundamental rights only obliged local governments to pay some lip service to scheduled caste representation. Even more significant was the suggestion that in the new atmosphere of secular and liberal democracy, communal or caste mobilisation could not exist – that it had been eliminated or was on the verge of eradication, by virtue of the very principles of freedom and democracy themselves. The bogey of communalism and caste mobilisation in such a presentation of citizens' fundamental rights was therefore an outdated product of a colonial system that was now defunct. Here was a powerful argument to support upper-caste dominance throughout the polity of north India: communalism and casteism had been eradicated through the constitution. Or, to put it

---

[58] This formula recommended that, in every state, three languages should be taught in schools: the language of the state (the mother tongue for the majority of its population); another modern Indian language (Hindi, where the first one was not Hindi); and one other language.

[59] Ralph Russell, 'Urdu in India since Independence', *Economic and Political Weekly*, 34, 1/2, 1999, 44–8. See also Mushirul Hasan, *Legacy of a Divided Nation: India's Muslims since Independence* (Delhi: Oxford University Press, 1997).

[60] Letter No. 37/B.R. (Ad) IA/52, 11 February 1952, in 'Amendment of para. 1699 of Revenue Manual requiring inspecting authorities to see that there is not a preponderance of the persons of any one caste in tahsils', Revenue (B), File 126(B)/52, Box 155, Uttar Pradesh State Archives.

another way, the principles of the constitution could be allowed to take their course in such a way that did not necessarily oblige local governments to pursue actively principles of equality or what would today be described as affirmative action.

Yet other voices in the debate about the 'preponderance of any particular caste' took a more pessimistic view. One note on the same file on the Revenue Manual suggested that:

... our society is riven by castes, creeds and so many other divisions. A large percentage of persons including those in public service, at least, in the lower ranks are sometimes guided in their actions not by the merits of a question, but by the birth, caste or religion of the individuals involved.[61]

The position of such realists was based in the idea of communalism and casteism as a problem of India unreformed. For these more critical voices, the propensity for interests to mobilise around caste or community identities was down to the failure of national and state-sponsored elites. National political organisations had set out to reform Indian society, and yet despite their best efforts, Indian rural localities were riven with older (or what Nehru would significantly describe as 'medieval') allegiances. Indian society could therefore, according to these kinds of state-driven discourses, be crudely divided into two sections: an educated, urban-based, middle-class, high-caste community, who endeavoured to propagate the benefits of a national agenda of fundamental rights, and an undefined morass of the Indian public, who would break out of primordial allegiances with great difficulty. Moments of communal antagonism, too, were viewed as points of failure in the control of elites to reform society of this particular 'evil'. As the reformers of the Revenue Manual put it '... if the history of the political disunity of our country and its consequent downfall is not to be repeated, positive, drastic steps will have to be taken towards eradication of this evil'. A section of those in positions of power in the national and state-level administrations believed that the overall context of fundamental rights and democracy would bring in their train mass education that supposedly obliterated this 'evil'. Other reformers, however, disagreed: 'whether we take these steps or not, mere refusal to recognise it does not solve the problem'.[62]

Most historians of the phase of 'Congress dominance' have suggested that the overall control of key aspects of the political system by the party meant that for most of India, parties of both the left and right were

[61] *Ibid.*
[62] *Ibid.*

marginalised. Certainly, the Congress was able to adapt its structures to local patterns of dominance.[63] And Nehru, alarmed at what he saw as the relative weakness of the Congress in the 1952 elections, continued through the next two general elections of 1957 and 1962 to allow the party to mobilise support on the basis of patronage and the authority of locally dominant men.[64] As we will see in the following chapters, this created a form of political fragility, which was to break relatively easily after the death of Nehru and in the early years of Indira Gandhi's prime-ministership. It also meant that by the mid to late 1960s, the liberty given to local leaders and intermediaries in the mobilisation of support also opened the way for different patterns of caste dominance, as new 'populist' coalitions and combinations came to the fore.

(III) PAKISTAN: RELIGION AND ETHNIC CONFLICT

Since Pakistan's inception in 1947, as in the case of India, the moves by its governments and leaders to consolidate a cohesive national identity, on the lines of either political culture or ethnicity, have been highly problematic. In comparison to India, attempts to create national unity have been more closely tied up with the operation of state power itself and the difficulties in establishing legislative government. In India, the continued salience of what political observers repeatedly describe as 'communalism' is often related to the idea of the failure of secularism. In Pakistan, in contrast, sectarian and ethnic conflict is not juxtaposed to a clearly defined national agenda but seems to have grown out of sectional competition to control the state itself. In this sense, such conflicts are not generally represented in academic discussion as the polar opposite of an idealised national culture based around the secular state. The role of religion in politics in Pakistan has also, from the outset in 1947, been based in a kind of paradox surrounding the nation state. On the one hand, the whole notion of a separate Muslim homeland suggested a theocracy. India's Muslim religious leadership were hesitant to commit themselves to a separate state that would be secular. Yet Pakistan's ruling elites refused to commit themselves to a constitution based on Islamic principles. Moreover, Pakistan served the interests of some Muslims in those Indian provinces

---

[63] See Harold Gould, *Grassroots Politics: A Century of Political Evolution in Faizabad District* (New Delhi: South Asia Books, 1994).
[64] See Francine R. Frankel and M. S. A. Rao, eds., *Dominance and State Power in Modern India: Decline of a Social Order* (Delhi: Oxford University Press, 1989).

in which they were in a minority, such as UP, and much less those areas of British India where, being in a majority, they already had political dominance. The Muslim League leadership, dominated by UP men, had won over these Muslim majority areas by making specific concessions about provincial autonomy for areas like Bengal and Punjab. However, when these two provinces were divided in 1947, such promises seemed empty, not least because some of the poorest parts of the provinces were on the Pakistani side of the border.

In the first months of 1948, the '*ulama* of Pakistan did make attempts to establish a theocracy, with the proposal for a Ministry of Religious Affairs. The Muslim League's Objectives Resolution offered a vague promise that Islamic principles would be incorporated in the future constitution, but League leaders had no intention of taking the demands for a theocratic state seriously – with both Liaquat Ali Khan (Pakistan's first Prime Minister) and M. A. Jinnah arguing that British-style constitutional principles were compatible with Islam and the idea of an Islamic state.[65] Most importantly, by retaining the colonial traditions of the civil service and by eventually allowing the bureaucracy to wield power as the dominant political institution, Pakistan as a state came to be based more forcefully on the secular principles inherited from the British. This highly centralised, executive government power meant that, in contrast to India, legislatures were not able to exercise supremacy. Importantly, this system of governance was based on the dominance of fairly clearly defined regional/linguistic elites. Whereas in India the identity of ruling elites was regionally dispersed, albeit based for the most part on a high-caste Hindu dominance, in Pakistan a small Punjabi–muhajir (immigrants from UP) combination held the reins for most of the period up to the early 1970s. The fact that Pakistan failed to ratify a constitution in the first eight years of independence, allowing the bureaucracy and eventually the military to entrench themselves in the systems of governance, reinforced the position and power of this dominant minority. Key in this process was also the need to create a strong central government, vis-à-vis the provinces, to coordinate the military challenge of India and Kashmir.

There were other factors behind the early failures of a legislative alternative to the dominance of the bureaucracy and military. In most regions of India, political parties could only hesitantly, partially and under certain

<hr/>

[65] Richard Symonds, 'State-Making in Pakistan', *Far Eastern Survey*, 19, 5, 1980, 45–50.

conditions appeal to particularistic interests. However, in Pakistan the relationship between party and ethnic constituency appeared to be more direct, at least in the years immediately following independence. In India too, in many states and particularly at the centre, the very complexity of political society has meant that parties at all levels of the electoral process have had to rely upon cross-communal agendas or build support bases around factional agreements. As we will see in the following chapter, since the 1980s, a range of parties have been more clearly based on the support of ethnic/caste constituencies, especially as the politics of caste reservations developed. These constituencies do not, in every case, consistently support the same party in any particular region, which has meant that parties have attempted to appeal to a range of ethnic/caste/religious interests. But in Pakistan, this process appears, at least on the surface, to be less ambiguous, and representations of ethnicity, region and language have defined more clearly access to or control of state institutions. An important factor here is that not only political parties but other politicised institutions are mapped onto an ethnic landscape whose boundaries and divisions are largely accepted by Pakistani citizens. For example, the military has been ostensibly dominated by two specific ethno-regional groups – Punjabis first and then Pushtoons. However, as the following section will explore, there is more to the definitions of ethnic or sectarian identity in Pakistan than these bare patterns of dominance would imply.

Most important in the years up to 1971 was the greatest symbolic regional/ethnic and linguistic division of them all – between the Punjabi–muhajir-dominated West Pakistan, and Bengali East Pakistan. Consolidation and cooperation between east and west might have been possible if the Muslim League had managed to retain dominance across Pakistan as a whole in the manner of the Congress in India. However, the League, being dominated by the political ambitions and outlook of the UP muhajirs – the same men who, along with Punjabis in the military, dominated the state executive – had too weak a popular base in Pakistan as a whole to risk elections and a popular mandate. Critical to this insecurity was the point that, in any election, Bengali East Pakistan would have to be the dominant region in the state on account of its population. As the Muslim League failed to call elections, knowing that it had no control over the outcomes in East Pakistan, the civil service entrenched itself further within the political system as a whole, and after 1954, the party largely disintegrated, lacking a popular base. The power of the military and bureaucracy within the Pakistani state was also reinforced by external

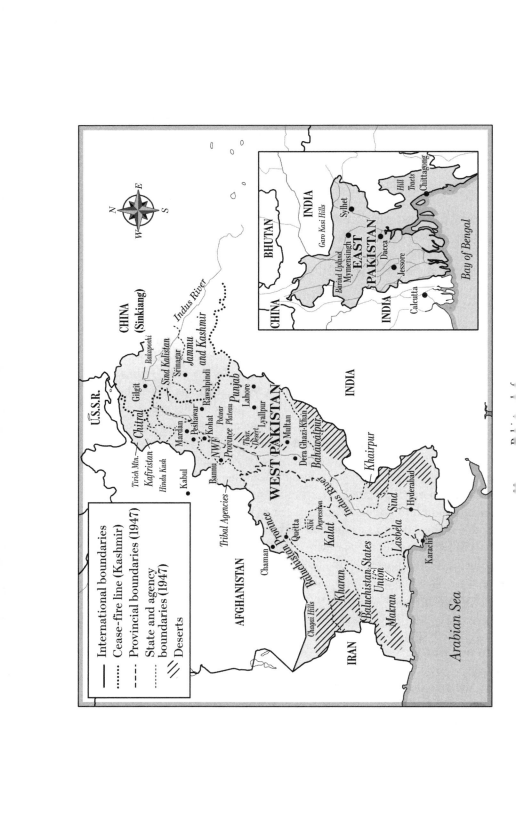

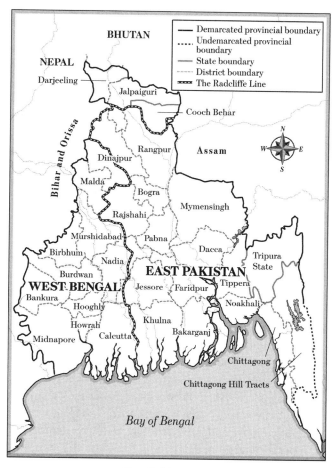

MAP 3. East Pakistan, 1947–1971

forces, most notably the geostrategy of the United States in backing Pakistan's non-representative regimes from 1954.[66]

The Constituent Assembly rarely met over the first five years of Pakistan's existence, and when it did, it was riven with disagreements about the relative constitutional position of East and West Pakistan.

---

[66] The first U.S. military aid to Pakistan occurred as early as 1950, but was extended during the Eisenhower administration as part of the U.S. strategy of Middle-East defence in a formal Mutual Defence Agreement. See James W. Spain, 'Military Assistance for Pakistan', *The American Political Science Review*, 48, 3, 1954, 738–51. The military coup of 1958 did not change the flow of military aid to Pakistan, although U.S. policy shifted more towards India following the latter's war with China in 1962. See Feroz Ahmed, 'Pakistan Forum: Partners in Underdevelopment: Pakistan and the U.S.', *Merip Reports*, 26, 1974, 23–7.

When parity was decided between East and West and entrenched in the 1956 constitution (an arrangement that obviously disadvantaged the more populous East), all the provinces of the West were forced into the 'one-unit scheme', leading to the dismissal of the resistant Sindh and NWFP ministries. The provinces were unwilling to surrender resources to the centre, especially when many of them had to face reconstruction following partition. This action was indicative of the relative power the central government would continue to play within the political system, but also meant that the leaders who dominated the centre would be even less able to rely upon political support from the provinces.[67] Moreover, the links between the Prime Minister and parliament were exposed as being weak too in April 1953, when the Governor General, Ghulam Mohammad, dismissed the Prime Minister. When in 1954, the Constituent Assembly attempted to hit back by legislatively curbing the power of the Governor General and by repealing the Public and Representative Office Disqualification Act (PRODA), used by the bureaucracy to investigate charges of corruption against politicians, Ghulam Mohammad dissolved the Constituent Assembly (October 1954). A military coup in 1958 was perhaps not surprising, given the gradual rise to dominance of the executive wings of government.[68] In addition, with no judicial autonomy from the executive, the state was practically free to infringe fundamental rights.[69]

Ayub Khan's coup in 1958 was followed by an attempt to build a clearer network of relationships between the bureaucracy and rural elites across Pakistan as a way of cultivating more stable networks of allies through 80,000 geographical units known as 'basic democracies'. This was just a superficial arrangement, and Pakistan still continued to be governed largely by an unreformed civil service. And, as in the colonial period, the limited structures of 'representation', in this case the basic democracies, had no mechanisms for accommodating political opposition, forcing groups and communities excluded from government patronage to mobilise more directly and violently in opposition. The regime was able to rule by ordinance and effectively control the media, academia, legal profession and judiciary.

[67] Ayesha Jalal suggests that the need to maintain military power vis-à-vis India and the requirements of taming the provinces were 'contradictory' requirements, since Pakistan had been left with such meagre resources after independence. Ayesha Jalal, *Democracy and Authoritarianism in South Asia: A Comparative and Historical Perspective*, pp. 49–50.

[68] Omar Noman, *Pakistan: A Political and Economic History since 1947* (London: Kegan Paul International), pp. 11–12.

[69] Jalal, p. 51.

Most importantly, the 1962 constitution institutionalised Ayub's racial thinking about Bengali ethnic and cultural inferiority and reinforced a form of centralisation that was focussed on the idea of West Pakistan Punjabi–muhajir power. Provincial governments were not granted even the semblance of autonomy, working more like local governments in a unitary state. In response, in 1966 the Awami League of East Pakistan made a demand for a confederation and reiterated it in their election manifesto in 1970. Sheikh Mujib-ur Rahman, the first leader of Bangladesh and figurehead of the Awami League (which he co-founded in 1949) had in the 1940s championed the cause of Pakistan under Suhrawardy's Muslim League in Bengal. From the beginning, the Awami League aimed to rout the Muslim League in East Pakistan on the basis of Bengali regional sentiment. However, after 1958, Ayub Khan banned political party activity and established military rule, which effectively pushed the leaders of the Awami League underground. This only enhanced the popularity of leaders such as Mujib in Bengal, however, especially when, from 1966, he formulated what came to be known as the 'six-point program' for regional autonomy. The six demands were fully acceptable within the legal constitutional set up of Pakistan. They called for: a parliamentary federal government based on universal adult franchise; the centre to only have powers over defence and foreign affairs, with all other power vested in provincial units; two separate but convertible currencies for East and West; taxation and revenue collection to be vested in provincial units; foreign exchange accounts and trade and commercial relations to be conducted separately; and, finally, the formation of a militia or paramilitary force for East Pakistan. However, Mujib and thirty-four other colleagues were charged with conspiring in the forcible dismemberment of Pakistan in collusion with India in the Agartala conspiracy case. Mujib was arrested, which eventually led to rioting and violence in early 1969 in East Bengal for his release.[70] This led to a step down by Ayub, his replacement by Yahya Khan and the massive success of the Awami League in the 1970 elections in East Pakistan.

Strong, regionally based opposition was generated too in Sindh, NWFP and Baluchistan. In Sindh, this manifested itself in the growth of the Pakistan People's Party (PPP), also mobilised on the back of class-based demands that opposed the regime's industrialisation programme. A series of mass demonstrations and riots against the regime across Pakistan

[70] Marcus Franda, *Bangladesh: The First Decade* (New Delhi: South Asian Publishers Pvt, 1982), pp. 12–14.

between November 1968 and March 1969, in which around 250 people died in clashes, forced Ayub to transfer power in 1969 to Yahya Khan.[71] Yahya had no real option but to allay criticisms by announcing a general election to be held in late 1970, which resulted in an absolute majority for the Awami League, with 160 of 162 seats from East Pakistan. The PPP won 81 of the 138 seats in West Pakistan.

It was in this context, then, of fragile centre-province relations with strong authoritarian overtones and with the dominance of particular and defined regional elites that ethnic and sectarian conflict in Pakistan took on quite specific characteristics. Whereas in India conflict between communities continued to be described in terms of 'communalism', in Pakistan this older colonial terminology has not been used so readily. This is not just down to the fact that specific 'Hindu–Muslim' conflict of the Indian kind has no clear or direct parallel in Pakistan. There is also a qualitative political difference here between how the violence of 'communalism' in India in its various guises is represented and ethnic conflict in Pakistan. The former involves a history in which national movements and parties delineated the 'communal' as essentially antagonistic to progress, development, national unity and internal security. In Pakistan, by contrast, discussions of ethnic conflict map more directly onto a competition for control of the state apparatus and state resources in such a way that makes a consensus (even one defined by high-status elites) about Pakistani national identity difficult to come by. In other words, such conflict in Pakistan is not presented as an essentially 'anti-national' activity, as it often is in India.

As a result, political scientists and historians have generally written in terms of the ethnicities of the main provincial areas of the nation: Muhajiri Urdu-speaking immigrants, Punjabis, Sindhis, the Pushto population of the North-West Frontier Province and Baluchis. The key identifiers of difference have been around region, 'custom' and language. Unequal distribution of resources, both in terms of economic development and political authority/opportunity, is seen by many scholars as the key driver of conflict at an inter-regional and national level. In many cases, this has manifested itself in resentment at migration of groups from one particular region into another. For example, Pushtoon migration into Baluchistan has led to the creation of the Pushtoonkhwa Milli Awami Party, which is not only anti-Pushtoon but also separatist in its ambitions.[72] The next

[71] Noman, 27–33.
[72] Irm Haleem, 'Ethnic and Sectarian Violence and the Propensity towards Praetorianism in Pakistan', *Third World Quarterly*, 24, 3, 2003, 463–77.

chapter will look at work that has largely deconstructed this focus on ethnicity, which in some cases essentialises the political interests of these groups, ignoring other contingent variables. Nevertheless, political discussion of ethnic difference has certainly characterised Pakistani politics at the national level. The division between the Sunni and Shi'a communities in Pakistan is also pertinent. Around seventy-five to eighty-five per cent of the total population is Sunni[73] and the religious divisions between the two sects have given rise to sectarian radicalism and militancy among a small minority. These so-called 'Jihadi' groups include the Sunni Sipah-I Sahaba Pakistan (SSP), the Shia Tahriki Jafaria Pakistan (TJP) and the Sipah-I Muhammed (SM). Some of the most destructive conflicts between these groups have taken place since the 1980s, and in some respects, their presence in the Pakistani political landscape has been strongly coloured by how they have been used as signifiers of everyday violence. Whenever a bombing or local shooting occurs, sectarian violence is commonly identified as a cause.

However, the ethnic and sectarian divisions mapped out in this way are open to the same queries as those surrounding 'community' in India. Whereas ethnicity, region and sect have clearly formed the basis for political *mobilisation* in many instances in Pakistan, these identities have been based on specific political contingencies, on the one hand, and deeper colonial representations, on the other. The Shi'a and Sunni communities of Pakistan, for example, are largely based on relatively modern notions of sectarian difference, albeit modelled around specific theological debates. The definitions of difference between the sects were clearly linked to modern technologies – the use of newspapers and pamphleting, for example, which promoted the distinctive beliefs and political institutions of each sect.[74] Also significant has been the establishment of new institutions along old models – the development of sectarian madrasahs, for example, which proliferated in Punjab particularly from the mid-1970s.[75] The basis for sectarian division also relates to protests against 'heresy' that go back to the late colonial period. The exposing of 'heresy' by a radical Punjabi Sunni leadership has been based around a long-standing opposition and

---

[73] Although there is no agreement on the exact Shi'a population of Pakistan, with estimates ranging from two per cent to twenty-five per cent.

[74] For an in-depth history of the formation of Shi'a political institutions, see Justin Jones, 'The Shi'a Muslims of the United Provinces of India'.

[75] For more detail on this, see S. V. R. Nasr, 'The Rise of Sunni Militancy in Pakistan: The Changing Role of Islamism and the Ulama in Society and Politics', *Modern Asian Studies*, 34, 1, 2000, 139–80.

persecution of the Ahmadi sect – a group who profess support for the notion of Mirza Ghulam Ahmad as a prophet. For the most part, from the end of the 1960s, the opposition has been to Twelver Shi'ism and has been based on sectarian struggles to define the role of Islam in politics.

Particular institutions of state, especially in the area of security and 'law and order', have largely thrived on these representations of community. The constitution of 1962 stressed that the revival of political parties would be conditional on their adherence to Islamic ideology. Such a requirement allowed the government to suppress left-wing movements and parties. Most notably, the Inter-Services Intelligence (ISI), expanded under Ayub and ostensibly set up to combat external threats to Pakistan, has been at the forefront in exploiting domestic tensions between these communities. In the anti-Ahmadi movements among radical Sunnis, the strong arm of the state and its representation of 'community' have also been highly influential. Efforts were made from 1974 to declare Ahmadis a non-Muslim minority, and the Sipah-I Sahaba also sought to redefine Islam further along these lines so as to exclude the Shi'a community too. The whole definition of what constitutes a 'true Muslim', then, connects sectarian conflict to the mechanisms of state representation and power in a direct way. As a result, the content of policies promoting 'Islam' in state institutions has been the subject of debate and contention. For example, Shias and Sunnis have been divided since 1979 over the imposition of an Islamic tax according to the Sunni Hanafi law – the Zakat – with the inception of the Islamicising policies of General Zia-ul-Huq.[76]

Whereas in India shortly after independence, one of the foundations of the 'secularism' was to position the state as constitutionally 'neutral' in relation to religious issues (albeit with important reforms of Hindu personal law and non-interference in Muslim personal law), in Pakistan the state has been expected to intervene actively. In India, there is ambiguity surrounding the extent to which the constitution promotes non-interference of the state in religious matters. This is not least because of the commitment, as described in the section above, to promote reservations on the basis of caste, which carries implications for religious cultures in some parts of the country. In the case of Pakistan, the ambiguity does not surround the basic principles of state interference but the control of that interference and involvement. In this sense, there is a clearer expectation in Pakistan that religion, sect and

---

[76] Muhammad Qasim Zaman, 'Sectarianism in Pakistan: The Radicalization of Shi'i and Sunni Identities', *Modern Asian Studies*, 32, 3, 1988, pp. 689–716.

ethnicity are categories around which state power can be legitimately controlled, and that Islam in particular can be used as a medium of state discipline.

Too much should not, however, be read into the salience of ethnic and regional division in state formation and democratic failures in Pakistan. Certainly, the ethnic background of the military in Pakistan was significant from the outset, since although direct military rule did not begin until the period of 1958–68, indirectly the military influenced the political process in the first decade of Pakistan's existence. One argument about the continued saliency of praetorian power in Pakistan suggests that as the utility of coercion increases, so the attractiveness of military rule arises. So, Pakistan's divided society with its ethnic and sectarian conflicts ultimately gives rise to non-democratic forms of government.[77] Burma, Sri Lanka and Malaysia are often presented as comparisons, where direct or indirect praetorianism was bolstered or legitimised partly by the need for the state to control ethnic and sectarian conflict. South America, Brazil, Peru and Bolivia present similar frameworks for comparison. In the case of Pakistan, the range of fluid political alliances that have, in the main, worked along ethnic or regional lines have clearly contributed to what is officially defined as the 'law and order' problem and more generally to relatively political instability.

But this is clearly not just a simple pattern of a multi-ethnic society in which a propensity for violence needs to be controlled by a state that stands above it. The locus of state power is clearly interwoven with fluctuating sectional alliances, sometimes based on factors such as linguistic or regional or sectarian background, sometimes based on alliances that are entirely separate from sectional interests. And the very definitions of such categories are, as in India, contested and challenged at multiple levels. In particular, the everyday practice of Islam cut across the categories of definition set out by political leaders and the media, suggesting that such identities were certainly not immutable. However, power was still obtained and conflicts were still resolved on the basis of this politics of representation. State actors, as in India, have been known to exploit other kinds of conflicts to justify military or military/civilian power.[78] Ethnic and religious conflict, then, becomes (as it did in the colonial period) a means by which representative processes can be bypassed or a justification for

---

[77] Irm Haleem, 'Ethnic and Sectarian Violence and the Propensity towards Praetorianism in Pakistan', p. 469.
[78] *Ibid.*, p. 466.

their suppression (in the case of Pakistan). But explanations for continued bureaucratic and military rule in Pakistan over this period must also be related to the basic structural weaknesses of Pakistan's economy and political system from 1947, the influence of U.S. military sponsorship and the political ambitions of bureaucrats and military men.

CONCLUSION

Following independence, the new governments of India, Pakistan and Ceylon all attempted (to varying degrees) to combine a commitment to 'secularism' with the problems of state building and national consolidation. Organisations like the Indian National Congress in colonial India and the Ceylon National Congress and UNP in Sri Lanka were based on the principle that the social plurality of South Asia necessitated at least a symbolic recognition of a politics of diversity. However, nationalism, not least in a colonial context, presupposes ideological decisions about a composite nation, which (often in an authoritarian way) grants civic rights only to those able to identify with a dominant national culture. These efforts of the South Asian post-colonial states were most obviously seen in the forceful projection of national integrity in the face of regional separatism and religious community mobilisations. In India, this involved the negotiation of linguistic reorganisation, on the one hand, to the benefit of the centre and the immediate suppression of outright attempts at secession in Junagadh and Hyderabad, on the other. In Sri Lanka, it comprised the eventual establishment of a Sinhala-only policy and a focus on Sinhalese identity as the principal component of national identity. Looking at these processes in relation to the late colonial period, then, it is clear that the focus on the establishment of a powerful centre was something inherited from the colonial period. But in the case of Pakistan, this process was complicated by the broad-stroke politics of ethnic division that cut across the key institutions of the state – the bureaucracy and the army – and the problems of consolidating national culture within obviously dominant regional/migrant identities.

These patterns of post-colonial state formation, and national consolidation, formed the background and context for a very different kind of religious and caste community politics in the independent South Asian states. In India, the bogey of 'communalism' was associated with the defeated Muslim League. For many years after independence, this often placed Muslim minorities in an ambiguous position, despite the secular pronouncements of governments at the centre. In this sense, the 'secularism' of the Indian state contained within it a number of tensions and contradictions, some of which effectively encouraged the dominant political cultures of powerful, high-status Hindu communities who largely dominated the early post-independence regimes. There was also an important gulf between the rhetoric of the secular state at a national level and the practices of state and district-level politicians.[79] These problems and contradictions were also implicit in the whole project of state modernisation. By suggesting that the very process of modernisation and state building would eventually destroy all 'backward' or primordial ethnic and religious associations, dominant politicians in the ruling Congress effectively bolstered high-caste, conservative definitions of Indian national identity. In these analyses, 'modernisation' effectively meant the assimilation of heterogeneous cultures and political organisations into this uniform political culture of Indian nationality. The assumption that a dominant (Hindu) political culture lay at the heart of Indian citizenship and identity also, however, in time, indirectly encouraged a new politics of caste-based mobilisation. In Pakistan, the ideology of 'secularism' did not feature as a political project of dominant elites. This, as well as the political and structural weaknesses of state-formation processes themselves, allowed certain elites to use ethnic identities in their challenge for control of the state apparatus in a much less ambiguous way. Yet, as earlier chapters have suggested, religious, caste and ethnic 'conflict' was not related to these broad divisions or state and national ideologies in an uncomplicated way – a theme to which we will return in the next chapter for the period after 1970.

[79] For an example of this for UP, see William Gould, 'Contesting "Secularism" in Colonial and Postcolonial North India between 1930 and 1950s'.

7

New Conflicts and Old Rivalries

The 1970s and 1980s

On the morning of 31 October 1984, Indira Gandhi set out from her prime-ministerial residence at 1 Safdarjung Road, New Delhi, to attend an interview with Peter Ustinov. As she passed through the gardens of the house, two of her Sikh bodyguards, Beant Singh and Satwant Singh, opened fire, spinning the Prime Minister of India around and leaving her prone and bleeding on the ground, after which multiple rounds of ammunition were fired at her immobile body. Although there was an ambulance on site, nobody could find the driver. Sonia Gandhi and Indira Gandhi's aides lifted her into a Hindustani Ambassador and she was rushed to the All India Institute of Medical Sciences, which held a special supply of her 'O' blood group Rh. negative. Meanwhile, the two arrested Sikhs were shot by their guards. Although attempts were made to remove some of the bullets, Indira Gandhi was pronounced dead by the early afternoon of the same day.[1]

The killing of Indira Gandhi illustrated in a brutal and dramatic way the interconnection between the violence of the locality – the indignation of Delhi's Sikh community – and decision making at the highest levels of the Indian state. Satwant and Beant Singh (who were shot at the scene of the incident) carried out the assassination in revenge for the government's operation against Sikh militants taking refuge in the grounds of the Golden Temple in Amritsar. Operation Blue Star was the final act in a disastrous policy of central interference in the complex factional divisions within Punjabi Sikh politics, as Indira Gandhi's regime attempted to

---

[1] This account is based on Pranay Gupte, *India: The Challenge of Change* (London: Methuen, 1989), pp. 29–35.

subdue the separatist ambitions of a section of its leadership. The assassination of Indira Gandhi had much more disturbing consequences. Over the first week of November 1984, thousands of Sikhs were killed in a pogrom that spread across the main cities of north India and was most pronounced in Delhi and Kanpur. Much of this violence appeared to be spontaneous, but over the following years, a series of official investigations and independent enquiries suggested that it may have been planned. As with the violence around India's partition, the quotidian was interlaced with the highest levels of state, and the formalities of political rivalry. And the apparent ferocity of popular indignation was not easily unravelled from a sense of political conspiracy.

The relationship between popular perceptions of the Indian state and the apparent spontaneity of 'religious' or 'ethnic' violence in South Asia will be one of the main concerns of this chapter. However, violence will not be the only concern: moments of direct conflict, as earlier chapters have argued, only represented one dimension of a much more complex array of political postures around religious and caste community. Throughout the 1960s, India experienced other social transformations, including the rise of new intermediate peasant classes, and by the end of that decade, the dominance of the Congress regime faced some of its first serious challenges. In the 1970s and 1980s, new economic pressures, in the shape of a global economic crisis and new political contestations – the loss of Congress power after the Emergency – altered the context of ethnic and religious mobilisation. This chapter will also examine three broad developments in terms of their impact on the politics of religious identity and conflict. First, it surveys the changing conditions surrounding ethno-political assertion in the context of separatism and regional political challenge, from the Emergency through to the intensification of Punjabi, Kasmiri and Assamese separatist movements. Second, it asks why the 1980s appeared to witness a new resurgence in communal conflict and rioting in areas such as Ahmedabad (1984) and Uttar Pradesh throughout the mid part of the decade. Why was it that the 1950s and 1960s appeared to be decades of relative cooperation and consensus but that apparent religious conflict re-emerged from the late 1970s? Finally, it looks at international factors in the changing contexts of religious identity politics. In particular, it examines the changing nature of Indo-Pakistan relations and the new conditions for religio-political movements under Zia's regime, and the moves towards economic liberalisation from the late 1980s.

(I) INDIA IN THE ERA OF 'CONGRESS DECLINE'

A common focus of academic and media attention on South Asia in the 1970s and early 1980s India was the apparent rise of 'challenges to national integrity' and the resurgence of extended and intensive incidents of reported Hindu–Muslim conflict. Historians and political scientists have related both of these themes to the notion of the crisis of state power and Congress legitimacy, which have examined, for example, weaknesses in Indira Gandhi's period of rule.[2] However, such themes have also been the product of a particular historical interest in Hindu–Muslim antagonism that has developed since the dramatic changes of the late 1980s/early 1990s, and the growing power of the Hindu right in India. Principally, the interests of historians and political scientists were affected by two interconnected sets of events. First, academic attention has been captured by the mobilisation of support for the parties and organisations of the Hindu right-wing Sangh Parivar – the BJP, RSS, VHP and others – around the attempt to destroy the Babri-Masjid at Ayodhya.[3] In this dispute, the parties of the Hindu right used the issue of Babar's mosque in the city of Ayodhya, built allegedly on the site of a temple to Ram, to mobilise broad political support across north India, which eventually resulted in the formation of state-level BJP governments. This will be explored in more detail in the next chapter. Second, following V. P. Singh's government's decision to implement further reservations in public bodies via the Mandal Commission Report, the parties of the Hindu right have also faced off against other powerful north Indian movements, promoting the interests of 'Backward' and 'Other Backward' caste communities.

Those looking back from the crisis years of 1990–2, reflecting on the changes brought by the Ayodhya dispute and the implementation of the Mandal Commission on caste reservations, noted a wider social acceptance of 'communal ideologies' and mobilisation. For a range of scholars working on India,[4] this was not just about the increasing popularity of the institutions of the Hindu right or the growing ubiquity of other organisations of the Sangh Parivar. It was also, and perhaps predominantly, about the indifference and neglect of the principle of state secularism itself and

---

[2] See, for example, Zoya Hasan, 'Changing Orientation of the State and the Emergence of Majoritarianism in the 1980s', *Social Scientist*, 18, 8/9, 1990, pp. 27–37.

[3] For example, Peter Van der Veer, *Religious Nationalism: Hindus and Muslims in India* (Berkeley: University of California Press, 1994); David Ludden, ed., *Contesting the Nation: Religion, Community and the Politics of Democracy in India* (Philadelphia: University of Pennsylvania Press, 1996).

[4] Including Mushirul and Zoya Hasan, Partha Chatterjee and Sudipta Kaviraj.

the flirtation with communal mobilisation by a range of parties.[5] These interpretations suggest a three-decade period of relative stability and 'communal harmony' in which the secular drives of the Nehruvian Congress controlled the resurgence of 'communal forces' – a suggestion that the last chapter argued was in need of revision. In some analyses, the expansion of fundamentalism and revivalism was a generalisable phenomenon, being present in other states, notably Pakistan in the 1980s.[6] However, the apparent resurgence of Hindu nationalism in India from the 1980s squarely related to contingent political events and the peculiar quality (and limitations) of secularism and the secular state.

In India, the authority of the Congress regime was radically affected by the rise of new peasant and low-caste organisations and parties, some of which had been advantaged by economic changes in the countryside. In particular, under the leadership of Chaudhuri Charan Singh and Ram Manohar Lohia in Uttar Pradesh in the mid-1960s, and in the formation of the Bharatiya Lok Dal and Samyukta Socialist Party, agricultural communities began to challenge the urban high-caste dominance of the political mainstream in north India. In other areas, for example Bihar, where Jayaprakash Narayan developed a student movement against the administration, challengers from the left also critiqued Congress-sponsored 'corruption' in state-level governments. By the late 1980s, the older Nehruvian consensus had broken down in more than just party politics too, as governments began to reconsider the older models of planned economic development and to countenance liberalisation. These political and economic changes accompanied the growing power of parties of the right in India for reasons that will be explored more below. In Pakistan, in contrast, the apparent rise of Islamic parties and movements in the 1980s often related to specific measures of military regime protection: particular parties and ideologies were promoted as a way of combating the political threat of the Sindhi PPP, which had dominated Pakistan in the middle part of the 1970s.

The 'weaknesses' of Indian secularism, however, were not entirely related to the problems associated with Congress's political 'decline' from the 1970s and 1980s, and to make such arguments wrongly presents the party as an uncomplicated champion of secular politics. As we saw in the last two chapters, 'secularism' was already set up on the basis of

---

[5] See Zoya Hasan, 'Changing Orientation of the State'.
[6] See, for example, the work of Mark Juergensmeyer, especially *The New Cold War? Religious Nationalism Confronts the State* (Berkeley: University of California Press, 1994).

political and ideological compromises, and the Congress organisation was certainly not a uniformly 'secularist' party. Nevertheless, there were important ways in which some of the confidence and political consensus of the early to mid-1960s was more rapidly broken down from the end of the decade, and this had implications for the rise of political challengers to Congress. As the older Nehruvian alliances between centre and state party bosses was broken apart from the late 1960s, Indira turned to a more 'personalised' politics in which there were shifts towards the tactics of the Hindu right in some areas, and in which a more dangerous system of intermittent alliances involved a range of separatist leaders and organisations. The obvious electoral weakening of Congress was most apparent from 1967 when Congress was defeated in eight states in the general elections.[7]

The breaking up of consensual alliances between the Congress regime at the centre and parties in the states and regions was, as we have seen, dramatically illustrated by Indira Gandhi's policies towards Punjab. Here, from the early 1970s, the central government attempted to divide Sikh leaders in a bid to consolidate Congress power in the state. The Akali Dal was forced into a position of pushing again for more radical separatist demands, including a separate sovereign state. Gandhi's response was to continue to label their activities as seditious, but also to divide and rule by forging alliances with selected Sikh leaders – most notoriously, Jarnail Singh Bhindranwale, leader of the Damdami Taksaal. The Congress won power in the state in 1980, but once Sikh militants had been mobilised, it was difficult for either the moderate leaders of the Akali Dal or the Congress to overcome the increasing popularity of the more genuine and radical Sikh proponents of a separate Sikh state. Over the early 1980s, a cycle of militancy and repression set in, as the centre was unable to accommodate the radical demands of the more extremist leadership. Crucially, Indira Gandhi turned down more moderate demands of the Akalis, involving control over agricultural subsidies, for fear of appearing to 'appease' minorities.[8] This effectively legitimised more radical Sikh leaders and factions further, and in particular placed Bhindranwale in a powerful and pivotal position in relation to Sikh factions as a result of his popular following.[9]

---

[7] Francine Frankel, *India's Political Economy, 1947–1977: The Gradual Revolution* (Princeton: Princeton University Press, 1978), pp. 352–60.
[8] Atul Kohli, 'Can Democracies Accommodate Ethnic Nationalism?', pp. 22–3.
[9] See Robin Jeffrey, *What's Happening to India?* (New York: Holmes and Meier, 1994), pp. 145–50.

Bhindranwale had already been involved in violent opposition to the Sant Nirankari Mission, a movement that was seen by orthodox Sikhs as an affront to true Sikhism. Most prominently, he was allegedly involved in instigating the murder of the Arya Samaj leader, Jagat Narain, and although he was released from arrest due to lack of evidence, he and his armed followers took refuge in a guest house in the precincts of the Golden Temple in 1982. Between 3 and 6 June 1984, the central government launched Operation Blue Star whereby the Indian army attempted to dislodge armed militants from the Temple complex. The operation, which was later popularly viewed as a national disgrace, resulted in the death of approximately 500 civilians and eighty-three army personnel, as well as Bhindranwale himself.[10] Following the assassination of Indira Gandhi by her Sikh bodyguards on 31 October 1984, a nationwide pogrom against Sikhs resulted in at least 3,000 deaths, with most of the violence concentrated in and around Delhi, where one estimate put the number of deaths at 2,733. The violence was then revisited and reproduced in the media and public sphere through official enquiries, which reiterated familiar means of describing Indian rioters and victims in ethnic terms. Between November 2004 and February 2005, ten Commissions and Committees submitted reports to parliament.[11] Most of these enquiries were concerned with culpability and punishment; they focussed predominantly on Congress party members (specifically Jagdish Tytler) and senior police officers.

The 1980s, as we will see, were extremely important, then, in terms of the shifting terrain of ethnic and communal politics and the apparent weakening power of an older Nehruvian rhetoric of national consensus. For Zoya Hasan, as the Congress lost some of its traditional following, for example among Muslims in north India, the parties like the BJS gradually stepped into the political vacuum in some areas. By the early 1980s, in response to these political challenges, the Congress increasingly adopted forms of political majoritarianism, which played upon similar ideological themes to the Hindu right. For example, in the 1984 elections, all opposition parties were described, in similar terms to the rhetoric used by the

---

[10] Harnik Deol, *Religion and Nationalism in India: The Case of the Punjab* (London: Routledge, 2000).
[11] These were the Marwah Commission, the Misra Commission of Enquiry, the Kapur Mittal Committee, the Jain Banerjee Committee, the Potti Rosha Committee, the Jain Aggarwal Committee, the Ahuja Committee, the Dhillon Committee, the Narula Committee and the Nanavati Committee.

Hindu right, as 'anti national' forces in the Indian political landscape.[12] To explore how the political tactics of majoritarianism came about, it is necessary to consider some of the longer-term political conditions: the main challenges to Congress authority and support at a national level came around the pre- and post-Emergency period between 1974 and 1978. In general, parties of the right and left made more significant and sustained gains (and garnered ideological support) at a regional or state level. Connected to this was relative stagnation of the industrial economy from the late 1960s and a turn away from U.S. to USSR support in an attempt to address the perceived loss of popular support in 1967.[13] But this was not just about political and international conditions. Related to the instability towards the end of Indira Gandhi's rule and life was the appearance of new forms of communication technology and publicity: the increasing coverage of television ownership and, importantly, the screening of Hindu 'classics' such as the Mahabharata and the Ramayana by the late 1980s, and the use of music and video cassettes to promote political messages using innovative media.[14] Changes in society and the economy, particularly in patterns of consumption, were of course related to the opening up of the economy in the later years of the decade – a context that accompanied the growing affluence of urban middle classes across India and Pakistan.

By the early 1980s, Congress party and government decisions about religion and religious communities were perhaps more sensitive than they had ever been before. Whereas for most of this period Congress governments asserted the party's legitimacy as the only truly 'national' movement, lip service was nevertheless paid to sectional interests by the leadership where it was felt that those interests might need to be re-engaged. This was illustrated in the controversy surrounding the court ruling and subsequent government action on the divorce of a Muslim woman, Shah Bano, in 1985–6. In 1978, Shah Bano had filed a petition for maintenance against her husband in the Indore Judicial Magistrate's courts after he divorced her under conditions in which he claimed such maintenance was not legally obligatory. The husband's case was based on the principle that the payment of maintenance was only obligatory, under Muslim personal law, for the period of *iddat*, which had by that time passed. However, his appeal to the High Court was dismissed following

---

[12] Zoya Hasan, 'Changing Orientation of the State', p. 30.
[13] Frankel, pp. 296–7.
[14] See Arvind Rajagopal, *Politics After Television: Hindu Nationalism and the Reshaping of the Public in India*.

lengthy courtroom considerations of Muslim Personal Law, which suggested the importance of adopting a Uniform Civil Code. The Muslim press across India and Muslim Personal Law Board were incensed by what they saw as the courts' interference with issues of Muslim Personal Law, some going so far as to argue that paying maintenance to a divorced wife went against sharia law and therefore was against Islam. Unsuccessful in the courts, the Muslim Personal Law Board took the case to Parliament. It was at this point that Rajiv Gandhi, whose ruling Congress (I) had recently suffered defeats in by-elections in UP, Gujarat and Assam, decided to pass the Muslim Women (Protection of Rights on Divorce) Act 1986, which reversed the Shah Bano case decision.[15]

This turn of events certainly pushed the Hindu right into a more searing critique of its main national rival, the Congress, who it claimed was acting in an 'anti-national' way by appeasing the Muslim minority. The Shah Bano affair has figured as one of the key moments in interpretations of the rise of the Sangh Parivar (the 'family' of Hindu nationalist organisations, such as the Bharatiya Janata Party, RSS and Vishwa Hindu Parishad, discussed more below) against the backdrop of questions surrounding the survival and strength of Indian secularism itself.[16] However, a problem with the 'crisis of secularism' arguments that appeared in the early 1990s is that, while they identified the social and political pressures that led to the declining hegemony of the Congress and the growing fortunes of the Hindu right, they did not adequately set out how this connected to a real crisis for the Indian state per se. In fact, not only are the organisations of the Sangh Parivar keen to uphold the modernising agendas of the Indian state, their cadres also claim to be the holders of a true rather than 'pseudo' secularism as they define it. The BJP, since its reformation in 1980 (previously BJS), has been keen to promote a form of majoritarian politics that eliminates the claims of specific minority groups within the Indian polity. It aims to do so by keeping the basic structures of state power in India intact, and in this sense is somewhat different to other 'revivalist' or 'fundamentalist' groups, which critique modern state structures.[17] One key context then for the relatively rapid rise of political parties

---

[15] Nawaz B. Mody, 'The Press in India: The Shah Bano Judgement and its Aftermath', *Asian Survey*, 27, 8, 1987, 935–53.

[16] See, for example, Stanley J. Tambiah, 'The Crisis of Secularism in India', in Rajeev Bhargava, ed., *Secularism and its Critics* (Oxford: Oxford University Press, 1998), pp. 430–1.

[17] See Partha Chatterjee, 'Secularism and Tolerance', in Rajeev Bhargava, ed., *Secularism and Its Critics* (Oxford: Oxford University Press, 1998), pp. 345–8.

and organisations that capitalise on community differences can be found in the social and political changes among those hitherto marginalised groups identified as a 'threat' to national unity. In this sense, the agendas of the Hindu right are not entirely different from the Indian National Congress, and it should not therefore surprise the historian to find overlaps in personnel and ideology, particularly the propensity to raise the bogey of 'antinational' threats to Indian integrity.

The rise of the Hindu right has relatively little to do with changed perceptions of Muslims in India or the changing context of the Islamic world beyond India's borders (although these are contextually important in their own way, as we will see in another part of the discussion). Instead, its fortunes (and the reappearance of 'communalism' as an issue of public concern) has rather more to do with changing patterns of social dominance in crucial regions of India against a backdrop of new forms of political communication, economic development and opportunity. From the mid-1960s, key groups of lower castes mobilised around both 'kisan' and OBC identities to challenge the hegemony of high-caste dominance in areas like the Hindi belt. Under the leadership of Chaudhuri Charan Singh in the 1960s, these political interests – largely represented in the north of India by Ahir, Jat and Gujar communities – combined at certain moments to arrange coalitions that pushed for the recognition of new forms of quota politics. The first significant taste of power at the centre came in 1977, in the aftermath of the Emergency, with the formation of the Janata government under the leadership of Morarji Desai. The Janata government of 1977 to 1980 was composed of a somewhat uneasy alliance of Bharatiya Lok Dal (led by Charan Singh), the Congress (O), the Jana Sangh led by Atul Behari Vajpayee, the Swatantra Party and the Socialists. So despite the relatively fresh faces, any kind of affirmative action policy could only be the outcome of political compromise within government.

This government came to power on the wave of discontent with the corruption surrounding the Emergency, not least the contested election of Indira Gandhi herself, but also controls of freedom of expression, public accountability and the disastrous government-led family planning and beautification campaigns. For his short six-month period of power in 1979–80, Charan Singh passed what was described in the press as a 'kulak budget', promising benefits for small- and medium-level peasant holders. The possibilities for affirmative action at this stage were of course limited by the presence of the coalition partners, especially the Jan Sangh. However, Desai (as Prime Minister between 1977 and 1979) had appointed a Commission under B. P. Mandal that concluded that the

OBC groups, which constituted around fifty-two per cent of India's population, warranted further reservations in government, and public-sector institutions of twenty-seven per cent of posts.[18] The Commission's proposals were not implemented from 1980, with the return of Gandhi to power, but were to resurface in 1989 under the Janata Dal government – a series of events that will be outlined in Chapter 8. In the lead up to the implementation of the Mandal Commission, then, a combination of social and political changes set the scene for new forms of confrontation around community mobilisation. The developments in rural society since the early 1960s, encouraged by the Green Revolution and the growing affluence and political assertiveness of particular north Indian lower castes, eventually manifested themselves in political authority, first in certain states of India and then at the centre.

The growing relevance of affirmative action on the basis of caste threatened the local, regional and national authority of an array of high castes and other dominant communities in an unprecedented way. Chapter 6 looked at the existence of an ideological consensus surrounding the narratives of Indian freedom and independence, in which a range of (largely high-caste) leaders across India were eulogised in bringing a set of universal liberal principles through the new Indian constitution. These principles, under the direction of this leadership, often allowed governments at all levels to obscure or obfuscate on-going social and communal tensions in the name of national unity and integrity. A comparable discourse was taken up by rejuvenated, high-caste-dominated parties staking their claim to be the champions of national integrity in the form of the Sangh Parivar or 'family' of institutions of the Hindu right. The national consensus surrounding the older Congress leadership no longer held out when a new generation of leaders from other regional, caste and occupational backgrounds started to critique openly not only the direction but the very honesty of a form of governance directed by the older, high-caste, English-educated elites.

There were (and had always been) more direct ways, then, to ostensibly represent and defend the idea of national integrity and to protect the interests of those with most vested in the mechanisms of state power. The Bharatiya Jana Sangh had begun to represent a kind of national alternative to the Congress for large parts of India, albeit one temporarily delegitimised for a time by the force of Nehruvian rhetoric. This alternative

---

[18] For a more detailed discussion of this political phase, see Christophe Jaffrelot, 'The Rise of the Other Backward Classes in the Hindi Belt', pp. 86–108.

national party spoke to the need to find a cultural rather than a broadly liberal-secular basis for Indian unity and homogeneity; an appeal to (a largely reinvented) idea of Hindu nationality, which had its roots in organisations that had slipped in and out of Congress membership or allegiance in the past.[19]

The Sangh Parivar claimed to be inheritors of a 'true' Indian nationalism, which had developed out of the Hindu Mahasabha and RSS of the 1920s in northern and western India. In the aftermath of Indira Gandhi's Emergency in March 1977, Hindu nationalists – particularly the Jana Sangh, some of whom had an RSS background – did well in the Lok Sabha and Vidhan Sabha elections. Many of these figures had been arrested under the Maintenance of Internal Security Act in the Emergency period. This gave the Jan Sangh a new kind of public respectability in the period of 1977–8.[20] A number of Sanghites joined the Janata party group, which formed a majority in the Lok Sabha and made up its strongest contingent, although many of them were uncomfortable with an alliance with socialists from the ex-Bharatiya Lok Dal. An issue of particular discord was the socialists' promotion of caste reservations policies contained within the state-level Backward Castes Commissions, which granted further reservations for 'Other Backward Castes' (OBCs). In 1978, Jan Sanghites were associated with Hindu–Muslim rioting in Aligarh, which further distanced them from their leftist partners. Charan Singh, as part of a factional competition with Morarji Desai, highlighted the latter's association with the Jan Sangh members and pushed for the expulsion of ministers who retained links to the RSS. This eventually resulted, in July 1979, in the fall of the Desai government and the formation of a government under Charan Singh.[21] On 5 April 1980, members of the BJS formed a new party, the Bharatiya Janata Party (BJP), under the presidentship of Atal Bihari Vajpayee. The BJP attempted to broaden and moderate its appeal, claiming some of the Janata Party's programme, including 'Gandhian socialism' and 'positive secularism', and developing clearer socio-economic agendas and policies.[22]

Despite the apparent moderation of its Hindu nationalist agenda, the reorganisation of the BJS into the BJP in 1980 accompanied a growing public interest in the ideologies of the Hindu right as the decade

---

[19] See William Gould, *Hindu Nationalism*.
[20] See Arvind Rajagopal, 'Sangh's Role in the Emergency', *Economic and Political Weekly*, 38, 27, 2003, 2797–8.
[21] Jaffrelot, *The Hindu Nationalist Movement*, pp. 300–9.
[22] *Ibid.*, pp. 315–18.

progressed. Much of the support for the Sangh Parivar, particularly in areas like Gujarat and the Hindi belt, related to high-caste fears surrounding the politics of reservations for OBCs. The growing support for the BJP over this period in parts of northern and western India was also linked to other social changes, notably the growth in relative prosperity and influence of Indian middle classes across both urban and rural India.[23] This heterogenous middle class is as complex as that discussed in earlier chapters for the late colonial period, including rich farmers, white collar and other professionals and those running small businesses. However, it is marked by upward mobility, conspicuous consumption and the acquisition of consumer products and services. These urban classes' fortunes changed largely as a result of the rapid growth in average family incomes over the mid-1980s, illustrated, for example, in the rapid increase in car/scooter and television ownership. By the end of the 1980s, one estimate of the numerical size of the Indian middle class put it at 176 million – making up forty-two per cent of urban households and thirteen per cent of rural families.[24] Significantly, these families are dominated by those from higher-caste communities who did not benefit from reservations policies. Also, it is this very group that have most strongly backed the idea of a strong unitary India. As in the late colonial period, part of the status enhancement/aspiration-raising projects for these middle classes was the support of religious observance. Having acquired wealth more rapidly than social status, a common way to assert status was through religious observance, as Chris Fuller has shown with the middle-class support for Hindu revivalism through temple renovation in south India. This is not to suggest that the support for parties like the BJP, particularly once it enjoyed a taste of real power from the 1990s, was exclusively drawn from these social groups and castes. As we will see in the final chapter, the BJP was obliged for electoral and state-level political reasons to attempt to draw more 'Backward Castes' into its support networks in the last years of the 1990s in states like UP.

(ii) 'communalism' in the 1980s

The political ferment of the period from the late 1970s to the mid-1980s seemed to coincide with a rise in popular or everyday violence, described by the media and government as 'communal'. The estimated number of

[23] For a complex discussion of this process, see Arvind Rajagopal, *Politics After Television*.
[24] Corbridge and Harriss, p. 124.

'riots' over the decade of the 1980s defined in this way increased fourfold when compared to the 1970s. Just in UP, there were sixty riots between February 1986 and the middle of 1988.[25] Accompanying this apparent rise in violence and conflict, and the growing fortunes of the Sangh Parivar, particularly in north and western India, was the appearance of new organisations and writers who protested against what was felt to be the 'communalisation' of Indian politics. Asghar Ali Engineer was a central figure in this from the early 1980s, writing in the *Economic and Political Weekly*, who presented some early observations on the tactics of the Hindu right in the thick of conflicts. An important dynamic of Engineer's observations, which represent an early foray into the subject in the light of the later voluminous work on the Hindu right in the early 1990s, were structural and socio-economic reasons for violence and conflict. For Engineer, communal riots commonly occurred in medium-sized towns, where the proportion of Muslim communities to the population as a whole was relatively high and where there were clear indices of economic and/or political competition between different religious communities or sects. This was clearly the background framework for his analysis of conflict between Shias and Sunnis in Bombay in 1988.[26]

Importantly, Engineer also ascertained that these moments of violence in the early 1980s appeared to be more 'planned' than in earlier times – an observation to which we will return below, but which certainly related to the long-term stockpiling of weapons specifically designed for a riot situation. In this sense, his work corresponded to that of 'constructivist' authors who looked at the ways in which social and ethnic identities were 'constructed' for particular political ends.[27] One of the key 'case studies' for Engineer was the violence in Meerut, Uttar Pradesh, in September to October 1982. Here, a key observation was the extent to which the predominantly high-caste leadership of the Sangh attempted to mobilise low castes and Dalits for a show of strength. Part of the reasoning behind this for Engineer was the prevention of low-caste conversion to Islam and the building of a low-caste Muslim political front, particularly in Uttar Pradesh.

---

[25] Zoya Hasan, 'Changing Orientation of the State', p. 28.
[26] Asghar Ali Engineer, 'Sectarian Clashes in Bombay', *Economic and Political Weekly*, 23, 39, 1988, 1993–4.
[27] For a discussion of these authors, see James D. Fearon and David D. Laitin, 'Violence and the Social Construction of Ethnic Identity'.

Perhaps more significant than building the image of Hindu unity, then, was the sense of manipulation and exploitation described in these reports: Dalits and low castes were excellent fodder for the violence itself, especially from the perspective of the RSS. These observations can now be seen to correspond to the later work of Paul R. Brass in looking at how political violence, especially in local politics in western and central UP, operated along the lines of violence by proxy. Brass shows how dominant communities used retinues of lower castes to carry out acts of violence against rivals,[28] sometimes as part of an institutionalised riot system.[29] Taking his own analysis further, Engineer suggested that such violence by proxy was also a method of 'dividing the have-nots' in any particular urban constituency by the Hindu right as a way of drawing them away from support for the Congress (I) – the main local rival of the BJP.[30] The RSS and BJP leadership in Meerut were also able to make use of the intimate connections between local political leadership and administration, as described in the last chapter, to mobilise support from the Superintendent of Police and the Additional District Magistrate. Reports on the 1982 violence in Meerut suggested that these two officials were instrumental in ordering firings on Muslims over the period of intense violence between 29 September and 1 October, which resulted in twenty-nine deaths. It was alleged that the Provincial Armed Constabulary (PAC) had a pre-arrangement with the Hindu parties to facilitate attacks against Muslims and systematically destroyed and looted Muslim properties in the town. They also managed to draw away a disgruntled Hindu leadership from the Congress (I) that had been passed over in elections when tickets were given to Muslims.[31]

There were broader factors at play in the mobilisation of the Sangh, including the scare of Hindu conversions to Islam and the use of international events to both intimidate and mobilise poorer Hindu communities. In its propaganda, the Sangh represented India as a unitary, pre-1947 entity, colouring maps of Pakistan and Bangladesh saffron. It also reflected on the rise of 'Islamic fundamentalism' in the Arab world and the India-wide debates about a uniform civil code.[32] Highly significant in

---

[28] Paul R. Brass, *The Politics of Northern India: 1937 to 1987, Volume I: An Indian Political Life: Charan Singh and Congress Politics, 1937 to 1961* (New Delhi: Sage, 2011), pp. 282, 289.
[29] Paul R. Brass, *The Production of Hindu–Muslim Violence in Contemporary India.*
[30] Asghar Ali Engineer, 'The Guilty Men of Meerut', *Economic and Political Weekly*, 17, 45, 1982, p. 1803.
[31] *Ibid.*, p. 1804.
[32] Asghar Ali Engineer, 'Behind the Communal Fury', *Economic and Political Weekly*, 17, 10, 1982, pp. 356-7.

the mobilisational techniques of the Sangh over this period, even where this was based in very localised cadres, were the constant references to the 'threat' of Pakistan or the need to take it back or destroy it. At Sholapur in 1982, the slogans during a VHP procession included 'jalado, jalado Pakistan jalado' ('burn, burn Pakistan') and 'Ek dhakka aur do, Pakistan tor do' ('give one more push and break Pakistan'). Perhaps most interesting here were slogans about the specific fortunes of migrant Muslims and their properties: 'Ye desh Hinduon ka, nahin kisi ke bap ka' ('this country belongs to the Hindus and is not of somebody's father's property'). In summary, Engineer suggested that 'The perpetuators of the status quo, whether they be Muslim fundamentalists of Saudi Arabia and Pakistan, or Hindu fundamentalists of India, need the spectre of external enemy to beat into submission the have-nots within' and connected this to the policies of Zia in Pakistan.[33]

In many of the conflicts instigated by the Sangh Parivar in places like Pune, Bombay, Meerut and Ahmedabad in the early to mid 1980s, it was clear that there was a connection between the targeting of Muslim communities and the fate of low castes, Dalits and tribal communities. For example, the 1985 riots in Ahmedabad, as we will see, demonstrated a direct transformation from caste to communal conflict. In a comparable way, Engineer outlined connections between the largely poor Muslim community of Pune and the economy of the city's Sweeper communities in the February 1982 Jan Jagran Andolan in the city, which led to the burning of extensive areas of Muslim properties. As suggested above, Dalits and low castes were mobilised in the violence against Muslims in Meerut. The relationship between Hindu-right instigated/encouraged violence and the participation/control of lower castes was perhaps even more common in Gujarat over the 1980s. In 1981, students in Ahmedabad protested against the abolition of reservations, as they had been promoted through the Mandal Commission proposals. In the city, it was clear from the early 1980s, too, that there was a socio-economic gulf between the vast majority of the Muslim population, alongside the Dalit communities, and the higher Hindu caste groups. Engineer suggests that in 1981–2, the RSS, which instigated much of the violence over those years, mainly recruited from particular conservative trading castes, such as the north Gujarat Patels.[34]

[33] *Ibid.*, p. 357.
[34] Asghar Ali Engineer, 'Communal Violence in Gujarat', *Economic and Political Weekly*, 17, 4, 1983, p. 100.

In her study of the Ahmedabad riots of 1985, Shani takes Engineer's arguments further and suggests that what had traditionally been analysed as 'Hindu–Muslim' antagonism in Gujarat should not be principally seen in that light in these years. Adopting the notion of ethno-nationalist mobilisation, Shani suggests that struggles between different caste communities of Hindus were very much at the root of conflict, which later revolved around a 'Hindu–Muslim' series of disputes.[35] In 1985, the key trigger to controversy between different communities was the state government's decision to extend educational and governmental reservations to 'socially and educationally Backward Castes' in the state from ten per cent to twenty-eight per cent as a result of the Gujarat government's Baxi Commission Report. Shani's account outlines competing narratives of the riots that took place in February 1985, from the official Dave Commission report of the local government, which largely obscured the detailed caste-basis of the background conflict, to individual accounts from survivors and witnesses. Shani, in agreement with Tambiah and Brass, suggests that the formation of a broader 'ethnoHindu' identity was part of a process whereby Hindu–Muslim divisions were perpetuated as self-fulfilling political discourses re-created in historical memory. Violence perceived to be 'communal' was often actually based on a range of social conflicts frequently involving the local state.[36] The intersection between religious community and caste was repeated again in conflict in Ahmedabad in 2002, as Chapter 8 will explore.

Below the media reports of Hindu–Muslim antagonism, other kinds of social struggle characterised these conflicts. The violence of the 1980s involved disputes about the control of land and local resources in which the mechanism of the local state and administration were intimately tied to changing pressures on resources, commercial opportunities and population pressure. Another way to look at this is to consider how these instances of violence took on a differential significance for different levels of the Indian state. For example, in Meerut in 1982, the immediate trigger for rioting related to a very specific dispute over land surrounding a Hindu well and the alleged existence of a temple. The claims of the RSS on the latter only appeared after contestation of ownership on the valuable urban land arose, and involved a powerful Muslim lawyer from the locality. Such

---

[35] Ornit Shani, *Communalism, Caste and Hindu Nationalism* and 'The Rise of Hindu Nationalism in India: The Case Study of Ahmedabad in the 1980s', *Modern Asian Studies*, 39, 4, 2005, 861–96.
[36] Shani, *Communalism, Caste and Hindu Nationalism*, p. 158.

disputed sites, then, became the terrain of competitive political authority, as leaders from all sides used the publicity of 'puja' (prayer) or opposition to the site to garner support. The mechanisms of judicial and executive action also became important dynamics in the respective strategies of each side, with preferential court rulings forming the focus for conflict. When a more serious outbreak of violence in 1987 occurred in Meerut, the UP state government's official administrative enquiry, led by Gian Prakash, obscured certain facets of government servant involvement in the violence – especially that of the PAC.[37] This survey of official obfuscation, as the work of Paul R. Brass on Aligarh also shows, suggests that 'communal violence' has been officially represented in ways that strategically generalise such violence, as part of an institutionalised riot system, or downplay its detailed political motivations.[38]

This leads us back to the question of how far violence, apparently generated between religious or other ethnic communities in 1980s India, was in fact based in more complex, varied and often local manifestations of antipathy. One of the key problems in sustaining the constructivist arguments of those studying communal riots and violence is the question of how and why large numbers of people appear to be either duped or convinced by the deliberate manipulation of religious and community symbols by those in positions of power. One of the most convincing of the many possible answers to this conundrum is the point that the large numbers of people involved in such violence as the Gujarat or Meerut riots in the 1980s are not necessarily motivated by the religious or ethnic symbols attached to the riots at all – that, in fact, the interpretations of these events are a post facto explanation, which allows political leaders or the state to present explanations that are politically expedient or convenient.

For example, in *Theft of an Idol*, Paul R. Brass suggests that local feuds and conflicts often provide the specific motivations for those involved in violence, and that the frame of a larger religious riot allows such conflicts to take place, even though the substantive reason for them is very different to how they are represented in general.[39] This seems to have been particularly the case, for example, where police involvement in apparent instances of communal violence linked to other forms of criminal behaviour, in which the exercise of social humiliation was used as a means of asserting local

[37] Asghar Ali Engineer, 'Gian Prakash Committee Report on Meerut Riots', *Economic and Political Weekly*, 23, 1/2, 1988, 30–1, 33.
[38] Paul R. Brass, *Theft of an Idol*.
[39] *Ibid.*

dominance. Also significant are complex instances of violence and conflict by proxy, in which those on the margins of a particular community assert their rights to be a part of it by undertaking violent action on behalf of that group.[40] One example of this process in the late colonial period was seen in the Adi Hindu movement in UP, which asserted its members' identities as 'protectors' of Hinduism. Here too, though, the motivations for such actions often related to discrete and local manifestations of local power and status rather than broader, national concepts of religious identity.

But how and why did conflict expand and develop (either in reality or representation) into what observers considered to be 'communal' violence from these more localised disputes? Certainly, some political organisations and structures (which themselves might benefit electorally from violence) were positioned to encourage such transformations and acquire knowledge about how the state operated at everyday levels, or how state agents could be corrupted. Significant here is the work of Ashutosh Varshney, which explores how civic institutions, particularly those with influence in local governments, may have deterred violence in some contexts in contemporary India. Observing that riots seem to reoccur in a relatively small number of towns and cities, including Ahmedabad, Bombay, Aligarh, Hyderabad and Meerut, Varshney has identified possible associational organisations of civic engagement that may prevent conflict in other contexts.[41] However, civic institutions could equally serve as means for controlling state servants and local politicians in the encouragement of violence. The legacies of bureaucratic and police traditions from the colonial era, which for pragmatic reasons permitted the autonomous exercise of local power in many cases, allowed, in a different, democratic context, the machinery of the state itself to be temporarily appropriated by local powerbrokers.[42] Added to this was the knowledge among political parties and ordinary citizens alike that local administrations could sometimes be influenced informally – a situation that could play into the hands of the religious right.[43] It has, at different moments and in different contexts across South Asia in the 1980s, for example, served the interests of parties such as the BJS/BJP to represent non-religious quarrels as broad

---

[40] Fearon and Laitin, p. 857.

[41] Ashutosh Varshney, 'Ethnic Conflict and Civil Society', pp. 375–90.

[42] William Gould, *Bureaucracy, Community and Influence*.

[43] For an example of this process, of linking national surveys of communalism, from the 'upper' levels of the state to local ethnography, see Amrita Basu, 'When Local Riots are Not Merely Local: Bringing the State Back In, Bijnor 1988–1992', *Economic and Political Weekly*, 29, 40, 1994, 2605–21.

Hindu–Muslim antagonism by controlling the levers of the local state. This appears to have been the case in some of the early to mid-1980s projects to broaden the significance of anti-reservation politics to wider audiences via propaganda that more broadly promoted communal hatred. In other contexts, violence between religious and ethnic communities has related to the longer-term exercise of state power, religious authority and social dominance. As we will see in the case of Sri Lanka, the identification of organised political agencies in moments of violence is perhaps more relevant over longer periods of time, and over even larger spaces within the state, when compared to India.

(iii) THE 1970S AND 1980S IN SRI LANKA

Any narrative of the intense political conflict and the formal depiction of 'terrorist' threats to 'the state' in Ceylon (renamed Sri Lanka in 1972) of the 1980s is perhaps most appropriately begun with the 1971 Janatha Vimukthi Peramuna or JVP (People's Liberation Front – a Marxist–Leninist party) insurrection. The April 1971 uprisings were essentially a youth rebellion against the incumbent Bandaranaike administration. Although they lasted only a few weeks, the insurrection broke out in seven of the nine provinces, and the JVP managed to hold onto significant areas in the southern and central provinces. The Ceylon government had been forced to rely upon military aid from India and Pakistan – at that time under the leaderships of Indira Gandhi and Benazir Bhutto. The uprising signalled a new level of commitment to internal security for Sri Lankan governments, but also, importantly, the increasing interconnection between the internal politics of Sri Lanka and India.[44]

It was in this atmosphere of political insecurity and competition that militant Tamil organisations also began to change their approach to the politics of protest. Key in the foregrounding of militant Tamil organisations was the policy of educational standardisation, introduced in 1973 by Mrs. Bandaranaike, ostensibly to control admissions to universities along 'ethnic' lines. Also important was the 1972 constitution, which gave formal recognition to the dominance of the Sinhalese Buddhist community. Third, sporadic incidents of violence between the two communities became a key election issue in the 1977 elections. The victory of the United National Party promised some honouring of Tamil autonomy, with the setting up in 1981 of district development councils. However, this

---

[44] *Sunday Observer* (Colombo), 8 May 2005.

supposed second tier of government was poorly funded and never seriously implemented.[45] The elections also signalled the decline of the mainstream left and the rise of the UNP trade union with their pro-Sinhalese stance. The Tamil United Liberation Front (TULF), which had evolved out of the TUF, was already pushing its separatist ambitions set out in the Vaddukoddai resolution of May 1976. This resolution firmly stated that the ambition of the TULF was the foundation of Tamil Eelam – a separate sovereign state.

The wording of the Vaddukoddai resolution represented a classic citation of ethnic history as a strategy for setting out a sense of political separation. In this narrative, the Tamil kingdoms, described as separate from the Sinhalese territories, were conquered by the Portuguese in 1619 and then the Dutch and British. The latter, for administrative convenience, unified these kingdoms on the island, yet it was the Tamils, the resolution claimed, who were the most genuine champions of political independence from colonial rule. These claims to the leadership of 'anti-colonial' protest reflected older Hindu nationalist arguments in India. But the principal part of the resolution listed the specific measures in which the Sinhalese majority had trampled upon the civic rights of the Tamil minority, which in 1971 made up around eleven per cent of the island's population (although there was also a significant Indian Tamil population of nine per cent), compared to the seventy-two per cent Sinhalese majority. Focus was also placed on the future project of economic planning, socialist redistribution and public ownership of key enterprises.[46] Work on the basis of ethno-nationalism on the island has suggested that the drives for separation are also characterised by the self-perception of Ceylon Tamils, as an economically advanced population, held back by discriminatory government policies.[47] Also key in the resolution, however, was mention of the imposition of Buddhism, which was given the 'foremost place', under the Republican Constitution, above Hinduism, Islam and Christianity.[48] The central document of Tamil separatism, then, evoked constitutional/state structures to make a formal argument about separate identity. But this historical separateness was also premised upon a clear sense of religious difference.

[45] James Manor, ed., *Sri Lanka in Change and Crisis.*
[46] 'The Vaddukoddai Resolution', available at http://www.satp.org/satporgtp/countries/ shrilanka/document/papers/vaddukoddai_resolution.htm, accessed on 15 January 2010.
[47] For details of this argument, see Amita Shastri, 'The Material Basis for Separatism', *Journal of Asian Studies*, 49, 1, 1990, 56–77.
[48] 'The Vaddukoddai Resolution'.

Work on the development of ethnic separatism and conflict in Sri Lanka bears certain similarities to research on Indian 'communalism' and religious separatism. First, a collection of older work has outlined the somewhat primordial sense of ethnic difference of the Tamil minority and Sinhalese majority illustrated in references to history, language and cultural difference. Other discussions have pointed out the ways in which, following independence and particularly in the 1950s, the Sinhalese majority used political and state structures to further economic opportunities for themselves. The evidence of the gradual displacement of Tamils from the civil administration certainly supports analyses of this process. So do the uneven 'development' policies, especially in paddy cultivation, which favoured the Sinhalese-dominated provinces.[49] Even more importantly, the electoral swing to the ruling coalition (the SLFP-led United Front) in 1971 gave it a large enough majority to change the constitution in 1972, thereby institutionalising the Sinhala language and Buddhism. Yet neither the more functionalist arguments looking at structures of economic and political opportunity nor the more primordialist arguments fully explain the conflicts and events that ensued from the late 1970s in Sri Lanka. As we will see, there are other ways of exploring the detailed mechanisms of violence in Sri Lanka that unpack the very meaning of everyday violence itself.

Following the Vaddukoddai resolution, the TULF was pushed into a somewhat contradictory position – espousing separatism for the North East, yet sitting in parliament in the south. Added to this insecurity was the increased authoritarian power of the state itself – enshrined in the new constitution of 1978, which granted enhanced executive powers to the president, J. R. Jayawardene – which allowed the ruling party to suppress the civic rights of opposition parties. The constitution, in introducing proportional representation, did contain overtures to the Tamil parties, since in any parliamentary or presidential election, their share of the vote could now 'count'. However, the growing authoritarian policies of the state quickly quashed any execution of these concessions in practice: Sinhalese security forces and police continued to suppress Tamil organisations in the north, and a 'fourth amendment' to the constitution in 1982 prolonged the parliament for six years.[50] The sixth amendment to the constitution, which, in July 1983, prohibited those subscribing to

[49] Amita Shastri, pp. 61–6.
[50] See James Manor, 'Introduction', in James Manor, ed., *Sri Lanka in Change and Crisis*, pp. 10–14.

separatism from sitting in the parliament, brought an end to the dualism between protests against Sinhalese dominance, on the one hand, and constitutional representation, on the other. Importantly, there were reflections, here, of India's 1963 sixteenth amendment, which was designed to combat the separatist ambitions of the Dravida Munnetra Kazagham (DMK) – the Dravidian successor to the Justice Party in the south. Into this political vacuum created by the resignation of the TULF leaders from parliament stepped the Liberation Tigers of Tamil Eelam (LTTE), under the leadership of Velupillai Prabhakaran. However, the Tamil communities in Sri Lanka were also divided politically, and over the early 1980s, the support for Jayawardene from some Tamil areas increased relatively – with some seeing his party as a secure alternative to the increasing chauvinism of the SLFP. Tragically, as these events unfolded, government security forces effectively targeted some of the UNP government's main minority support over the late 1970s and early 1980s.[51]

The intimidatory and violent tactics used by the LTTE and Sinhalese parties around the middle of 1983 generated increasing militarisation in Sri Lanka politics. Organised violence was a feature of both sides of the Tamil–Sinhalese conflicts from this point. Over July and August 1983, several hundred were killed (mostly Tamils), tens of thousands were driven into refugee camps and countless businesses looted and burned. Much of this violence was reported at the time as being 'systematic', and in some cases involved gruesome 'symbolic' forms of execution. Specific Tamil business and professional communities were targeted in Colombo. Opinion on the roots of the violence, as in most 'communal' riots in India for example, is divided. The spark was an LTTE attack on Sinhalese forces on 23 July, resulting in the deaths of thirteen soldiers. Thereafter, government security forces and party members, over which the president had poor control, were central in sustaining the violence, promoting massacres and pogroms.[52] As Brass has shown for north India in the same period, the 'terrorism' and 'anti-state' activity of the Tamil community, as propounded by key Sinhalese leaders, became a central theory in explaining and justifying the violence, especially from the perspective of the state.[53]

Certainly, the events of 1983 helped to generate further support for Tamil separatist organisations. However, the Tamil movements were also

---

[51] M. P. Moore, 'The 1982 Elections and the New Gaullist-Bonapartist State in Sri Lanka', in James Manor, ed., pp. 51–76.
[52] Eric Meyer, 'Seeking the Roots of the Tragedy', in James Manor, ed., pp. 137–52.
[53] Elizabeth Nissan, 'Some Thoughts on Sinhalese Justifications for the Violence', in James Manor, ed., p. 176.

MAP 4. Sri Lanka

not unified, and the 'separatist' movement cannot be generalised into a single organisation. It was made up of around thirty or so factions, some of which were Marxist and most of which rejected the structure of parliamentary democracy for the setting up of Tamil Eelam in the north and east of the country. The factions were also divided on the basis of caste, with the upwardly mobile Karaiyars and Koviars in Jaffna challenging the traditional dominance of the Vellalars. As well as the LTTE, other significant groups included the Eelam People's Revolutionary Liberation Front or People's Liberation Army (EPRLF), the Tamil Eelam Liberation Organisation (TELO), the Eelam Revolutionary Organisation of Students (EROS) and the People's Liberation Organisation of Tamil Eelam (PLOTE or PLOT). The first four of these merged into a kind of loose federation of the Eelam National Liberation Front (ENLF) in March 1985.[54]

The LTTE was the forerunner organisation, founded in 1972, and is also the organisation responsible for the assassination of the thirteen Sinhalese soldiers, which sparked the island-wide riots against the Tamil population. By contrast, EROS, formed in London in 1975, is based upon a consortium of Tamil intellectuals concentrating more on economic sabotage and generally opposing the use of armed resistance. A very different organisation again, PLOT, is Marxist, using hit-and-run guerrilla tactics and generally attempting to avoid non-combatant casualties. Its leader, Uma Maheshwaran, has become something of a rival to Prabhakaran of the LTTE, which has at times escalated into armed conflict between the two groups. Highly significant has been the link between these movements and parties in Tamil Nadu itself – with opposition parties in the state often basing their agendas against the Congress on the basis of lack of support for Tamil separatism in Sri Lanka. The AIADMK in particular has been instrumental in highlighting its positive support for Eelam. Most importantly, at a more informal level, it is fairly clear that training camps for Tamil movements exist in Tamil Nadu.

The Sinhalese forces have been largely concentrated in the building up of the Special Task Force of paramilitary police, operating in the eastern provinces. Specific government initiatives have encouraged the militarisation of the wider Sri Lankan population, for example the formation of the Manpower Mobilization Office, which has trained cadets of young men since 1985. Sinhalese settlers in the Vanni jungle area of Jaffna have also been trained by the central government, and Sinhalese settlements have been encouraged to tip the population balance. Here, government grants led to central government involvement in the everyday concerns of Sinhalese settlers, as they attempted to navigate state interracial policy.

However, as was the case in India, in exploring these conflicts and ethnic rivalries in Sri Lanka, it is also necessary to look more closely at the nature of the violence associated with it. In the early 1980s, we see a range of examples of retributive killings in the Sinhalese–Tamil conflict in Sri Lanka. For example, in the summer of 1983, killings of Sinhalese soldiers, which formed the backdrop to a public funeral in Colombo, led to extreme retributive killings and violence against Tamil populations – whole suburbs of the city were razed to the ground and some of the towns

---

[54] Bruce Matthews, 'Radical Conflict and the Rationalization of Violence in Sri Lanka', *Pacific Affairs*, 59, 1, 1986.

to the south destroyed, leading to the death of around 2,000 to 3,000 Tamil civilians.[55] The UNP government, since the early 1980s, has been involved in the organisation of systematic violence against its opponents, which is semi-official in nature. Indeed, no government in South Asia has managed to retain power in quite the same way with the complicit acquiescence of agents of intimidation and violence. But of course, this is a situation in which the governments themselves are rarely able to control the actions of their own cadres. In the 1980s violence in Sri Lanka too, it appears that civilian Tamil populations were very often tarred with the brush of being 'Tigers', even when the Tigers had not operated within hundreds of miles. This identification of Tamil populations was fuelled by the press, despite the fact that one of the principal reasons for the on-going failure to establish Tamil autonomy by guerrilla tactics has been the presence of mainstream Tamil parties and populations in southern parts of Sri Lanka that vehemently oppose violence.

There is much more for the historian to think about here, however, than simply the issue of Sinhalese–Tamil conflict or Buddhist–Tamil conflict. Recent research has shown that there were important changes in the 1980s around the traditions of Buddhist monks, which pushed the monasteries directly into the public political sphere. Widely circulated Buddhist newspapers, like *Budusarana*, suggested that the new young monk should not ignore the contemporary issues of nation, language and religion. This idea emerged in argument with the more traditional stance that monks should follow a religious ideal that transcended the temporal concerns of nation or religious difference. However, the new ideal of monks as brave and fearless came through very strongly in the early to mid-1980s against a discourse that described the corrupt and amoral influences of Westernisation and the market.[56] These more militant discourses linked Sinhalese identity to the Buddhist *sangha* as a response to a particular political moment and, importantly, a time when aspects of state power were being critiqued. These will be further explored in the next chapter in looking at how violence in Sri Lanka involves and affects ordinary people.

None of these considerations, however, existed entirely in a vacuum on the island, and its politics were also related to other kinds of states – most notably, India. In 1985, Rajiv Gandhi's assessment of the problems in Sri Lanka were that there were in fact 'two terrorisms' – that of the Tamil Tigers, on the one hand, and that of Sri Lankan soldiers who 'lose their

[55] Jonathan Spencer, 'Collective Violence and Everyday Practice in Sri Lanka', p. 616.
[56] Ananda Abeysekara, 'The Saffron Army, Violence, Terror(ism)'.

composure'.[57] Critical to the failure of the Tamil separatists for most of this period was the reluctance of any Indian government to aid militarily the movements against the Sri Lankan government. Here, the issue of separatism in Sri Lanka linked very strongly to anticipation of separatism in India itself. Faced in the 1980s with powerful separatist movements in the Punjab and Assam, Indira Gandhi and Rajiv Gandhi were aware that Eelam would set a very dangerous precedent. More directly, there was a concern that the links between Tamil separatism and the Dravidian movement in Tamil Nadu might add another tangled separatist agenda to the long list of challenges of national integrity, as set out in the last chapter. For both of these leaders, as we have already seen in the case of Indira Gandhi, action against regional separatism was to cost them their lives. For Rajiv Gandhi, this was at the hands of an LTTE suicide bomber, on 21 May 1991 while he campaigned in Tamil Nadu. The bomber was angered at the alleged atrocities of the Indian Peace Keeping force in Sri Lanka and Gandhi's role in over-throwing a military coup in the Maldives in 1988 supported by PLOTE.

(IV) PAKISTAN AND BANGLADESH: SECULARISM AND 'ISLAMIZATION'

In 1971, the broad divisions between West Pakistan and Bengali East Pakistan finally came to a head to change the political geography of South Asia completely. We saw in the last chapter how, for most of the first two decades of its independence, Pakistan was ruled without recourse to democratic conventions, and that when the Constituent Assembly did meet in the early years, it was the site for arguments about the relative constitutional position of East and West. Military and bureaucratic authority within Pakistan was also bolstered by the geostrategy of the United States, but within the country itself, it quickly became apparent that military regimes had few mechanisms for accommodating political opposition, leading to further authoritarian measures of rule by ordinance. These measures were the result, at another level, of enforced state centralisation, which initially suppressed the political ambitions of the powerful Awami League in East Pakistan. The arrest of Mujib ur Rahman led to violence in 1969 in Bengal, eventually resulting in the stepping down of Ayub Khan and his replacement by Yahya Khan. But in the elections that

---

[57] Bruce Matthews, 'Radical Conflict and the Rationalization of Violence in Sri Lanka'.

ensued the following year, the Awami League scored a landslide victory in East Pakistan.

In Pakistan, the division between east and west and the failures of the political system to accommodate the logic of the Bengali majority, then, reached a crisis point after the first general elections for the country in 1970. Whereas Mujib ur Rahman's Awami League won 151 of the total 153 seats in East Pakistan, Zulfikar Bhutto's PPP was the major party in the west, winning 81 of the 148 seats there. Importantly, the PPP dominated the two provinces of Punjab and Sindh. However, despite the successes of the Awami League, its six-point programme (see Chapter 6) was stalled by the Legal Framework Order under which the 1970 elections had been held. This allowed the army, which controlled the office of president, to oppose the League's demand for a confederation between two regions, being incorporated into a constitution. Whereas for a while before the elections accommodation between the army and Mujib seemed possible, it soon became clear that neither the hawks in the army nor the less compromising members of the League would be able to come to an agreement about any future constitution. At the same time, Bhutto had more successfully manoeuvred the PPP around the more resistant members of the army establishment to push for the indefinite postponement of the National Assembly. In 1971, Pakistan was racked by a civil war between its two wings, with India siding with Bengal, which resulted in a new breakaway state from East Pakistan – Bangladesh.

In a curious parallel with the pronouncements of leaders of the Congress right in the mid-1940s in agreeing to cut off 'the diseased limb', the PPP cautiously welcomed its control of the new, more physically viable smaller Pakistan from 1972. Yet, once again, it seemed that the promises of true representative popular government were constrained by the insecurities of political power and the continued hold of the military and bureaucratic elites in Pakistan. The PPP's creation of the paramilitary Federal Security Force (FSF) became a means of intimidating opponents to the new regime with what became an officially sponsored army of thugs. Not surprisingly, the PPP largely failed to accommodate the demands and aspirations of the minority provinces and, despite the provisions of the 1973 constitution, which granted a greater degree of provincial autonomy, stamped down on political opposition in Baluchistan and NWFP. And as a result, the severe underrepresentation of ethnic minorities such as Baluchis in the political and military establishment continued. Since 1947, guerrilla groups in Baluchistan had opposed the power of the central Pakistani government, particularly the Pararis, who had been encouraged by the creation of Bangladesh in 1971. Attempts to reform the customary author-ity of tribal chiefs in the region also met with fierce opposition, and a more serious conflict arose over the suspected succession plans of the National Awami Party (NAP) in the province. This latter smear campaign of the PPP against the NAP in Baluchistan served to marginalise the more moderate NAP leadership, which had, since the elections, been keen to work within the institutional structures of the constitution. Most signifi-cantly, the removal of the NAP government in Baluchistan made a mock-ery of the so-called representative nature of the PPP government, as military rule was once again imposed in the province. Effectively, the army became an institution that, in many different ways, was perceived as a force for the control of corrupt and treacherous politicians who threatened Pakistani national security.[58] Failures in accommodation of minority interests occurred elsewhere. In Sindh, the PPP-dominated gov-ernment passed a bill that made Sindhi the official provincial language in July 1972 and led to riots between muhajir organisations and the provin-cial police.[59]

Over the period of PPP rule, the eventual ditching of the radical left within the party and reorientation with landlord interests in the Punjab and Sindh pushed the PPP closer to compromise with Islamic conserva-tives. In the 1970 elections, the conservative and religious parties had, collectively, polled a larger number of votes than the PPP, and so the latter was always under pressure to appeal to similar constituencies. For exam-ple, in 1974, in the aftermath of the anti-Qadiani riots, the Qadianis (who claimed that their founder, Mirza Ghulam Ahmed, was a prophet, thereby questioning the finality of the prophethood of Mohammed) were declared a non-Muslim sect. Also significant in this flirtation with the religious right were the PPP's relations, which improved over the mid-1970s, with the Gulf States, whose economic power had been enhanced as a result of the 1973 oil crisis. A summit of Islamic heads of state was held in Lahore in 1974, signalling Pakistan's ambitions to be seen as one of the leaders of the Muslim world. The influence of states like Saudi Arabia on the PPP regime were evident in the eventual banning of alcohol and nightclubs and the moving of the weekend break from Sunday to Friday. But it was economic measures and the dissatisfaction with the corruption of the regime that eventually resulted in the popular protests led by the Pakistan National

---

[58] Noman, *Pakistan: A Political and Economic History since 1947*, pp. 65–8.
[59] Moonis Ahmar, 'Ethnicity and State Power in Pakistan: The Karachi Crisis', *Asian Survey*, 36, 10, 1996, 1031–48.

Alliance (PNA) against the PPP-rigged elections of 1977. Once again, the military were asked to take power on the (mistaken) understanding that there would eventually be transfer to the rule of another civilian government.

Given this political context, it was not surprising that specific state institutions continued to be involved in the development of sectarian and ethnic clashes. This has been especially the case since the 1970s, when the Bhutto regime was continually challenged by the military, by building alliances of regional and ethnic parties. For example, in the mid to late 1970s, the army sought alliances with the Jamaat-e-Islami as a way of creating a broader base for its eventual coup.[60] However, it was the regime of General Zia-ul-Huq that most clearly illustrated the extent to which government flirtation with sectarian organisations complicated the nature of conflict and violence around ethnicity or sect. By the late 1970s, the fragile legitimacy of the army (especially since its 1977 coup was illegal under the 1973 constitution) meant that the regime under Zia-ul-Huq needed to seek legitimacy by other means. It is of course wrong to assume that the turn towards theocracy and the courting of the religious right was confined to this period: Bhutto's regime was also drifting in that direction in the mid-1970s as a result of political imperatives and international factors. However, Zia's government raised the formal powers of the central state to the point of defining a comprehensive ideology that promoted new forms of social organisation. And its more blatant use of arbitrary power to enforce obedience to the state did allow Islamicist conceptions of the state and society to dominate in an unprecedented way in the 1980s. Zia overtly stated that all aspects of social and political life, all offices of the state, politics and administration would be 'regulated in accordance with Islamic Principles'.[61] Islamisation projects also affected policies of 'development', particularly in relation to women, effectively reinforcing male-centred patrilinear conceptions of law and the legal process.[62]

These patterns of state power closely emulated the ideas of Maududi's Jamaat-e-Islami. Both before the Zia coup and throughout the phase of Zia's power, the Jamaat and particularly the ISI was courted but just as quickly ditched when political expediency allowed. Even more directly,

[60] Irm Haleem, 'Ethnic and Sectarian Violence and the Propensity towards Praetorianism in Pakistan', p. 470.
[61] Speech of Zia-ul-Huq, 14 August 1977. Quoted in Noman, p. 145.
[62] See Anita M. Weiss, 'Women's Position in Pakistan: Socio-Cultural Effects of Islamization', *Pacific Affairs*, 25, 8, 1985, 863–80.

there is evidence that intelligence agencies, particularly the ISI, have deliberately fomented both ethnic and sectarian conflict in Pakistan from at least the 1980s as a means of maintaining the power of the military. The classic example here is the formation of the Islamic Jamhoori Ittihad (IJI) with the assistance of the ISI in the late 1980s. This coalition of centre-right Punjabi-dominated interests and Islamicists was headed up by a handpicked leader, Nawaz Sharif, as a way of combating the power and influence of the predominantly Sindhi Pakistan People's Party (PPP). In 1984 too, the Mohajir Quami Movement was also courted by the IPI to oppose the PPP.

Islamisation of the state in Pakistan in the 1980s was also linked to the proliferation of madrasahs and the growing power of their students in local and national politics. The number of madrasahs increased two-and-a-half times between 1975 and 1996, from around 700 to 2,463, partly financed by Saudi Arabia and the United Arab Emirates.[63] The Jamaat-e-Islami founded its own madrasahs over the same period. The motivation for this funding in the 1970s was fear about Pakistan's apparent turn to the left under Bhutto. This was despite the fact that Bhutto's regime, too, had used the idea of state promotion of Islam as a means of regime legitimisation and started a process that Zia effectively continued.[64] In the early 1980s, Gulf State financial support was also linked to a desire to provide an Islamic bulwark against the invaders of Afghanistan, with some of the madrasahs' activitists being trained up to fight against the USSR. Many of the graduates of the new madrasahs were therefore keen to promote jihad in relation to events in Afghanistan, and some of the 'ulama modelled themselves on the example of the Taliban. Some of the madrasahs became training grounds for the main religio-political organisations in the country, which competed for funding from the Gulf States. Although the extent to which these developments were related to specific state reforms under Zia should be treated with caution,[65] it is generally acknowledged that strident Sunni militancy since the 1980s has contributed to violence between the main sects in Pakistan. In 1988, 150 Shi'i were killed in Gilgit by vigilante Sunni groups, and over the late 1980s and early 1990s, significant Shia and Sunni leaders were assassinated, including an Iranian cultural attaché in Lahore.[66]

---

[63] Nasr, 'The Rise of Sunni Militancy', p. 142.
[64] See Nikki Keddie, 'Pakistan's Movement Against Islamization', *MERIP Middle East Report*, 148, 'Re-Flagging the Gulf', 1987, 40–1.
[65] This note of caution is sounded by Charles H. Kennedy, 'Islamization and Legal Reform in Pakistan, 1979–1989', *Pacific Affairs*, 63, 1, 1990, 62–77.
[66] Nasr, 'The Rise of Sunni Militancy', p. 141.

Importantly, sectarian conflict and, in particular, Shi'i assertion through radical organisations had been enhanced with the impact of the Iranian revolution of 1978–9. In July 1980, a large group of Shias marched on Islamabad to demand that the Islamic Zakat tax, as set out by Sunni Hanafi law, should not be imposed on them and that the Ja'fari Law should be implemented. The Tahrik-I Nifaz-I Fiqh-I Ja'fariyya organisation (TNFJ) spearheaded this campaign. But also highly significant was the demand that the Shia community should be represented in the highest levels of the state. Here again, we see reflections of comparable demands in India on the basis of 'Backward Caste' and 'Other Backward Caste' representation. Significant too was the fact that this demand was made irrespective of the numerical strength of the Shia community – an idea that very much picked up on the notion of representation by 'qaum' rather than by proportion, akin to the pre-independence north Indian Muslim population.[67] In the case of Pakistan, one of the important drives for this demand was that the Shia community should have adequate representation in think tanks concerned with the overall process of Islamisation. The program of the TNFJ set out that each recognised school of Islamic thought should be given the right to be governed by its own specific interpretations of the Quran and Sunna. Each school should also be given 'effective representation' on the Council of Islamic Ideology – a government-constituted body whose aim was to advise government about Islam and everyday life.[68]

Violence between other regional communities, however constituted, has occurred on a large scale too. Between 1985 and 1992, more than 3,000 people lost their lives reportedly as a result of what is officially (and in the media) reported as 'ethnic' violence between Sindhis and Muhajirs in Sindh. The Mohajir Quami Movement (MQM) has since this time strongly reacted to what it has perceived as Sindhi violence against its 'community', leading in April to May of 1994 to a 'six-day insurgency' against the provincial government involving MQM armed snipers. As suggested in Chapter 6, such incidents have largely encouraged the operation of military curfew, which in a larger sense has legitimised military rule in general. Over the 1990s, conflicts between the main sectarian extremist organisations – the Sunni Sipah-I Sahaba Pakistan (SSP), the Shia Tahriki Jafaria Pakistan (TJP) and the Sipah-I Muhammed (SM) – claimed around 900

---

[67] For more detail on the notion of representation by religious community in colonial India, see the work of Farzana Shaikh, *Community and Consensus in Islam*.
[68] Muhammad Qasim Zaman, 'Sectarianism in Pakistan'.

lives. Whether or not these conflicts were uncomplicated cases of direct clashes between sects (a conclusion that is confused by state involvement), their representation as such is important.

As in Pakistan, there has been ambivalence about the extent to which Bangladeshis can point to Islam as a defining aspect of Bangladeshi national identity.[69] But in this case, the significance of religion in national identity is intimately tied to the specific circumstances of the country's foundation. The creation of Bangladesh was intimately related to the balance of power between the main states of South Asia and the failure of Pakistan to accommodate a federal democratic system in which the political aspirations of each unit were managed under an overarching central government. But most importantly, it was the outcome of a strong historical sentiment of Bengali identity,[70] which came into conflict with the uneven exercise of power in the Pakistani state. The events surrounding the dramatic defeat of Pakistan with the help of Indian forces in 1971 also contributed to a scenario in which Mujib emerged as a death-defying regional/national hero. According to his own accounts, the Pakistani authorities repeatedly failed to 'finish him', and on one occasion, a grave was dug for him in the confines of the Mianwali jail where he was held during the conflict. In his own testimony, on that occasion, he was shielded and saved by a prison warden with whom he had struck up a close friendship.[71] Because West Pakistanis had so dominated the bureaucracy and military before 1971, the new state had to build many structures from scratch. Added to this, cyclones and floods ravaged East Pakistan in November 1970, which meant that the effort was one of economic reconstruction too. Most of the members of the first Bangladeshi cabinet had little experience in government, and for most of the first two decades of its existence, Bangladesh was beset with natural disaster, not least flooding, and political instability. Added to this, the population as a whole was among the poorest in the world by the standard measures of per capita income.

Bangladesh, then, had come into being as a result of an alliance between Muslim Bengal and 'Hindu' India, which cast further doubt over the

---

[69] Keddie, 'Pakistan's Movement Against Islamization', also argues that in Pakistan in the mid-1980s, there were a range of movements actively opposing state moves towards Islamisation.

[70] To a great extent, this was based in the idea of the distinctive national culture of Bengali speakers – a claim of linguistic nationalism which has been echoed elsewhere in Pakistan, for example among Siraiki speakers in Punjab – see Feroz Ahmed, 'Ethnicity, Class and State in Pakistan', *Economic and Political Weekly*, 31, 47, 1996, 3050–3.

[71] Franda, pp. 14–15.

MAP 5. Bangladesh

political purchase of the old 'two-nation' theory. Whereas Pakistani regimes have directly acknowledged the significance of Islam in the founding of the nation and, from the 1980s, have allowed Islamic parties and pressure groups to press for the incorporation of sharia into executive governance, in Bangladesh Islam holds a more uncertain position. Stress on language and regional identity again pushed Bangladesh much closer to West Bengal, as did the existence of a substantial Hindu minority of around 12.5% (in 1991). Moreover, while still East Pakistan, West Pakistani political and religious elites tended to promote the notion of Bengalis as low-caste converts to Islam, something that added to the branding of Bengalis as 'kafirs' during the 1971 war. Bangladesh's constitution, promulgated in 1972, set out one of its fundamental principles as 'secularism' and contained other articles around which freedom of religious association was granted but which prohibited the operation of a number of 'politico-religious' parties that had attempted to establish an Islamic state.

However, Mujibur Rahman was more or less obliged to pay some lip service to Islamic institutions within the first few years of the state's existence, particularly as the state was largely dependent upon financial aid from Arab states. For example, the Islamic Academy, which had been initially abolished in 1972, was revived and upgraded to a foundation in 1975. After his assassination in the same year, the association of Mujibur Rahman with secular nationalism, on the one hand, and corruption and dictatorship, on the other, made it easier for his successors, Khandakar Moshtaque Ahmed (whose regime was quickly recognised by the government of Saudi Arabia and who sought to crush the Awami League) and later Ziaur Rahman to make more political use of Islam. Islamic organisations had gained further popular legitimacy in their relief work during a famine in 1974. Islam and the principles of the Shariat were also promoted via radio and television and *azan*, or prayer five times a day, was popularised by the media.[72] In 1976, the constitutional ban on religio-political parties was amended. The word 'secularism' was taken out of the preamble of the constitution and replaced with 'faith in the Almighty Allah' in 1977, the term *joy Bangla* was abolished as 'un Islamic' and, most importantly, Bangladesh's foreign policy moved away from the previously friendly stance towards India.

After Zia ur Rahman's assassination on 31 May 1981, Bangladesh's new leader, Hossain Mohammad Ershad, continued the trend of promoting the official connection between the state and Islam, with the formal declaration of Bangladesh as an Islamic state. In 1983, the Fourteenth Conference of Islamic Foreign Ministers was held in Dhaka. Important in this move away from the secular leftism of the Awami League and similar parties in Bangladesh was the significance of the Arab world as a source of aid and jobs for Bangladeshi migrant workers. In June 1988, Ershad announced the eighth amendment to the constitution of Bangladesh, which declared Islam the state religion. And between 1976 and 1988, the number of madrasahs increased in number from 1,830 to

---

[72] Emajuddin Ahamed and D. R. J. A. Nazneen, 'Islam in Bangladesh: Revivalism or Power Politics?', *Asian Survey*, 30, 8, 1990, 796–7.

2,700.[73] Since regimes have moved away from the secular foundations of the state, Islamic parties have also proliferated, including the Muslim League, the Islamic Democratic League, the Jamaat-e-Islami, the Nizam-i-Islam, the Jamiat-e-Ulema-e-Islam, the Islamic Republican Party and the Bangladesh Khilafat Andolan. Some of these parties were electorally successful in the mid-1980s, particular in local government bodies. However, popular responses to the implementation of Islamic law in Bangladesh have been even less enthusiastic than in Pakistan in the 1980s. Religious observance at a popular level also involves worship at the shrines of Sufi saints and pirs, traditionally rural society is marked by cross-communal cultures and there are ambiguities surrounding the place of Islam in Bangladeshi identity, despite state attempts at Islamisation. This has meant that, for the most part, women's rights, for example, have been pursued in a more welcoming context than in Pakistan.[74] Despite the formation of the Women's Action Forum in Pakistan in 1981 opposing Islamisation, Benazir Bhutto, faced with opposition from religious organisations, was unable to modify significantly Zia's moves in that direction once she came to power in November 1988.

In both Pakistan and Bangladesh, Islam has been used by regimes for the purposes of legitimacy but has also repeatedly featured as a basis of national integration: first, in efforts to hold East and West Pakistan as a unitary state; and second, as a means of establishing an over-arching national identity in both states after 1971. On the other hand, the apparent 'Islamisation' of Pakistan (and to some extent Bangladesh) since the mid to late 1970s, although uneven and highly contested in its effects, has contributed to sectarian conflict and has been used in Pakistan as an ideological means of labelling Bengalis as 'kafirs'. For both states too, the promotion of Islam in cultural and political institutions has been a means, especially since the early 1980s, of gaining support internationally, particularly from some of the Gulf States. For Bangladesh in its early years, this was also about state recognition, but it was a process that accelerated from 1976 with the re-admittance of religious parties into the mainstream.[75] However, despite these moves from the highest levels of the state, powerful opposition movements in both states have consistently critiqued the effects of religious conservatism on the constitutional rights

[73] *Ibid.*, p. 798.
[74] Naila Kabeer, 'The Quest for National Identity: Women, Islam and the State in Bangladesh', *Feminist Review*, 37, 1991, 38–58.
[75] Ahmed Shafiqul Huque and Muhammad Yeahia Akhter, 'The Ubiquity of Islam: Religion and Society in Bangladesh', *Pacific Affairs*, 60, 2, 1987, 200–25.

of citizens. In particular, women's movements have pushed, especially in Bangladesh, for the rights of citizens' organisations to have a voice in the reform of systems of personal law. Just as the parties of religious revival have fed off changes in communication technology and international developments over the 1970s and 1980s, so too have 'secularist' movements. But, as we will see in the next chapter, tension and competition between these differing views of 'modernity' have themselves created new kinds of violence, which has reached even the poorest communities in rural Pakistan and Bangladesh.

CONCLUSION

Although the period from the early 1970s to the end of the 1980s has been depicted as one of 'crisis of the state' in South Asia, in other respects it was a period in which the authoritarian powers of the state were enhanced in ways not seen since British rule. In India, Indira Gandhi's Emergency allowed her to control political opposition, and thereafter incidents of communal conflict implicated local state agencies, particularly the police. In Pakistan, the regime of General Zia promoted in the most forthright manner ever an ideology of state now more closely wedded to the development of 'Islamic' institutions. However, over this period too, the particular experiences of the local state for ordinary Indians and Pakistanis were quite different. In reality, there were many ways of mediating state agencies, for example getting around the state-driven policies of family planning in India in the mid-1970s[76] or finding other means of building local power and legitimacy. This process involved, too, the playing off of different intermediaries to the local state – a process in which local conflict, often around religious or community-based antagonism, was crucial. It has become apparent to ordinary citizens in all of our contexts that the differences between the rhetoric of the state at national levels and its complex mediation in the locality has further implications. Those attempting to get things done in their day-to-day lives use informal means of influencing bureaucrats and politicians. This has contributed to the continued pertinence of quasi-state organisations, which either (in the case of NGOs) promote welfare and educational development or put pressure on government via religious community organisations. The latter process has often

---

[76] For a detailed study of how the actions of the state were complicated at local levels in mid-1970s India, see Emma Tarlo, *Unsettling Memories: Narratives of the Emergency in Delhi* (London: Hurst, 2003).

played into the hands of the religious right. It has, at different moments across India in the 1980s, for example, served the interests of parties such as the BJP to relate quotidian struggles to a sense of broad Hindu–Muslim antagonism. This appears to have been the case in some of the early to mid-1980s projects to broaden the significance of anti-reservation politics to wider audiences via propaganda that more broadly promoted communal hatred.

Governing regimes have also profited from the representation of violence along broad religious or ethnic lines. This can be seen from the point of view of the Hindu right in the 1980s and the political establishment in Pakistan. However, regimes promoting Islamisation, on the one hand, and Hindu nationalist movements, on the other, are not straightforward phenomena that simply promote authoritarianism or project religious ideologies. Both have been intimately tied into the promotion of unitary state power in ways that very much go against other forms of religious revivalism, particularly Islamic radicalism. Second, they have come about as a result of a political struggle with other social forces in each context: in India, this has been the result of the growing political ambitions of peasant movements and the attempts to extend the politics of caste reservations. In Pakistan and Bangladesh, secularist, reformist and regional movements have all challenged, in different ways, patterns of apparent Islamisation. Just as, in the 1920s, the development of Hindu *sangathan* took place in relation to the apparent organisation of other religious communities, so too has the Hindu right in India been based, in some respects, on a struggle with the exponents of a new form of ethnic reservation. In both India and Pakistan, movements of the religious right have also evolved through national debates about the ways in which South Asian societies mediate the wider world: the challenges of rapid technological change, accelerating economic development and consumerism, the changing structures of the family and the empowerment of women.

8

The Resurgence of Communalism?

1990 to the 2000s

On 27 February 2002 at around 8:00 A.M., the S6 carriage of the Sabarmati Express burst into flames as it pulled out of Godhra station in Gujarat. Hindus returning from a pilgrimage to Ayodhya organised by the Vishwa Hindu Parishad were either burned or asphyxiated in the carriage. The fifty-nine deaths involved in this incident became a mantra for the Hindu right, and a spur for calculated retribution. The incident was sparked by an altercation between the travellers in the carriage and Muslim hawkers on the platform, and a rumour that the former had abducted a Muslim girl. The event triggered revenge killings, largely orchestrated by organisations of the Hindu right, against Muslims across the state, with estimates of deaths ranging between 790 and 2,000 and involving more than a thousand towns and villages. Some of the worst violence occurred in Ahmedabad where specific businesses were also attacked. In the years following the violence, a range of enquiries have attempted to ascertain whether the initial attack on the carriage was a preplanned Muslim attack on the *kar sevaks*, an act of spontaneous aggression or simply an accident. What had become clear by early 2005 was that a number of state agencies (in particular, the police) had sought to represent the incident, as well as the ensuing violence, in terms of a preplanned Muslim conspiracy theory. The evidence collected on the Godhra incident was highly unreliable for the most part and largely contradictory.[1] Nevertheless, the Gujarat police invoked the Prevention of Terrorism Act to arrest 123 alleged conspirators, including Deobandis and alleged

---

[1] 'The truth about Godhra', *The Hindu*, Online Edition, 23 January 2005, http://www.hindu.com/2005/01/23/stories/2005012303901400.htm, last accessed on 20 March 2010.

Islamic militants. In the post-Godhra violence too, a range of complaints and independent enquiries were targeted at the Gujarat police who allegedly stood by or actively participated as the violence (against Muslims in particular, although not exclusively) progressed. India's National Human Rights Commission reported that much of the violence was premeditated by organisations of the Hindu right. There have also been allegations that acquiescence in and support for the violence reached the very top of the BJP-led Gujarat administration.

Once again, Gujarat in 2002 illustrated the interconnections between the local and quotidian and the national and international via the politics of religion. The Godhra incident and the mass violence that followed amply illustrate the Byzantine complexity of state agents' involvement in such violence and the political incentives that drive the actions of police investigators as they force confessions and testimonies from witnesses. Perhaps even more significant has been the political afterlife of the violence. On the one hand, this has affected the politics of Gujarat itself and the growing popularity of the Narendra Modi regime there. The violence has also brought about different politically motivated accounts and commissions. Two principal commissions of enquiry – the Nanavati and the Banerjee commissions – have been based around the alternative viewpoints of the Hindu right/Gujarati state government and Laloo Prasad Yadav (Railway Minister) respectively. Nanavati concluded that the incident was caused by a conspiracy and Banerjee that it was an accident. Those implicated in the attacks on Mumbai between 26 and 29 of November 2008 also used as one of their justifications the Muslim pogrom in Gujarat. The significance of the violence also links backwards to earlier events. The pilgrims killed in the Godhra incident were returning from Ayodhya, from the site of one of the main symbolic issues for the mobilisation of the Hindu right in India since the early 1990s. The Ayodhya temple-mosque controversy, as we will see, has been one of the main and on-going controversies around which the Sangh Parivar has built support. There were other, deeper histories behind this violence. The Godhra Muslims were associated with the Ghanchi community who, in the manner of old colonial ethnographies, were described by previous studies of communal violence as 'backward' and 'aggressive'.[2]

The more recent political successes of the Hindu right or Sangh Parivar in India, which will form one of the main themes of this chapter, are not,

---

[2] Asghar Ali Engineer, 'Communal Riots in Godhra: A Report', *Economic and Political Weekly*, 16, 41, 1981, 1638–40.

however, directly comparable to the growth of religious movements in states that have promoted 'Islamisation'. This chapter will argue that there are complex processes at work, which relate as much if not more to the politicisation of ethnic conflict as to the promotion of a new kind of religiosity in India. The situation in most of the other South Asian states is quite different, although there are some parallels here with Sri Lanka, as we will see. Ethnographies of Indian religions and religious practice have shown that local religious movements are central to the social identities of many Indians, and sometimes influence everyday understandings of political processes.[3] And one of the main themes of religious revival and community mobilisation over the twentieth century involved the project of defining and homogenising such traditions. However, neither 'religion' nor especially 'Hinduism' can be approximated to ontological categorisation. Most of the critical writing on the Sangh Parivar has argued that its rise has relatively little to do with changes or developments in private and individual religious worship and a lot more to do with the specific formations of Indian nationalism. In fact, unlike other fundamentalist movements, the institutions of the Hindu right are content to work within the rubric of the 'modern' state and offer no thorough ideological critique of it.[4] The rise of the Hindu right in India has much more to do with the politics of community mobilisation than it does with the promotion of a particular religious agenda. It has suited the purposes of a range of parties on the Hindu right, for example, to represent the central narratives of India's political history around the 'Hindu–Muslim' problem or the issues of 'communalism' and 'sectarianism'. And most importantly of all, it has suited the purposes of those attempting to dominate or control the agencies of South Asia's states (whether from a colonial or democratic perspective) to make a play on such broad divisions.

As we saw in earlier chapters, the specific forms taken by India's secular culture have meant that the state has not always been able to maintain neutrality in relation to all religious communities, and, certainly, secularism has not halted the politicisation of religion. This is not, however, to argue, as others have done, that secularism cannot provide the means to challenge the Hindu right. As we saw in the last chapter, the attempts of the state to promote forms of affirmative action were oriented around the principle of community as 'caste', which necessarily related to older forms of religious identity. But the state's involvement, by default, with

---

[3] See Chris Fuller, *The Camphor Flame: Popular Hinduism and Society in India.*
[4] Partha Chatterjee, 'Secularism and Tolerance'.

religious practice took place in other areas too. The Hindu Code Bill was an attempt to rationalise the varied 'customary' systems of law that governed the transfer of property and defined the material basis of conjugal relationships. The aim was to 'modernise' and rationalise these systems of personal law in ways that would benefit Indian women. In this process of reform, the state was effectively 'interfering' in or changing customs for one broad community and not the other. In the process, a Hindu majoritarian sentiment was easily championed in areas of the country where the movements of minority religions were still important. Not surprisingly, then, Indian secularism meant one thing in theory and quite another in practice in different regions of India.[5] In reality, in north India, for example, the secularism set out in the Indian constitution catered for the interests of very specific and somewhat privileged high-status communities, for whom the politics of religion could be relegated to the quotidian levels and concerns of the village and gully. The assumed 'violence' of ordinary Indians was assumed by those in positions of power to be a product of their inability to grasp the civic principles of state secularism. Yet, where the state did indeed interfere with religious traditions and practices, as inevitably it did, not least through policies of reservations, the interests of those most able to influence the political process were most easily protected by political reference to state 'secularism'. The following section will examine how the politics of religion and religious identity in India and, in particular, the growing power of Hindu nationalism was related, too, to significant social, economic and technological changes across South Asia.

(1) TECHNOLOGY, COMMUNICATION AND ECONOMIC CHANGE: THE HINDU RIGHT IN INDIA

Economists have tended to view the Indian economy in terms of missed opportunities and slow rates of growth, particularly leading up to the early 1980s. However, from the mid-1990s, India's international image came to be associated with the other 'tiger' economies in many respects, but with some crucial differences. The roots of India's recent success were often related to the skills and business acumen of its rapidly expanding urban middle classes and entrepreneurs. Yet behind the glamour of the wealthy appearing in the pages of glossy periodicals, India was still strongly associated with social and economic inequality. Although rarely described as

---

[5] For a case study of this process, see William Gould, 'Contesting "Secularism" in Colonial and Postcolonial North India between 1930 and 1950s'.

such in explicit terms, India's economic fortunes have, for a variety of reasons (many relating to the ideologies of the Congress regimes themselves), been related by economists to the perpetuation of social customs that reinforced differences of education and opportunity. And the same emphasis on culture and custom has underlain the continued relevance of 'communal' violence in India. This is despite the fact that some of the most ferocious rioting to have taken place since the early 1990s has been in one of the most wealthy cities and regions of India – Ahmedabad in Gujarat. Here, as the opening section of the chapter suggested, some of the key targets of violence were middle-class Muslim neighbourhoods and businesses, and there were suggestions that business rivalry played its part. A great deal of support for the BJP and its associated organisations in Gujarat also comes from communities that have been traditionally described as 'affluent', 'forward' or 'educationally advanced'.

Such associations between religion, tradition and custom and economic backwardness have a deeper history. Between 1950 and 1989, the rate of economic growth in India averaged around 3.7%, which was below the average of all 'developing' economies as a group, eliciting the comment by Indian economist Kakkadan Nandanath Raj who had worked on the First Five Year Plan and by Raj Krishna that India suffered from 'Hindu' rates of growth. The term was then picked up by the American economist and anticommunist of the 1960s, Robert McNamara, for whom Indian socialism had resulted in stultified growth and the perpetuation of social inequality. Since then, the term has become a powerful idea for comparing India's pre-1990s political economy to the apparent 'success' thereafter. In its original form, the term had nothing directly to do with religion, religious identity or community. Yet, it was clear that the use of the term 'Hindu' conjured up a deliberate contrast between the promises of socialist development and the apparent realities of social inequality and the perpetuation of tradition. And the idea of a backward-looking religious tradition, stultified in the preservation of dated social conventions and practices, was juxtaposed in stark contrast to the rhetoric and modernising aspirations of Nehruvian India.[6] Moving beyond the bald figures of economic growth, the commentary on the social and cultural backgrounds to development also suggested problems in the mobilisation of what Amartya Sen has defined as 'social capital'. The 'Hindu' rate of growth also suggested high levels of illiteracy, particularly among women; a skewed gender ratio and relatively low

---

[6] See M. Shiviah, 'Behind Hindu Growth Rate: Glimpses of Upper Class Statecraft', *Economic and Political Weekly*, 28, 14, 1993, 594–6.

female employment in skilled work.[7] There is also a correlation between regions in which levels of female literacy and educational achievement are low and 'communal' violence.

The BJP eventually embraced the implications of the economic changes of the early 1990s – but only did so after a series of complex compromises around their own supporters' advocacy of anti-'foreign' ideologies. Once economic liberalisation began to open up India's economy to greater levels of foreign investment and multinational companies, ending the controls of the Nehru era, it was the Hindu right itself that benefited, arguably, in political terms. Indeed, the notion of 'Hindu' eventually came to be associated with privatisation and India's new open market economy as it faced the rest of the world, and was eventually embraced by the Hindu right as part of the critique of Nehruvianism.[8] This was particularly the case by the time of the 2004 election campaigns in which the BJP used the ill-fated slogan of 'India Shining'.[9] The main beneficiaries of more rapid rates of economic growth, changing patterns of consumerism and national self-confidence appeared to be those very middle-class urban communities most attracted to the ideologies of the Sangh Parivar, as introduced in the last chapter. This was a class made up of upper-caste rural communities with enough disposable income to engage with the mass consumerism set off by economic liberalisation, on the one hand, and a middle-class urban population keen to assert their status through displays of support for religious revival, on the other.

In the late 1980s, and particularly after 1991, the opening of India to market forces dovetailed with economic liberalism, accompanied by strident post–cold war nationalism in other parts of the world. It was not until 1991, though, that the Finance Minister, Manmohan Singh, pushed India firmly towards economic liberalism, with a set of reforms aimed to integrate India more directly into the global economy and to promote India's capacity to supply cheap knowledge-orientated goods and services to the rest of the world. Singh aimed to cut the fiscal deficit in India, created by excesses in the 1980s, by reducing defence spending and by cutting subsidies for exports, sugar and fertilisers. Industrial licensing – the system that had marked the era of 'license-permit-raj' – was dismantled, foreign investment was now encouraged, private-sector industries were promoted in

[7] Amartya Sen, 'Indian Development: Lessons and Non-Lessons', *Daedalus*, 118, 4, 1989, 369–92.
[8] Jay Dubashi, 'Hindu Rate of Growth', *Organiser*, New Delhi, 9 June 1985.
[9] See Andrew Wyatt, 'Building the Temples of Postmodern India: Economic Constructions of National Identity', *Contemporary South Asia*, 14, 4, 2005, 465–80.

areas traditionally held back for state enterprises and tariffs were reduced to free up trade. To some extent, these reforms were successful, in that they led eventually to much faster rates of overall growth. Certainly, the relative incidence of rural and urban poverty decreased between the early 1970s and early 1990s, even though the sheer number of people living in poverty increased. However, Indian agriculture, despite being the principal occupation of a large majority of the population to date, had not been significantly reformed. And rather than leading to changes in older structures of social dominance, economic liberalisation appeared to reinforce some of those older patterns of inequality, both social and regional. In general, while investment freed up opportunities for those with the educational and social assets to take advantage of them, the specific nature of investment and business in India in all sectors tended to trap poorer men, women and children into vulnerable, short-term and often dangerous jobs.[10] Some data also suggest an increase in inequality during the 1990s, with gaps widening between urban and rural areas and between different states and cities. Whereas public-sector salaries increased by five per cent per year, increases in real agricultural wages only rose by roughly two-and-a-half per cent per year.[11]

The reforms process in India has been, according to one influential academic, one of stealth with no particular master plan or narrative, but which has allowed certain influential politicians, particularly at the state level, to redistribute political patronage.[12] However, there is also a sense in which certain class and community formations have been reinforced by liberalisation. Arvind Rajagopal has argued that there were cultural aspects to this shift, as well as economic ones. In the United States, UK and India, the very classes that benefitted from the opening up of the economy – whose higher levels of expenditure were now being financed by higher levels of public borrowing – were precisely the constituencies to whom strident nationalist rhetoric appealed.[13] And it was these same communities who appeared to be buying into 'foreign technology fetishism' brought about by the appearance of multinationals in India from the early 1990s.[14] In the case of India, this also

---

[10] Corbridge and Harriss, pp. 145–6.
[11] Angus Deaton and Jean Dreze, 'Poverty and Inequality in India: A Re-examination', *Economic and Political Weekly*, 37, 36, 2002, 3740.
[12] R. Jenkins, *Democratic Politics and Economic Reform in India* (Cambridge: Cambridge University Press, 1999).
[13] Arvind Rajagopal, 'Ram Janmabhoomi, Consumer Identity and Image-Based Politics', *Economic and Political Weekly*, 29, 27, 1994, 1659–68.
[14] Thomas Blom Hansen, 'The Ethics of Hindutva and the Spirit of Capitalism', in Thomas Blom Hansen and Christophe Jaffrelot, eds., *The BJP and the Compulsions of Politics in India* (Delhi: Oxford University Press, 1998), pp. 296–9.

manifested itself in the appearance of new kinds of media that were consumed largely by upper-caste, middle-class urban Indians, particularly in the big cities. The products of this media were also quite new. Some of the most popular 'national' television programmes to appear from the late 1980s included the serialisation by Doordarshan of the Ramayana (January 1987–August 1989) and the Mahabharata. Rajagopal has described this as the unprecedented centralisation of cultural production in India, which privileged a catch-all high-caste Hindu approach to Indian national identity and which manifested itself in the attempts of right-wing parties' elite leaders to employ intermittent communal mobilisation.[15]

The Sangh Parivar as a whole was placed in a difficult position by these developments, as the RSS was keen to promote swadeshi demonstrations against what it perceived as the threat of foreign and exploitative multinationals. Many in the BJP saw advantages in political support for liberalisation. However, in 1992, it accepted a kind of 'corrective' from the RSS, and set out its own economic policy, which, while welcoming certain aspects of liberalisation and foreign investment, also pushed for protection of indigenous markets and capital. This double discourse was largely maintained by the BJP right up to the late 1990s, and still figures in its attempts to create a sense of national strength and pride vis-à-vis international capitalism.[16] However, once it gained power at the centre in 1998, and even more so by the time of the 2004 election campaign, the BJP attempted to capitalise on this enhanced national culture of middle-class consumerism. In 2004, this manifested itself in the electoral slogan 'India Shining'. In this link between the building of a new vision of national identity and forms of consumerism and economic change, India was projected by parties like the BJP as a 'brand' that had moved away from the master narrative of the Nehruvian-planned economy. Whereas the Congress through the early period of economic reforms had sought to push through change without any large-scale public statements to India's population as a whole, the BJP in the late 1990s began to forge more clearly the rhetorical links between Indian identity and economic liberalism. In order to overcome internal divisions and to present a set of symbols around which the party could unite, the BJP could present India as a new superpower. Once, by the early 2000s, that translated into global economic success, the Hindu right, via the BJP, was at the forefront of associations with the

[15] Arvind Rajagopal, *Politics After Television*, pp. 24–9, 42.
[16] Hansen, 'Hindutva and Capitalism', pp. 307–9.

new external image.[17] The BJP was also very quick to pick up on the interrelationships between mass consumerism and mass politics, as it presented its alternative economic visions for India, which critiqued older Congress agendas.

Over this period of celebration of middle-class consumerism and market liberalism, the older roots of 'Hindu' mobilisation surrounding direct critiques of Western modernity now seemed to have shifted. Moreover, the idea of Hindu nationalism as a form of 'fundamentalism' did not seem to fit such consumerist desires. Clearly, the forms of Hindu nationalism that emerged from the late 1980s, as suggested by Christophe Jaffrelot, were heterogenous, and it is perhaps not entirely surprising that a range of apparently Hindu extremist movements might coexist with a (relatively) liberal political agenda of the BJP. These somewhat unusual features of the Hindu right can be examined in a number of ways, but the approach here will be to look at three particular elements. First, the relationship between these movements and the idea of the 'Hindu' when compared to other 'fundamentalist' movements was quite specific and unusual, particularly when it came to perceptions of the state. Whereas Islamic movements in South Asia have tended to stress specific aspects of religious reform and change as part of a broader political agenda to present a powerful and pristine Islam, there is no clear or definitive position in the Hindu right or even a dominant notion of a purified Hinduism. In this sense, it is not like most other movements of religious mobilisation, largely for reasons linked to its development within the context of Indian democracy. To some extent, however, the shifting politics of the Jamaat-e-Islami in Bangladesh in moving towards the promotion of certain kinds of reformism as a result of political pressure is comparable, as we will see.

In contrast, some of the most important Islamic and Sikh movements in South Asia and beyond have critiqued the Western idea of the separation of state and religion. They have also identified clear symbols of political authority in relation to unquestionable aspects of religious scripture or dogma and in many cases proposed theocratic institutions. The latter have never been called for by the Sangh Parivar. The notion 'Hindutva' does not involve the enforcement of scriptural injunctions, a role for religious institutions in the judiciary and other wings of the state or the outright censorship of scientific knowledge – although it has deliberately targeted other intellectual freedoms. The Sangh Parivar, in contrast, embraces the modern state and uses it to critique what it sees as other forms of

---

[17] Andrew Wyatt, 'Building the Temples of Postmodern India'.

fundamentalism among different religious traditions.[18] However, within the Hindu right, there were a range of differing attitudes towards the state, some working within the existing structures of Nehruvian India and others directly challenging its redistributive tendencies. While the promotion of urban consumerism may have suited the electoral interests of the BJP (and, in many respects the Congress), it worked against some of the abiding features of RSS and VHP ideology and strategy. Parts of the RSS and Bajrang Dal were particularly wedded to the ongoing idea of swadeshi and direct critiques of Western decadence or moral corruption – an ideology that went hand in hand with attacks on Christians in north India,[19] Orissa and Tamil Nadu, and the targeting of multinational fast-food outlets. And some sections of the Sangh also appeared to support the perpetuation of cultural practices such as *sati* in defence against what it saw as foreign-inspired, neo-colonial reformism.[20]

Second, and connected to the last point, within the Sangh, the chasing of 'modernity' and consumerism has sat side by side with forms of mobilisation that are reminiscent of militant movements of the right. If anything, particularly in its demonisation of minorities, the Parivar bears a closer relationship to European Nazism than it does to South Asian religious radicalisms from other traditions. From the perspective of 1993, certainly, following intense rioting across north India around the demolition of the Babri Masjid and then even more intense anti-Muslim violence in Bombay, it appeared that, as in Italy and Germany between the wars, street violence might bring the Hindu right to power. Attacks on Muslim minorities have been directly compared to Nazi policies towards European Jews.[21] Important too in this comparison was infiltration of the main arms of the state – the police, bureaucracy and then political authority at all levels of the representative system. The far right in Europe had also taken power in a context of constitutionalism and respect for legal procedures and increasingly suppressed expressions of independent intellectual dissent. For the leading Delhi historian of this period, such violence was broadly tolerated as a result of years of political acquiescence in communal

[18] Chatterjee, 'Secularism and Tolerance', p. 1768.
[19] 'Bajrang Attacks Christians in Agra', *Asian Age*, 24 April 2000.
[20] C.K. Viswanath, 'Sati, Anti-Modernists and Sangh Parivar', *Economic and Political Weekly*, 34, 52, 1999, 3648.
[21] Sumit Sarkar, 'The Fascism of the Sangh Parivar', *Economic and Political Weekly*, 28, 5, 1993, 163–7.

incidents, in which the Hindu right attempted to instil its ideology beyond its core petit bourgeois/high-caste urban trader base.[22]

Finally, there was a crucial overlap between the BJP and other parties like the Congress when it came to attempts to represent the whole of Indian political society. Ultimately, and perhaps not at all surprisingly, both parties attempted to win over dominant communities (that had largely controlled the Congress party in different Indian localities) or to devise symbols of Indian identity that embraced consumer desires. And both parties were best placed to make a serious bid for power at the centre. This relates to the historical formation of both parties from the late colonial period in which, as we saw in earlier chapters, the Congress and organisations like the Hindu Mahasabha shared personnel. Over the 1990s, the BJP, as the party political wing of the Sangh, has come to the realisation that it could not continue to trample over the constitutional rights of religious minorities and still succeed politically within a democratic system. This is despite the fact that throughout its promotion of violence and the suppression of human rights, it has been granted space within the democratic system.[23] In the phase of the BJP's increasing success at the state level of politics, from the early 1990s, the need for the party to compromise on some of its more hardline 'Hindutva' policies is apparent in areas where it has formed governments. For example, in the mid-1990s in Uttar Pradesh and parts of western India, the BJP has formed deals with other parties in the formation of state-level administrations, some of which are directly opposed to its ideologies. In UP, this has been created by the caste fragmentation of the 'Hindu' vote, which has offered some possibilities but also some obstacles in the light of the 'Hindutva' ideology.[24] In attempts to get an all-India presence, the BJP has also had to break out of its focus areas of northern and western India to make appeals to the southern states – something that proved very difficult over the 1990s.[25] Overall, its political compromises have, like those of the Congress, been ultimately geared towards the winning of power at the centre.

Despite the need for deals at the time of the elections, the rising importance of the Hindu right in Indian politics rejuvenated the politics of public

---

[22] *Ibid.*

[23] Sumanta Banerjee, 'Sangh Parivar and Democratic Rights', *Economic and Political Weekly*, 28, 34, 1993, 1715–18.

[24] Jasmine Zerinini-Brotel, 'The BJP in Uttar Pradesh: From Hindutva to Consensual Politics?', in Hansen and Jaffrelot, eds., *The BJP and the Compulsions of Politics*, pp. 72–100.

[25] James Manor, 'Southern Discomfort: The BJP in Karnataka', in *Ibid.*, pp. 163–201.

symbolism in the 1990s – the use of religious imagery, mobilisation around moments of public spectacle and the reworking of the Indian epics. The new importance of mass media and the imagery associated with the reworking of religious epics, as described by Rajagopal, played an important part in the design and presentation of some of the large movements and *yatras* of the Hindu right, and related to anticipation of international 'threats'. This was also assisted by changes in modern communication technology. The tools of modern media and communication were used in the Ayodhya campaigns through the early 1990s (the Ram Jamnabhoomi movement) to contest older Nehruvian views of Indian secularism. Under the presidency of L. K. Advani, the BJP led a campaign (which had been championed by the VHP years previously) to rebuild a temple to Ram on the site of the Babri Masjid (built in 1528) in Ayodhya, on the claim that the mosque had been built on the ruins of an ancient temple site. In 1990, Advani launched a *yatra* to Ayodhya to the disputed site, a movement that helped the BJP to increase its electoral presence in the 1991 general elections. On 6 December 1992, the Babri Masjid was attacked and largely destroyed by *kar sevaks*, and following the demolition, rioting spread across north India and south-west to Mumbai, resulting in roughly 2,000 deaths.[26] Between 1993 and 1998, when the BJP won power at the centre within the National Democratic Alliance under the leadership of Atul Bihari Vajpayee, the BJP for the most part reaped political dividends from the Ayodhya dispute. Vajpayee formed another government in 1999, which ruled until 2004.

Just as much of the communal violence around the early 1990s, for example, the ferocious riots in Mumbai in 1993 cannot be simply explained away as the result of basic religious antagonism between religious communities, neither was this a case of the straightforward manipulation of passions by political parties of the right. Clearly again, in many of these instances of violence, local turf wars could be fought out and specific power contests decided around issues that often had little to do with the broader themes attached to the riots. As Amrita Basu has convincingly argued in work on Bijnor district in the early 1990s, and as previous chapters have implied, communal violence, especially in the complex phase of coalition electoral politics, has to be studied 'from below', as well as from above.[27]

---

[26] For a detailed account of the political symbolism surrounding the Ram Jamnabhoomi movement in Ayodhya, see Peter Van der Veer, *Religious Nationalism*.

[27] Amrita Basu, 'When Local Riots are Not Merely Local: Bringing the State Back In, Bijnor 1988–1992', *Economic and Political Weekly*, 29, 40, 1994, 2605–21.

The new forms of religio-political activism promoted by the Sangh were, in some parts of India, connected to women's organisations and female leaders. In the interwar period, as we saw in Chapters 3 and 4, Hindu nationalist publicity was often marked by discussions of the 'sexualised' Muslim male, whose masculinity was represented as threatening to Hindu female purity. By picking out the issue of female rape and abduction, organisations of the Hindu right have attempted to align themselves with particular feminist agendas. For example, the BJP has aligned itself with support for a uniform civil code, which would enhance women's rights but which also seeks to highlight the inequities of Muslim personal law. Such a stance has attracted some prominent female leaders to the BJP – for example, Vijayraje Scindia and Uma Bharati. The latter came to prominence on the back of the Ram Jamnabhoomi movement around Ayodhya. These women have taken a vow of celibacy – a form of chastity that 'heightens their iconic status' by being based in the principle of renunciation. However, in posing as the moral protectors of the Hindu community, these figures have often served to reinforce the patriarchal attitudes of the Hindu right. In particular, the political imagery of the Hindu right has continued to be highly gendered, promoting social roles for women that reinforce conservative notions of male–female relations and sexuality, and associating the Indian land with 'motherhood'.[28]

The rise of the BJP from the early 1990s, then, was related to a wide range of complex factors and historical legacies, some of which link it to other mainstream nationalist parties and organisations. Because of the dramatic events surrounding the Babri Masjid dispute and the implementation of the Mandal Commission report (explored in the pages that follow), there has been a tendency in the literature to relate its modern successes to relatively recent tensions in the 'decline' of secularism. However, parties of the Hindu right and the constituencies and semi-formal political movements to which they appeal have a much deeper history. We need to consider the nature of Hindu nationalism in the light of changes over the entire late colonial and early post-independence period to understand fully the nature and appeal of its nationalism and the ongoing significance of violence against minorities. Most importantly, the idea that India's 'secularism' has been threatened is difficult to maintain in the face of the Sangh Parivar's claims to represent 'true' Indian secularist politics and its embrace of the modern state. Indian secularism has always

---

[28] Amrita Basu, 'The Gendered Imagery and Women's Leadership of Hindu Nationalism', *Reproductive Health Matters*, 4, 8, 1996, 70–6.

contained contradictions and tensions, which as early as the 1950s and 1960s could be exploited by religio-political organisations. The apparent electoral successes of the BJP, if anything, have signalled a weakening of its core Hindutva ideology as it has attempted to come to terms with power sharing and the need to appeal outside its Hindi heartlands. Since the early 1990s, then, its political appeal has shifted to quite wide and sometimes surprising social constituencies. For example, some of the institutions of the Sangh Parivar have managed to bridge the political gap between the middle-class beneficiaries of Nehruvian modernity and national progress, and vernacular cultures and disenfranchised communities.[29] Certainly, in the promotion of specifically Indian products through swadeshi projects, and the rejection of the immoralities of Western influence, relatively diverse communities in north and western India can be engaged.

However, the social bases of the Hindu right should be related to deeper political histories, taking us back to the early part of the century. Here, the development of theories of secularism, not just in the parties of the right but also those of the national mainstream, created an ideological space in which the Sangh Parivar could claim to represent the Indian interpretation of a 'true' Indian secularism. This is not to suggest that Nehruvian secularism was a 'sham' – something apparently doomed to failure in the light of the events of the 1990s. Scholars who have attempted to make this kind of argument – Ashish Nandy, T. N. Madan and Partha Chatterjee – have sought to re-establish the 'virtues of the fragmentary, the local and the subjugated' as a way of unmasking the violence of modernity. Nandy in particular effectively presents an anti-secular front in his argument that secularism and Hindu nationalism have much in common in their fear and intolerance of ethnic diversity and dissent. Like secular nationalists, Hindu nationalists for him are principally interested in governing and shaping the margins and forcing people into a false religious consciousness.

Yet this comparison can serve to legitimise aspects of right-wing religious nationalism by suggesting that 'secularism' is a purely Western concept doomed to failure in India, or that Indian religious cultures contain within them forms of secular toleration. There are alternatives to this approach to secularism. One of the most powerful forces challenging the Hindu right in India since the 1960s, and even more powerfully since the 1990s, has been the adoption of Indian secular nationalism by lower-caste parties. For example, the Bahujan Samaj party in UP, led by Mayawati, has embraced ideologies of secular modernity as a means of

---

[29] Corbridge and Harriss, p. 192.

challenging what it perceives as high-caste dominance. Mayawati's governments have been keen to promote large-scale capital projects of infrastructure modernisation (albeit by dubious or controversial means) and modern education for Dalits. This follows in the tradition of Ambedkar in his modernist attacks upon the hierarchical social structures of Hinduism. Nandy and Madan's focus on religious cultures on the margins, in contrast, runs the danger of privileging Brahmanical cultures anew, somewhat in the style of older Gandhian Congress claims to represent Dalits as 'harijans' and objectified recipients of social reform.

The work of the anti-secularist critics of the Hindu right has also tended to overstate the Hindu right's potential ability to control the Indian state. It is of course easier to see this in retrospect than from the position of the early 1990s. The changing political fortunes of the BJP since about the mid-1990s clearly show that the political landscape of India effectively forced the party to downplay crucial elements of the ideology that drove, among other things, the Ayodhya publicity stunts. In many states where the party has been successful since the 1980s – UP, Rajasthan and even, to a lesser extent, Gujarat, for example – the BJP has been obliged to take into account new constituencies in Indian politics, on the one hand, and to play the game of coalition politics, on the other. The BJP has been forced to accommodate, at certain moments, OBCs and their political representatives in UP, for example, since the late 1990s.[30] Although the Hindu right probably represents one of the most serious challenges to the hegemony of parties like the Congress at the centre, it can never effectively establish the kind of 'Hindu rashtra' suggested by the likes of Savarkar, while its power is so dependent upon the coalition of a range of convergent political interests in each local power base.

From the 1980s, the Hindu right began to articulate more clearly the idea of threats to Indian national integrity (and 'Hindu' integrity) from broader, often international, sources. As India began to connect more clearly to the global economy, and as the successes and wealth of NRIs began to seep back into India, organisations like the VHP identified external 'threats' and challenges to the Hindu body politic. Such threats included, alongside internal fears related to the politics of caste reservations, the Rushdie Affair, in which a range of South Asian Muslim organisations had supported a *fatwa* against the author of *The Satanic Verses*, the visit of Pope John Paul II and Bangladeshi migration into Assam. However, alongside this, within the Sangh Parivar, there has been a battle

---

[30] Corbridge and Harriss, p. 126.

between the proponents and opponents of modernity, which has often revolved around the BJP and the RSS. The Sangh was able to take advantage of changes in communication technologies and the new consumerist spirit following economic liberalisation from the early 1990s. But liberalisation has also contributed to the disaggregation of representative politics and the development of an array of regional challenges to the 'all Indian' parties. In order to win power, the BJP (and the Congress) need to compromise their ideologies to accommodate broader political constituencies. A politics of religious hatred can still, however, surface at moments when it suits the purposes of regional parties, as was seen in Gujarat in 2002–3, or when it suits such parties to highlight 'foreign' threats to Indian national strength and integrity.

(ii) HINDU NATIONALISM AND CASTE IN INDIA

The growth in support for the institutions of the Sangh Parivar in the early 1990s was therefore closely tied to complex India-specific social and political changes. These included, most notably, high-caste reactions to the renewed policies of caste reservations in government employment and educational institutions following the implementation of the Mandal Commission report in 1990. The debates about caste reservations were inherited from older public discussions about 'communalism' and religious identity politics. The architects of India's constitution, in an attempt to establish a liberal democracy, devised systems of affirmative action for 'Scheduled Castes' (SC), which resembled the colonial state's religious minorities policies. The very definitions of 'depressed class' or 'Scheduled Caste' had a ritual and religious dimension, since they were based on ethnographic work defining caste difference around the socio-economic implications of custom and ritual. Low-status Muslim communities could not be defined as SCs, since the key dynamic of caste in these ethnographies was the ritually prescribed hierarchy that could only exist within one particular religious tradition. In this sense, reservation on the basis of caste effectively implied state interpretations of religious practice.

The outcome of these measures has for the most part been almost exactly the opposite of what was intended. The Constituent Assembly in the late 1940s, and the later framers of recommendations for caste reservations, consistently asserted that the ultimate aim was to eliminate caste as a category of social differentiation. Yet the very process of affirmative action, reservation and special consideration through the constitution served to reinforce the political significance of caste by the 1990s. This was partly a result, as in previous years, of low-caste and Dalit movements' reaction to attempts by organisations like those within the Sangh Parivar to formulate high-caste notions of Hindu unity. And, as we have seen in the last chapter, much of the violence against Muslims in the latter part of the twentieth century was also connected to attacks on (or the cynical cooption of) lower castes. Changing caste identifications, then, were not simply a reaction to state ethnographies, but also to the politics of 'Hindu nationalism' or, in the south, the historical significance of Brahman domination.

Low-caste or Dalit movements have been instrumental in these debates about reservations and reactions to Hindu nationalism, especially since the 1970s and 1980s. Organisations such as the Dalit Panthers, for example, expressed caste disadvantage along the lines of racial discrimination and identified high-caste Hindu prejudice as a socio-racial phenomenon.[31] The identification of caste disadvantage along the lines of race, in ways that emulated African American movements, is also founded on a complete rejection of Hinduism but does not dispense with religious ideas entirely. The ideology of the Panthers is based on a synthesis of Marxist and Buddhist philosophies, although the organisation has been subject to internal debate about the incompatibility of the two. Important in this debate has been the on-going attachment to Ambedkarite thinking and his decision to lead a group of western Indian Dalits to convert to Buddhism in 1956.[32]

But, apart from in areas like Tamil Nadu, under the leadership of the DMK, it was not really until the 1990s that parties exclusively representing the interests of low castes and Dalits managed to gain *power* at the level of Indian states. The Bahujan Samaj party, founded by Kanshi Ram in 1984, a Chamar from Punjab, was able, like the BJP in Uttar Pradesh, to take advantage of the weakening political position of the Congress in the early 1990s. One factor in the rise of 'Backward Castes' and Dalit organisations, as well as movements like that of the BSP, was the decision in 1990 of the V. P. Singh government to implement the Mandal Commission recommendations. These extended reservations to 'Other Backward Castes' by adding a further twenty-seven per cent level of reservation in government posts and the public sector. This development has been the bedrock of the growing power of another party based on Backward Caste constituencies (particularly Yadavs and Kurmis) in north India – the Samajwadi Party

---

[31] Corbridge and Harriss, p. 214.
[32] Janet A. Contursi, 'Political Theology: Text and Practice in a Dalit Panther Community', *Journal of Asian Studies*, 52, 2, 1993, 320–39.

(SP). The latter grew out of the BJD, which as we saw in the last chapter, represented the interests of middle-caste peasant groups, particularly communities like the Jats. The SP, in contrast, under the leadership of Mulayam Singh Yadav, appealed more directly to communities now included within systems of reservations that had been extended after the implementation of the Mandal Commission. We should be hesitant, however, in putting too much emphasis on the context of state reservations in the rising power of these parties. The BSP's regional power in UP, for example, also has much to do with the specific context of the decline of the Congress there as one of the principal parties of choice for Dalit communities in the region.[33]

The unity of communities represented by the BSP and those Backward Castes supporting Mulayam Singh Yadav's SP has been very hard to maintain in a political atmosphere of horse-trading and house crossing. At first glance, it would appear that the BSP and SP represent narrow ethnic/caste communities compared to the Congress, who claim to represent Indians across a range of cultures, communities and social backgrounds. But exclusive backing of a coherent or consistent collection of 'Backward Castes'/Dalits by either of these new challengers to the Congress would have spelt political suicide for both parties at the state level of politics. There is a parallel here, then, with the BJP. For the BSP, 'Bahujan' (meaning 'majority') includes all those castes not in the top three *varnas*. This means the 450 castes constitutionally identified as historically 'untouchable' (SC), many of which had traditionally voted for the Congress as the erstwhile champion of minority interests. However, its success in winning the majority of the SC vote has varied from state to state. Generally speaking, there are usually specific local reasons for this variation, but one trend has been the extent to which the reservation of caste groups in the administration as a whole has allowed the BSP to increase electoral support. Also important for the BSP has been the failure of parties like the Congress to accommodate upwardly mobile SCs into its own party organisation. This scenario has been complicated by the internal organisational incentives that any particular party may be able to offer a particular caste or ethnic group. For example, the BSP leadership has traditionally encouraged factional competition between different caste clusters within the party, which has marginalised some lower-caste groups

[33] See Oliver Mendelsohn and Marika Vicziany, *The Untouchables: Subordination, Poverty and the State in Modern India* (Cambridge: Cambridge University Press, 1998), ch. 8.

and created a disincentive for accommodation within the organisation – for example, the Adharmis and Ramdasias in Punjab.[34]

The administrative and social authority of particular caste constituencies, then, connects to the political organisation of different parties. An added complication is the tendency of parties since the 1990s to mobilise and hold power around temporary political alliances, which appear to cut across ideology. Here, election alliances take place within states but also with a consideration for the links between the politics of the state and the politics of the centre. From about 1993–4, the BSP began to extend its mobilisational strategies beyond its immediate SC constituencies to appeal to 'Backward Caste' groups that traditionally followed the SP and eventually even to high-caste constituencies in north India. This was partly achieved through electoral alliances and power sharing at the state level.[35] The Janata Dal in Bihar, too, under the leadership of Laloo Prasad Yadav and the related party – the SP in UP – competed for the leadership of the Yadav community across the Hindi belt in north India in the mid-1990s. The two parties also competed for a section of the north Indian Muslim vote.[36] In the same period across north India, the Congress has made alliances with parties like the BSP as a means of garnering a broader constituency of support, without threatening the privileged position of upper castes within its own party organisations.[37]

In Tamil Nadu, a similar picture of shifting caste and ethnic alliances around electoral opportunism is evident, but the circumstances are very different compared to the north. Although the DMK represents the non-Brahman movement as a whole, and this has had a dramatic effect on the opening up of opportunities for non-Brahman communities in public office and politics, electoral opportunism has also overrun ideology. By the 1990s, it was also clear, despite decades of DMK dominance in the state, that some non-Brahman communities had benefited while others had been largely left out of these political changes. Chettiars, Gounders, Kallars and Nadars have dominated in administration and politics, whereas Adi

---

[34] For details of how this played out in Hoshiarpur, Punjab, see Kanchan Chandra, 'The Transformation of Ethnic Politics in India: The Decline of Congress and the Rise of the Bahujan Samaj Party in Hoshiarpur', *Journal of Asian Studies*, 59, 1, 2000, 26–61.

[35] For a survey of the different stages in the BSP's mobilisation of non-SC communities, see Sudha Pai, *Dalit Assertion and the Unfinished Democratic Revolution: The Bahujan Samaj Party in Uttar Pradesh* (Delhi: Sage, 2002).

[36] See, for example, 'Janata Dal Under Pressure', *Economic and Political Weekly*, 30, 45, 1995, 2833.

[37] Kanchan Chandra, pp. 54–5.

Dravidas and Vanniars have not been so fortunate over these years. As communities such as the Chettiars have been able to form a new state-level elite, they have been less inclined to back the core ideologies of socialism and caste uplift traditionally associated with the DMK. And in this context, they have been willing to form alliances with high-caste parties and organisations. Feeling excluded from the elitist politics of the DMK, the Vanniars – the largest caste group in the northern districts of Tamil Nadu – formed their own political party, the PMK, which since the early 1990s has been actively hostile to the older Dravidian party.[38] In other states, bipolar party competitions exist – for example in Kerala, Orissa, Andhra Pradesh, Karnataka and Punjab. But in these regions too, caste reservations have played a part in complicating existing factional political alliances.

These relatively unstable (often multipolar) politics of election deals, rivalries and horse-trading have been associated with a rise in political corruption. Significant numbers of MLAs at the state level in some areas of India (e.g. Bihar and UP) have criminal records, many of them for heinous crimes. Most famously, Laloo Prasad Yadav was at the centre of a fodder scam involving Rs. 950 crores, and more recently in the new millennium, Mayawati's administration has run up even greater bills in the construction of monuments to BSP heroes and leaders. In Tamil Nadu in 2001, the Election Commission succeeded in rejecting the nomination papers of the leader of the AIADMK for state assembly elections, Jayalalitha, as a result of conviction in two corruption cases.[39] Perhaps most importantly of all, the ideological raison-d'etre of many of these state-level parties in 1990s India has seemed shallow to the public at large and based on the same political opportunism that generated such scandals. As with the religious symbolism and exclusivism of the BJP, the parties that initially appealed to low castes and Dalits have not been able to sustain a political stance that continues to privilege those communities that they aspire to represent. The nature of Indian political mobilisation, electoral politics and the uses to which political power is put vis-à-vis the local state means that alliances have to be more fluid, cutting across community-based loyalties.

Nevertheless, the growing importance of the Hindu right in politics since the early 1990s and, even more importantly, the growing power of parties taking advantage of the politics of reservations have led to dramatic changes in the representation of public and political spaces. Some have

[38] M. S. S. Pandian, 'Crisis in DMK', *Economic and Political Weekly*, 29, 5, 1994, 221–3.
[39] B. Venkatesh Kumar, 'Criminalisation of Politics and Election Commission', *Economic and Political Weekly*, 36, 24, 2001, 2119–21.

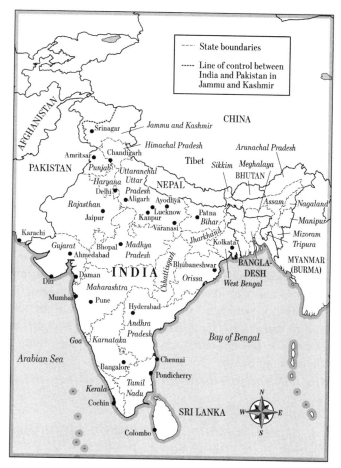

MAP 6. India, 2000

argued that it has led to a kind of revolution in the very nature of politics across India since the early 1990s.[40] This has manifested itself in much more ambitious and confident public displays of cultural identity – for example, the Dalit mela around Ambedkar Jayanti in UP and Bihar, which has been popularised and extended by the BSP since the early 1990s. These occasions have literally been moments for Dalit communities to reclaim street spaces and for the dissemination of Dalit pamphlet literature. In the work of Omprakash Valmiki, for example, participants in the mela can

---

[40] See Christophe Jaffrelot, *India's Silent Revolution.*

read about their community's historical descent, following an older Adi Hindu ideology of the 1930s, which describe Dalits as ancient India's original inhabitants. Other pamphlets invert the popular Hindu mythology of the beneficent ancient Ram Rajya and reinterpret some of the central Brahmanical epics.[41]

In parallel with the Hindu right, the Mayawati BSP government in UP has attempted to remould north Indian political identities and the public sphere of politics, even where they have failed to improve substantially the lot of the lower-caste constituencies that they represent. Since the late 1990s, many of the public spaces of the UP state capital, Lucknow, have been transformed with the renaming of parks, roads and even adjoining districts after key low-caste and untouchable leaders. The transformation has been taken to the extent of the building of overbearing civic monuments and statues to BSP leaders, which dwarf the older chauraha statues of the likes of Patel, Gandhi and Bose. Clearly, the BSP is attempting to redefine the meanings of Indian citizenship with its own forms of civic identity building. This has taken place in ways that compare to the religio-political mobilisations of the Hindu right, as was seen in the early 1990s around the *rath yatra* movements. The difference here is that the religious imagery of cultural and national unity mobilised by the Hindu right has been deliberately subverted, particularly through projects of informal popular education and mass mobilisation.

(III) SRI LANKA: FORMAL AND INFORMAL VIOLENCE IN THE 1990S AND 2000S

Political violence in Sri Lanka, which, as we have seen in previous chapters, appeared to revolve around ethnic and religious difference, had effectively become a full-scale civil war by the mid-1980s. The involvement of international agencies and, most importantly, the Indian army and security forces in the country from the late 1980s complicated an already multi-faceted conflict over the 1990s and early 2000s. Teasing out the on-going significance of ideas about religion and ethnicity in this context of war is particularly difficult, especially since, as we will see, violence and assertions of 'national' identity have been highly contingent on locality and context.[42] In the conflict between Sinhala and Tamil communities and

---

[41] Sarah Beth, 'Taking to the Streets: Dalit *mela* and the Public Performance of Dalit Cultural Identity', *Contemporary South Asia*, 14, 4, 2005, 397–410.
[42] For a discussion of this, see Ananda Abeysekara, 'The Saffron Army, Violence, Terror(ism)'.

organisations in Sri Lanka, most radical Tamil organisations deny the effective existence of a unitary nation of Sri Lanka. Analyses of this violence cannot be easily consolidated into an overarching narrative, especially as the perpetrators of atrocities have not always acted on the basis of a clearly defined political agency. Some of the worst atrocities have been carried out by rapidly formed death squads, third-party organisations and armed movements, which, while supported or trained by government or the LTTE, actually act on the basis of localised disputes. Nevertheless, most of the reporting on the civil war conflicts quantifies its casualties in such a way that the representation of the various 'atrocities', 'abuses of human rights' and 'massacres' has become a very part of the political publicity war between the different parties involved.

In order to trace how this war in the *representation* of violence has progressed and how the actions of the state in conflicts in Sri Lanka has created ambiguities about responsibility, it is important to consider the changing political context. Since the late 1980s, Indian involvement in Sri Lanka increased, particularly from July and August of 1987, when aid was dropped on Jaffna. Indian policy of the early 1980s was largely sympathetic to the Tamil insurgents in the context of politics in and pressure from Tamil Nadu. However, over the late 1980s, India's position shifted. In the Indo–Sri Lankan peace accord of 19 July 1987, the Sri Lankan government agreed to a number of concessions around the recognition of Tamil as an official language and provincial devolution. The Indian Peace-Keeping Force (IPKF) was sent to northern and eastern regions of the country, and India agreed to no longer support Tamil insurgents. From this point, although some Tamil organisations agreed to lay down their arms, the LTTE was reluctant, not least because Indian control of the north had allowed the Sri Lankan government to divert its attentions on the south and quell the Janatha Vimukthi Peramuna (JVP) uprisings there.[43] The JVP had, over the 1980s, shifted its ideological base from Marxism to a more outright militant Sinhalese nationalism. In an attempt to demobilise the LTTE, the IPKF ended up in conflict with the separatist organisation. A range of Sinhalese organisations also began to oppose the IPKF, which was involved (according the reports of some human rights organisations) in human rights abuses. Rajiv Gandhi was reluctant to withdraw from Sri Lanka, but following his defeat and the instatement of the V. P. Singh government in December 1989, the IPKF was withdrawn within three

[43] Partha S. Ghosh, 'Sinhala-Tamil Ethnic Conflict in India', *Economic and Political Weekly*, 30, 25, 1995, 1486–8.

months. Rajiv Gandhi's involvement in Sri Lanka led, on 21 May 1991 in the lead up to the next general elections, to his assassination by Thenmuli Rajaratnam, a member of the LTTE.

Following the withdrawal of the IPKF, the LTTE managed to set up quasi-government structures in the north of the country. Throughout the early 1990s, a number of organisations, including those associated with the government, were implicated in acts of what have been described in the popular media as 'ethnic cleansing'. For example, in October 1991, roughly 75,000 Muslims were expelled from the Northern Province by the LTTE, and more than 100 Muslims were killed in Palliyagodella, after the latter had requested military assistance and protection from the Sri Lankan government. Significant in this violence was the involvement of female LTTE members, or the 'birds of independence', many of whom received military training in India.[44] In response, government forces and armed Muslim groups took revenge on Tamil villages in the region. Significant in the retributive violence against both the LTTE and the JVP was the semi-formal nature of armed organisations acting at the behest of the 'state'. Both sides have used civilians as human shields and have allowed 'security' forces and death squads to act out retributive killings of suspected opponents with complete freedom of action. For example, much of the violence against the Tamil communities in the north was perpetrated by government-armed and -trained Muslim home guards. In late 1990, the government also admitted to arming and training rival Tamil organisations to the LTTE – for example, the Eelam People's Democratic Party (EPDP) and the Tamil Eelam Liberation Organisation.[45] Yet above this chaotic situation of inter-party conflict, which clearly cuts across ethnicity, governments have justified the use of militias to 'protect' innocent minorities on each side.

In 1994, a People's Alliance government came to power in Sri Lanka, with the central aim of establishing peace. Although some progress was made to that end in early 1995, the peace was broken again by April. From this point onwards, the extent to which local state agents were able to control systematic violence against particular communities was complicated by the mass exodus of people away from the conflict. Over the second half of the decade, an all-out government offensive, aimed at taking

---

[44] Peter Schalk, 'Women Fighters of the Liberation Tigers in Tamil Ilam. The Martial Feminism of Atel Palacinkam', *South Asia Research*, 14, 2, 1994.
[45] 'Human Rights Watch World Report: Sri Lanka, 1990', http://www.hrw.org/legacy/reports/1990/WR90/ASIA.BOU-11.htm, last accessed on 23 February 2010.

hold of the Jaffna peninsula, resulted in the mass displacement of civilians (by the end of the decade more than one million were estimated by human rights organisations to have been 'internally displaced') and the continued terrorist bomb attacks of the LTTE against public transport and buildings in the south of the country. Since, as we have seen above and in the previous chapter, governments and parties had difficulties in controlling the excesses of their own cadres in the 1980s conflict,[46] this was still more the case in a context of mass migration: very often, for example, violence against Tamil civilians would take place on the basis of a rumour that they were Tigers, and that could be enough evidence for the mobilisation of formal and semi-formal units against them. In the panic and uncertainty created by mass movement and displacement, popular rumour about the violent intentions of the 'other' community could be more widespread and regionally dynamic. Women outnumbered men among the internally displaced, and the number of accusations of rape, often by security forces, increased over the late 1990s. In other areas of Jaffna, the LTTE forced civilians into military training.[47] Important here from the Sinhalese perspective was the image of the all-powerful Tamil terrorist, whose image was built up around a cultural repertoire of beliefs about violence. But even more significant was the nature of the violence itself – often quite ritualistic, planned and executed in a manner that sought to humiliate the victim socially.[48] The symbolic character of terror in the meantime continued: the LTTE carried out a massive suicide bombing attack on Bandaranaike International Airport in July 2001. The conflict effectively reached a stalemate with government control of Jaffna city but LTTE military successes in other parts of the region.

A cease-fire agreement was again signed in December 2001. The conflict had now involved a range of international efforts to restore peace and 'stability', and the 9/11 attacks led the U.S. government to offer support to the Sri Lankan government as part of its global 'war on terror'. This allegedly had an effect on the LTTE in its decision to negotiate, and during the ensuing talks, it largely dropped its long-standing demand for a separate state. The peace largely fell apart by April 2006, as the LTTE (which had also split in 2004) pulled out of the increasingly fragile peace negotiations. Over the next two years, retributive killings, usually styled as

---

[46] Spencer, 'Collective Violence and Everyday Practice', p. 617.
[47] Mario Gomez, 'National Human Rights Commissions and Internally Displaced Persons: The Sri Lankan Experience', in Ujjwal Kumar Singh, *Human Rights and Peace: Ideas, Laws, Institutions and Movements* (New Delhi: Sage, 2009), p. 306.
[48] Spencer, 'Collective Violence and Everday Practice', pp. 618–22.

'massacres' and publicised in the regional media with emotive imagery, pushed the conflict further, as in earlier phases of the civil war. In the context of mass PC ownership and Internet access, news websites such as Tamilnet have been extremely important in distributing news about the war (from an LTTE perspective) not only in South Asia but also to the Tamil and Sri Lankan diasporas overseas. On 17 May 2009, the LTTE admitted military defeat and, officially, the civil war in Sri Lanka ended, with enormous costs to civilian life and livelihoods. Hundreds of thousands of internally displaced persons were still for the most part confined to refugee camps as a result of the conflict.

The theme of 'violence' in Sri Lanka, then, is complicated by the production of state discourses and ideologies that essentialise the identities of different minority communities, as in other parts of South Asia. Culpability for acts of violence is also complicated by the ways in which it has connected to everyday and local concerns, on the one hand, and to the employment of (often autonomous) local militias, on the other. There are other ways in which what appears to be a largely 'ethnic' conflict contains much more than just questions of ethnic or linguistic difference around which we might define the 'national' aspirations of the different parties to conflict. First, although this conflict has not been based around 'religion' directly, it is not necessarily the case that the LTTE's call for a separate 'secular state' has disengaged it from the religious significance of militant mobilisation for the Tigers. For the most part, the Tigers' secularism has been juxtaposed to the militant religious mobilisation of Hindu and Muslim movements. However, the LTTE has for a long time used commemorative rites, such as the use of 'hero stones' (*natukal*), at the sites of the burial of fallen members and suicide bombers. In this way, they have dispensed with the Hindu practice of cremation, but replaced it with a ritual deification of humans to 'sacralise localities', since the positioning of stones as shrines establishes guardian deities. Tiger propaganda has deliberately employed a combination of Christian and Saivite symbolism, and a concept of the afterlife is, for some scholars, implicit in the motivation of self-sacrificing fighters.[49]

Second, although language, region and ethnicity are central to the conflict at large in Sri Lanka, the broad state (and international) discourses around these themes can be broken down in other ways. Significant in historical interpretations of the civil war are not only the participants but

---

[49] Michael Roberts, 'Tamil Tigers: Sacrificial Symbolism and "Dead Body Politics"', *Anthropology Today*, 24, 3, 2008, 22–3.

also the non-involvement of communities that have largely remained aloof. In the central region of the island – the up-country area – 'Indian' Tamil populations had for the most part not been involved in the conflicts of the mid-1980s. In October 2000, some Tamil prisoners were massacred at Bindununwewa, which provoked a few days of riots, but in general, these communities have remained separate from the main Sinhalese–Tamil conflicts of the island. The leaders of the up-country Tamils have generated rumours about the possibilities of violence among the youth of their community. However, it is probably the case that they do not possess the political connections in India (being overshadowed by the Tigers) or the powerful mobilising Marxist ideology of the JVP to position themselves against governing regimes. Instead, the up-country Tamils have tended to focus their complaints across the ethnic divide, blaming both Sinhala-dominated governments and Sri Lankan Tamil organisations for their inability to get access to government employment.[50]

Third, the conflict in Sri Lanka (as we have seen in the conflicts in north India surrounding the Hindu right) is complicated by the cross-cutting and peculiar circumstances of gender difference and the part women have played in the violence. On the one hand, over the course of the civil war, instances of ritualised humiliation have been used as a means of reinforcing notions of community dishonour on the 'other' community. Custodial rape and the torture of women and children have, as in the case of India's partition, been employed as a means of marking indices of power, creating victims and destroying the abilities of those involved to exercise their civic rights. On the other hand, women have been instrumental in perpetrating violence, particularly in the LTTE, in a way that subverts some of the common notions of gendered violence.

In the final analysis, the question still remains as to how conflicts in Sri Lanka since the 1980s have led to the legitimisation of acts of violence, which in many cases do not appear to have furthered the political interests of organisations implicated. At one level, the very insecurity of state power in Sri Lanka has led formal government agencies to encourage, occasionally, paramilitary organisations to act, in the meantime furthering their own agendas. At another level, local and regional rivalries have become entangled in larger national disputes, sometimes working against the grain of the larger conflict or complicating it. Significant, here, is the on-going

---

[50] Daniel Bass, 'Paper Tigers on the Prowl: Rumors, Violence and Agency in the Up-Country of Sri Lanka', *Anthropology Quarterly*, 81, 1, 2008, 269–95; S. Nadesan, *A History of the Up Country Tamil People* (Colombo: Nandalla Publishers, 1993).

relevance of state myths, which focus on themes of ethnicity, culture and territory as a justification for the maintenance of military power for reasons of 'state security'. For one researcher on the Sri Lankan civil war, the insecurity of governments in Sri Lanka about the sovereignty of the state has meant that communities on the margins have been more vigorously controlled and sometimes brutally disempowered, with no claims or rights under law or as 'citizens'.[51] Yet around these brutal realities for those targeted, displaced or caught in the crossfire, governments have still promoted an external image of acquiescence with international law and the promotion of human rights.

(IV) PAKISTAN AND BANGLADESH: AUTHORITARIANISM AND POLITICAL CONFLICT

In Pakistan and Bangladesh, as in Sri Lanka and India, commentators have tended to associate acts of violence with the high politics of ethnic division or religious controversy. Much of the research on contemporary Pakistan, for example, has reflected on the growth of inter-ethnic or inter-regional conflict or the impact of the 'war on terror' on Islamisation in the country. However, as in other South Asian countries, these broad divisions around community and ethnicity, as they play out at the highest levels of state, are complicated and sometimes subverted at the levels of everyday life, where most citizens actually experience politics. This section of the chapter will explore some of the major controversies in which the mobilisation of religion and ethnicity appear to have generated forms of conflict and violence since the late 1980s. It will argue that there is no necessary connection between the practice of religion for ordinary people and sectarian violence, but that institutions that have promoted religious revivalism and extremism have formalised and legitimised their political authority in the context of specific local, national and international developments. Second, the articulation of ethnicity or religious sentiment has, in many cases, taken place in support of direct action and political protest around specific political issues. In this sense, the actual (and, importantly, popularly perceived) weaknesses of state power and institutions of political representation have given religious organisations the space and political opportunity to thrive. Third, violence, as we have seen in Sri Lanka,

---

[51] Mangalika de Silva, 'Stripping Women: Securing the Sovereign "National" Body', in Nvanita Chadha Behera, ed., *International Relations in South Asia: Search for an Alternative Paradigm* (New Delhi: Sage, 2008), pp. 306–28.

has been used as a means of resolving specific *local* disputes in the first instance, even where it has connected to events at the national level.

Over the 1990s in Pakistan, political parties aligned strongly with what appeared to be the major ethnic divisions – the PML representing the interests of Punjabis, the PPP largely (although not exclusively) Sindhis and organisations such as Baluch National Party representing Baluchistanis. The Mohajir Quami Movement (MQM), renamed Muttahida Qawmi Movement in 1997, formed in 1984 and represented Muhajir communities, with a focus in the city of Karachi.[52] At least by the late 1980s, it seemed possible that a civilian government could hold power for a time –a situation that changed the context of competition between these groups. In the elections of November 1988, following the death of General Zia in a plane crash in August, the PPP under the leadership of Benazir Bhutto became the largest party in the National Assembly, followed by the Islami Jamhuri Ittehad, despite the attempts of the military and state-controlled media to obstruct Bhutto's campaign. When in power, Bhutto attempted to establish civilian control over the ISI but increasingly antagonised the military brass. Even more problematic for the new regime was the fact that, for the first time, there was a government at the centre that did not hold power in the state government of Punjab, the latter being controlled by Nawaz Sharif. Sharif made moves towards provincialisation, with the support and encouragement of the president and military. Bhutto was dismissed in August 1990 for 'corruption, inefficiency and misconduct of power' under pressure from the military, but following an interim period under Nawaz Sharif, she regained power in October 1993.

The 1993 elections again demonstrated the extent to which apparent differences in ethnicity across the political system destabilised the ruling regime. However, to a great extent, the so-called Sindhi–Muhajir conflicts in urban Sindh in the 1990s are not easily characterised in terms of 'ethnicity'. The Muhajir community is composed of groups from a range of different Indian regions – Bihar, Madhya Pradesh, Gujarat and, most prominently, Uttar Pradesh. Its ideological unity is based, therefore, largely on language (Urdu). Organisationally, the MQM has resembled right-wing organisations in Europe, with its focus around a single leader. However, by the early 1990s, the organisation appeared to shift away from the promotion of Pakistani nationalism and forms of regionalism. And from the mid-1990s, the MQM has enforced its position as the leading organisation of 'Muhajir patronage', extorting *chanda*

---

[52] Ameen Jan, 'Pakistan on a Precipice', *Asian Survey*, 39, 5, 1999, 699–719.

(contributions) in some cities from local businesses. This, some scholars argue, has been a response to the growing 'ethnic' nationalism of other communities in Pakistan.[53]

In this development, the relative significance of Karachi to the Pakistani economy and revenue base and the relatively high levels of educational achievement and literacy among Muhajirs was important. But so too was the distinctive and fragmented nature of urban violence in Karachi, in which the local state had been largely usurped by competing organisations. The population of Karachi increased over the 1980s and 1990s, and there was increasing pressure on its housing resources and employment opportunities. While the PPP dominated Sindh as a whole, the MQM under the leadership of Altaf Hussain was predominant in Karachi. In 1992, the military launched 'Operation Cleanup', targeted against MQM urban militancy in Karachi. In response, the latter organisation exercised a form of urban warfare against the government and the PPP, which involved the deaths of thousands in 'terrorist' attacks. This violence has, since 1994, involved paramilitary forces, who have carried out extra-judicial killings of MQM members.[54] The violence in Karachi is, however, also marked by the actions of violent entrepreneurs – local militant organisations – who use ethnic and religious divisions to further local agendas and whose exercise of terror in the locality fragments and complicates supposed political polarisation around ethnicity.[55]

Conflict in Pakistan in the 1990s has not been confined to either sectarian or regional/ethnic disputes either. So much of what has happened for those mobilising around the symbols of religious identity in either India or Pakistan has involved events in the 'other' state. The demolition of the Babri Masjid in India had a knock-on effect in Pakistan, where more than thirty temples were attacked and some destroyed in retributive violence. The popular media in Pakistan reacted to the Ram Jamnabhoomi movement by reasserting doubts about the integrity of Indian secularism and the extent to which Indian regimes were able or indeed interested in validating

---

[53] Farhat Haq, 'Rise of the MQM in Pakistan: Politics of Ethnic Mobilization', *Asian Survey*, 35, 11, 1995, 990–1004.
[54] Moonis Ahmar, 'Ethnicity and State Power in Pakistan: The Karachi Crisis'.
[55] For a study of urban warfare in Karachi, see Laurent Gayer, 'Guns, Slums and "Yellow Devils": A Genealogy of Urban Conflicts in Karachi, Pakistan', *Modern Asian Studies*, 41, 3, 2007, 514–44. See also Oskar Verkaaik, *Migrants and Militants: Fun and Urban Violence in Pakistan* (Princeton: Princeton University Press, 2004).

its legal principles.[56] In Bangladesh too, riots broke out in Dhaka on receipt of the news of the demolition of the mosque in Ayodhya. The Indian Airlines office was attacked, the Indian Cultural Centre burned, the Bangladeshi Communist Party offices were targeted and a number of temples were demolished. However, the Awami League made political capital out of the Jamaat-e-Islami's association with these protests, and also ran rallies condemning the 'communalism' of both the Islamic party and that of the Sangh Parivar in India.[57]

An important spur for direct action on the streets of Pakistan's cities over the 1990s was the continued attempts of regimes to consolidate power and silence opposition movements within the formal institutions of the state. This occurred under civilian regimes too. From February 1997, Nawaz Sharif and the Pakistan Muslim League (PML) held an absolute majority in the national parliament and quickly moved to consolidate his power. Holding 137 out of 205 seats in the National Assembly, he was able to nullify the eighth constitutional amendment, which allowed the president to dismiss the government and to call for new elections. In early 1999, the opposition to Nawaz Sharif was mostly composed of ethnic parties, on the one hand, and an increasingly powerful religious leadership, which in some instances sought to overthrow the whole basis of parliamentary government, on the other. Sharif also introduced legislation preventing members of the National Assembly from violating party discipline, which limited their ability to make deals with opposition parties. Sharif increased the power of the centre, declaring president's rule in Sindh and using the judiciary to convict Bhutto and her husband of corruption. The freedoms that the press had enjoyed under Benazir Bhutto were curbed and 2,000 NGOs were banned.

The battles for control over the principal arms of the state and the undermining thereby of the judiciary and constitutional norms intensified from the late 1980s in Pakistan as regimes used the threat of 'international terrorism' to stamp down on opposition parties. Since September 2001, the authoritarian arms of the state in Pakistan have also been used to ban all manner of sectarian organisations and, in the process, have served to control other forms of political opposition. However, this has meant that organisations such as Lashkar-i-Jangvi and Jaish-i-Mohammad – both

---

[56] Mahmoud Monshipouri, 'Backlash to the Destruction at Ayodhya: A View from Pakistan', *Asian Survey*, 33, 7; South Asia: Responses to the Ayodhya Crisis (1993), pp. 711–21.
[57] Partha S. Ghosh, 'Bangladesh at the Crossroads: Religion and Politics'.

militant groups connected by the authorities to specific terrorist attacks against U.S. consulates and luxury hotels in Pakistan and kidnappings – were more easily turned towards the Taliban and al-Qaeda over the porous border with Afghanistan.[58] In 2003, the Legal Framework Order under General Musharraf allowed the president to dissolve the National Assembly once again and to introduce a National Security Council for discussion of 'democracy, governance and interprovincial harmony'. And again, it was in political opposition to these authoritarian moves that religious organisations in Pakistan attempted to build popular opposition against Pakistan's alignment with the United States, particularly around the invasion of Iraq. Here, the Muttahida Majlis-i-Amal (MMA) was at the forefront, providing opposition in the absence of the key secular leaders Benazir Bhutto and Nawaz Sharif. Increasingly too, an embattled military regime at the centre has been challenged by organisations based on provincial power, who have sought to push Pakistan more in the direction of a theocratic state, for example, in the NWFP.[59]

To a great extent, radical sectarian movements and parties in Pakistan have attempted to uphold conservative principles of family organisation and sharia law in an attempt to establish and foreground Islam in every aspect of society and politics in the region. Yet the recent strengthening of radical religious organisations in Pakistan, in the light of international and national developments, has also involved the support of women activists, for example, in parties such as Jamaat-e-Islami. Islamist ideology has become a means of exposing what is thought of, by many subject to the authoritarian rule of military regimes in Pakistan, as Western decadence in Pakistani society. It has also been a means of opposing the 'orientalist' ambitions of Western powers in the Muslim world and mobilising large numbers around symbols of political resistance to the 'corruption' of non-Islamic influences. The MMA has hundreds of women representatives in local and regional councils. Some academics have suggested that the existence of women in such organisations poses problems for feminist organisations in Pakistan, but also suggests a defiant negation of Western ideas about social development and secular modernity. For such women, 'women's rights' cannot be furthered according to the normative agendas of a separation of state from society, and they instead promote

[58] Ian Talbot, 'Pakistan in 2002: Democracy, Terrorism and Brinkmanship', *Asian Survey*, 43, 1, 2003, 198–207.
[59] Ian Talbot, 'Pakistan in 2003: Political Deadlock and Continuing Uncertainties', *Asian Survey*, 44, 1, 2004, 36–42.

women's roles as protectors and 'mothers' of the righteous.[60] However, the relationship between women's political mobilisation and Islamisation is a highly differentiated one across the country. In other regions of Pakistan, women's organisations have championed resistance to official moves towards Islamisation, suggesting its largely unfinished nature and presenting alternative means of being a pious Muslim. In Chitral in northern Pakistan, women have been critical of the paternalistic 'men of piety' and have forcefully entered debates about how far local Islamist moves affect issues of everyday morality.[61]

In Bangladesh, debates among feminist scholars have to a great extent focussed on women workers in low-paid sectors, such as ready-made garment workers, sex workers and migrant labourers to the Gulf states, as well as gendered violence against women, including 'acid violence'. It is likely that the latter has increased since the late 1980s, partly as a result of a reassertion of patriarchy in the face of high levels of unemployment, economic insecurity and the perceived (by men) 'threat' of female employment and independence.[62] The rise in employment of women in Bangladesh over the 1980s and 1990s coincided with the growing popularity and strength of the Jamaat-e-Islami, and the rising number of fatwas against women who work in NGOs or the export sector.[63] A fatwa is an opinion on a point of law rendered by a *mufti* or legal consultant in response to a question submitted by a private individual. It is not legally enforceable or bound to be accepted. However, between January 1993 and December 1996, more than sixty incidents of fatwa-instigated violence were reported in Bangladesh, and nearly all were directed against poor rural women. In most cases, these fatwas were issued by unqualified men by the standards of Islamic jurisprudence.[64] Much of this violence has targeted basic schools and health centres providing education for women in rural communities. Crucially, the state in Bangladesh did little or

---

[60] Amina Jamal, 'Feminist "Selves" and Feminism's "Others": Feminist Representations of Jamaat-e-Islami Women in Pakistan', *Feminist Review*, 81, Bodily Interventions, 2005, 52–73. See also Farhat Haq, 'Militarism and Motherhood: The Women of the Lashkar-i-Tayyabia in Pakistan', *Signs*, 32, 4, 2007, 1023–46.

[61] Magnus Marsden, 'Women, Politics and Islamism in Northern Pakistan', *Modern Asian Studies*, 42, 2–3, 2008, 405–29.

[62] Afroza Anwary, 'Acid Violence and Medical Care in Bangladesh: Women's Activism as Careworker', *Gender and Society*, 17, 2, 2003, 305–13.

[63] Shelley Feldman, 'Exploring Theories of Patriarchy: A Perspective from Contemporary Bangladesh', *Signs*, 26, 4, 2001, 1097–127.

[64] Elora Shehabuddin, 'Contesting the Illicit: Gender and the Politics of Fatwas in Bangladesh', *Signs*, 24, 4, 1999, 1012, 1017.

nothing in response to these incidents, – a situation that is widely publicised in Bangladeshi society. Instead, the institution of a *salish* or local village judgement has been common. However, the Jamaat-e-Islami (JI), the main party of the religious right, has argued that such events result from the 'absence' of Islam in the public sphere, which has permitted 'unqualified' men to condone or promote acts of violence.[65] In fact, since the late 1990s, the JI has attempted to compete with secular organisations and has strenuously argued that Islam recognises the rights of women as individuals and their rights to study, work and vote.[66]

Feminists, as in Pakistan, have also had to contend with the fact that many women have been attracted to Islamist organisations. In particular, Islamist Quranic study circles have been important in organisations like the student-based Bangladesh Islamic Chatri Sangstha, and have promoted the idea that modern life can be related to scriptural conventions.[67] The consensus has been that women's groups need to work from within such organisations to further women's rights. However, specific issues have made attempts to develop the health, independence and work prospects of women in Bangladesh, the focus of condemnation from institutions and movements of the Islamic right. On 30 June 1994, a nationwide hartal was called by a number of Islamic organisations in support of a fatwa against Taslima Nasrin who had published a novel – *Lajja* – that criticised the persecution of women and Hindus in Bangladesh. An alliance of thirteen Islamic groups, named the United Actions Council, observed Koran day on 29 July 1994, again calling for the punishment of Taslima and other 'atheist', 'apostate' or 'blasphemous' authors; that NGOs refrain from 'anti-Islamic' activities; that a blasphemy law be passed by the parliament; and that there be no foreign 'interference' with religious issues in the country. But, as in party political confrontation, so again here there were counter-demonstrations from those opposing the religious right: 'Liberal' organisations and movements staged their own mass rallies over the same period in support of the right to freedom of expression and against the mobilisation of the religious right. There was some ambivalence among these protestors about the specific writings of Taslima Nasrin, which also offended moral sensibilities more broadly in Bangladesh by advocating sexual freedom for women. *Lajja* also provided symbolic capital for the

---

[65] *Ibid.*, p. 1013.
[66] Elora Shehabuddin, 'Jamaat-e-Islami in Bangladesh: Women, Democracy and the Transformation of Islamist Politics', *Modern Asian Studies*, 42, 2/3, 2008, 577–603.
[67] Maimuna Huq, 'Reading the Qur'an in Bangladesh: The Politics of "Belief" Among Islamist Women', *Modern Asian Studies*, 42, 2/3, 2008, 457–88.

Hindu right in India. It became a best-seller on the other side of the border, and the BJP promoted its translation into other Indian languages.[68]

Around these protests, there were other casualties in parts of Bangladesh where overseas emigration has been common. The Bangladesh Women's Health Coalition office in Sylhet was attacked shortly following the hartal in a spate of violence and intimidation that linked local concerns to national events. This organisation had provided reproductive health services, literacy classes and awareness classes on family law on marriage, inheritance, divorce and guardianship of children. However, in the early 1990s, it was opposed by a local powerful *pir* who had the support of the Jamat-i-Islami and who felt he was losing many of the women who had previously visited him for his 'healing powers', favours and connections.[69] The Bangladesh Rural Advancement Committee and the Grameen Bank, both well-established NGOs in the country, complained of harassment and vandalisation of properties and, in some cases, the destruction of offices and schools. Foreign NGOs were also attacked.[70]

Although many of the formal organisations of the religious right in Bangladesh have seemed to sponsor demonstrations against developmental organisations, it is wrong to suppose that Islam necessarily reinforces patriarchy. As in Pakistan, women have used Islam to liberate themselves from men: in parts of Sylhet in Bangladesh, the worship of female saints has helped to empower women in the locality.[71] Instead, the connection between religious radicalism and everyday violence relates more to the (actual and perceived) weaknesses of political and state structures. Political changes in the 1990s epitomised these instabilities. In December 1990, the military regime of General H. M. Ershad resigned in Bangladesh, and elections were held in February 1991. The surprise victory of the Bangladesh National Party (BNP), who managed to form a government as a result of accommodation with the Jamat-i-Islami, resulted in the appointment of Bangladesh's first female Prime Minister – Khaleda Zia.

---

[68] M. Rashiduzzaman, 'The Liberals and the Religious Right in Bangladesh', *Asian Survey*, 34, 11, 1994, 974–90; and 'Islam, Muslim Identity and Nationalism in Bangladesh', *Journal of South Asian and Middle Eastern Studies*, 18, 1994, 36–60. See also S. M. Shamsul Alam, 'Women in the Era of Modernity and Islamic Fundamentalism: The Case of Taslima Nasrin of Bangladesh', *Signs*, 23, 2, 1998, 429–61.

[69] Sandra M. Kabir, 'An Experience of Religious Extremism in Bangladesh', *Reproductive Matters*, 4, 8, 1996, 104–9.

[70] Rashiduzzaman, 'The Liberals and the Religious Right', p. 975.

[71] Alyson Callan, 'Female Saints and the Practice of Islam in Sylhet, Bangladesh', *American Ethnologist*, 35, 3, 2008, 396–412.

Over the early 1990s, the BNP was faced with widespread political boycott both within and outside Bangladesh's parliament. Following a mass resignation of opposition members – from the Awami League (AL), the Jatiya Party (JP) and the Jamaat-e-Islami (JI) – at the end of 1994, the parliament was eventually dissolved in 1995 and public protests followed across the country, which eventually culminated in the resignation of the BNP in March 1996. A powerful element within the JI was a radical group of educationalists and university professors, who, along with the JI's student wing, Islami Chatra Shibir, organised mass demonstrations and public meetings against the government over the mid-1990s.[72] For one prominent scholar, the failure of Bangladeshi governments over the 1980s and 1990s to allow broader political participation among wider sections of society has pushed 'demand groups' to use direct action and violence to further their agendas. Political divisions encouraged leading business interests in the country to push for political accommodation for the sake of the economy, touching off a rumour that the top business houses were attempting to unduly influence politics and play the role of kingmaker.[73]

Politics in Bangladesh, then, was characterised by forms of party confrontation, in which each party attempted to gain control fully of the levers of the state and where protest and opposition were highly adversarial. These confrontations have created instabilities and a lack of political accommodation that one political scientist suggests are related to Bangladesh's long experiences of military regimes and the fundamental weakness of democracy in the country.[74] One outcome of this situation, in particular, the contests between the BNP and AL since the early 1990s, has been the courting, by each of these main parties, of the JI – the party of the religious right – as a means of unseating or challenging the main opposition party. This has added authority and legitimacy to the main political representatives of Islamic organisations.[75] Certainly, a patrimonial form of dynastic leadership has also encouraged the sharply adversarial nature of party politics under the premierships of the daughter of the leader of the war for Bangladeshi liberation, Sheikh Hasina Wajid (AL), between 1996

---

[72] Golam Hossain, 'Bangladesh in 1995: Politics of Intransigence', *Asian Survey*, 36, 2, 1996, 196–203.
[73] Stanley A. Kochanek, 'The Rise of Interest Politics in Bangladesh', *Asian Survey*, 36, 7, 1996, 704–22.
[74] Akhtar Hossain, 'Anatomy of Hartal Politics in Bangladesh', *Asian Survey*, 40, 3, 2000, 508–29.
[75] M. Rashiduzzaman, 'The Liberals and the Religious Right', p. 985.

and 2001 and that of the widow of General Ziaur Rahman, Begum Khaleda Zia (BNP), between 1991 and 1996 and 2001–6.

The insecurities of the larger 'secular' parties and their inability to forge a politics of consensus, then, has to some extent provided opportunities for the religious right in Bangladesh since the mid-1990s. Following new elections in June 1996, an AL government was elected, and this time it was the turn of the BNP to organise street demonstrations, *hartals* and parliamentary boycotts. This time too, among the usual protests about the mismanagement of the economy was an Islamic JI-run protest in July 1997, which campaigned around the issue of Israeli policies towards Palestine. Also common over this phase were accusations about the government's 'pro-Indian' bias. This lack of stability, in a context of patronage politics in Bangladesh, has led to a range of controversies around development policies for the urban poor. In the late 1990s, the Bangladeshi government came under intense pressure as a result of its bungling of a policy for the eviction of sex workers and slum dwellers without a clear strategy of rehabilitation.[76] Such mistakes have encouraged accusations of religious organisations about the 'corruption' or misgovernment of the mainstream parties in Bangladesh. Confrontational politics continued into the 2000s, with the AL publishing a list of the 101 'Godfathers' in the ruling BNP in October 2003.[77] One of the crucial pawns in this BNP–AL contest has been the JI – a coalition partner in the BNP-led government – along with the Islami Oikya Jote. Under pressure from these groups, in 2004, the government banned the publications of the sect of Ahmadiyyas. With Islamic parties in positions of power, the government was even weaker in dealing with sectarian violence – for example, the gang terror of the Taliban-inspired 'Bangla Bhai' in north-western Bangladesh.[78]

Political observers of Pakistan and Bangladesh have noted some similarities between the two states, particularly in relation to the role of intermittent civilian/military regimes, and the apparent 'Islamisation' of politics and society from the 1980s. However, these narratives need to be complicated by region and attention to the politics of local communities and specific urban or rural spaces. At first glance, both states appear to be threatened at multiple levels by ethnic and sectarian conflict. But this

---

[76] Stanley A. Kochanek, 'Governance, Patronage Politics and Democratic Transition in Bangladesh', *Asian Survey*, 40, 3, 2000, 530–50.

[77] Rounaq Jahan, 'Bangladesh in 2003: Vibrant Democracy or Destructive Politics?', *Asian Survey*, 44, 1, 2003, 58.

[78] Ali Riaz, 'Bangladesh in 2004: The Politics of Vengeance', *Asian Survey*, 45, 1, 2005, 112–18.

violence is highly differentiated and fractured once we look at some of the
underlying motivations for apparent militant mobilisation, for example, in
some of Pakistan's larger cities or Bangladesh's rural locales. Recent
anthropological work has also reoriented our view of the significance of
'Islam' and the politics of religion in Pakistan by looking at the role of
emotion, the structure of the family and the idea of individual sentiment.[79]
There is a gulf, then, between the narrative histories of the state and high
politics and the quotidian experiences of each state's civilians. For example, even though Bangladesh had two consecutive female Prime Ministers,
this has had little or no effect on the ability of women's movements or
NGOs to promote women's education and health. With the inability of the
state to do anything about women's rights or to rein in the violence
associated with religious fundamentalism, it falls to feminist organisations
such as the Women's Social Collective.[80] Or it has fallen to women to
reform such organisations of religious mobilisation from within.

Each state has also been faced with dual and competing international
pressures – from the UN, on the one hand, and Saudi Arabia, on the other.[81]
Religious and ethnic organisation has therefore provided a means of protest
and mobilisation in the face of the weak state, itself subjected to intense and
violent political competition, and the pressures of widely differing international agencies. At certain moments too, such organisations have become a
vehicle for violence. And the shortcomings of the state at all levels are well
known for all of Pakistan and Bangladesh's citizens. For some, then, religious
and ethnic mobilisation has provided the means to make a protest, where
representative institutions have failed. For others, religious mobilisation has
been a means of responding to a rapidly changing and uncertain political and
economic future. Finally, for many, it has been a means of upholding social
stability, paternalism and local power in the face of globalisation, the impact
of the wider world on every aspect of society and the increasing autonomy
(and desire for independence) of the country's most underprivileged citizens.

CONCLUSION

In all of the states of South Asia from the early 1990s, parties and organisations of religious revivalism and mobilisation were forced to come to

---

[79] For another case study of local critiques of Islamisation policies in northern Pakistan, see
     Magnus Marsden, 'All Male Sonic Gatherings, Islamic Reform and Masculinity in
     Northern Pakistan', *American Ethnologist*, 34, 3, 2007, 473–90.
[80] Alam, p. 458.
[81] Shehabuddin, 'Contesting the Illicit', p. 1013.

terms with increasingly close connections between South Asia and the wider world via economic liberalisation, changes in media and communications and increasing domestic consumerism. For some organisations, like the BJP and its associated movements in the Sangh Parivar, this created divisions and dilemmas, as it was forced to compromise an earlier commitment to swadeshi. Older critiques of Western modernity were also altered or moderated, to some extent, by parties of the religious right in Pakistan and Bangladesh, especially those that attempted to accommodate women. In all cases, these movements then found themselves having to alter their politics on the basis of the demands of new constituencies. And in the case of the BJP, gaining political power at state and national levels meant accommodation of parties that had largely benefitted from India's implementation of caste reservations. However, this has not meant that such organisations have turned their back on the methods of mobilisation around religious symbolism, as the on-going episodes connected to the Ram Jamnabhoomi movement illustrate. To some extent, this is the result of the differences between the Sangh Parivar organisations at different levels of the Indian polity. Neither have these institutions eschewed the promotion of religious intolerance at moments when it suits the purposes of regional parties or movements, as was seen in Gujarat in 2002.

Since the late 1980s, the Hindu right in India and the Islamic parties in Pakistan and Bangladesh also promoted their own visions and symbols of the united nation. For both sets of organisations, threats to national integrity often appeared to come from foreign or international sources. As India began to connect more clearly to the global economy and as diasporic wealth drained back into India, sources of funding were, however, also found from overseas. In the case of Bangladesh and Pakistan, regimes have had to position themselves, too, in relation to particular foreign governments, and at certain moments have been keen to garner support from the Arab states – a situation that in some cases has encouraged the establishment of religious institutions. And political decisions in each of our states have been made in reference to one or more of the others: for example, the course of the civil war in Sri Lanka was affected by Indian involvement both directly and militarily and via support for Tamil separatism from the south.

Yet each of our states has continued to be insecure, vulnerable to the demands of regional and ethnic groups (in the case of Pakistan and Sri Lanka) and subverted at local levels by those able to gain leverage with the local administration (in the case of India). For Pakistan and Sri Lanka, popular awareness of the state's weaknesses in this respect has encouraged

Religion

paramilitary organisations to act in the meantime furthering their own agendas. These entrepreneurs of violence in the cities and countryside have carried out atrocities that have served to entangle local and regional rivalries with larger national disputes, sometimes working against the grain of the larger conflict or complicating it. In response or in anticipation of this, in some of our case studies, military power and associated myths of national unity have been promoted for reasons of 'state security'. In other places, such as Bangladesh, the inability of the main political parties to reach a national consensus has given a space for movements of religious mobilisation to thrive. Ordinary citizens of each of our states have been caught in the crossfire and sometimes implicated in conflagrations of violence. But their experience of state violence has been very different to that projected to international news agencies, which represent the region in terms of broad ethnic and religious divisions. In reality, for many in India, Bangladesh, Pakistan and Sri Lanka, everyday experience does not correspond to these images of conflict. And religious practice and sentiment only connects in a tangential way to the agendas of the political mobilisers of religious community. Indeed, it is the very refusal of most inhabitants of South Asian states to acquiesce in the idea that the traditions of Islam, Hinduism, Buddhism, Sikhism or Christianity can be reduced to a political posture that continues to offer one of the greatest challenges to organisations of communal mobilisation.

Conclusion

Anyone glancing at a library catalogue or bookshelf on the politics or history of India, Pakistan, Bangladesh and Sri Lanka may be forgiven for thinking that religious cultures have defined some of the most important political developments in the region over the twentieth century. This is partly the result of the dominance of long-standing Western academic frameworks. A key aspect of British colonial knowledge was that religious traditions largely defined distinctively 'Indian' political and social organisations – an idea that also served to justify British power for most of the late colonial period. Although this book has focussed on religion and conflict, it has attempted to oppose suggestions that South Asian societies should be defined principally in relation to religious cultures. Throughout, it has also argued for a clear distinction between structures of religious belief and practice and the phenomenon of religious community mobilisation. The latter has taken place for largely political ends, often for purely secular purposes. And it is the latter that has formed the main focus of this book, since such movements have been implicated in moments of dramatic confrontation between different organisations and communities. The book has also attempted to show that violence and conflict were not the only or even the principal manifestations of 'communal' mobilisation. Even where the casualties of violence inspired by religious or ethnic difference have been extensive, such as Sri Lanka since 1983, the psychological motivations for violence and its extreme implications for local societies have often clouded deeper-seated political differences. This is not to suggest that violence itself is not significant to our analysis, but that its manifestation does not epitomise or necessarily explain religious and communal conflict. This is not least because it has been the practice of political parties and of states to use and recreate information about extreme violence as a means of furthering broader political agendas. 'Violence' has become a loaded term, an ontological category if you will, as much as 'communalism' in South Asia.

To this end, the book has looked closely at the state in South Asia, and our first concluding point lies in an examination of the nature and actions of those states. The phenomenon of communalism or religious conflict cannot be fully explored, it has argued, without a careful analysis of not only the nature of the state but also how different social groups in South Asia perceived it. This means taking into account the fact that the state is not an autonomous entity, which acts out agendas largely separated from social networks of power. The state is effectively either made up of social interest groups or interacts very closely with them. The nature of the state is important to our study because of the way it changed too. What political freedom actually meant, for example, after 1947 for most Indians was not always clear-cut, since popular views of everyday governance did not change dramatically or suddenly. There was, for many, a palpable gulf between the high-level rhetorical narratives of national freedom and the mundane realities of making contact with local governments, bureaucrats and police officers. The experience of partition as a process of state change, too, created ambiguities for minorities in India and Pakistan, in which national identity and a sense of belonging was not certain for many.[1]

These changes brought other kinds of implications for ideas about religious community. From the early 1950s, the Indian state ostensibly aimed to promote secularism. Yet, even at the highest levels of the state, this was often compromised by the stance taken in relation to Pakistan or in connection to movements of regional separatism, as we saw in Chapter 6. The implication of colonial governments' decisions in dividing communities from each other has been well rehearsed. This had an afterlife after 1947. But after independence too, the issue of 'communalism' or sectarianism changed in other ways and took place against the backdrop of the attempts of national regimes to define a broader and consolidated 'national' culture. In Sri Lanka, this involved the eventual establishment of a Sinhala-only policy and attempts to focus on Sinhalese identity as the principal component of national identity. In Pakistan, this process was complicated by the broad-stroke politics of ethnic division, which cut across the key institutions of the state – the bureaucracy and the

[1] For an exploration of this process, see Ansari, Gould and Sherman, 'The Flux of the Matter'.

army – and the problems of consolidating national culture within obviously dominant regional/migrant identities.

State power was experienced by most people in relation to a range of different governmental spaces, and was therefore dependent on where contact took place with government servants or politicians. At local levels, ordinary Indians may have had recourse to local political leadership as a way of mediating its structures and rules. This was of course limited in the pre-1947 period by the fact that the colonial system was primarily based on resource extraction rather than responsible self-government and tended to promote sectional rather than universal representation. In the late colonial period, religious communities were rapidly established in the context of new (albeit limited) institutions of political representation. However, in general it was the *absence* of adequate political representation for most Indians that made religious community organisations pertinent to political leaders and lobbying groups. And connected to this, it was the locally contingent nature of the state that allowed certain interest groups to exercise some leverage. The points at which religious community became important in these processes have been one of the main elements of this book. And critical, here, was the anticipation by political leaderships of how the system might change in the future. This was a dynamic history of representative politics. Elections are one obvious area in which religious community mobilisation, around organisations such as the Hindu Mahasabha or Muslim League, became important, particularly in phases like the mid-1920s, when the context of political mobilisation changed rapidly. The specific areas in which 'communal' conflict emerged also related to the nature of party political (or factional) mobilisation.

There was no necessary political confrontation between different communities around elections or other moments of political engagement. But at certain moments, it suited the purposes of factional leaders to mobilise on this basis. This was sometimes for direct and practical reasons: systems of local patronage now overlapped with local representative institutions, which could control religious spaces and institutions and, through them, religious practices. As we saw in Chapters 2, 3 and 4, the control of municipal government was important in the determination of routes for religious processions or in permitting the work of slaughterhouses. For example, urban traders in Bombay and the area of Gujarat promoted public and religious reform as part of the complex agenda of municipal domination and professional solidarity. These activities could be crucial to the livelihoods of large numbers but were of greater symbolic significance in the delineation of space. It was no accident that some of the main direct conflicts between communities took place over specific ideas about territory, locality, neighbourhood or space.

Work on the 'crisis of the state', which looked at South Asia (in particular, India) from the early 1970s to the end of the 1980s, explored some of the problems and contradictions in an Indian secular state whose leaders were unable to protect its core values of religious tolerance. This was also a period, though, of enhanced state authoritarianism in India and Pakistan. It was a time in which Indians, faced with increasingly complex political demands and a more intrusive bureaucracy and police, developed new ways of mediating state institutions. Getting things done in India, Pakistan and Sri Lanka has often involved the employment of intermediaries to the state and political system and semi-formal approaches to officialdom.[2] Here too, ordinary Indians have found it expedient to employ organisations of religious representation or to build lobbying movements on the basis of community. This has been particularly useful since the 1980s, with the rise of regional parties in most parts of India, which have catered to the interests of specific caste-based communities. But at other moments, this need to mediate state agencies has benefitted the Hindu or Islamic right across all of our case studies. In particular, incidents of communal conflict, often around quite local issues, have been used as a means of building broader electoral support for religious parties.

A second set of arguments and themes in this book concerns the politics surrounding the representation of religious community. To a great extent, the history of communalism and conflict in South Asia is a history of projects of political definition and boundary drawing, both physical and metaphorical. But it is also a history in which the ability of institutions to represent populations on the basis of community related to specific structures of power. Most of the projects, for example, in the delineation of a broad Hindu community were not based in a desire to find religious synthesis between different sects or castes or even to reform religious practices. Rather, they were largely concerned with the secular aim of maintaining the power of existing (largely urban) elites, sometimes differentiated by region, as they competed with other broadly defined communities. It was for this reason that Hindu mobilisation was most prominently related (in the late colonial period) to Hindu nationalism, since the definition of national community was central to the project of those promoting Hindu identities.

---

[2] See William Gould, *Bureaucracy, Community and Influence*, pp. 130–5.

Crucially, the power of representation situated in these organisations was partially a product of (or informed by) colonial ideas about religious community and Indian society at large. For institutions like the Congress, Muslim League, Hindu Mahasabha, Singh Sabha, Arya Samaj and Sanatan Dharmas, the politics of the 'masses' coincided with colonial stereotypes of Indian social disorganisation. The essential politics of the ordinary peasant or worker, for these ideologues, involved superstitious attachments to religious rituals. They were, according to their analyses, deaf to arguments based on rationality and could be best mobilised with reference to simple evocations of religious symbolism or moments of religious observance. For many thinkers too, the belief that modern education could break down traditional attachments to religious ritual and belief was part and parcel of the term 'communalism', as the phenomenon came to be associated with political 'backwardness'. As Chapters 6 to 8 explored, for the post-colonial period, 'modernisation' entailed attempts to assimilate or integrate heterogeneous cultures and political organisations into more uniform political cultures. In India, for many institutions, this was based on the assumption that a dominant (Hindu) political culture lay at the heart of Indian citizenship and identity. By the mid-1990s, this was a modernised Hindu culture, which embraced technological and global achievements and international commerce, as Chapter 8 explored. In Pakistan, core national political cultures were more clearly polarised around officially defined ethnic and regional differences by the 1990s, but there were experiments in the 1980s to promote a unified Islamic identity. However, in all of our states, attempts to associate dominant religious or ethnic cultures with national development faced resistance. In India, this came about through movements of lower-caste or Dalit mobilisation. In Sri Lanka, in a very different way, resistance was much more direct and manifested itself in the increasing radicalisation of demands for Tamil Eelam.

The whole basis of what 'religion' meant in public life in India also changed in the late nineteenth and early twentieth centuries, as intellectuals attempted to define religious communities in relation to world religions and the belief structures of other traditions. 'Religion' did not simply feature, in these discussions, as a matter of belief or even social organisation. It also related to cultural production, the means of communication and ideas about the Indian nation. Culture overlapped with political authority, particularly around the delineation of how literature, art and music should be consumed or enjoyed and who might be privileged to enjoy it. In this sense, the relationship of the arts to changing ideas about

religious community entailed projects of cultural standardisation – forms
of colonial knowledge production, perpetrated by those with the wealth,
education and taste to create and disseminate artistic products. In a more
practical sense, the promotion of the vernaculars coincided with the control of institutions, some of which, such as those associated with education,
provided the basis for forming political networks. This was most obviously
the case in the Aligarh movement and the institutions promoted by the
Arya Samaj.

Third, this book has argued throughout that attempts to define, represent and mobilise broad religious communities exposed much more complex solidarities and conflicts that critiqued or mobilised religion in their
own ways. At one level, this involved debates about the position of women
in relation to men, the family, the community and nation. To a great
extent, attempts to define Hindu and Muslim cultures in South Asia were
largely driven by men, and involved a stricter delineation of the practical
and symbolic roles of women. This was not unchallenged by women,
though – a point that was increasingly seen by the 1970s and 1980s across
South Asia in women's involvement both inside and outside organisations
of religious community mobilisation. Most projects of representation were
therefore highly problematic and, as well as gendered, were socially and
regionally limited. In the late colonial period, as Chapters 2 to 4 argued,
some of the main organisations of communal mobilisation failed to mobilise fully even a small section of India's vast population. For most Indians,
religious community served quite different purposes – the means of asserting higher status locally, the basis for rebellion or reform or a process
whereby they could seek local accommodation. In this sense, ideas about
religious community were shaped by other solidarities: low-caste migrants
to north Indian cities championed forms of Hindu mobilisation and revivalism in the 1920s and 1930s as a means of asserting local status and
power. In tribal areas at the turn of the twentieth century, it became a
means of rebellion, and for urban workers in some of the mill cities in the
interwar period, it could be a means of mediating the workplace. By the
late 1930s and 1940s, those disadvantaged by the religious polarisation of
Hindu–Muslim confrontation were in other ways able to promote ideas of
'minority status' in response to new constitutional proposals. But religious
'community' also complicated other social structures and, in particular,
cut across the potential solidarity of occupational groups between different
regions, cities or even neighbourhoods. Neither was the role of religious
community in this process entirely functional. In each particular locality,
the importance of intermediaries at all levels of the Indian economy and

workplace meant that patterns of domination and subordination worked according to their own forms of internal logic. In a similar way, the struggles to assert a unified sense of Hindu or Muslim community identity were complicated and challenged by localised forms of quotidian authority, other ritual or social hierarchies or other contingent associations.

Fourth, this book has been about violence. The very phenomenon of the communal riot itself entailed much more than just apparent violence between two or more communities. Observers, the state and local politicians attached other signifiers to such events, most notably publicising them as examples of how India's violent local populations needed to be controlled, educated or governed. In this sense, this book has supported the notion that, throughout, violence was to some extent 'produced' by powerful political and state agents as a means of furthering other agendas. But bearing in mind this point that the representation is often more politically significant than the event of violence, we are immediately faced with the question of how important violence is, ultimately, for understanding religious community conflict. In any violent event, there was evidently a whole range of detailed, complicated and contingent variables at play. In many cases, the decision of people to act in a violent manner related to individual and psychological motivations. Some people were attracted to ways of life because they enjoyed violence. For others, violence was vicarious or related to localised patterns of revenge. Moreover, the statistics of violence, and the very language surrounding it, has become a system of representation behind which the real experience of those involved in violent events disappears. The longer-term human effects are often written out of history as a result of the focus on the larger picture of destruction. This appears to be the case in some of the early analyses of partition, and only relatively recently have individual testimonies or work on the broader 'refugee' predicament come to the surface.

Finally, we are left with the question of why so many appeared to act in a violent manner at the behest of religious or community leaders. How were people led to acts of violence over our period? This book has argued that in many instances of officially defined 'communal' conflict, communities were rarely 'led', although background political actors may have played a role in provoking conflicts. In many cases, members of religio-political organisations have actively sought out targets to kill during riots and pogroms. And in many, state agents – policemen and other government servants – have been co-opted into the whole complicated drama of conflict, particularly since such events are often as much about the failure to protect the public as they are about active engagement. In other cases, policemen and other state agents were actively involved. But most incidents were much more than that. Just as institutional representations of 'Hindu' or 'Muslim' communities, for example, only very vaguely captured the sentiments of South Asia's populations, so too does the rallying cry of community only inadequately explain ordinary people's involvement in large-scale acts of violence. In the final analysis, no single set of motivations probably ever leads groups of people to act violently. As we saw throughout, most had their own reasons to enter a conflict. But there is no doubt that the effects of violence have been evoked, reproduced and publicised to further the social dominance of those championing organisations of religious community mobilisation.

Bibliography

Manuscript Sources

All Indian Congress Committee Papers, Nehru Memorial Museum and Library, New Delhi.
Papers of Charles Canning, Brotherton Library, Leeds.
Papers of W. A. Chaning Pearce, IPS, UP, 1947. MSS.EUR.F/161/144, Oriental and India Office Records, British Library, London.
Papers of Frampton, Centre of South Asian Studies, Cambridge.
Papers of Malcolm Hailey, MSS.EUR.E220/15A, Oriental and India Office Records, British Library, London.
Papers of Viceroy Hardinge, University Library, Cambridge.
Papers of K. M. Munshi, Nehru Memorial Museum and Library, New Delhi.
Papers of Narendra Dev, Nehru Memorial Museum and Library, New Delhi.
Papers of G. B. Pant, Nehru Memorial Museum and Library, New Delhi.
Papers of Sri Prakash, Nehru Memorial Museum and Library, New Delhi.
Papers of Mridula Sarabhai, Nehru Memorial Museum and Library, New Delhi.
Papers of P. D. Tandon, National Archive of India, New Delhi.
Papers of the United Society for the Propagation of the Gospel, Rhodes House Library, Oxford.

Government Records

Appointments Department Files, Uttar Pradesh State Archives, Lucknow.
Colonial Office Files, Public Record Office, London.
Food and Civil Supplies Department, Uttar Pradesh State Archives, Lucknow.
General Administration Department, Uttar Pradesh State Archives, Lucknow.
Home Department Files, National Archives of India, New Delhi.
Home Political Files, National Archives of India, New Delhi.
Police Abstracts of Intelligence, Central Record Room, CID Headquarters, Lucknow.
Public and Judicial Department (L/PJ), Oriental and India Office Records, British Library, London.
Public Works Department, Uttar Pradesh State Archives, Lucknow.
Revenue Department, Uttar Pradesh State Archives, Lucknow.

Service and General Files (L/SG), Oriental and India Office Records, British Library, London.

Official Publications

The Despatch on 'General Education in India', Bristol Selected Pamphlets, 1880.
General Report on the Administration of the United Provinces, 1939 (Lucknow, 1941).
Report of the Backward Classes Commission, Vol. I (Simla, 1955).
Report of a Commission Appointed by his Excellency the Governor to enquire into and report upon the circumstances connected with the shooting of L. Romanis Perera and nine others (1917).
Report of the Linguistic Provinces Committee, Appointed by the Jaipur Congress, December, 1948 (New Delhi, 1949).
Report on the Newspapers Published in the Bombay Presidency for the week ending 4 January 1919, L/R/5/175, Oriental and India Office Collections, British Library.
Report on the Newspapers Published in the Bombay Presidency for the week ending 11 January 1919, L/R/5/175, Oriental and India Office Collections, British Library.
Report on the Newspapers in the United Provinces for the week ending 14 April 1934, L/R/5/101, Oriental and India Office Collections, British Library.
Report on the Representation of Muslims and other minority communities in the Subordinate Railway Services. Vol. 1 Report (New Delhi, 1932).
Representation of the Muslims of the United Provinces (India) to the Indian Statutory Commission, July 1928 (Allahabad).
'The Vaddukoddai resolution', available at www.satp.org/satporgtp/countries/shrilanka/document/papers/vaddukoddai_resolution.htm, accessed on 15 January 2010.

Newspapers

Chamd
Camd (Allahabad).
Census of India, 1931, The United Provinces, Part I Report (Allahabad, 1932).
Citizen Weekly (Kanpur).
The Hindu (New Delhi).
The Leader (Allahabad).
National Herald (Lucknow).
Organiser (New Delhi).
Sunday Observer (Colombo).

Books, articles and unpublished theses

Aaron, Sushil J., 'Contrarian Lives: Christians and Contemporary Protest in Jharkhand', *Asia Research Centre Working Paper No. 18* (London: London School of Economics, 2007).

Abeysekara, Ananda, 'The Saffron Army, Violence, Terror(ism): Buddhism, Identity and Difference in Sri Lanka', *Numen*, Vol. 48, No. 1 (2001).

Adarkar, Neera, 'In Search of Women in History of Marathi Theatre, 1843–1933', *Economic and Political Weekly*, Vol. 26, No. 43 (1991), pp. WS87–WS90.

Agnes, Flavia, 'Women, Marriage and the Subordination of Rights,' in Partha Chatterjee and Pradeep Jaganathan, eds., *Community Gender and Violence: Subaltern Studies XI* (New Delhi: Permanent Black, 2000), pp. 106–37.

Ahamed, E. and Nazneen, D. R. J. A. 'Islam in Bangladesh: Revivalism or Power Politics?', *Asian Survey*, Vol. 30, No. 8 (1990).

Ahmar, Moonis, 'Ethnicity and State Power in Pakistan: The Karachi Crisis', *Asian Survey*, Vol. 36, No. 10 (1996), pp. 1031–48.

Ahmed, Feroz, 'Pakistan Forum: Partners in Underdevelopment: Pakistan and the U.S.', *Merip Reports*, No. 26 (1974), pp. 23–27.

'Ethnicity, Class and State in Pakistan', *Economic and Political Weekly*, Vol. 31, No. 47 (1996), pp. 3050–3.

Ahmed, Rafiuddin, *The Bengal Muslims, 1871–1906: A Quest for Identity* (Delhi: Oxford University Press, 1981).

Ahmed, Talat, *Literature and Politics in the Age of Nationalism: The Progressive Episode in South Asia, 1932–1956* (London: Routledge, 2008).

Alam, S. M. Shamsul, 'Women in the Era of Modernity and Islamic Fundamentalism: The Case of Taslima Nasrin of Bangladesh', *Signs*, Vol. 23, No. 2 (1998), pp. 429–61.

Alter, Joseph S., *The Wrestler's Body: Identity and Ideology in North India* (Berkeley: University of California Press, 1992).

'Gandhi's Truth: Nonviolence and the Bimoral Imperative of Public Health', *The Journal of Asian Studies*, Vol. 55, No. 2 (1996), pp. 301–22.

'Indian Clubs and Colonialism: Hindu Masculinity and Muscular Christianity', *Comparative Studies in Society and History*, Vol. 46, No. 3 (2004), pp. 497–534.

Ambedkar, B. R., *Annihilation of Caste, and The Untouchables: A Thesis on the Origins of Untouchability* (Jullundur: Bheem Patrika Publications, 1971).

Amin, Shahid, 'Gandhi as Mahatma: Gorakhpur District, Eastern UP, 1921', in Ranajit Guha, ed., *Subaltern Studies III: Writings on South Asian Society and History* (Delhi: Oxford University Press, 1984).

Andersen, Walter K. and Damle, Shridhar D., *The Brotherhood in Saffron: The Rashtriya Swayamsevak Sangh and Hindu Revivalism* (Boulder: Westview Press, 1987).

Ansari, Sarah, *Life After Partition: Migration, Community and Strife in Sindh, 1947–1962* (Oxford: Oxford University Press, 2005).

Anwary, Afroza, 'Acid Violence and Medical Care in Bangladesh: Women's Activism as Careworker', *Gender and Society*, Vol. 17, No. 2 (2003), pp. 305–13.

Arnold, David, *The Congress in Tamilnad: Nationalist Politics in South India, 1919–1937* (London: Curzon Press, 1977).

'Rebellious Hillmen: The Gudem-Rampa Risings 1839–1924', in R. Guha, ed., *Subaltern Studies I: Writings on South Asian Society and History* (Oxford: Oxford University Press, 1982).

'The Congress and the Police', in Mike Shepperdson and Colin Simmons, eds., *The Indian National Congress and the Political Economy of India, 1885–1985* (Aldershot: Avebury, 1998), 208–30.

Arora, Jagnath Prasad, *Beriyom ki Jhankar* (Banaras: Sangrakantra Va Prakashak, 1930), PP.Hin.B.298 OIOC.

Arya, Mahashay Nandlal, *Devotional Songs of a National Complexion, Kranti Bhajnavali* (Ghazipur: Arya Bhajnopadeshak, 1937), PIB 77/2 OIOC.

Aziz, K. K., ed., *Muslims Under Congress Rule, 1937–1939: A Documentary Record* (Islamabad: NIHCR, 1978).

Baker, Christopher John, *The Politics of South India, 1920–1937* (Cambridge: Cambridge University Press, 1976).

Bakhle, Janaki, *Two Men and Music: Nationalism in the Making of an Indian Classical Tradition* (Oxford: Oxford University Press, 2005).

Banerjee, Sumanta, 'Sangh Parivar and Democratic Rights', *Economic and Political Weekly*, Vol. 28, No. 34 (1993), pp. 1715–18.

Baran Ray, Anil, 'Communal Attitudes to British Policy: The Case of the Partition of Bengal 1905', *Social Scientist*, Vol. 6, No. 5 (1977).

Bardhan, Pranab, *The Political Economy of Development in India* (Oxford: Oxford University Press, 1984).

Barrier, N. Gerald, 'The Arya Samaj and Congress Politics in the Punjab, 1894–1908', *The Journal of Asian Studies*, Vol. 26, No. 3 (1967), pp. 363–97.

Banned: Controversial Literature and Political Control in British India, 1907–1947 (Columbia: University of Missouri Press, 1974).

Basra, Amrit Kaur, 'The Punjab Press and the Golden Temple Controversy (1905): An Issue of Sikh Identity', *Social Scientist*, Vol. 24, No. 4/6 (1996), pp. 41–61.

Bass, Daniel, 'Paper Tigers on the Prowl: Rumors, Violence and Agency in the Up-Country of Sri Lanka', *Anthropology Quarterly*, Vol. 81, No. 1 (2008), pp. 269–95.

Basu, Amrita, 'When Local Riots are Not Merely Local: Bringing the State Back In, Bijnor 1988–1992', *Economic and Political Weekly*, Vol. 29, No. 40 (1994), pp. 2605–21.

'The Gendered Imagery and Women's Leadership of Hindu Nationalism', *Reproductive Health Matters*, Vol. 4, No. 8 (1996), pp. 70–6.

Basu, Subho, 'Strikes and 'Communal' Riots in Calcutta in the 1890s: Industrial Workers, Bhadralok Nationalist Leadership and the Colonial State', *Modern Asian Studies*, Vol. 32, No. 4 (1998), pp. 949–83.

Bayly, C. A., 'Patrons and Politics in North India', *Modern Asian Studies*, Vol. 7, No. 3 (1973).

The Local Roots of Indian Politics: Allahabad 1880–1920 (Oxford: Oxford University Press, 1975).

'The Pre-History of "Communalism"? Religious Conflict in India, 1700–1860', *Modern Asian Studies*, Vol. 19, No. 2 (1985).

'The Origins of Swadeshi (Home Industry): Cloth and Indian Society, 1700–1930', in C. A. Bayly, ed., *Origins of Nationality in South Asia: Patriotism and Ethical Community in the Making of Modern India* (Delhi: Oxford University Press, 1998).

Bayly, Susan, 'Caste and Race in the Colonial Ethnography of India', in Peter Robb, ed., *The Concept of Race in South Asia* (Delhi: Oxford University Press, 1997).

Caste, Society and Politics in India from the Eighteenth Century to the Modern Age (Cambridge: Cambridge University Press, 1999).

Saints, Goddesses and Kings: Muslims and Christians in South Indian Society, 1700–1900 (Cambridge: Cambridge University Press, 1989).

Beaglehole, J. H., 'Indian Christians – A Study of a Minority', *Modern Asian Studies*, Vol. 1, No. 1 (1967), pp. 59–80.

Beth, Sarah, 'Taking to the Streets: Dalit *Mela* and the Public Performance of Dalit Cultural Identity', *Contemporary South Asia*, Vol. 14, No. 4 (2005), pp. 397–410.

Bhatt, Chetan, *Liberation and Purity: Race, New Religious Movements and the Ethics of Postmodernity* (London: UCL Press, 1996).

Blackburn, Stuart H., *Singing of Birth and Death: Texts in Performance* (Philadelphia: University of Pennsylvania Press, 1988).

Blom Hansen, Thomas, 'The Ethics of Hindutva and the Spirit of Capitalism', in Thomas Blom Hansen and Christophe Jaffrelot, eds., *The BJP and the Compulsions of Politics in India* (Delhi: Oxford University Press, 1998).

Wages of Violence: Naming and Identity in Postcolonial Bombay (Princeton: Princeton University Press, 2001).

Brass, Paul R., *Factional Politics in an Indian State: The Congress Party in Uttar Pradesh* (Berkeley: University of California Press, 1965).

'Muslim Separatism in United Provinces: Social Context and Political Strategy Before Partition', *Economic and Political Weekly*, Vol. 5, No. 3/5 (1970).

Theft of an Idol: Text and Context in the Representation of Collective Violence (Princeton: Princeton University Press, 1997).

The Production of Hindu–Muslim Violence in Contemporary India (London: University of Washington Press, 2003).

Forms of Collective Violence: Riots, Pogroms and Genocide in Modern India (New Delhi: Three Essays Collective, 2006).

The Politics of Northern India: 1937 to 1987, Volume I: An Indian Political Life: Charan Singh and Congress Politics, 1937 to 1961 (New Delhi: Sage, 2011).

Brown, Judith M., *Gandhi's Rise to Power: Indian Politics 1915–1922* (Cambridge: Cambridge University Press, 1972).

Butalia, Urvashi, *The Other Side of Silence: Voices from the Partition of India* (London: Hurst, 2000).

Callan, Alyson, 'Female Saints and the Practice of Islam in Sylhet, Bangladesh', *American Ethnologist*, Vol. 35, No. 3 (2008), pp. 396–412.

Caplan, Lionel, *Class and Culture in Urban India: Fundamentalism in a Christian Community* (Oxford: Clarendon, 1987).

Carritt, Michael, *A Mole in the Crown* (Hove: Author, 1985).

Chakrabarty, Bidyut, 'The Communal Award of 1932 and Its Implications in Bengal', *Modern Asian Studies*, Vol. 23, No. 3 (1989), pp. 493–523.

'Fluidity or Compartments: Hindus, Muslims and Partition', in Bidyut Chakrabarty, ed., *Communal Identity in India: Its Construction and Articulation in the Twentieth Century* (New Delhi: Oxford University Press, 2003) pp. 78–105.

Chakrabarty, Dipesh, 'Trade Unions in a Hierarchical Culture: The Jute Workers of Calcutta 1920–1950', in Ranajit Guha, ed., *Subaltern Studies III: Writings on South Asian History and Society* (Delhi: Oxford University Press, 1984).

Chandavarkar, Rajnarayan, *The Origins of Industrial Capitalism* (Cambridge: Cambridge University Press, 1994).

'Customs of Governance: Colonialism and Democracy in Twentieth Century India', *Modern Asian Studies*, Vol. 41, No. 3 (2007), pp. 441–70.

Chandidas, R., 'Electoral Adjudication in India', *Economic and Political Weekly*, Vol. 3, No. 24 (1968), pp. 901–11.

Chandra, Kanchan, 'The Transformation of Ethnic Politics in India: The Decline of Congress and the Rise of the Bahujan Samaj Party in Hoshiarpur', *Journal of Asian Studies*, Vol. 59, No. 1 (2000), pp. 26–61.

Chatterjee, Partha, 'Agrarian Relations and Communalism in Bengal', in Ranajit Guha, ed., *Subaltern Studies I* (Delhi: Oxford University Press, 1982).

'The Nationalist Resolution of the Women's Question', in Kumkum Sangari and Sudesh Vaid, eds., *Recasting Women: Essays in Colonial History* (New Brunswick: Rutgers University Press, 1990), pp. 233–53.

Nationalist Thought and the Colonial World: A Derivative Discourse (Minneapolis: University of Minnesota Press, 1993).

The Nation and its Fragments: Colonial and Postcolonial Histories (Princeton: Princeton University Press, 1996).

'Secularism and Tolerance', in Rajeev Bhargava, ed., *Secularism and Its Critics* (Oxford: Oxford University Press, 1998).

The Politics of the Governed: Reflections on Popular Politics in Most of the World (New York: Columbia University Press, 2004).

Chatterji, Joya, *Bengal Divided: Hindu Communalism and Partition, 1932–1947* (Cambridge: Cambridge University Press, 1994).

The Spoils of Partition: Bengal and India 1947–1967 (Cambridge: Cambridge University Press, 2007).

Chaturvedi, Acharya Vithal, *Rajyakranti aur Bharatiy* (Saharanpur, 1932), PIB 27/24 OIOC.

Cohn, Bernard, *Colonialism and Its Forms of Knowledge: The British in India* (Princeton: Princeton University Press, 1996).

'Congress Report on the Punjab Disorders', *Collected Works of Mahatma Gandhi*, 20, 1, 25–38.

Contursi, Janet A., 'Political Theology: Text and Practice in a Dalit Panther Community', *Journal of Asian Studies*, Vol. 52, No. 2 (1993), pp. 320–39.

Corbridge, Stuart and Harriss, John, *Reinventing India: Liberalization, Hindu Nationalism and Popular Democracy* (Malden: Polity, 2000).

Dalmia, Vasudha, *The Nationalisation of Hindu Traditions: Bharatendu Hariscandra and Nineteenth Century Banaras* (Oxford: Oxford University Press, 1997).

Das, Suranjan, *Communal Riots in Bengal, 1905–1947* (Delhi: Oxford University Press, 1991).

Deaton, Angus and Dreze, Jean, 'Poverty and Inequality in India: A Re-examination', *Economic and Political Weekly*, Vol. 37, No. 36 (2002), pp. 3729–48.

Deol, Harnik, *Religion and Nationalism in India: The Case of the Punjab* (London: Routledge, 2000).

Deshpande, Vamanrao H., *Indian Musical Traditions: An Aesthetic Study of the Gharanas in Hindustani Music* (Mumbai: Popular Prakashan, 2001).

Dewey, Clive, 'The End of the Imperialism of Free Trade', in Clive Dewey and A. G. Hopkins, eds., *The Imperial Impact: Studies in the Imperial History of India and Africa* (London: Athlone Press, 1978).

Anglo-Indian Attitudes: The Mind of the Indian Civil Service (London: Hambledon Press, 1993).

Dirks, Nicholas B., *Castes of Mind: Colonialism and the Making of Modern India* (Princeton: Princeton University Press, 2001).

Downs, Frederick S., *History of Christianity in India Volume V*, Part 5: *North East India in the Nineteenth and Twentieth Centuries* (Bangalore: Church History Association of India, 1992).

Dubashi, Jay, 'Hindu Rate of Growth', *Organiser*, New Delhi, 9 June 1985.

Dumont, Louis, *Homo Hierarchicus: An Essay on the Caste System* (London: Weidenfeld and Nicolson, 1970).

Dutt, Romesh Chander, *The Economic History of India in the Victorian Age: From the Accession of Queen Victoria in 1837 to the Commencement of the Twentieth Century* (London: Kegan Paul, 1904).

Engineer, Asghar Ali, 'Communal Riots in Godhra: A Report', *Economic and Political Weekly*, Vol. 16, No. 41 (1981), pp. 1638–40.

'Behind the Communal Fury', *Economic and Political Weekly*, Vol. 17, No. 10 (1982), pp. 356–7.

'The Guilty Men of Meerut', *Economic and Political Weekly*, Vol. 17, No. 45 (1982).

'Communal Violence in Gujarat', *Economic, and Political Weekly*, Vol. 17, No. 4 (1983).

'Sectarian Clashes in Bombay', *Economic and Political Weekly*, Vol. 23, No. 39 (1988), pp. 1993–4.

'Gian Prakash Committee Report on Meerut Riots', *Economic and Political Weekly*, Vol. 23, No. 1/2 (1988), pp. 30–1, 33.

Farquhar, J. N., *Modern Religious Movements in India* (London: Macmillan, 1915).

Fearon, James D. and Laitin, David D., 'Violence and the Social Construction of Ethnic Identity', *International Organization*, Vol. 54, No. 4 (2000), pp. 845–77.

Feldman, Shelley, 'Exploring Theories of Patriarchy: A Perspective from Contemporary Bangladesh', *Signs*, Vol. 26, No. 4 (2001), pp. 1097–127.

Fernando, P. T. M., 'The British Raj and the 1915 Communal Riots in Ceylon', *Modern Asian Studies*, Vol. 3, No. 3 (1969), pp. 245–55.

Fox, Richard, 'Urban Class and Communal Consciousness in Punjab: The Genesis of India's Intermediate Regime', *Modern Asian Studies*, Vol. 18, No. 3 (1984), pp. 459–89.

Franda, Marcus, *Bangladesh: The First Decade* (New Delhi: South Asian Publishers, 1982).

Frankel, Francine, *India's Political Economy, 1947–1977: The Gradual Revolution* (Princeton: Princeton University Press, 1978).

Frankel, Francine R. and Rao, M. S. A., eds., *Dominance and State Power in Modern India: Decline of a Social Order* (Delhi: Oxford University Press, 1989).

Freitag, Sandria, 'Sacred Symbol as Mobilizing Ideology: The North Indian Search for a "Hindu" community', *Comparative Studies in Society and History*, Vol. 24, No. 4 (1980), pp. 597–625.

'Ambiguous Public Arenas and Coherent Personal Practice: Kanpur Muslims 1913–1931', in Katherine P. Ewing, ed., *Shari'at and Ambiguity in South Asian Islam* (Berkeley: University of California Press, 1988), pp. 147–53.

Collective Action and Community: Public Action and the Emergence of Communalism in North India (Berkeley: University of California Press, 1989).

Frykenburg, Robert, *Christianity in India: From Beginnings to the Present* (Oxford: Oxford University Press, 2008).

Fuller, C. J., *The Camphor Flame: Popular Hinduism and Society in India* (Princeton: Princeton University Press, 1992).

and Harriss, John, 'For an Anthropology of the Modern Indian State', in C. J. Fuller and Veronique Benei, eds., *The Everyday State and Society in Modern India* (London: Hurst, 2001), pp. 1–30.

and Spencer, John, 'South Asian Anthropology in the 1980s', *South Asia Research*, Vol. 10 (1990), pp. 85–105.

Gallagher, John and Seal, Anil, 'India Between the Wars', *Modern Asian Studies*, Vol. 15, No. 3 (1981), pp. 387–414.

Gandhi, M. K., 'Hindu–Muslim Conflict, Its Causes and Cure', *Young India*, 29 May 1924.

An Autobiography or The Story of My Experiments with Truth (London: Penguin, 1982).

Gayer, Laurent, 'Guns, Slums and "Yellow Devils": A Genealogy of Urban Conflicts in Karachi, Pakistan', *Modern Asian Studies*, Vol. 41, No. 3 (2007), pp. 514–44.

Ghosh, Partha S., 'Bangladesh at the Crossroads: Religion and Politics', *Asian Survey*, Vol. 33, No. 7 (1993), pp. 697–710.

'Sinhala–Tamil Ethnic Conflict in India', *Economic and Political Weekly*, Vol. 30, No. 25 (1995), pp. 1486–8.

Gillion, K. L., *Ahmedabad: A Study in Indian Urban History* (Berkeley: University of California Press, 1968).

Godsmark, Oliver, 'The Mobilisation of Regional Identities in Post-Colonial Maharashtra: Responses to the Centre's Construction of a Nationalist Hegemony', Unpublished MA dissertation, University of Leeds, 2008.

Gomez, Mario, 'National Human Rights Commissions and Internally Displaced Persons: The Sri Lankan Experience', in Ujjwal Kumar Singh, ed., *Human Rights and Peace: Ideas, Laws, Institutions and Movements* (New Delhi: Sage, 2009).

Gooptu, Nandini, 'The "Problem" of the Urban Poor Policy and Discourse of Local Administration: A Study in Uttar Pradesh in the Interwar Period', *Economic and Political Weekly*, Vol. 31, No. 50 (1996), pp. 3245–54.

'The Urban Poor and Militant Hinduism in Early Twentieth-Century Uttar Pradesh', *Modern Asian Studies*, Vol. 31, No. 4 (1997), pp. 879–918.

The Politics of the Urban Poor in Early Twentieth Century India (Cambridge: Cambridge University Press, 2001).

Gordon, Richard, 'Non-Cooperation and Council Entry, 1919–1920', *Modern Asian Studies*, Vol. 7, No. 3 (1973).

'The Hindu Mahasabha and the Indian National Congress, 1915–1926', *Modern Asian Studies*, Vol. 9, No. 2 (1975), pp. 145–203.

Goswami, Manu, 'From Swadeshi to Swaraj: Nation, Economy, Territory in Colonial South Asia, 1870–1907', *Comparative Studies in Society and History*, Vol. 40, No. 4 (1998), pp. 609–36.

Gould, Harold, *Grassroots Politics: A Century of Political Evolution in Faizabad District* (New Delhi: South Asia Books, 1994).

Gould, William, 'Congress Radicals and Hindu Militancy: Sampurnanand and Purushottam Das Tandon in the Politics of the United Provinces', *Modern Asian Studies*, Vol. 36, No. 3 (2002), pp. 619–56.

Hindu Nationalism and the Language of Politics in Late Colonial India (Cambridge: Cambridge University Press, 2004).

'The U.P. Congress and "Hindu Unity": Untouchables and the Minority Question in the 1930s', *Modern Asian Studies*, Vol. 39, No. 4 (2005), pp. 845–60.

'Contesting "Secularism" in Colonial and Postcolonial North India between 1930 and 1950s', *Contemporary South Asia*, Vol.14, No. 4 (2005), pp. 481–94.

'"The Dual State: The Unruly Subordinate", Caste, Community and Civil Service Recruitment in North India, 1930–1955', *Journal of Historical Sociology*, Vol. 20, No. 1–2 (2007), pp. 13–43.

Bureaucracy, Community and Influence: Society and the State in India, 1930–1960s (London: Routledge, 2011).

'From Subjects to Citizens? Rationing, Refugees and the Publicity of Corruption over Independence in UP', *Modern Asian Studies*, 42, 6 (2011).

Graham, Bruce, *Hindu Nationalism and Indian Politics: The Origins and Development of the Bharatiya Jana Sangh* (Cambridge: Cambridge University Press, 1990).

Gunasinghe, Newton, 'The Open Economy and Its Impact on Ethnic Relations in Sri Lanka',*The Ethnic Conflict*.

Gupta, Charu, 'Articulating Hindu Masculinity and Femininity. Shuddhi and Sangathan Movements in United Provinces in the 1920s', *Economic and Political Weekly*, Vol. 33, No. 13 (1998), pp. 727–35.

Sexuality, Obscenity, Community: Women, Muslims, and the Hindu Public in Colonial India (Delhi: Permanent Black, 2001).

Gupte, Pranay, *India: The Challenge of Change* (London: Methuen, 1989).

Haleem, Irm, 'Ethnic and Sectarian Violence and the Propensity towards Praetorianism in Pakistan', *Third World Quarterly*, 24, 3 (2003), pp. 463–77.

Haq, Farhat, 'Rise of the MQM in Pakistan: Politics of Ethnic Mobilization', *Asian Survey*, Vol. 35, No. 11 (1995), pp. 990–1004.

'Militarism and Motherhood: The Women of the Lashkar-i-Tayyabia in Pakistan', *Signs*, Vol. 32, No. 4 (2007), pp. 1023–46.

Hardiman, David, 'Adivasi Assertion in South Gujarat: The Devi Movement of 1922–3', in Ranajit Guha, ed., *Subaltern Studies III: Writings on South Asian History and Society* (New Delhi: Oxford University Press, 1984), pp. 196–230.
Peasant Nationalists of Gujarat: Kheda District 1917–1934 (Delhi: Oxford University Press, 1984).
Hardy, Peter, *The Muslims of British India* (Cambridge: Cambridge University Press, 1972).
Hasan, Mushirul, *Nationalism and Communal Politics, 1885–1930* (New Delhi: Manohar Publications, 1991).
Legacy of a Divided Nation: India's Muslims since Independence (Delhi: Oxford University Press, 1997).
Hasan, Zoya, 'Communalism and Communal Violence in India', *Social Scientist*, Vol. 10, No. 2 (1982).
Dominance and Mobilisation: Rural Politics in Western Uttar Pradesh 1930–1980 (New Delhi: Sage, 1989).
'Changing Orientation of the State and the Emergence of Majoritarianism in the 1980s', *Social Scientist*, Vol. 18, No. 8/9 (1990), pp. 27–37.
Hawley, John Stratton, 'Modern India and the Question of Middle-Class Religion', *International Journal of Hindu Studies*, Vol. 5, No. 3 (2001), pp. 217–25.
Haynes, Douglas, *Rhetoric and Ritual in Colonial India: The Shaping of a Public Culture in Surat City 1852–1928* (Berkeley: University of California Press, 1991).
Heimsath, Charles H., *Indian Nationalism and Hindu Social Reform* (Princeton: Princeton University Press, 1964).
Hossain, Akhtar, 'Anatomy of Hartal Politics in Bangladesh', *Asian Survey*, Vol. 40, No. 3 (2000), pp. 508–29.
Hossain, Golam, 'Bangladesh in 1995: Politics of Intransigence', *Asian Survey*, Vol. 36, No. 2 (1996), pp. 196–203.
Huq, Maimuna, 'Reading the Qur'an in Bangladesh: The Politics of "Belief" Among Islamist Women', *Modern Asian Studies*, Vol. 42, No. 2/3 (2008), pp. 457–88.
Huque, Ahmed Shafiqul and Akhter, Muhammad Yeahia, 'The Ubiquity of Islam: Religion and Society in Bangladesh', *Pacific Affairs*, Vol. 60, No. 2 (1987), pp. 200–25.
Ilaih, Kancha, 'Productive Labour, Consciousness and History: The Dalitbahujan Alternative', in Shahid Amin and Dipesh Chakrabarty, eds., *Subaltern Studies IX: Writings on South Asian History and Society* (Delhi: Oxford University Press, 1996).
Inden, Ronald, *Imagining India* (London: Hurst, 2000).
Jaffrelot, Christophe, *The Hindu Nationalist Movement and Indian Politics: 1925 to the 1990s* (London: Hurst, 1996).
'The Rise of the Other Backward Classes in the Hindi Belt', *The Journal of Asian Studies*, Vol. 59, No. 1 (2000), pp. 86–108.
India's Silent Revolution: The Rise of the Lower Castes in North India (London: Hurst and Co., 2003).

Dr. Ambedkar and Untouchability: Analyzing and Fighting Caste (New York: Columbia University Press, 2005).

Jahan, Rounaq, 'Bangladesh in 2003: Vibrant Democracy or Destructive Politics?', *Asian Survey*, Vol. 44, No. 1 (2003), 58.

Jalal, Ayesha, *The Sole Spokesman: Jinnah, The Muslim League and The Demand for Pakistan* (Cambridge: Cambridge University Press, 1985).

Democracy and Authoritarianism in South Asia: A Comparative and Historical Perspective (Cambridge: Cambridge University Press, 1995).

Self and Sovereignty: Individual and Community in South Asian Islam Since 1850 (London: Routledge, 2000).

Jamal, Amina, 'Feminist "Selves" and Feminism's "Others": Feminist Representations of Jamaat-e-Islami Women in Pakistan', *Feminist Review*, Vol. 81, Bodily Interventions (2005), pp. 52–73.

Jan, Ameen, 'Pakistan on a Precipice', *Asian Survey*, Vol. 39, No. 5 (1999), pp. 699–719.

Jayawardena, Kumari, 'Ethnic Consciousness in Sri Lanka: Continuity and Change' in *Sri Lanka The Ethnic Conflict: Myths, Realities and Perspectives* (New Delhi: Navrang, 1984).

Jefferey, Keith, '"An English Barrack in the Oriental Seas"? – India in the Aftermath of the First World War', *Indian Economic and Social History Review*, Vol. XII, No. 4, pp. 367–84.

Jeffrey, Robin, 'The Punjab Boundary Force and the Problem of Order, August 1947', *Modern Asian Studies*, Vol. 8, No. 4 (1974).

What's Happening to India? (New York: Holmes and Meier, 1994).

Jenkins, R., *Democratic Politics and Economic Reform in India* (Cambridge: Cambridge University Press, 1999).

Johnson, Gordon, 'Partition, Agitation and Congress: Bengal 1904–1908', *Modern Asian Studies*, Vol. 7, No. 3 (1973), pp. 533–88.

Jones, Justin, 'The Shi'a Muslims of the United Provinces of India, c. 1890–1940', PhD Dissertation, University of Cambridge, 2007.

Jones, Kenneth W., 'Communalism in the Punjab: The Arya Samaj Contribution', *Journal of Asian Studies*, Vol. 28, No. 1 (1968), pp. 39–54.

'Ham Hindu Nahin: Arya-Sikh Relations, 1877–1905', *The Journal of Asian Studies*, Vol. 32, No. 3 (1973), pp. 457–75.

'Religious Identity and Indian Census', in N. G. Barrier, ed., *The Census of British India: New Perspectives* (Delhi: Manohar, 1980).

Joshi, Chitra, 'Kanpur Textile Labour: Some Structural Features of Formative Years', *Economic and Political Weekly*, Vol. 16, No. 44/46 (1981), pp. 1821–9, 1831–6.

'Bonds of Community, Ties of Religion: Kanpur Textile Workers in the Early Twentieth Century', *The Indian Economic and Social History Review*, Vol. 22, No. 3 (1985), pp. 251–80.

Joshi, Ram, 'Politics in Maharashtra – An Overview', in Usha Thakkar and Mangesh Kulkarni, eds., *Politics in Mahashtra* (Delhi: Himalaya, 1995).

Joshi, Vijaya Chandra, *Lala Lajpat Rai: Writings and Speeches, Volume 1, 1888–1919* (Delhi: University Publishers, 1966).

Juergensmeyer, Mark, *The New Cold War? Religious Nationalism Confronts the State* (Berkeley: University of California Press, 1994).

Kabeer, Naila, 'The Quest for National Identity: Women, Islam and the State in Bangladesh', *Feminist Review*, Vol. 37 (1991), pp. 38–58.

Kabir, Sandra M., 'An Experience of Religious Extremism in Bangladesh', *Reproductive Matters*, Vol. 4, No. 8 (1996), pp. 104–9.

Kannangara, A. P., 'The Riots of 1915 in Sri Lanka: A Study in the Roots of the Communal Violence', *Past and Present*, Vol. 102 (1984), pp. 130–65.

Kapferer, Bruce, *Legends of People, Myths of State: Violence, Intolerance and Political Culture in Sri Lanka and Australia* (Washington DC: Smithsonian Institution Press, 1986).

Katzenstein, Mary Fainsod, Mehta, Uday Singh and Thakkar, Usha, 'The Rebirth of Shiv Sena in Maharashtra: The Symbiosis of Discursive and Institutional Power', in Amrita Basu and Atul Kohli, eds., *Community Conflicts and the State* (New Delhi: Oxford University Press, 1998), pp. 215–38.

Kaviraj, Sudipta, 'On State, Society and Discourse in India', in James Manor, ed., *Rethinking Third World Politics* (London: Longman, 1991), pp. 225–50.

Kearney, Robert N., *Communalism and Language in the Politics of Ceylon* (Durham: Duke University Press, 1967).

Kearney, Jayawardene and Blackton, Fernando, 'The 1915 Riots in Ceylon: A Symposium', *Journal of Asian Studies*, Vol. xxix (1969–70), pp. 219–66.

Keddie, Nikki, 'Pakistan's Movement Against Islamization', MERIP Middle East Report, 148, 'Re-Flagging the Gulf', Sept.–Oct. 1987.

Kennedy, Charles H., 'Islamization and Legal Reform in Pakistan, 1979–1989', *Pacific Affairs*, Vol. 63, No. 1 (1990), pp. 62–77.

Khaliquzzaman, Chaudhuri, *Pathway to Pakistan* (Lahore: Longmans, 1961).

Khan, Yasmin, *The Great Partition: The Making of India and Pakistan* (London: Yale University Press, 2007).

King, Christopher R., *One Language, Two Scripts: The Hindi Movement in Nineteenth Century North India* (Bombay: Oxford University Press, 1994).

Kochanek, Stanley, *The Congress Party of India: The Dynamics of One-Party Democracy* (Princeton: Princeton University Press, 1968).

Business and Politics in India (Princeton: Princeton University Press, 1974).

'The Rise of Interest Politics in Bangladesh', *Asian Survey*, Vol. 36, No. 7 (1996), pp. 704–22.

'Governance, Patronage Politics and Democratic Transition in Bangladesh', *Asian Survey*, Vol. 40, No. 3 (2000), pp. 530–50.

Kohli, Atul, 'Can Democracies Accommodate Ethnic Nationalism?', in Amrita Basu and Atul Kohli, eds., *Community Conflicts and the State in India* (New Delhi: Oxford University Press, 1998).

Kothari, Rajni, 'The Congress System', in Zoya Hasan, ed., *Parties and Party Politics in India* (New Delhi: Oxford University Press, 2004), pp. 39–55.

Kumar, B. Venkatesh, 'Criminalisation of Politics and Election Commission', *Economic and Political Weekly*, Vol. 36, No. 24 (2001), pp. 2119–21.

Kumar, Krishna, 'Hindu Revivalism and Education in North-Central India', *Social Scientist*, Vol. 18, No. 10 (1990), pp. 4–26.

Kumar, Nita, *The Artisans of Banaras: Popular Culture and Identity, 1880–1986* (Princeton: Princeton University Press, 1988).

Lelyveld, David, 'Three Aligarh Students: Aftab Ahmad Khan, Ziauddin Ahmad and Muhammad Ali', *Modern Asian Studies*, Vol. 9, No. 2 (1975), pp. 227–40.

Aligarh's First Generation: Muslim Solidarity in British India (Princeton: Princeton University Press, 1978).

'Disenchantment at Aligarh: Islam and the Realm of the Secular in Late Nineteenth Century India', *Die Welt des Islams*, New Series, Bd. 22, Nr. 1/4 (1982), pp. 85–102.

Ludden, David, ed., *Contesting the Nation: Religion, Community and the Politics of Democracy in India* (Philadelphia: University of Pennsylvania Press, 1996).

McGuire, John, 'The World Economy, the Colonial State, and the Establishment of the Indian National Congress', in Mike Shepperdson and Colin Simmons, eds., *The Indian National Congress and the Political Economy of India 1885–1985* (Aldershot: Avebury, 1988), pp. 40–60.

McLane, John R., *Indian Nationalism and the Early Congress* (Princeton: Princeton University Press, 1977).

Malik, Kenan, *The Meaning of Race: Race, History and Culture in Western Society* (Basingstoke: Macmillan, 1996).

Mallampalli, Chandra, *Christians and Public Life in Colonial South India, 1863–1937: Contending with marginality* (London: Routledge, 2004).

Manor, James, ed., *Sri Lanka in Change and Crisis* (London: Croom Helm, 1984).

The Expedient Utopian: Bandaranaike and Ceylon (Princeton: Princeton University Press, 1988).

'Southern Discomfort: The BJP in Karnataka', in Thomas Blom Hansen and Christophe Jaffrelot, eds., *The BJP and the Compulsions of Politics in India* (Delhi: Oxford University Press, 1998), pp. 163–201.

Markovits, Claude, ed., *A History of Modern India, 1480–1950* (London: Anthem, 2002).

Marsden, Magnus, *Living Islam: Muslim Religious Experience in Pakistan's North West Frontier* (Cambridge: Cambridge University Press, 2005).

'All Male Sonic Gatherings, Islamic Reform and Masculinity in northern Pakistan', *American Ethnologist*, Vol. 34, No. 3 (2007), pp. 473–90.

'Women, Politics and Islamism in northern Pakistan', *Modern Asian Studies*, Vol. 42, No. 2–3 (2008), pp. 405–29.

Matthews, Bruce, 'Radical Conflict and the Rationalization of Violence in Sri Lanka', *Pacific Affairs*, Vol. 59, No. 1 (1986).

Meillassoux, C., 'Are There Castes in India?', *Economy and Society*, 2, 1, 85–211.

Mendelsohn, Oliver and Vicziany, Marika, *The Untouchables: Subordination, Poverty and the State in Modern India* (Cambridge: Cambridge University Press, 1998).

Menon, Dilip, *Caste, Nationalism and Communism in South India: Malabar 1900–1948* (Cambridge: Cambridge University Press, 1994).

Menon, Rita and Kamla, Bhasin, 'Recovery, Rupture, Resistance: Indian State and Abduction of Women during Partition', *Economic and Political Weekly*, Vol. 28, No. 17 (1993), pp. WS2–WS11.

Borders and Boundaries: Women in India's Partition (New Brunswick: Rutgers University Press, 1998).

Metcalf, Thomas, *Ideologies of the Raj* (Cambridge: Cambridge University Press, 1994).

Meyer, Eric, 'Seeking the Roots of the Tragedy', in James Manor, ed., *Sri Lanka in Change and Crisis* (London: Croom Helm, 1984) pp. 137–52.

Minault, Gail, *The Khilafat Movement: Religious Symbolism and Political Mobilization in India* (New York: Columbia University Press, 1982).

'Sayyid Mumtaz Ali and 'Huqquq un-Niswan': An Advocate of Women's Rights in Islam in the Late Nineteenth Century', *Modern Asian Studies*, Vol. 24, No. 1 (1990), pp. 147–72.

Secluded Scholars: Women's Education and Muslim Social Reform in Colonial India (Oxford: Oxford University Press, 1999).

Minault, Gail and Lelyveld, David, 'The Campaign for an Indian Muslim University, 1898–1920', *Modern Asian Studies*, Vol. 8, No. 2 (1974), pp. 145–89.

Misra, B. B., *The Indian Middle Classes. Their Growth in Modern Times* (Oxford: Oxford University Press, 1961).

Mody, Nawaz B., 'The Press in India: The Shah Bano Judgement and its Aftermath', *Asian Survey*, 27, 8 (1987), pp. 935–53.

Monshipouri, Mahmoud, 'Backlash to the Destruction at Ayodhya: A View from Pakistan', *Asian Survey*, Vol. 33, No. 7, South Asia: Responses to the Ayodhya Crisis (Jul. 1993), pp. 711–21.

Moore, M. P., 'The 1982 Elections and the New Gaullist-Bonapartist State in Sri Lanka', in James Manor, ed., *Sri Lanka in Change and Crisis* (London: Croom Helm, 1984), pp. 51–76.

Moore, R. J., 'Jinnah and Pakistan Demand', *Modern Asian Studies*, 17, 4 (1983), pp. 529–61.

Morris, Morris David, 'Labor Discipline, Trade Unions and the State in India', *The Journal of Political Economy*, Vol. 63, No. 4 (1955).

'The Effects of Industrialisation on "Race Relations" in India', in G. Hunter, ed., *Industrialization and Race Relations: A Symposium* (London: Oxford University Press, 1965).

Mufti, Aamir R., 'A Greater Story-Writer than God: Genre, Gender and Minority in Late Colonial India', in Partha Chatterjee and Pradeep Jeganathan, eds., *Subaltern Studies XI: Community, Gender and Violence* (Delhi: Permanent Black, 2000), pp. 13–36.

Myrdal, Gunnar, *Asian Drama: An Enquiry into the Poverty of Nations* (Harmondsworth: Penguin, 1968).

Nadesan, S., *A History of the Up Country Tamil People* (Colombo: Nandalla Publishers, 1993).

Naregal, Veena, *Language Politics, Elites and the Public Sphere: Western India Under Colonialism* (London: Anthem Press, 2001).

Nasr, S. V. R., 'The Rise of Sunni Militancy in Pakistan: The Changing Role of Islamism and the Ulama in Society and Politics', *Modern Asian Studies*, Vol. 34, No. 1 (2000), pp. 139–80.

Natrajan, Balmurli, 'Caste, Class, and Community in India: An Ethnographic Approach', *Ethnology*, Vol. 44, No. 3 (2005), pp. 227–41.

Newbigin, Eleanor, 'The Hindu Code Bill and the Making of the Modern Indian State', PhD dissertation, University of Cambridge, 2008.

Nissan, Elizabeth 'Some Thoughts on Sinhalese Justifications for the Violence', in James Manor, ed., *Sri Lanka in Change and Crisis* (London: Croom Helm, 1984).

Noman, Omar, *Pakistan: A Political and Economic History since 1947* (London: Kegan Paul International, 1990).

Obeyesekere, Gananath, 'Personal Identity and Cultural Crisis: The Case of Anagarika Dharmapala of Sri Lanka', in Frank E Reynolds and Donald Capps, eds., *The Biographical Process: Studies in the History and Psychology of Religion* (The Hague: Mouton and Co., 1976).

'The Origins and Institutionalisation of Political Violence', in James Manor, ed., *Sri Lanka in Change and Crisis* (London: Croom Helm, 1984), pp. 152–66.

O'Hanlon, Polly, 'Acts of Appropriation: Non-Brahman Radicals and the Congress in Early Twentieth Century Maharashtra', in Mike Shepperdson and Colins Simmons, eds., *The Indian National Congress and the Political Economy of India 1885–1985* (Aldershot: Avebury, 1988), pp. 102–46.

Omissi, David, *Indian Voices of the Great War: Soldiers' Letters, 1914–1918* (London: Palgrave Macmillan, 1999).

Omvedt, Gail, *Cultural Revolt in Colonial Society: The Non-Brahman Movement in Western India 1873–1930* (Bombay: Scientific Socialist Education Trust, 1976).

Openshaw, Jeanne, *Seeking Bauls of Bengal* (Cambridge: Cambridge University Press, 2004).

Orsini, Francesca, *The Hindi Public Sphere 1920–1940: Language and Literature in the Age of Nationalism* (Oxford: Oxford University Press, 2002).

Page, David, *Prelude to Partition: The Indian Muslims and the Imperial System of Control 1920–1932* (Delhi: Oxford University Press, 1982).

Pai, Sudha, *Dalit Assertion and the Unfinished Democratic Revolution: The Bahujan Samaj Party in Uttar Pradesh* (Delhi: Sage, 2002).

Pandey, Gyanendra, *The Ascendancy of the Congress in Uttar Pradesh: A Study in Imperfect Mobilisation* (Oxford: Oxford University Press, 1978).

'Peasant Revolt and Indian Nationalism: The Peasant Movement in Awadh, 1919–1922', in Ranajit Guha, ed., *Subaltern Studies I: Writings on South Asian History and Society* (New Delhi: Oxford University Press, 1982), pp. 143–97.

'Liberalism and the Study of Indian History: A Review of Writings on Communalism', *Economic and Political Weekly*, Vol. 18, No. 42 (1983), pp. 1789–1791, 1794.

'Rallying Round the Cow: Sectarian Strife in the Bhojpuri Region, c. 1888–1917', in Ranajit Guha, ed., *Subaltern Studies II: Writings on South Asian History and Society* (Delhi: Oxford University Press, 1983).

The Construction of Communalism in Colonial North India (Delhi: Oxford University Press, 1990).

'In Defence of the Fragment: Writing about Hindu–Muslim Riots in India Today', *Economic and Political Weekly*, Vol. 26, No. 11/12 (1991), pp. 559–61.

'India and Pakistan, 1947–2002', *Economic and Political Weekly*, Vol. 37, No. 11 (2002), pp. 1027–33.

Routine Violence: Nations, Fragments, Histories (Palo Alto: Stanford, 2005).

Pandian, M. S. S., 'Crisis in DMK', *Economic and Political Weekly*, Vol. 29, No. 5 (1994), pp. 221–3.

Parel, Anthony, *Gandhi: Hind Swaraj and Other Writings* (Cambridge: Cambridge University Press, 1997).

Peabody, Norbert, 'Tod's Rajast'han and the Boundaries of Imperial Rule in Nineteenth Century India', *Modern Asian Studies*, Vol. 30, No. 1 (1996).

Phadke, Y. D., *Politics and Language* (Bombay: Himalaya Publishing House, 1979).

Pinney, Christopher, 'Colonial Anthropology in the "Laboratory of Mankind"', in C. A. Bayly, ed., *The Raj: India and the British, 1600–1947* (London: National Portrait Gallery, 1990), pp. 278–304.

Ponnambalam, Satchi, *Sri Lanka: The National Question and the Tamil Liberation Struggle* (London: Zed Books, 1983).

Qureshi, Regula Burckhardt, *Sufi Music of India and Pakistan: Sound, Context and Meaning in Qawwali* (Cambridge: Cambridge University Press, 1986).

Rajagopal, Arvind, 'Ram Janmabhoomi, Consumer Identity and Image-Based Politics', *Economic and Political Weekly*, Vol. 29, No. 27 (1994), pp. 1659–68.

Politics After Television: Hindu Nationalism and the Reshaping of the Public in India (Cambridge: Cambridge University Press, 2001).

'Sangh's Role in the Emergency', *Economic and Political Weekly*, Vol. 38, No. 27 (2003), pp. 2797–8.

Ramanathan, P., *Riots and Martial Law in Ceylon, 1915* (London: St. Martin's Press, 1915).

Ramaswamy, Sumathi, 'En/Gendering Language: The Poetics of Tamil Identity', *Comparative Studies in Society and History*, Vol. 35, No. 4 (1993), pp. 683–725.

Passions of the Tongue: Language Devotion in Tamil India, 1891–1970 (Berkeley: University of California Press, 1997).

Rashiduzzaman, M., 'The Liberals and the Religious Right in Bangladesh', *Asian Survey*, Vol. 34, No. 11 (1994), pp. 974–90.

'Islam, Muslim Identity and Nationalism in Bangladesh', *Journal of South Asian and Middle Eastern Studies*, Vol. 18 (1994), pp. 36–60.

Riaz, Ali, 'Bangladesh in 2004: The Politics of Vengeance', *Asian Survey*, Vol. 45, No. 1 (2005), pp. 112–18.

Robb, P. G., *The Government of India and Reform: Policies Towards Politics and the Constitution 1916–1921* (Oxford: Oxford University Press, 1976).

Roberts, Michael, 'Tamil Tigers: Sacrificial Symbolism and "Dead Body Politics"', *Anthropology Today*, Vol. 24, No. 3 (2008).

Robinson, Francis, *Separatism Among Indian Muslims: The Politics of the United Provinces Muslims 1860–1923* (Cambridge: Cambridge University Press, 1973).

'Municipal Government and Muslim Separatism in the United Provinces, 1883–1916', *Modern Asian Studies*, Vol. 7, No. 3 (1973), pp. 389–441.

Rogers, John D., 'Social Mobility, Popular Ideology and Collective Violence in Modern Sri Lanka', *The Journal of Asian Studies*, Vol. 46, No. 3 (1987), pp. 583–602.

Roy, Modhumita, '"Englishing" India: Reinstituting Class and Social Privilege', *Social Text*, Vol. 39 (1994), pp. 83–109.

Russell, Ralph, 'Urdu in India Since Independence', *Economic and Political Weekly*, Vol. 34, No. 1/2 (1999), pp. 44–8.

Saiyid, M. H., *Mohammad Ali Jinnah* (Lahore: Elite Publishers, 1945).

Sampurnanand, *Evolution of the Hindu Pantheon* (Bombay: 1963).

Samuel, John, 'Language and Nationality in North-East India', *Economic and Political Weekly* Vol. 28, No. 3/4 (1993), pp. 91–2.

Sarkar, Sumit, *The Swadeshi Movement in Bengal, 1903–1908* (New Delhi: People's Publishing House, 1973).

Modern India 1885–1947 (London: Macmillan Press, 1983).

'The Conditions and Nature of Subaltern Militancy: Bengal from Swadeshi to Non-Cooperation, c. 1905–1922', in Ranajit Guha, ed., *Subaltern Studies III: Writings on South Asian History and Society* (New Delhi: Oxford University Press, 1984), pp. 271–320.

'The Fascism of the Sangh Parivar', *Economic and Political Weekly*, Vol. 28, No. 5 (1993), pp. 163–7.

Sarkar, Tanika, 'A Pre-History of Rights: The Age of Consent Debate in Colonial Bengal', *Feminist Studies*, Vol. 26, No. 3 (2000), pp. 601–22.

Hindu Wife, Hindu Nation: Community, Religion and Cultural Nationalism (Delhi: Permanent Black, 2001).

Schalk, Peter, 'Women Fighters of the Liberation Tigers in Tamil Ilam. The Martial Feminism of Atel Palacinkam', *South Asia Research*, Vol. 14, No. 2 (1994).

Schultz, Anna, 'Hindu Nationalism, Music and Embodiment in Marathi Rashtriya Kirtan', *Ethnomusicology*, Vol. 46, No. 2 (2002), pp. 307–22.

Seal, Anil, *The Emergence of Indian Nationalism: Competition and Collaboration in the Late Nineteenth Century* (Cambridge: Cambridge University Press, 1968).

Sen, Amartya, 'Indian Development: Lessons and Non-Lessons', *Daedalus*, Vol. 118, No. 4 (1989), pp. 369–92.

Development as Freedom (Oxford: Oxford Paperbacks, 2001).

Sen, Amiya P., *Hindu revivalism in Bengal, 1872–1905: Some Essays in Interpretation* (Delhi: Oxford University Press, 1993).

Sen, Uditi, 'Refugees and the Politics of Nation Building in India', PhD Dissertation, University of Cambridge, 2009.

Shaikh, Farzana, *Community and Consensus in Islam: Muslim Representation in Colonial India, 1860–1947* (Cambridge: Cambridge University Press, 1989).

Shani, Ornit, 'The Rise of Hindu Nationalism in India: The Case Study of Ahmedabad in the 1980s', *Modern Asian Studies*, Vol. 39, No. 4 (2005), pp. 861–96.

Communalism, Caste and Hindu Nationalism: The Violence in Gujarat (Cambridge: Cambridge University Press, 2007).

Shastri, Amita, 'The Material Basis for Separatism', *Journal of Asian Studies*, Vol. 49, No. 1 (1990), 56–77.

Shehabuddin, Elora, 'Contesting the Illicit: Gender and the Politics of Fatwas in Bangladesh', *Signs*, Vol. 24, No. 4 (1999), pp. 1012, 1017.

'Jamaat-e-Islami in Bangladesh: Women, Democracy and the Transformation of Islamist Politics', *Modern Asian Studies*, Vol. 42, No. 2/3 (2008), 577–603.

Sherman, Taylor C., *State Violence and Punishment in India* (London: Routledge, 2010).

and William Gould and Sarah Ansari, 'From Subjects to Citizens: Society and the Everyday State in the India and Pakistan', *Modern Asian Studies*, 44, 7, 2011.

Shetty, Sandhya, '(Dis)figuring the Nation: Mother, Metaphor, Metonymy', *Differences: A Journal of Feminist Cultural Criticism*, 7, 3, 1995.

Shiviah, M., 'Behind Hindu Growth Rate: Glimpses of Upper Class Statecraft', *Economic and Political Weekly*, Vol. 28, No. 14 (1993), 594–6.

Shukla, J. D., *Indianisation of All-Indian Services and Its Impact on Administration 1834–1947* (New Delhi: Allied, 1982).

Sidhwa, Bapsi, Urrvashi Butalia and Andrew Whitehead, *History Workship Journal*, 50, 2000, 230–8.

de Silva, Mangalika, 'Stripping Women: Securing the Sovereign "National" Body', in Nvanita Chadha Behera, ed., *International Relations in South Asia: Search for an Alternative Paradigm* (New Delhi: Sage, 2008), pp. 306–28.

Singh, Anita Inder, *The Origins of the Partition of India* (Delhi: Oxford University Press, 1990).

Singh, K. S., *Dust Storm and Hanging Mist: A Study of Birsa Munda and His Movement in Chota Nagpur 1874–1911* (Calcutta: Firma K. L. Mukhopadhyay, 1966).

Sinha, Mrinalini, *Colonial Masculinity: The 'Manly Englishman' and 'The Effeminate Bengali' in the Late Nineteenth Century* (Manchester: Manchester University Press, 1995).

Specters of Mother India: The Global Restructuring of an Empire (Durham: Duke University Press, 2006).

Sontheimer, G. and Kulke, H., eds., *Hinduism Reconsidered* (Delhi: Manohar, 1997).

Spain, James W., 'Military Assistance for Pakistan', *The American Political Science Review*, Vol. 48, No. 3 (1954), pp. 738–51.

Spencer, Jonathan, 'Collective Violence and Everyday Practice in Sri Lanka', *Modern Asian Studies*, Vol. 24, No. 3 (1990).

Srinivas, M. N., *Caste in Modern India and Other Essays* (London: Asia Publishing House, 1962).

Stark, Ulrike, *An Empire of Books: The Naval Kishore Press and the Diffusion of the Printed Word in Colonial India, 1858–1895* (New Delhi: Permanent Black, 2007).

'Statement of Communal Riots in the UP Between 1922 and 1927', L/PJ/6/1890 OIOC.

Stokes, Eric, *The English Utilitarians and India* (Oxford: Oxford University Press, 1959).

Symonds, Richard, 'State-Making in Pakistan', *Far Eastern Survey*, Vol. 19, No. 5 (1980), pp. 45–50.

Talbot, Ian, 'Pakistan in 2002: Democracy, Terrorism and Brinkmanship', *Asian Survey*, Vol. 43, No. 1 (2003), pp. 198–207.

'Pakistan in 2003: Political Deadlock and Continuing Uncertainties', *Asian Survey*, Vol. 44, No. 1 (2004), pp. 36–42.

Tambiah, Stanley Jeyaraja, *Sri Lanka: Ethnic Fratricide and the Dismantling of Democracy* (London: I. B. Taurus, 1986).

Buddhism Betrayed? Religion, Politics and Violence in Sri Lanka (Chicago: University of Chicago Press, 1992).

'The Crisis of Secularism in India', in Rajeev Bhargava, ed., *Secularism and its Critics* (Oxford: Oxford University Press, 1998).

Tarlo, Emma, *Unsettling Memories: Narratives of the Emergency in Delhi* (London: Hurst, 2003).

Thapar, Romila, 'Syndicated Moksha?', *Seminar*, Vol. 313 (1985), pp. 14–22.

Thielemann, Selina, *Singing the Praises Divine: Music in the Hindu Tradition* (New Delhi: A.P.H. Publishing Corporation, 2000).

Tomlinson, B. R., *The Political Economy of the Raj 1914–1947: The Economics of Decolonzation in India* (London: Palgrave, 1979).

'The Historical Roots of Indian Poverty: Issues in the Economic and Social History of South Asia', *Modern Asian Studies*, Vol. 22, No. 1 (1988), pp. 123–140.

Torri, Michelguglielmo, '"Westernised Middle Class", Intellectuals and Society in Late Colonial India', *Economic and Political Weekly*, Vol. 25, No. 4 (1990), pp. PE2–PE11.

Trivedi, Lisa, *Clothing Gandhi's Nation: Homespun and Modern India* (Bloomington: Indiana University Press, 2007).

Upadhyaya, Prakash Chandra, 'The Politics of Indian Secularism', *Modern Asian Studies*, Vol. 26, No. 4, 1992.

Van der Veer, Peter, *Religious Nationalism: Hindus and Muslims in India* (Berkeley: University of California Press, 1994).

Vanaik, Achin, *The Furies of Indian Communalism* (London: Verso, 1998).

Varshney, Ashutosh, 'Ethnic Conflict and Civil Society: India and Beyond', *World Politics*, Vol. 53, No. 3 (2001), pp. 362–98.

Ethnic Conflict and Civic Life: Hindus and Muslims in India (New Haven: Yale University Press, 2002).

Verkaaik, Oskar, *Migrants and Militants: Fun and Urban Violence in Pakistan* (Princeton: Princeton University Press, 2004).

Viswanath, C. K., 'Sati, Anti-Modernists and Sangh Parivar', *Economic and Political Weekly*, Vol. 34, No. 52 (1999), p. 3648.

Washbrook, David, 'Gandhian Politics', *Modern Asian Studies*, 7, 1, 1973, 107–14.

'Development of Caste Organization in South India 1880–1925', in C. J. Baker and D. A. Washbrook, eds., *South India Political Institutions and Political Change* (Delhi: Macmillan, 1975).

'Orients and Occidents: Colonial Discourse Theory and the Historiography of the British Empire', in Robin Winks, ed., *The Oxford History of the British Empire Volume V: Historiography* (Oxford: Oxford University Press, 1999).

Watt, Carey A., 'Education for National Efficiency: Constructive Nationalism in North India, 1909–1916', *Modern Asian Studies*, Vol. 31, No. 2 (1997), pp. 339–74.

Weidman, Amanda J., *Singing the Classical, Voicing the Modern: The Postcolonial Politics of Music in South India* (Durham: Duke University Press, 2006).

Weiss, Anita M., 'Women's Position in Pakistan: Socio-Cultural Effects of Islamization', *Pacific Affairs*, Vol. 25, No. 8 (1985), pp. 863–80.

Wickremeratne, L. A., 'Religion, Nationalism and Social Change in Ceylon, 1865–1885', *Journal of the Royal Asiatic Society*, Vol. 2 (1969), pp. 123–50.

Wilkinson, Steven I., 'India, Consociational Theory, and Ethnic Violence', *Asian Survey*, Vol. 40, No. 5 (2000), pp. 767–91.

Votes and Violence: Electoral Competition and Ethnic Riots in India (Cambridge: Cambridge University Press, 2004).

Wolpert, Stanley, *Jinnah of Pakistan* (New York: Oxford University Press, 1984).

Wyatt, Andrew, 'Building the Temples of Postmodern India: Economic Constructions of National Identity', *Contemporary South Asia*, Vol. 14, No. 4 (2005), pp. 465–80.

Yang, Anand, 'Sacred Symbol and Sacred Space in Rural India', *Comparative Studies in Society and History*, Vol. 22 (1980), pp. 576–96.

Zaman, Muhammad Qasim, 'Sectarianism in Pakistan: The Radicalization of Shi'i and Sunni Identities', *Modern Asian Studies*, Vol. 32, No. 3 (1988), pp. 689–716.

Zamindar, Vazira, *The Long Partition and the Making of Modern South Asia: Refugees, Boundaries, Histories* (New York: Columbia University Press, 2007).

Zastoupil, Lynn, 'J. S. Mill and India', *Victorian Studies*, Vol. 32, No. 1 (1988), pp. 31–54.

Zavos, John, 'The Arya Samaj and the Antecedents of Hindu nationalism', *International Journal of Hindu Studies*, Vol. 3, No. 1 (1999), pp. 57–81.

The Emergence of Hindu Nationalism in India (Delhi: Oxford University Press, 2000).

Zerinini-Brotel, Jasmine, 'The BJP in Uttar Pradesh: From Hindutva to Consensual Politics?', in Thomas Blom Hansen and Christophe Jaffrelot, eds., *The BJP and the Compulsions of Politics in India* (Delhi: Oxford University Press, 1998), pp. 72–100.

Index